*Piers Plowman*

AN ESSAY IN CRITICISM

# Piers Plowman

AN ESSAY IN CRITICISM

BY

JOHN LAWLOR

LONDON

EDWARD ARNOLD (PUBLISHERS) LTD

FIRST PUBLISHED 1962

by
Edward Arnold (Publishers) Ltd
41 Maddox Street, London W. 1

Printed at Leiden in the Netherlands by
A. W. SIJTHOFF'S UITGEVERSMAATSCHAPPIJ N.V.
and bound by Webb Son & Co., London

# Contents

|  | page |
|---|---|
| Preface. | 9 |
| Introductory Note. | 12 |

## *Part I   The Argument*

| | |
|---|---|
| CHAPTER   I The Middle-Earth of Man (Prologue, Passus I-IV) | 17 |
| CHAPTER   II An End of Evasion (Passus V-VII) | 45 |
| CHAPTER   III A Dreamer's Progress (Passus VIII-XIV) | 87 |
| CHAPTER   IV Ascent and Return (Passus XV-XX) | 139 |

## *Part II   The Poetic Techniques*

| | |
|---|---|
| CHAPTER   V Rhythm, Speech and Argument | 189 |
| CHAPTER   VI Allegory, Similitude and Wordplay | 240 |
| CHAPTER VII The Poet and the Dreamer | 281 |
| Appendix: Some problems of a true text of *Piers Plowman* | 323 |
| Index | 331 |

For

THELMA

# Acknowledgements

Some parts of this book incorporate material which has previously appeared in the *Review of English Studies, Modern Language Review* and *Medium Aevum*, here revised and in part re-written. I am grateful to the Editors for permission to reprint. A shortened form of the present Chapter VII was delivered as a paper at a meeting of Cambridge members of the Medieval Society, to whom I am grateful for helpful discussion.

The lines of W. H. Auden on p. 319 are quoted by permission of the poet and Messrs. Faber and Faber; and those of Walter de la Mare on p. 324 by permission of the executors and Messrs. Faber and Faber.

All text-references to Chaucer are to the edition of F. N. Robinson (London, Oxford University Press, 2nd. edn. 1957); Gower, the edition of G. C. Macaulay (Oxford, Clarendon Press, 1901); Shakespeare, the Complete Works edited by Peter Alexander (London, William Collins, 1951).

For the translation of Scriptural references in *Piers Plowman* I have drawn mainly on the Authorized or King James Version (1611), as being most familiar to the majority of English-speaking readers.

Dr. J. A. W. Bennett and Professor E. Talbot Donaldson did me the considerable kindness of reading through a first draft. I have tried to profit from their most helpful observations.

This book is mainly concerned with the B Text of *Piers Plowman*, with references to A and C readings only when they seem of special interest in relation to B. Professor Donaldson placed me further in his debt by suggesting various readings from collations made for the forthcoming new edition of the B Text. He must not, of course, be thought of as necessarily approving those readings I have selected or the interpretations I have placed upon them. Professor Kane's welcome edition of the A Text (*Piers Plowman: the A Version*, London, Athlone Press, 1960) arrived too late for me to make extensive use of it; but I have verified that my quotations from the A Text accord (though not necessarily in orthography or line-numbering) with what is certain to be the standard edition for many years to come. Dr. G. H. Russell,

who with Professor A. G. Mitchell is preparing a new edition of the
C Text, has very kindly answered my questions about certain C Text
readings. The text of *Piers Plowman* here used is, therefore, that of
W. W. Skeat (*The Vision of William concerning Piers the Plowman* etc.,
Oxford, 1886, 2 vols.) with occasional variants from the sources I have
mentioned, each being particularized as it occurs. I have removed
Skeat's medial point, a cumbersome and misleading device, and have
altered punctuation where necessary.

It will perhaps save misunderstanding if I add that the englishing
attempted at the page-foot is designed to give the readiest help to a
reader wholly unfamiliar with Middle English, and not to constitute
translation of any more ambitious kind. I ordinarily give the Modern
English form in parenthesis if it enables the reader to penetrate unfamiliar
spelling: as, *pens* (pence) money; *sone* (soon) at once. For a similar
reason I have usually retained Skeat's hyphenations: as, *ther-myde*;
*y-graced*. I have occasionally consulted existing versions, but have not
troubled to indicate where my interpretation agrees with or differs
from them.                                                    J. L.

# *Preface*

I have tried in this book to interest a reader who has no previous knowledge of *Piers Plowman* or of medieval poetry at all, except perhaps Chaucer's General Prologue and one or two of *The Canterbury Tales*, but who has some interest in English poetry—say, from Wyatt or the Elizabethans onwards. The criticism proposed is literary criticism, the worth of the object under review without undue reference to its genetic origins or the period of its composition, but involving some comparison with English poetry as it has been written at various times, including our own.

We hear a good deal from both sides about the need for the specialist to open—or re-open—communication with the non-expert public. But what methods are to be adopted? With *Piers Plowman*, a single long poem, it seemed to me that two salient lessons of modern criticism were most relevant. They are: firstly, the need to experience the poem serially, to take it in order, so that its highly individual terrain is not flattened into a relief-map, however faithfully plotted and exactly drawn to scale. The ups and downs of the journey are to be encountered, not viewed from a single comprehensive standpoint, if we are to make any but the least helpful sense of the poem. Secondly, and of quite crucial importance where a body of systematic thought is variously drawn upon, we must examine the 'ideas' of a work of art as they exist in the work and not as they may be otherwise stated, however authoritatively, by philosopher, theologian, or scientist. If the poem, play, or novel has any justification at all, it must be, at the very least, that it expresses not thought but what it is to think—not religion but religion as men may hold it, not science but what it is to be a scientist. Moreover, when in the course of the argument misunderstandings occur, they come as false paths and blind alleys which must be explored before their nature can be known. Any tendency to omniscience, either as knowing the end from the beginning, or being ever-prepared to apply a systematic pattern of interpretation, is certainly dangerous and may be wholly disastrous.

I cannot hope to have entirely avoided these dangers. But awareness of them has suggested the shape of this book. Part I offers a step-by-step reading of the poem. My aim is to place the reader, so far as possible, in direct touch with *Piers Plowman*. One version of the poem, the B Text, is consistently followed, with a glance at the other two versions only when the difference is striking. Langland's lines are quoted freely, and glossed minutely at the foot of the page, so that the reader who follows Part I through to the end will have read the poem in its essential nature and scope. Nothing has been omitted that bears on the developing argument; least of all have I been tempted to omit or abridge what may strike a modern taste as digressive. The circuitous shape of the argument, its successive rather than sequential quality, and thus the nature of the Dreamer's progress, are certainly not less important to grasp than any simple account of the main conclusions. Again, when considering such terms as *Kynd*, *Wit*, *Will*, etc. I try to concentrate on the meanings which a reader without previous knowledge of medieval discussion can identify in the poem and relate to his own experience. Above all, with the progression 'do well, do better, do best' I have dealt in turn with each of the definitions which the Dreamer is given at different times, while keeping touch, throughout, with that generic non-technical sense of 'doing well' which is prior to all such definitions and comprehends them all.

Part II is wholly similar in conception. Here I try to discuss the poem in its distinctive techniques—diction and rhythms, allegory and word-play, the role of the Dreamer—in terms the reader should not find forbidding, whatever the views he forms. On rhythm, and metre in general, I have thought it desirable to say something about the varying relations between English speech and 'measure', and to consider the suitability of particular speech- and rhythmic-patterns to different kinds of argument. On allegory, it seemed necessary to oppose the claims of those who would detect complex and multiple significance at almost every turn. This is done in the hope of returning the reader to the plain text; I do not supply (what will certainly be found helpful to subsequent reading of the poem) any account of the allegorical works and devices with which the poet may have been familiar. Finally, in the account of the Dreamer the emphasis is placed not on the poet but on the *persona* deployed in the poem. Concentration on unity of authorship (in itself welcome) has caused some critics to insist unduly on the identity of that author, 'William Langland' in a narrow, quasi-autobiographical, sense.

I would emphasize that the treatment throughout is designed to assist an unskilled reader in a first reading of the poem. With some misgivings, I have accepted a degree of repetition, notably between Part I and Part II, as inevitable if this purpose were to be consistently followed out. I particularly ask the reader's indulgence for referring him more than once, in various parts of the book, to the same passage, when different approaches seemed necessary and potentially rewarding. This book will have succeeded if the reader is drawn to such excellent helps to further study as already exist, and from which I have learned much, both in agreement and dissent, and to that increasing number of works which we may expect in the general current of scholarly interest in this poem.

In the study of *Piers Plowman*, as in other fields, problems of disproportion arise for the learned no less than the uninstructed. The palmary achievements of the last thirty years have removed any reproach that the thinker and visionary was being neglected in favour of the satiric observer. There is now no danger that scholarship will ignore or underrate the profound matters that absorb the Dreamer as the argument develops. But there is perhaps the danger of overlooking the simplicity with which he begins—and ends. There is evident (and not in *Piers Plowman* studies only) a decided over-compensation, as a sturdy professionalism sets itself to remove all traces of former disparagement for a 'Gothic' middle age. It is the more important to be on our guard where Langland's poem is concerned; for the nature of the Dreamer's progress is distinctly unusual. The method of the poet, we may feel, is not so much to develop an argument as to make us undergo its development. He gives us thinking rather than thought; all the Dreamer's perplexities are before us, the riddles he cannot solve as well as the truths he can triumphantly affirm. This is complex enough; but, paradoxically, it proceeds from a simple beginning—the vision of an England so far astray that it can find at need only one guide to truth. We advance into complexity when it is found that the guide is himself subject to criticism and must in his turn repent. Perhaps I have said enough to show that the 'inwardness' of the poem—the real connexions and transitions of the poet's creative imagining—is peculiarly liable to be missed in any analysis. So, at the first turning-point, we are still puzzled by the Pardon granted to the Plowman; and in our haste to interpret it we resort to its implications in the poet's developed thought, missing its devastating simplicity and thus the real transition it effects between the satirist's work of destruction and the thinker's task of construction. Scholarship can come too soon to the Dreamer's awakening and his pondering the implications of what he has been shown. Langland *may* be a poet of confused purpose. But we would do well, before assenting to the judgement, to banish any preconceived notions of the kind of poem we are offered. It will be best, then, to proceed in strict sequence with the poet, to follow without anticipating his leading. The Dreamer's own progress is a sufficient guide, if we will but attend to it.

# Introductory Note

*Piers Plowman* exists in three versions, generally referred to as the A, B, C Texts, each consisting of two parts, a Vision (*Visio*) followed by a Life *(Vita)*. In A, which has thirteen Passus in all (including the Prologue), the *Vita* consists of four books of the Life of Do Well. B, used in this book, is twenty-one Passus in all, and here (as in C, which has twenty-three Passus) the *Vita* is the Life of Do Well, Do Better and Do Best.

It is generally held that these three versions are all the work of one man; and they have been given approximate dates of composition as follows: A about 1370; B between 1377 and 1379; C after 1390.

The name 'Will' is applied to the Dreamer on several occasions in the poem, and a number of colophons refer to the author by this name. At B XV 148 the Dreamer says, 'I haue luyed in *londe*. . .my name is *Longe* Wille'. 'William Langland' is given as the author's name in one MS (Dublin D. 4.1). A Latin *memorandum* there asserts that 'the father of William Langland, Eustace de Rokayle, was a gentleman living at Shipton-under-Wychwood and holding land of Lord Despenser in Oxfordshire, and the aforesaid William wrote the book called *Perys ploughman*'. It has been established that there was an adherent of the Despensers called Eustace de Rokayle living at Shipton-under-Wychwood, and it has been noted that the Despensers were patrons of the monasteries of Great Malvern and Tewkesbury. The fact that the son did not take his father's surname cannot be regarded as a proof that he was illegitimate. Another MS (Huntington Lib. Hm 128, formerly Ashburnham 130) records that 'Robert or william langland made pers ploughman'; but 'Robert' may be thought to have arisen from a misunderstanding of 'Thus, yrobid in russet, I rombide aboute' (A IX 1, where one MS, for *yrobid*, actually reads *Roberd*). From certain passages in the poem it has been inferred that the author was born about 1332 near the Malvern hills, perhaps educated at the monastery of Great Malvern, took minor clerical orders (which did not require celibacy), and came to London where he lived with his wife Kit and his daughter Nicolette on Cornhill, making a living by saying prayers for the souls of his benefactors. Other details concern his dress, his scant respect for the self-important, his reluctance to work manually, his persistence in writing verses, and his admission that he had led an unprofitable life. Concerning a historical William Langland nothing has come to light.

In the B Text, the first part, the *Visio*, consists of a Prologue and Passus I to VII; the second part, the *Vita*, dealing with Do Well, Do Better and Do Best, runs from Passus VIII to XX. The *Visio* is concerned with the relatively simple situation of 'man's disobedience'. The theme is law (reaching beyond society's laws to the Law of God) and universal blameworthiness. The all-pervading evil is the mercenary motive; and society is set to rights by insistence on just rewards for co-operative effort. The leader found to organise men and women of different classes is the Plowman, the type of honest labour, a provider as opposed to the 'wasters' who abound on every hand. The question of rewards is renewed when approval for this man's outstanding virtues is forthcoming. The indulgence or 'pardon' which the Plowman then receives once more reveals the Law of God as absolute in its demands. Piers tears up his 'pardon', announces his resolve to be less anxious about his daily sustenance, and, quarrelling with a Priest, passes from the Dreamer's sight (*Prologue*, Passus I-VII).

In Part II, the Dreamer ponders intently, with many set-backs and some false turnings, a group of closely-related problems which arise in any protracted consideration of the possibilities of fulfilling God's law. Such are the relation between righteousness (considered as fulfilment of a moral code) and salvation; elaborate learning as opposed to unlettered faith; the free will of human creatures set over against predestination; and so on. All these remain within the orbit the *Visio* had marked out, man's relations with a Divine Lawgiver. But, first sounded in the Prologue to the whole poem, and heard at intervals since, has been another theme—a Love which is higher than Law. Man can envisage a rule of Reason which, as loving obedience freely given, will resolve all discords, in the individual as in society. But first the Dreamer must learn to travel in the company of Patience and to attend to what he is taught (*Life of Do Well*, Passus VII—XIV). The Dreamer is then ready to learn what Love is and to see Love fulfilling Law in the Saviour's earthly career, with its triumphant consummation at Calvary and in the Harrowing of Hell. This takes up and perfects another theme, the vision of simple dependence upon the Creator, which had come upon the Plowman in the moment that Law was disclosed in all its rigour. So it is fitting that at this stage of the Dreamer's journey Piers Plowman reappears to instruct him. This part or 'movement' of the poem ends with the Easter peal of triumph (*Life of Do Better*, Passus XV-XVIII). Lastly, the state of the Church is considered, and the poem ends in a swift return from a perfected past to a disordered present, where the truth is still to be sought by the individual conscience as long as life lasts (*Life of Do Best*, Passus XIX-XX).

# PART I

# *The Argument*

Virtue is like hunger or thirst; it must be satisfied or we die.
JEREMY TAYLOR

'*Contra*', quod I as a clerke and comsed to disputen,
And seide hem sothli, '*sepcies in die cadit iustus.*'
VIII 20-21

# CHAPTER I

# The Middle-Earth of Man

(Prologue, Passus I-IV) CARLYLE, *Past and present*

... he lives in an element of miracle; Heaven's splendour over his head, Hell's darkness under his feet. A great Law of Duty, high as these two Infinitudes, dwarfing all else, annihilating all else...

## I

*Prologue*

We begin with a Prologue in which certain facts are established. The world is one in which the good are heavily outnumbered, and its law is self-interest. It is, of course, a world under authority; just as the field of folk is seen in relation to the Castle aloft and the dungeons beneath, so the world of sinful men and women lies below both Papal and regal authority. But if law is commonly disregarded, the sanction of authority at its highest is not in law but love; and love is to be found among the virtues. The Dreamer

> parceyued of the power that Peter had to kepe,
> To bynde and to unbynde, as the boke telleth,
> How he it left with loue, as owre lorde hight,
> Amonges foure vertues, the best of all vertues,
> That cardinales ben called . . .

The cardinal virtues are one thing; those Cardinals at Rome, who have taken the same name and have the authority to appoint St Peter's successors, are another. We can be sure that the election of a Pope requires both love and learning:

> in loue and letterure the eleccioun bilongeth.

But the poet will not say more about the Papal Court; and similarly, though the King is to rule mercifully as well as justly (a warning sounded

*To bynde and to unbynde* (see Matt. xvi 19); *the boke* the Bible; *hight* bade; *letterure* learning.

from on high), yet for his people there must be a simple *de facto* recognition of his authority:

*Precepta Regis sunt nobis vincula legis.*

We must be concerned with the realities of the world we know; and in this middle-earth the struggle is for power. The fable of Who shall bell the Cat? points back to the only lesson for the prudent—let each look to his own. So the world of workshys, the purveyors of creature-comforts and the Pardoners who give absolution for cash, includes a mob of barristers, practising the law 'not for love of Our Lord' but for gain. With them, truly,

> Thow my3test better mete the myste on Maluerne hulles,
> Than gete a momme of here mouthe, but money were shewed.

The picture that Langland gives us is well-known: but perhaps its perspectives are not always appreciated. He is able to concentrate on a foreground of varied and animated action, a world in which the good are heavily outnumbered, and a world in which everything is for sale, including law. But this is made possible by a setting in which the law thus disregarded or placated is still not the final truth, the ultimate background. Man's law, the angel proclaims from on high, must be tempered with mercy. There is no resting in law, for law will be met with law, measure for measure:

> *Si ius nudatur, nudo de iure metatur.*
> *Si seritur pietas, de pietate metas!*

It is the first challenging antithesis we meet, the characteristic two-edged thrust that cuts through so many of the arguments we shall hear. If we choose law, then let us be sure we do not omit to be merciful. Merely on the level of self-interest, of each looking to his own, this is no more than common-sense. The world we are shown thus falls into a perspective more dynamic than the simple contrast of good and bad, law and offence. The final truth is that Divinely-appointed power lies with 'love', and is to be found with righteousness, the Cardinal virtues. But this is placed on the margin of our picture: the world we see squarely before us is experience as we encounter it. More, it is a world to which we readily grow accustomed; the poet need show us, he says, only the seventh

*Precepta* etc. The King's decrees bind us as the law; *mete* measure; *myste* mist; *hulles* hills; *momme* 'mum', the least sound; *here* their; *but* unless; *Si ius* etc. If justice is stripped bare (of mercy), naked justice will be your portion. If mercy is sown, mercy will be reaped.

part, so familiar is the whole. It is the more necessary that we should be awakened from our acceptance of man's habitual folly and evasion. The poem proper therefore begins with the entry from above of one who will explain: and it is appropriate that the explanation throws light upon the observer, the Dreamer, as well as upon the reality we, with him, behold. We are, throughout the poem, not to remain at a safe remove from reality; for in this—man's natural disposition to see evil as external to himself—there lies a danger which is perhaps deeper than any.

## II

*Passus I*

A beautiful Lady, clothed in linen, summons the Dreamer to consider what he has seen—the general condition of humanity:

> Haue thei worschip in this worlde thei wilne no better;
> Of other heuene than here holde thei no tale.

For all her courtesy and beauty, the Dreamer is afraid; as well he may be, for to question this ordinary state of affairs is to raise incalculable issues. The Lady, however, begins with a simple and sufficient statement; to do right is to live according to Truth's teaching, and this is given its particular application to the world the Dreamer has seen—men are to observe *mesure* in the use of creature-comforts. The Dreamer at once asks a large question: to whom does the wealth of the world belong? The answer repeats the Lady's first statement—the individual is to look to himself. He is to render unto Caesar the things which are Caesar's; and this, we may note, is the true application of the base principle of self-interest everywhere evident in the Prologue. She concludes her explanation of the field by referring it to its setting. On the margin of our picture is Love; but Love is hindered by the lord of the dungeon which dominates the crowded plain. Wrong is given his ultimate title when he is called

> letter of loue, and lyeth hem alle;
> That trusten on his tresor bitrayeth he sonnest.

The 'explanation' given, we turn to the observer; the Dreamer asks her who she is. The reply carries its own mild reproof:

*Haue thei* provided they have; *worschip* respect, worldly success; *wilne* desire; *holde thei no tale* they take no account; *mesure* lit. 'measure', a reasonable use; *letter of loue* one who hinders love; *lyeth hem alle* deceives everyone; *That trusten* those who trust; *sonnest* soonest.

'Holicherche I am', quod she, 'Thow ou3test me to knowe,
I vnderfonge the firste and the feyth tau3te'.

The Dreamer at once cries to be taught how to save his soul. Holy
Church's answer is in keeping with this note of baptismal simplicity.
The truth is not hard—those who do good and purpose no evil to their
fellow-men shall have their reward. This simple truth is, be it noted,
set in the widest perspectives, as was the Prologue picture. The truth she
has uttered is common knowledge to all men, Christian and Pagan alike:
'cristene and vncristne clameth it vchone'. We should not miss the gentle
rebuke that this implies. But it is not dwelt upon. Holy Church continues
by emphasizing the good as obedience to Truth, incumbent upon all
men. Her conclusion is fittingly pragmatic; those whose actions evidence
true faith will go to heaven, where Truth is enthroned. Nothing simpler
nor more directly concerned with the practice of the individual soul
could be conceived. It seems, for the moment, that the way is clear from
the turbulent middle-world to that higher region from which Holy
Church has descended. But the Dreamer responds with another of his
large questions—How does Truth come to man? and disclaims any
natural knowledge upon the point. He does not know

> By what craft in my corps it comseth and where.

Now Holy Church is less gentle: how stupid, she declares, to say he does
not know something revealed by common experience! This is the first
scolding the Dreamer receives, and we may think he deserves it. An
apparently radical question has been asked; and the answer is, in effect,
'look in thy heart'. Something known to all men has been overlooked
by this searcher after knowledge:

> 'It is a kynde knowyng', quod he, 'That kenneth in thine herte
> For to louye thi lorde leuer than thi-selue;
> No dedly synne to do, dey thou3 thow sholdest'.

The Dreamer's question is foolishness indeed. But he is not left without
some concession to his desire for knowledge. Holy Church concludes,

> This I trowe be treuthe; who can teche the better,
> Loke thow suffre hym to sey and sithen lere it after.
> For thus witnesseth his worde, worche thow there-after.

*vnderfonge* received (in baptism); *the* thee; *tau3te* taught; *clameth* claim (to know
the truth); *vchone* each; *craft* power, faculty; *comseth* begins; *kynde knowyng*
natural knowledge; *he* she; *kenneth* tells, makes known; *leuer than* rather than,
more dearly than; *dedly synne* mortal sin; *dey* die; *I trowe* I assure you; *sithen* then;
*lere* learn; *worche* work.

Holy Church's reproof should be clear to the reader, if it is long in coming home to the Dreamer. There is something 'better' than this 'treuthe'—not better than truth, absolutely considered, but better than that truth which is all that can be revealed to the Dreamer in his present condition. And in the moment that Holy Church withholds the 'better' she gives her reasons for doing so; it is a teaching which must be carefully attended to, and it must be *practised*. At the outset of the poem the Dreamer is established in one line by both the neat glance at his impetuosity—'suffer him to sey'—and the sterner counsel to pass from theoretical inquiry to earnest application. We have taken the decisive step away from the world of the Prologue, where the Dreamer was merely a spectator of the actions of others. Now we are alert to a Dreamer in whom the desire to intervene, to search out the imagined heart of the problem, may overbear the simple and prior necessity of an attempt to practise the life about which he would know all. Again, the vexation of Holy Church with this inquirer who overlooks the knowledge written ineffaceably in his own heart sharpens our attention. We shall look more closely at what the Dreamer sees, to avoid looking merely with his eyes. In this way we are released from mere dependence upon the Dreamer: from this point forward the poem offers us the interlocking of two main themes—the 'evidence' and man's capacity for apprehending it as applying to himself.[1]

Holy Church concludes on the highest plane to which we were introduced in the Prologue—the Love which is above law ('Riȝt so is loue a ledere and the law shapeth') and is known to all men in their hearts. It is a final reminder that mercy is to guide all our actions. A lesson sufficient for his needs has been offered to the Dreamer. Now that he knows

> what treuthe is, that no tresore is bettere,

the stage is set for the entry of *tresore*. We have heard from Holy Church the principle that guided the few good folk in the Field; they 'Al for loue of owre lorde lyueden ful streyte'. Now we turn to examine more closely the moving principle of the workaday world, Lady Meed, the treasure that the 'most part of men' desire.

## Passus II

At first sight, Meed is a simple enough figure. The pairing of opposites—Holy Church's white linen as against Meed's scarlet, unadorned

*ledere* leader; *tresore* treasure; *ful streyte* with great strictness.

beauty opposed to lavish jewellery—starts us on the level of direct contrast.
We learn, too, that just as Holy Church will be wed to the merciful
man (he 'Schal be my lorde and I his leef in the heiʒe heuene') so,
conversely, the man who 'takes Meed' will lose Charity. Meed is
therefore the direct enemy of the teaching which Holy Church has
enjoined upon the Dreamer, whether that teaching be thought of
primarily as doctrine (Meed is the daughter of Falsehood) or, more
searchingly, as love. The Dreamer is now enabled to perceive a world
of interlocked interests—Meed is to be married, and the company at
her wedding, high and low, will reveal the extent of her sway. And,
indeed, it is a vast throng:

> I can nouʒt rekene the route that ran aboute Mede.

But it is the lawyers who are closest to her, headed by Simony and Civil
Law. We begin to see that the specific charge in the general indictment
against the world of the Prologue is venality—all is for sale, and this is
ratified by law, which also, and principally, is for sale. It is therefore
appropriate that a legal instrument is forthcoming, a formal contract
for the marriage of Meed: and in it we have the first sharp taste of the
poet's sustained ironic power. Meed is to be married

> more for here goodis,
> Than for ani vertue or fairenesse, or any free kynde.

So the settlement confers the 'earldom of envy and wrath together', the
'domain' of strife and senseless chattering, 'the County of Covetousness
and all the adjoining regions,' 'all the borough of theft' and 'the lordship of Lechery'. It is a fierce little burlesque which fittingly concludes
with the terms of the bargain, parodying the common forms of contract:

> to have and to holde and here eyres after
> A dwelling with the deuel, and dampned be for eure,
> With al the purtenaunces of purgatorie in-to the pyne of helle.
> ʒeldyng for this thinge at one ʒeres ende
> Here soules to Sathan to suffre with hym peynes,
> And with him to wonye with wo, whil god is in heuene.

The witnesses are headed by Wrong, and include Piers the Pardoner,
standing first in the list of such well-known occupational twisters as
Beadle, Reeve and Miller. The contract is then sealed:

*leef* beloved; *route* crowd; *goodis* goods (in the material sense, suggesting the ironic
contrast which follows—the lack of 'goods' in any other sense); *free kynde* noble
nature; *thinge* agreement; *wonye* dwell, live.

In the date of the deuel this dede is asseled[2]
Bi siȝte of sire Symonye and Cyuyles leue.

It is Theology's objection to this marriage-contract that makes the
matter less a simple affair of black-and-white than we may have supposed.
And we may note, in passing, that one of Langland's most marked
characteristics is the unusual combination of uninhibited mockery
(as here, the sardonic sweep of the 'contract') with a penetrating sense
that the truth is finally not simple. It is a characteristically double
awareness which the modern reader may miss; for generations of
moralists have accustomed us to purchase *élan* at the cost of complexity,
or to win insight by discounting broad and comprehensive effects.
Perhaps this may in some measure account for a fundamental
difference in standpoint between Langland's earlier and his later readers,
from the sixteenth century to the present. Those who were engrossed
by the satirist and those who today find themselves absorbed in the
thinker may profit from sharing their separate observations. The day
is past when the author threatened to disintegrate into five separate
persons. Perhaps a more lasting, because more insidious, threat is the
tendency to concentrate upon the one set of qualities to the exclusion
of the other. This I comment on in a later chapter[3]; for the moment,
we are concerned with Theology, rounding upon Civil Law, who has
assented to the marriage of Meed and Falsehood.

Theology's objection is that there is a right use of 'meed' or reward:
the labourer is worthy of his hire. Meed should therefore be allied to
Truth, not Falsehood. This, Theology says hotly, is one more proof
that Simony and Civil Law, acting together, are destroying Holy
Church. They would perpetrate a great wrong, for

> Mede is moylere, a mayden of gode,
> And myȝte kisse the kynge for cosyn, an she wolde.

Civil Law's notion of 'law' (and thus that of his 'notaries', too) must be
tested in the King's Court. And even there, if judgement should go
against Theology, let Civil Law beware, for Truth is a formidable
opponent, and with Conscience, who knows these rogues, will exact a
final penalty which they may well dread. The notaries and witnesses
are then bribed (Simony will make no move of assent until he receives
his silver) and the rout sets out for London. Here we may notice a

(*in the date of the deuel* parodying 'in the Year of Our Lord'); *moylere* woman;
*of gode* of good standing (*cf.* the ironic play upon 'goods' in the account of her
forthcoming marriage, above); *cosyn* cousin.

technique which we are to meet again—a crisis in the story is preceded
by a mass-movement; things grow to a head.

We shall examine Theology's case in a moment. What is immediately
noteworthy is the action that follows the setting-out for London. The
King, hearing that Falsehood and Flattery and their like are on the way,
sends to arrest them. Above all, Liar is to be taken; Meed will be
examined alone. But word reaches the offenders, and they go to ground.
Whatever the verdict in Meed's case, these ancient enemies will survive.
Their hiding-places are full of interest: Falsehood is received by the
Friars; and Guile, in terror of his life, is apprenticed by the Merchants.
Liar, that arch-rogue, has a harder time:

> He was nawhere welcome for his manye tales,
> Ouer-al yhowted and yhote trusse . . .

But there is one class of 'professional men' who gladly take him in;
and the phrases which tell of their anxious care are a sardonic echo of the
story of the Good Samaritan:

> pardoneres haued pite and pulled hym in-to house.
> They wesshen hym and wyped hym and wonden hym in cloutes . . .

It is an instance of that medieval taste which finds the essentially comic
in a strict inversion of truth, an upside-downness of equal and opposite
error which is possible only in a thoroughly authoritative framework
of belief. But the effect is not gratuitous. Like the comic blasphemies
and solemn palinodes of which it is a counterpart, it witnesses to unchanging truth and is the check to any merely theoretical victories.
Here, the enemies of good are not to be easily disposed of; the fight
continues. So the motive of the Pardoners, in their apparently charitable
care of Liar, is not far to seek; they

> sente hym with seles on sondayes to cherches,
> And gaf pardoun for pens poundmel aboute.

It is a re-planting of evil; other crooked trades are quick to follow this
lead. Wickedness has merely gone to ground, to await warily the out-
come of Meed's trial. In this way, the momentousness of the issues is
preserved without any loss of realism. The world of evil waits upon
the event. Similarly, the focus of the poem alters: after the crowded

*for* in spite of; *Ouer-al yhowted* hooted at everywhere; *yhote trusse* sent packing;
*wesshen* washed; *wonden* (wound) wrapped; *cloutes* rags, patched clothes; *seles*
seals (affixed to the Pardoner's warrant); *pens* (pence) cash; *poundmel aboute*
pounds-worths all round.

scene of the cavalcade *en route* for London, we narrow to a single figure, Meed, weeping and wringing her hands as she is arrested. The scene is cleared so that we can attend without interruption; for the world of the Prologue hangs in the balance. It is the first major turning-point in the poem.

### III

*Passus III*

The King declares that if Meed is obedient she shall be forgiven. But it is at once apparent that Meed has friends at Court. Some of the justices promise her that they will persuade the King to allow her to work her will, whatever Conscience may say. Meed thanks and—of course—rewards them. Similarly the Clergy plight their troth—

> for we beth thine owne,
> For to worche thi wille the while thow my3te laste—

and Meed guarantees preferment; however incompetent they may be, her followers are sure of office. This is Meed in her ordinary aspect— the evil of 'filthy lucre', poisoning all motive and thus thwarting justice and learning alike. It is both ground and foretaste of an aversion from the merely learned and authoritative which meets us with redoubled force later. We advance now to a particular instance of corruption. Meed is offered, and accepts, shrift from a Friar—on his terms. Whatever her offences—

> Thei3 lewed men and lered men had leyne by the bothe,
> And falsenesse haued yfolwed the al this fyfty wyntre—

he will not only give absolution but will be 'beadsman' and messenger. It is an absolute 'pardon', and we may think it cheap at the price of 'a seme of whete'. Meed agrees, and shamelessly (it is the poet's word) kneels to him. Perhaps it is Langland's sense of humour that is uppermost when we find that the Friar is one ahead in the moves of the game— it happens that his convent is putting up an expensive new window; meeting the cost would guarantee salvation. But we see at once that the Friar is in the hands of an expert. Meed readily agrees and goes beyond the immediate proposal. She will be the Friar's friend for ever; for she can rely upon the Friars not to be hard upon lechery. Indeed, with this understanding she will thoroughly re-furbish the convent; and everyone

---

*the while* etc. as long as you exist; *lewed* lay; *lered* (learned) clerics; *seme* load.

will have visible proof that she is 'sister of their house'. The comedy springs from the final truth that the world of evil is a world of ruthless individualism.

What is immediately evident is the extent of Meed's sway. The association of 'conscience-money', especially in point of lechery, with the visible splendour of houses of religion, drives deeper the case against Meed which is being built up in the reader's mind; and while it makes the more urgent a solution, it makes desperate the prospect of success. Meed, the reader feels, is too well entrenched in society. What could be further from God's ordinance than this ostentatious 'charity'?—and what more widespread? The powerful may well be warned against it —but with what prospect of success? So much for Meed as perverter of spiritual authority. Now her power is seen in corrupting secular justice. Here the guilty are 'Mayors and mace-bearers'

> that menes ben bitwene
> The kynge and the comune to kepe the lawes.

Through them we reach to the lowly poor. It is the poor who suffer, for those who defraud them by selling food at high prices buy immunity from the law by bribes and 'presents'.[4] From top to bottom, society is poisoned: Meed works her will, perverting divine and secular justice. Her present activities are wholly evil, a stranglehold upon society. If there is to be any question of marrying this 'maid', it must be a question of finding an effective partner.

The King is now ready, having taken counsel, to deal with the prisoner. With formal gravity he reproves her: she has often erred, but never so grossly as in this matter of the proposed marriage. She is forgiven, on condition that she renounces this course for ever. Will she marry instead Conscience, the King's knight, newly arrived from afar, if he is willing to take her? Meed's assent is immediate, and, one supposes, easy:

> 'ʒe, lorde,' quod that lady, 'lorde forbede elles!
> But I be holely at ʒowre heste lat hange me sone!'

This is surely an ironical protestation; she will in fact be punished— if not 'hanged'—if she is disobedient to the monarch, who is her judge.[5] But the ever-present liveliness of Langland's imagination goes deeper

---

*menes* intermediaries; *the comune* the people (the King's subjects); *ʒe* yes; *forbede* forbid; *elles* (else) otherwise; *holely* wholly; *heste* bidding, command; *lat hange me* may I be hanged; *sone* (soon) at once.

than overt mockery. There is no mistaking the utter inappropriateness of this eager compliance with the King's proposal, coming from the shameless creature who had knelt to the mercenary Friar. The general point is important; as one critic has well remarked, we learn what Meed represents

> just as we get to know a character in any good play, or narrative, by observing what she says, about herself or about others, what she does, what others say about her, how she reacts to what is said about her and what is done to her.[6]

It is unexceptionable advice; and here the critic understands Meed's immediate consent to the King's proposal as 'in keeping with Meed's character. She is always ready to do anyone's will'. If we have attended to what the poet has shown us of her universal success, we may feel that in fact it proclaims her conviction that she can work her own will in any circumstances whatever. At all events, Conscience is horrified; and in a single spate of denunciation he reviews all her misdeeds. The truth of this catalogue is evident; for it summarizes the very misdeeds of which we have already had proof. Meed has brought down Kings and Popes; she is a lecher; she corrupts the civil law; she perverts the Church through Simony; through her the poor are without redress. At the end of it, there is little prospect, it appears, that Meed can defend herself. 'Excuse the 3if thow canst', are the King's words to her. If Conscience's indictment is upheld, it means lifelong banishment.

Meed's reply, however, is formidable. It includes, most cleverly, the ground of Theology's objection to the original mariage; and it contains much more. It is in fact a counter-attack upon Conscience. The topical point is made that it was he who was responsible for the ill-success of the French campaign that ended ingloriously in the Treaty of Bretigny (1360). But the general point from which this arises is that made originally by Theology: *dignus est operarius* ('the labourer is worthy of his hire') — reward and merit are not to be easily divorced. Meed is thus enabled to carry her counter-attack up to the judgement-seat itself. It is not merely prudent for a King to reward his followers; it is his duty:

> It bicometh to a Kynge that kepeth a rewme,
> To 3iue mede to men that mekelich hym serueth.

rewme realm; mekelich dutifully.

'Mede' is thus an obligation that runs throughout society; so that she can assert with triumphant finality

> No wi3te as I wene with-oute mede may libbe.

Meed's appeal has been most cleverly couched. As directed to a King, it has appealed to 'organisation'—the ordered society which runs in the familiar grooves of habitual self-interest. This has followed well upon her earlier device of turning the argument *ad hominem*, first upon Conscience, then the King, with the reference to the ill-fated French venture. It is, apparently, an unanswerable case, as was Conscience's indictment upon her. All the medieval love of dialectic is here, in these apparently irreconcilable views, poised for final judgement. The King cries his appreciation of Meed's case:

> bi Criste! as me thynketh,
> Mede is well worthi the maistrye to haue!

It is here that we meet the first strong instance of Langland's poetic power. Action supervenes on debate, and the focus narrows to a single figure; Conscience kneels. The matter is now one of the highest solemnity. It is no longer merely a question of adjudging the better case: as, for the poet, it is no longer a demand, which he has brilliantly fulfilled, upon his skill in dialectical exchange. Now we come to a crucial issue. Conscience had dealt in formal courtesy earlier, when the trial had begun:

> Knelynge, Conscience to the kynge louted,
> To wite what his wille were and what he do shulde.

It is time to ask for a final deliverance from Meed's power. So Conscience literally makes his 'submission'; with one grave word of denial he kneels and continues as a suppliant:

> 'Nay,' quod Conscience to the kynge and kneled to the erthe.

The solemnity of the action is matched by the formal tone of address to the King, who is thus called from the heat of debate to his final responsibilities:

> There aren two manere of medes, *my lorde, with 3owre leue* . . .

This ceremonious but quiet opening, following immediately upon the brisk verbal exchanges of Conscience and Meed, may remind us of the

*wi3te* man, creature; *wene* think; *libbe* live; *maistrye* upper hand, favourable verdict; *louted* made obeisance; *manere* kinds; *leue* leave.

decisive moment in Act I of *King Lear* when Kent would recall his ruler to a sense of kingly responsibilities:

> Royal Lear,
> Whom I have ever honour'd as my king,
> Lov'd as my father, as my master follow'd,
> As my great patron thought on in my prayers...

The loyal subject seeks to recall his liege-lord to the sense of final responsibility; for the choice to be made is momentous. When, in Shakespeare's play, it fails, the subject goes on to speak with undeviating bluntness of false appearance and inward reality. So, though more mildly, Conscience distinguishes the 'two manere of medes'. For Kent, the ruler's folly can lead only to a world where values are precisely inverted ('Freedom lives hence, and banishment is here'). It is a similar danger that Conscience proclaims; and we have already seen it established in the field of folk—'Of other heuene than here holde thei no tale'. As in *King Lear*, so here; given only its opportunity, humanity will prey upon itself. If Kent's words are prophetic, Conscience's are, in one way, retrospective: they sum up and explain what we have already witnessed. Yet Conscience's account leads forward, too, in a manner that may surprise us.

Conscience points out that the term *mede* (or 'reward') can properly be applied only to two things—God's great reward to the virtuous; and the bribes or favours given in this life to those who do ill. Here extremes meet: for each is a *mede mesurelees*, a reward wholly disproportionate to the merits of the recipient. A surprising link is thus forged between the merits of the righteous and the palpable sins of the unrighteous. Surely and inevitably the scope of the poem is altering from the clear opposition 'good'-'bad', 'crime'-'punishment', 'virtue'-'reward'; the truth, on investigation, proves complex. It is Meed who has brought this on herself: to look into the commonly-accepted scheme of things must be, sooner or later, to contrast the Divine with the merely human standard. So here, Conscience makes short work of Meed's case.[7] Payment for services rendered or goods delivered is not a 'reward' at all; it is *mesurable hire*, a proportionate wage. Now it is Conscience's turn to drive a shrewd thrust home. Meed has adroitly made out a case for herself as a counsellor of Kings. Let the King recall (appropriately, from the Book of Kings) the Divine vengeance upon Saul for his disobedience through cupidity:

> Such a myschief mede made Saul the kynge to haue,
> That god hated hym for euere and alle his eyres after.

*eyres* heirs.

It is a telling stroke and parries Meed's confident conclusion upon the duties of a King. But Conscience ends with an ironic glance not at the ruler but at the possible fate of those who tender good advice. He will not, he says, draw out the moral of Saul's downfall, in case it causes offence:

> For so is this world went with hem that han powere,
> That who-so seyth hem sothes is sonnest yblamed.

This double-edged thrust at 'advisers' (if the good are reproved, the implication is that the bad, like Meed, are 'sonnest' applauded) fittingly concludes the case against Meed, where at one stroke 'reward' had been separated from due payment, the *mesurelees* from the *mesurable*, *meed* from *mercede*, as Langland calls it in the C Text. But Conscience has not done. The distinction between *mesurable* and *mesurelees* disposes forever of Meed's claim to make the world go round. In so far as she is active, she is active for ill. The world of rewards and services has been set to rights. It now remains to place it in its true perspective: and this is to be done by looking beyond it. A world of contractual obligation is not the highest good known to man. Now Conscience proudly asserts his title to knowledge—the same ground of judgement that had been revealed in the Prologue and in Holy Church's admonition to an inattentive Dreamer. It is 'natural knowledge', a law of nature written in all men's hearts, which both prompts Conscience—the awareness of right and wrong in particular situations[8]—and also gives assurance that the moral conflict will one day have an end:

> I, Conscience, know this, for kynde witt me it tauȝte,
> That resoun shal regne and rewmes gouerne.

This is the day when 'one Christian king' shall rule over all men. The return from the millennial vision to the present, where a Christian king is to give judgement in Meed's case, is well marked. Conscience, I fancy, underlines it. Meed may be *maistre* now—Conscience admits it; but not in that day:

> Shal na more Mede be maistre, as she is nouthe,
> Ac loue and lowenesse and lewte togederes,
> Thise shul be maistres on molde, treuthe to saue.

*went* changed; *sothes* truths; *sonnest* (soonest) first; *rewmes* realms; *nouthe* now; *Ac* but; *lowenesse* humility; *molde* earth.

It is perhaps a deliberate taking up of the King's cry at the end of Meed's defence:

> Mede is well worthi the *maistrye* to haue!

More than a successful plea, the upper hand in the present debate, is at stake. Conscience continues by opposing to Meed, the corrupter of law, *lewte*, whom we had earlier heard of in the Prologue (122, 126) and again from Holy Church (II 21). To counter Meed men must have *lewte*, scrupulous regard for law[9]; and thus there will be an end of that mere litigation which is Meed's greatest opportunity, placing her in reality above law, so that she

> Ouer lordes lawes reuleth the rewmes.

But obedience to law at its highest is love. We recall that *Lewte* was described by Holy Church as her lover. So we leave the *mesure* principle, and the hazards it offers, when we look beyond the mere reform of secular society. The great goal is not the triumph of law but its subordination:

> kynde loue shal come ʒit and conscience togideres,
> And make of lawe a laborere.

In that great day, the law-loving people, the Jews, shall know the truth. They

> shall wene in here witte, and waxen wonder glade,
> That Moises or Messie be come in-to this erthe,
> And haue wonder in here hertis that men beth so trewe.

Conscience speaks in character; it is natural to him, as it is for the Jews, to apprehend truth as perfect conformity with Divine injunction. With Langland we are never far from the realities of a world where the primary aspect of 'truth' is obedience to moral law; men's spiritual state is to be seen in their actions, and law implies punishment. The present vision is of universal peace; but there is the penalty of death for any who do not comply. The clergy will say their offices and keep away from the hunting-field; no oppressor shall rig the law to his own ends; there can be only one criterion and only one judgement:

> after the dede that is don, one dome shal rewarde,
> Mercy or no mercy, as treuthe wil acorde.

*Ouer* above; *kynde* natural; *wene* believe, suppose; *here witte* their understanding; *waxen* grow, become; *beth* are; *after* according to; *dome* judgement; *acorde* agree.

There is thus to be an end of the multiplicity of courts—one court only, and only one judge to pronounce sentence, 'True-tongue', who has never offended against Conscience. Then, to conclude, as though he has spoken too openly and thus ignored his own awareness of the likely fate of those who advise monarchs, Conscience utters a dark prophecy, which serves to distance his vision, recalling us to the present and deadly enemy of all that we might hope for:

> And er this fortune falle, fynde men shal the worste,
> By syx sonnes and a schippe and half a shef of arwes;
> And the myddel of a mone shal make the Iewes to torne,
> And saracenes for that si3te shulle synge *gloria in excelsis, &c.*,
> For Makomet and Mede myshappe shal that tyme;
> For, *melius est bonum nomen quam diuicie multe.*

The linking of 'Makomet' and Meed is a superb parting thrust. Now Meed is completely enraged. All her self-possession deserts her in a moment: and it is a telling insight that reveals her taking up the readiest weapon to hand—a plea for sympathy which is at the same time a shrewd appeal to duplicity. It is not for her, she cries, to pretend to learning; but even she knows that authorities can be quoted on both sides.

This concluding scene is of great importance if we are to see Meed in her true colours. One critic has invited our sympathy for her as a woman whom Conscience has 'bluntly and insultingly' refused. For such a reader, it is 'quite wrong to interpret the speeches of Meed as if she were aware of wrongdoing in herself'; she is 'almost morally neutral'.[10] I have already called attention to Meed's shameless acceptance of bogus shrift (III 35-63). Her blazing anger at Conscience is similarly revealing. But her true nature is put beyond doubt by her last piece of 'argument'. Meed has her place in a well-defined tradition of poetic moralizing. It is a tradition which proceeds upon a firm association between the contemptible and the ridiculous, and is nourished by that taste for comic inversion of the truth which underlies much medieval humour— in blasphemy, parody, or the Fescennine licence of appointed holiday, when the Boy Bishop, the Lord of Misrule, and other carnival kings-for-a-day hold their brief sway. The range of effect is wide; and the greatest single figure in this tradition is one of outright comedy—Alice, Wife

*er* before; *falle* befall, occur; *arwes* arrows; *the myddel of a mone* a full moon; *torne* be converted; *saracenes* Saracens (Mohammedans); *Makomet* Mohammed; *myshappe* come to grief (disaster); *melius est* etc. 'A good name is rather to be chosen than great riches' (Prov. xxii 1).

of Bath, with her magnificent contempt for *auctoritee* and thus her devastating opening gambit

> Experience, though noon auctoritee
> Were in this world, is right ynogh for me—[11]

which sweeps before it any lingering protest. The effect need not always be so boldly evident. For an instance which closely resembles this of Langland's, we may recall, from the Canterbury Tales, the Merchant's story of January and May. Pressing his lecherous attentions on his young bride, January asserts

> A man may do no synne with his wyf,
> Ne hurte hymselven with his owene knyf.[12]

We find another Canterbury pilgrim, the Parson, turning this truth the right way up when he comes to deal with *Luxuria*, Lechery, in his long discourse:

> And for that many man weneth that he may nat synne, for no like-rousnesse that he dooth with his wyf, certes, that opinion is fals. God woot, a man may sleen hymself with his owene knyf . . .[13]

Wilful misunderstanding is the characteristic of the sinful. Their errors as such are comic—but that is not to say they are innocent, much less amoral. On its serious side, the perversion of intelligence is not the least significant characteristic of the wicked. We need not go to Dante to learn that losing 'the good of the intellect'[14] is a process that, once set in motion, is irreversible; Shakespeare, Spenser and Milton will furnish examples enough. In the present instance, Meed makes a last attempt to counter Conscience's insistence upon the complexity of notions of reward and deserving, by equating complexity with confusion or inherent contradiction. She again quotes Scripture for her own ends: 'He who bestows gifts wins honour'. But her error is characteristic of perverted intelligence; to attempt to subvert truth is to leave out a major part of it. It is a fatal move; and Conscience closes for the kill. He can now afford to be humorous, for the real danger is almost past.

He begins with the ordinary form of address, the 'thou' that is familiar and here is condescending. Certainly, he says, her 'Latin' (the authority cited) is sound enough; but there is a slight objection:

*ynogh* enough; *weneth* thinks; *sleen* slay.

> thow art like a lady that redde a lessoun ones
> Was, *omnia probate*, and that plesed here herte,
> For that lyne was no lenger atte leues ende.
> Had she loked that left[15] half, and the lef torned,
> She shulde haue founden fele wordis folwyng therafter,
> *Quod bonum est tenete;* treuthe that texte made!

The tone is lightly ironical; and the irony is now deepened, as Conscience changes to the polite mode of address. His exaggerated deference is the last note of respect Meed is to hear, and parodies the respect paid her at her first coming to Westminster:

> And so ferde ʒe, madame!; ʒe couthe namore fynde,
> Tho ʒe loked on Sapience sittynge in ʒoure studie.

But if she were to look to her text again she would find a qualification of the phrase that gave such comfort. It is in fact

> A ful teneful tixte to hem that taketh mede,
> And that is, *animam autem aufert accipientium, &c.* :[16]
> And that is the taille of the tixte of that that ʒe schewed,
> That theiʒe we wynne worschip and with mede haue victorie,
> The soule that the soude[17] taketh bi so moche is bounde.

Meed is not the innocent creature a later, naturalistic tradition would have her. To be sure, Langland has ample room for sardonic humour in his presentation of the veritable *radix malorum*. But it is Meed's very universality that allows of energy and lifelikeness in her portrayal. What men cannot hope to change decisively they must find a place for in the scheme of things; and a thorough-paced, all-pervasive roguery is better ridiculed than merely denounced or piously suppressed. The medieval way is seen in gargoyle and misericord; the wicked is fantastic rather than utterly frightening. For the Devil, the Middle Ages knew, is, in More's phrase, 'the proud spirit' that 'cannot endure to be mocked'. The humour thus released is by no means incompatible with true insight. It is not a question of predetermining the merely moral status of human folly or weakness, and thus evoking a 'stock response'. It is rather a

---

*omnia probate* 'Prove all things'; *Quod bonum est tenete* 'hold fast that which is good' (I Thess. v 21); *lenger* longer; *atte* at the; *fele* the remaining; *ferde* fared; *couthe* could; *Sapience* Wisdom (here, a reference to the book of Proverbs which Meed has quoted); *teneful* vexatious; *hem* them; *animam aufert*, etc. 'he takes away the soul of those who receive them' (gifts); *taille* conclusion; *soude* pay, bribe.

matter of probing to the essential failing—the lack of integrity, if we will
—and thus revealing the streak of self-importance or of modest self-
congratulation in the apparently disinterested act or statement. In all
wickedness, thus considered, there is a fatal element of self-contradiction.
This satiric penetration should not come amiss to modern readers. Its
quality in Langland is that of tonic high spirits, not an inflexible and
grudging moralizing. For, as we have in part seen, and shall see in
abundance, his satiric understanding does not fail to include the Dreamer
himself. Meed, then, is not a 'character' for naturalistic appraisal. When
Langland tells us that she is

> As comune as a cartwey to eche a knaue that walketh,

his purpose is to show the universal compliancy behind Meed's outward
attractiveness. We must not allow an accident of literary history to
create for us another Doll Tearsheet, who, though 'as common as the
way between Saint Albans and London', is yet invested with her own
truth and dignity. It is Doll, a mercenary in her own line, who will be
friends with Falstaff for no lesser reason than that he is going to the
wars; 'and whether I shall ever see thee again or no, there is nobody
cares'.[18] There is no such disinterestedness in Lady Meed.

*Passus IV*

What follows is her utter downfall. But it is by no means a foregone
conclusion; indeed, Meed's final boldness is very nearly successful.
Conscience cannot be compelled to kiss Meed—unless Reason assents.
There is thus an interval, while Conscience is absent in search of Reason;
and it is an interval which presents Meed with her very last opportunity.
For the King has undertaken that a new order shall begin with Conscience's return; he, with Reason, will govern the realm as advisers
to the King. Reason makes ready for his journey, in the first of the
stiff, signpost-like 'allegories' that commonly mark a gathering-
point in the argument. They embody those names that, as Skeat notes,
remind us of Puritan worthies:

> And called Catoun his knaue, curteise of speche,
> And also Tomme Trewe-tonge-telle-me-no-tales-
> Ne-lesyng-to-lawȝe-of-for-I-loued-hem-neuere—
> 'And sette my sadel uppon Suffre-til-I-se-my-tyme,

*eche a* every; *Catoun* Cato (the name given to the author of a celebrated collection
of *Moral Distichs*); *knaue fellow; curteise* courteous; *lesyng-to-lawȝe-of* loose
tales to laugh at.

And lete warrok it wel with Witty-wordes gerthes,
And hange on hym the heuy brydel to holde his hed lowe,
For he wil make wehe tweye er he be there'.

This type of 'allegorical' work, which is little to the taste of the modern reader, will be discussed more fully in a later chapter. But I have quoted this first 'signpost' at length for its oblique reminder to us of the Dreamer's besetting sin of impetuosity—and thus the limitations of mere dialectical endeavour.[19] In the very moment that we await Reason as a deliverer we must learn that his horse needs to be restrained. The moral virtues are never very far from the poet's mind; and there must come a time when the Dreamer's merely argued progress towards his goal, failing, will bring him to recognize the need 'to see much and to suffer more.' For the moment, we may notice that the opposition is also aroused. 'Warren Wisdom', whom we may regard as Mr. Worldly Wise, and his friend Mr. Crafty ('Witty') ride to the Court.

Arrived at the Court, Reason is given a place on the Bench. Peace now appears, to complain of Wrong. This is no isolated interruption of Meed's examination. It is in fact the last and greatest instance of Meed's potential power. As it is revealed that the King knows Wrong for the rogue he is, Wrong in fear turns to 'Wisdom', who has been awaiting his opportunity, and beseeches him

To make pees with his pens, and profered hym manye.

But these experienced knaves tell their client plainly that

But if Mede it make, thi myschief is vppe,
For bothe thi lyf and thy londe lyth in his grace.

So Wrong redoubles his entreaty to 'Wisdom'

To make his pees with his pens handi-dandi payed,

and the fee is paid over. It is the last stand of evil—

Wisdome and Witte thanne wenten togideres,
And toke Mede myd hem, mercy to winne.

There is no room for illusion about Meed as she is joined by these most powerful of allies; and no pretence of formal proceeding on their part remains:

warrok gird; make wehe neigh; pees peace; pens (pence) money; But if Mede it make unless Meed can manage it otherwise; vppe in the ascendant (i.e. will prevail); his the King's; handi-dandi payed slipped from hand to hand as (corrupt) payment; myd with.

> Wisdom and Witt were about faste
> To ouercome the kyng with catel, ȝif thei myȝte.

But it is characteristic of evil to overreach itself. There is a clear justice in this revelation to the Court of Meed at work. The C text puts it very plainly in the one line:

> Thoruh Wrong and hus werkes ther was Mede yknowe. (C VI 71)

The King orders Wrong to be imprisoned. But Wrong's advocate has an ingenuous plea against this rigorous sentence; let him be bailed, in hope of amendment. 'Wit' joins in with the pious reflection

> Bettere is that bote bale adoun brynge,
> Than bale be ybette and bote neuere the bettere.

The whole tactic is a pretended acknowledgement of authority, to escape the realities of punishment. The law, it is now admitted, is the law—but need it press so hard? And the defence is very near gaining its end; for Meed asks mercy of Peace, handing over

> a present al of pure golde.

It is an amends—if over-handsome, as we should expect from Meed— for the wrong done; and it comes with Meed's assurance—for form's sake—that there will be no recurrence:

> 'Haue this, man, of me', quod she, 'to amende thi skathe,
> For I wil wage for Wronge he wil do so namore.'

The plaintiff is entirely satisfied, and now turns prisoner's friend:

> I forgyue hym that gilte with a goode wille;
> So that the kynge assent I can seye no bettere;
> For Mede hath made me amendes, I may namore axe.

It is a limit we have not reached before. There is no corruption of witnesses here: satisfaction has been made, on the promise of amendment. All we are seeing, after the earlier dramatic episodes of the trial, are the ordinary and approved processes of the law. It is thus that Meed is revealed as most dangerous of all. For, grant exemption from the law without a true guarantee of amendment, and law is brought into contempt; immunity has been merely purchased. We are back at the venal world of the *Visio*. It is a vital issue; can there be any question of *purchasing* forgiveness? The King is on to the present evasion at once:

*were about faste* set to at once; *catel* wealth; *Bettere is* etc. It is better that some recompense should be made, thus lessening the harm done, than that the offence be punished and no recompense made; *skathe* injury; *wage for* guarantee on his behalf; *So that* provided that; *axe* ask.

'Nay', quod the kynge tho, 'so me Cryst helpe!
Wrong wendeth nouȝte so awaye, arst wil I wite more;
For loupe he so liȝtly, laughen he wolde,
And efte the balder be to bete myne hewen'.

There is only one condition on which Wrong can be released:

But Resoun haue reuthe on hym he shal rest in my stokkes,
And that as longe as he lyueth, but lowenesse hym borwe.

Pressure is brought to bear on Reason, as before it was on Conscience.
Now we see that if these two can be divided, evil may yet win the day.
Reason is besought
                              to haue reuthe on that schrewe,
            And for to conseille the kynge and Conscience after
            That Mede moste be meynpernour.

If granted, the demand would of course bring back the rule of Meed,
and thus would constitute her acquittal from the charges brought against
her. It is an interesting reflection on her power that the threat to Wrong
is now occupying the forefront of our attention. Do we not forget that
Meed is still before the King under examination? Reason, however, is
vigilant; his answer is unyielding, and fits exactly the progress of events.
Meed has revealed herself by her own act; actions, Reason says, speak
truth. There can be no question of *reuthe* before there is a change of
heart. Reason can finally relent only when the world is set to rights.
We may notice that among the ills to be redressed is that of empty
pilgrimage. Once again, a movement of the poem is preluded, as Reason
looks ironically to the day when

            seynt Iames be souȝte there I shal assigne,
      That no man go to Galis but if he go for euere;
      And alle Rome-renneres for robberes of byȝonde
      Bere no siluer ouer see . . .

Reason can have no mercy on Wrong

      While Mede hath the maistrye in this moot-halle.

*tho* then; *wendeth* goes; *arst* first; *wite* know; *loupe he* if he were to escape;
*balder* bolder; *hewen* servants; *But* unless; *lowenesse hym borwe* contrition ransoms
him; *reuthe* pity; *schrewe* wretch; *meynpernour* surety; *seynt Iames* St James the
Great, whose shrine at Santiago de Compostella in *Galis* (Galicia) was a favourite
goal of pilgrimage; *renneres* runners; *for robbers of byȝonde* to enrich robbers living
abroad; *moot-halle* meeting-hall.

It is law, in all its sanctity, that must be upheld, without the least deviation, if the King is truly to care for his realm. [20] No concession can be made for 'gifts'; and so for Meed there can be no mercy 'but mekenesse it make'.

In this emphasis on fulfilment of law there is beginning to grow a sense that nothing less than the absolute is demanded. There begins to rise, above the dead level of this middle-earth, where the *mesurable* is the truth to be contended for, the cliff-like outline of perfection. Like the Dreamer's own Malvern Hills, seen from far off, the shape is at first indistinct. But the case against Meed is ended with one more of those two-edged pronouncements which summon us beyond habitual notions into full clarity:

> For *nullum malum* the man mette with *inpunitum*,
> And badde *nullum bonum* be *irremuneratum*.

It is an enigmatic utterance which will need to be interpreted. And, there, concludes Reason, lies danger:

> Late ȝowre confessoure, sire kynge, construe this *vnglosed*.[21]

The vital consideration is that the truth be applied, practised; upon that condition the millennial state foretold by Conscience is at hand. Langland repeats the telling phrase he had used earlier; law shall be a labourer. The plane on which we end is that on which the *Visio* has so far been wholly placed, the middle-earth which cries out for Christian reformation:

> Law shal ben a laborere and lede a-felde donge,
> And Loue shal lede thi londe as the lief lyketh!

It is the final comment on mere legal process. We see Meed imprudently winking to the lawyers, and their returning the greeting. But there is no doubt of the verdict: and Meed is hailed with contempt. It is Langland's characteristic fidelity to the fact that shows us a juryman and a Summoner following hard on her heels, while a Sheriff's clerk sourly rounds on the crowd who have never given him a pennyworth of consideration. Not only is Meed very much alive, but welcome for the judgement against her is by no means universal. The continuing problem of Meed's existence and influence is certainly not solved. The immediate threat to right government is ended; that is all. She is sternly rebuked by

*nullum malum* etc. adapted from a celebrated treatise by Pope Innocent III, 'On Despising Worldly Things' (*De Contemptu Mundi*). The passage in the original runs, 'He only is the just judge ... who leaves no evil unpunished, no good unrewarded'; *vnglosed* without a 'gloss' or comment, *i.e.* the plain sense; *lede a-felde donge* lead the muck-cart afield; *the lief lyketh* in accordance with your wishes (the change from the dignified plural 'you' to the singular 'thou' emphasizes the simple truth).

the King; for she has almost destroyed authority—'Mede ouer-mais-trieth lawe and moche treuthe letteth'. Judgement upon all offenders will be according to desert, uninfluenced by mercenary considerations:

> Mede shal nouȝte meynprise ȝow, bi the Marie of heuene!

There is to be only one criterion—steadfast compliance with justice, 'leute in lawe'; and that makes an end of all legal wrangling—'lete be al ȝowre Ianglyng'. It is the essential beginning: and now we may turn to the deeper problem which intended reform uncovers. Unless all assent to this new state of things it will be indeed difficult for the King to carry out his intention. We end the theoretical aspect of government, the right ordering of secular society, when Conscience and Reason are united with the Monarch in one resolve:

> Als longe as owre lyf lasteth lyue we togideres.

Authority is thus set to rights. There remains the problem of fulfilling the demand for right conduct which now falls unambiguously upon each subject.

How has this been brought about? In particular, how are we to follow Reason's bidding and 'construe' the two enigmatic lines which seal Meed's fate? To answer that question, we must first turn back to what we have seen of the main themes and their development up to this point. It is the more important to do this, since it is characteristic of the poet—as the reader will by now begin to recognize—that with this ending we are in fact at a new beginning.


## IV

We began with a Dreamer who, when his opportunity to ask funda-mental questions came, was over-ambitious. Looking outward rather than nearer home, he ignored the knowledge written in his own heart. But his questioning, though ill-directed, did serve to bring out two great truths which are at the heart of all Langland has shown us. Man has a sufficient guide in the Moral Law written in his heart; and law is yet not the highest attribute of Deity:

> This I trowe be treuthe; who can teche the better,
> Loke thow suffre hym to sey and sithen lere it after,

ouer-maistrieth overmasters; letteth hinders, thwarts; meynprise stand surety for; togideres together; sithen then; lere learn; after accordingly.

> For thus witnesseth his worde, worche thow there-after;
> For trewthe telleth that loue is triacle of heuene . . .

Truth is the inalienable possession of all men ('a kynde knowyng'); and its meaning is love—on the creature's side allegiance to his Lord which is above self-interest ('to louye thi lorde leuer than thi-selue'); on the Creator's side, a love that became incarnate:

> For heuene my3te nou3te holden it, it was so heuy of hym-self,
> Tyl it hadde of the erthe yeten his fylle . . .[22]

So all the concern with right conduct and correct doctrine, the search for a merely argued truth, whether in the individual or in society, the insistence that men are to be judged by their actions and not their professions merely, the sharp awareness of discrepancy between what man is and what he ought to be—all is placed in its true perspective. Man knows what is right; and his Creator is not only or even primarily a Divine Lawgiver. These two truths are central to the whole design. The application they are given immediately to an over-impetuous and over-theoretical Dreamer ('Loke thow suffre hym to sey and sithen lere it after') is of the highest importance in the later development of the poem, where the Dreamer is to ponder at length the significance of what he has seen, and to earn a further scolding or two before the end is in sight. The general application to society is immediately evident in the career of Lady Meed. It is Conscience, whose teacher is 'Kind Wit', who opposes Meed and ends the first confusion of terms by the clear distinction between 'reward' and 'payment' (the *mercede* of the C Text), and thus between the *mesurelees* and the *mesurable*. His doing so enables us to see afresh that God is not a God merely of due rewards and punishments: the 'reward' available to all is sheerly disproportionate to sinful man's deserving. It is a disproportion to be made manifest in that great day when 'kynde loue . . . and conscience togideres' will

> make of lawe a laborere; such loue shal arise,
> And such a pees amonge the people and a perfit trewthe,
> That Iewes shal wene in here witte, and waxen wonder glade
> That Moises or Messie be come in-to this erthe.

The fundamental truth is utterly simple; its application, though far-off, is the final comment on a world of rewards and punishments, and thus of bargains, evasions and substitutions. But if it is to a Promised Land that

---

*worche* work; *triacle* a sovereign remedy; *yeten* eaten; *wene* believe, suppose; *here witte* their understanding; *waxen* grow, become.

we are journeying, the road nevertheless must lead through Sinai. We may not, like Meed, attempt to evade Law; the satisfaction of Law is the question man must confront. The 'sentence' that sounded Meed's downfall was two-edged. As the poet will say of a later statement, 'Al in two lynes it lay'; it is as absolute as a naked sword:

> For *nullum malum* the man mette with *inpunitum*,
> And badde *nullum bonum* be *irremuneratum*.

This is the definition of the just man; and it reaches beyond the immediate situation. Its application to Meed is clear. Justice is to deal evenhandedly; but Meed will pervert its operations. She will stand alike between the good man and his reward, and the wicked and his punishment: so she is condemned. But what is of the highest importance to the poem is that in rejecting a world of payment for service (which includes payment in lieu of service) we make an end of all proximate measures. We must consider for once the *practicability* of the ideal of right conduct. The King may desire to rule justly; but what of the demand thus made upon all his subjects? We are to see how far humanity, desiring to make a new start, can obtain a sufficient guide. Already in the poem there has risen above the level of middle-earth the rock-like eminence of Law—the Law in all its rigour, with its undeviating demand for absolute fulfilment. It is well to know that love is the final truth; but how to satisfy the law's demands? We are at a new beginning in the inquiry.

In all this, Langland's art is at its most vigorous. I have already commented on the techniques employed—after the bustle and confusion of middle-earth, the isolated figure of Holy Church; after the cavalcade on its noisy way to Westminster, the solitariness of Meed: so, too, after the excitement of Meed's spirited defence, the kneeling of Conscience as he makes his gravest plea. We may add the final focus upon the three enthroned figures, King, Conscience and Reason as the clamour of the Court insulting Meed dies away. Above all, we must not fail to notice Langland's continuing realism—after the millennial vision of the rule of Reason, we return to the case awaiting trial; when sentence has been given upon Meed, we see that she has her friends still (just as Falsehood, Guile and Liar had found friends at need when Meed was arrested). This is the most striking single quality of Langland. He, least of all, we may feel, at the outset of our journey, is likely to lose himself in visionary ardour. His penetrating scorn has not failed to include the Dreamer, who is thus less our guide than our nearer companion. The themes of both the remainder of the *Visio* and the *Vita de Dowel* have been sounded—if the Law is to have final validity it must be perfectly fulfilled; then man, in his turn, must seek perfection. If we hurry over these early stages of the poem, or—worse—if we attend to them in the light of what we know comes later, we shall fail to see the organic connexion between the two great divisions of the *Liber de Petro Plowman* —the *Visio* in which the sight of a wicked world leads to the great question 'How shall the Law be fulfilled?', and the *Vita* in which perfect fulfilment of Law is at last apprehended by a Dreamer whose questionings, often ill-advised, bring him at last to understanding—so that he can take up once more his continuing search for the just man. Over all these first four Passus of the *Visio* rises the 'great Law of Duty'. To its final demand we now turn.

## Notes

1. As Miss Stella Maguire observes, 'The Prologue presents the world as it appears to a spiritually unenlightened man'. Miss Maguire appears, however, to take for granted the Dreamer's aptitude for Holy Church's instruction, believing that thereafter 'the Dreamer can never return to his original limited perception. All subsequent events must be judged by him in the light of her teaching'. ('The Significance of Haukyn, *Activa Vita*, in *Piers Plowman*', *Review of English Studies*, XXV (1949), 97-109; 101.) The fact is rather that this is what *ought* to happen. The Dreamer's actual inaptness enables us to observe without being dependent on him; and to apprehend—what is of the greatest importance as the poem develops in the *Vita*—that a failure to relate the wickedness of others to the self is a universal condition. On the characterization of the Dreamer, see Chapter VII, below.

2. *is asseled* is suggested by Donaldson for Skeat's *I assele*.

3. See pp. 306-13, below.

4. The C Text follows a stage further the successful career of the false traders. So far from being put down by the authorities, they become freemen of the city (C IV 108) —a telling instance of Lady Meed's power to subvert the authority that should restrain her.

5. The note of impudent assurance is well caught in Professor Coghill's version: 'I am wholly in your hand; hang me if I'm not!' (*Visions from Piers Plowman*, London, 1949, p. 32).

6. A. G. Mitchell, 'Lady Meed and the Art of *Piers Plowman*', Chambers Memorial Lecture, London, 1956, p. 4.

7. The C Text at this point turns decisively away from drama to sustained ratiocination. Conscience does not kneel; the striking equation between corrupt rewards and God's generosity towards sinful man is dropped; and in its place we have a determined insistence upon all true reward as in a sense merited—even the

'reward' of God is a return for the loyalty of His followers. This shift is by no means all loss; it gives us the useful term *mercede* to denote reward-as-due-payment; and, more important, a link is forged between this issue and that of Faith and Works, of which more is to be heard in due course.

8. As Randolph Quirk observes, 'conscience . . . is inwit's awareness of right and wrong brought to bear upon one's actions; it is inwit in action' ('Langland's Use of *Kind Wit* and *Inwit*', *Journal of English and Germanic Philology*, LII (1953), 18)8.

9. On the close connexion between *lewte* and law-keeping, see E. Talbot Donaldson, *Piers Plowman: the C-Text and its Poet* (New Haven, 1949), p. 66, n. 4.

10. Mitchell, *loc. cit.*, 9, 22.

11. *Canterbury Tales* D 1-2.

12. *ibid.*, E 1839-40.

13. *ibid.*, I 858.

14. *Inferno* iii 17-18.

15. *left* is suggested by Donaldson for Skeat's *other*.

16. The citation is from Prov. xxii 9, which is variously translated in Knox and A.V. See Knox's note and *cf.* p. 86, n. 24, below.

17. *soude* (Donaldson) for Skeat's *sonde* ('gift', 'present').

18. 2 *Hen.* IV ii 2 161-2; 4 63-4.

19. The reference to the human failing of impetuosity, and thus to a Dreamer, whose name is yet to be disclosed, becomes more pointed in the C Text:

> it is the wone of *Wil* to wynse and to kyke;
> Forthy lat peitrel hym and pole hym with peyntede wittes. (Russell)

It is a touch that foreshadows much of the Dreamer's erratic progress in the *Vita de Dowel*.

20. The emphasis in the C Text is transferred from the present proceedings to Meed's power over process of law in general:

> Whyl Mede hath the maistrye ther motyng is atte barre. (C V 132)

21. Donaldson suggests for *vnglosed* the reading *on englissh* 'in English', 'in plain language'.

22. For a discussion of this passage and a suggested new reading, see Appendix, pp. 328-9, below.

*wone* habit; *wynse* wince; *lat peitrel* etc. restrain him (as a horse is restrained by weight of breast-armour and head-guard); *motyng* legal pleading; *atte barre* at the Bar.

CHAPTER II

# An End of Evasion

## (Passus V–VII)

He has signed the death-warrant of sin in our nature, so that we
should be fully quit of the law's claim, we, who follow the ways of the
spirit, not the ways of flesh and blood.    Rom. viii 4 (Knox)

### I

*Passus V*

It fits well with the King's resolve that he takes his lords to Church;
and there, momentarily, the Dreamer leaves them, as he awakes. But—
however odd this may sound to us—he soon grows faint from lack of
sleep (meaning that what he has seen in his dream is incomplete; he
must know more): and with a prayer he is asleep once again.

Now we are introduced to what we might easily overlook, through
the concentration up to this point on rewards. Reason preaches before
the King, and his theme is punishment—the Wrath of God, manifest
both in this life, as in pestilence and hurricane, and for the guilty in
the life to come, which this present life foreshadows. Let the guilty
take heed; there is a Power not to be withstood:

> Beches and brode okes were blowen to the grounde,
> Torned vpward her tailles, in tokenynge of drede
> That dedly synne at domesday shal fordon hem alle.

The sermon is apposite. We may too easily have thought of punishment
as something to be averted; Meed and Wrong, for all that judgement has
gone against them, have not been visibly punished. But, more important,
the argument is now to lead from imperfect secular justice to the Divine
requirement of all men. So it is fitting that we are reminded of the power
of God—a God Who is not mocked. We turn at once to thoughts of
repentance: against *this* summons no stay or evasion is thinkable.

Reason's sermon is eminently practical, and thus can be brief. Let

---

*Torned vpward her tailles* turned bottom upwards; *in tokenynge of drede* as a terrible
sign; *dedly synne* mortal sin; *domesday* Judgement Day; *fordon* destroy; *hem* them.

wasters go to work, extravagance be reduced, and children (especially those of tradesmen) be strictly brought up. Above all, let those who would teach others look to themselves:

> That ȝe prechen to the peple preue it on ȝowre-seluen,
> And doth it in dede, it shal drawe ȝow to good;
> If ȝe lyuen as ȝe leren vs, we shal leue ȝow the bettere.

It is one more glance at that characteristic failing of the knowledgeable which Holy Church had touched upon in her admonition to the Dreamer. 'Practise what you preach' is the central lesson for any who would teach in a sinful world. So, too, professed religious must be obedient to their rule, on pain of secular intervention if they cannot manage their own affairs. There is only one precept for King and Pope alike; let each love and pity his following:

> And er he gyue any grace gouerne firste hym-selue.

So, too, for all who maintain the laws:

> ȝe that han lawes to kepe, late treuthe be ȝowre coueytise,
> More than golde or other gyftes, if ȝe wil god plese.

The whole emphasis is upon the individual's application of the truth to himself. True reform thus begins at home; there is no need to externalize the search. Let those who seek 'seynte Iames and seintes of Rome' seek instead

> seynt Treuthe, for he may saue ȝow alle.

We end with a prayer for blessing on all those who will follow Reason's teaching. It is a crucial moment; Repentance, 'rehearsing Reason's theme',

> gert Wille to wepe water with his eyen.

The proud spirit of independence, the creaturely disposition which, of itself, would choose individual existence even at the cost of separation from its Creator, is humbled. If the author's name was in fact Will, there is a happy accident in the relevance of his 'Christian name' to his characteristic standpoint in scrutinizing Christian truth.[1] We may notice, too, that when Wrath's confession is ended, and Repentance counsels

*That* that which; *on* in; *drawe* bring; *leren* teach; *leue* believe; *kepe* maintain, administer; *late* let; *coueytise* desiring; *gert* caused.

sobriety in future, the lesson is appropriated to a penitent who speaks in the first person:

> 'And drynke nou3te ouer delicatly, ne to depe noyther,
> That thi wille bi cause ther-of to wrath my3te torne.
> *Esto sobrius,* ' he seyde, and assoilled me after,
> And bad me wilne to wepe, my wikkednesse to amende.

The energy of the description of the Seven Deadly Sins is too well known to bear elaboration; but the artistry calls for some comment in more general terms. In relation to the imaginative quality of the whole, this is the first considerable taste of an ironic penetration that coexists in Langland with visionary ardour; and on this more must be said later. In structural terms, this is the place where the follies and knaveries of the world the poet knows are subsumed under the great traditional heads. We must not think of it as licensed diversion. The parallel is rather with Jonson's categorization of the 'Humours', which, so far from restraining insight, in fact intensifies, so that creative power is released into bold demonstration of the limited span of a self-interest that works its own destruction. It is idle to ask that the categorization—the 'Humour' or the Sin—should be complex or many-sided. The objection is not merely that in proportion as it attempted to do so it would lose its generalizing power. The true point is that it is not and must not attempt to be 'representational' at all in that way. As Coleridge said of 'narrative allegory', 'where it is too strongly individualized, it ceases to be allegory'; and he justifiably went on to complain that in *The Pilgrim's Progress* often 'the characters are real persons with nick-names'.[2] Like the axioms in Euclidean geometry, these pre-existing categorizations are indispensable to the economy and penetration of the demonstration in hand. Only grant that Greed can be simply and singly dominant—then see how far and how fast we can go with an Auaricia, as with a Volpone! Once we agree that 'a point has no magnitude' we can penetrate a great way into essential relationships. Useless to object, at any later stage, that the abstraction is 'unreal', that every point we encounter in reality has magnitude. The demonstration of essential properties is not to be hampered by exact delineation of a complex and ambiguous reality. The personifications who thus play their part in Langland's poem seem particularly well-placed at this stage in its development. Behind us lies the field of folk, a holiday scene, with work too long postponed. Before us is the prospect of a workaday

*to depe* too deep; *Esto sobrius* be sober; *assoilled* gave absolution.

world, where the host of men and women must settle to producing and distributing the wealth which Meed would misappropriate. It is time to call a halt to the free play of man's fundamental characteristic, an unvarying self-interest.

The graphic art of this Passus is thus the true counterpart not only of Langland's visionary power but also of his great capacity for tenderness, for pity on the victims of callous exploitation or contemptuous indifference. His scorn plays like flickering lightning across the sins, bringing individual features into strong relief, as the pale eyes of Wrath, or Envy's pendulous cheeks, framing a face like a leek which *hadde yleye longe in the sonne*—a snapshot which unmistakably highlights the unnaturalness of envy. Equally, there is the searing irony that allows these creatures to declare with an awesome simplicity their best understanding of the truths that are offered them. Speak to Envy of sorrow, and he can only reply in surprise

> I *am* sori . . . I am but selde other.

*Naïveté* works its own undoing, for its conclusions are at least unambiguous. Vice is natural; how then should envy and malice be expelled, save by convulsive drugs or outright surgery?

> May no sugre ne swete thinge asswage my swellynge,
> Ne no *diapenidion* dryue it fro myne herte,
> Ne noyther schrifte ne shame, but ho-so schrape my mawe[3].

Envy speaks from darkness, the darkness in which anything is conceivable other than a change of heart. Yet his is still not the despair that would welcome oblivion as a healing art, to

> Pluck from the memory a rooted sorrow,
> Raze out the written troubles of the brain,
> And with some sweet oblivious antidote
> Cleanse the stuff'd bosom of that perilous stuff
> Which weighs upon the heart.

The answer to that question is always the same:

> Therein the patient
> Must minister to himself.[4]

So Langland's Envy makes the better end:

> I will amende this, ȝif I may, thorw myȝte of god almyȝty.

*yleye* lain; *selde* seldom; *diapenidion* medicinal sweet; *but ho-so* unless someone; *schrape* scrape; *mawe* stomach; *thorw* through.

Again, we have not only the brilliant malice-in-action of Wrath as gardener and cook to the convent, setting all at odds with one another; there is also the penetration that allows us to see the real significance of game and set in these encounters. Of the Friars, suitably egged on, we learn:

> Thus thei speken of spiritualte that eyther despiseth other,
> Til thei be bothe beggers and by my spiritualte libben.

Those who dispute upon precedence will find themselves under Wrath's domination, ironically pointed by using *spiritualte* to denote both his power and the ruthless treatment his dependants can expect from him. The equivocation on the word declares a fatal divorce of tongue and heart. It is a penetration which takes us beyond mere moralizing or fulmination to ask a radical question—Is this in fact an incurable condition of humanity? When the passions of enclosed sisters are suitably fed, we see, firstly, the manifest evil:

> Of wykked wordes I, Wrath, here wortes i-made,[5]
> Til 'thow lixte' and 'thow lixte' lopen oute at ones,
> And eyther hitte other vnder the cheke.

But the real mischief does not end there. The power of evil is not only in the overt act but in its implications; for

> Hadde thei had knyues, bi cryst, her eyther had killed other.

As is everywhere evident in the poem, Langland's imagination is not static; the wish and its fulfilment, given only opportunity, are indissoluble.[6] With him it is not simply a matter of lively illustration to diversify a moral theme. When Langland is at his most spirited he is at his most penetrating. Thus, Avarice is graphically presented when we are told that he is a poor haven for vermin:

> But if that a lous couthe haue lopen the bettre,
> She sholde nou3te haue walked on that welche, so was it
> > > > thredebare.

But the truth of the Vice is deepened when we hear the easy blasphemy that accounts for his success as a trader. He depends not upon the Grace of God but upon 'the grace of guile'. Again, we come to an instance of ignorance-all-but-invincible, in the limit of this creature's understanding of the restitution necessary before contrition can be accepted:

*spiritualte* spiritual authority; *libben* live; *wortes* vegetables; *lixte* liest; *lopen* leapt; *eyther* one, each; *her* of them; *welche* (Welsh) flannel.

'Repentedestow the euere,' quod Repentance, 'ne
                 restitucioun madest?'
'3us, ones I was herberwed,' quod he, 'with an hep of
                              chapmen;
I roos whan thei were arest and yrifled here males.'

As we have seen with Lady Meed, the ignorance of the determinedly
sinful is unalterable—and therefore comic:

'I wende ryflynge were restitucioun,' quod he, 'for I
                 lerned neuere rede on boke,
And I can no Frenche in feith but of the ferthest ende of
                                        Norfoke.'

In this broad comedy we should not fail to notice the continuing note
of irony. Usury, Avarice says, he has been guiltless of, save in youth,
when he would trim currency and lend it 'for loue of the *crosse*'. The
blasphemous collocation (of the Redemption and the 'tail' side of coin),
like his earlier 'grace of guile', and Wrath's cookery of *wordes* and
*wortes*, at once proceeds from and expresses a fully inverted scheme of
values. The outright comedy of situation and act in Langland's account
of the Sins—as, above all, in the never-to-be-forgotten progress of a
repentant Gluttony not to the church but homewards by way of the
ale-house—should not divert us from this vivid penetration. Even on
very simple levels—the turn of a phrase or the search for an analogy—it
stabs home. When, for instance, Sloth tells us of his devotions—

And 3if I bidde any bedes, *but if it be in wrath*,
That I telle with my tonge is two myle fro myne herte—

the saving clause floods the understanding. We see not only how
burning anger focuses the will; but equally how very far habitual
'devotion' can be from any real intentness. So, too, an old truth is
presented with new vividness when the same authority tells us

3if any man doth me a benfait or helpeth me at nede,
I am vnkynde a3ein his curteisye and can nou3te vnderstonde it;
For I haue and haue hadde some dele haukes maneres,
I nam nou3te lured with loue, but there ligge au3te vnder the
                                              thombe.

*herberwed* lodged; *chapmen* tradesmen; *arest* at rest (asleep); *males* bags; *wende*
thought; *ferthest ende* farthest part; *but if* unless; *benfait* benefit, good turn;
*vnkynde* uncivil; *a3ein* in return for; *some dele* partly; *haukes* hawk's; *but* unless;
*ligge* lie; *au3te* something (to eat).

The image of the hawk brings to us with unmistakable force the wholly 'natural', and therefore finally untamable, quality of vice; and, at the same time, the reality behind the appearance of indolence—its unsleeping alertness to its own interest. With Sloth, indeed, we nearly reach a sense of hopelessness. The very call to Repentance causes him to swoon (and here again outright comedy makes its own contribution to fundamental truth). It is fitting that a creature so faint-hearted should be warned against despair ('ware the from wanhope wolde the bitraye'). Salvation begins to appear the all-but-impossible undertaking. To reach so far is typical of Langland; for now we have left behind all qualified under-standing of repentance. Nothing less will serve than direct appeal to the Saviour. The injunction to render to all their dues (Rom. xiii 8), so hard of human achievement, is fulfilled by One who had had mercy on a dying thief:

> Robert the robbere on *reddite* lokede,
> And for ther was nouȝte wher-of he wepe swithe sore.
> Ac ȝet the synful shrewe seyde to hym-selue,
> 'Cryst, that on Caluarye vppon the crosse deydest,
> Tho Dismas my brother bisouȝte ȝow of grace,[7]
> And haddest mercy on that man for *memento* sake,
> So rewe on this robbere that *reddere* ne haue,
> Ne neuere wene to wynne with crafte that I owe.
> But for thi mykel mercy, mitigacioun I biseche;
> Ne dampne me nouȝte at domesday for that I did so ille.'

It is perhaps the plainest, as it is certainly the most moving, appeal that we have yet heard. And it is simply and wholly a cry for mercy. Resti-tution, on any scale proportionate to our offending, we cannot make; this, too, God must do for us. It is the great turning-point. All confusion is stilled as Repentance bids them kneel and prepares to pray for them. His act exemplifies and preludes the leadership that they will need if they are to advance in their new-found resolution; for it is leadership by example.

*wanhope* despair; 'eddite Reddite ergo omnibus debit' (the text quoted above); *nouȝte wher-of* no wherewithal (nothing with which he could make restitution); *swithe* very; *shrewe* wretch; *Tho* when; *memento* 'Domine, memento me cum uen-eris in regnum tuum' ('Lord, remember me when thou comest into thy kingdom' Luke xxiii 42); *rewe* have pity; *wene* expect; *wynne* earn; *crafte* skill, knowledge; *owe* possess; *mykel* great; *dampne* damn.

## II

Repentance's opening words are suited to a new beginning of all things. He sets the framework of Divine Purpose in which the sinners find themselves. The long range of Langland's mind is perfectly evident as we look all the way from the present hubbub back to the original purposes of God—

> that of thi goodnesse gonne the worlde make,
> And of nou3te madest au3te, and man moste liche to thi-selue—

and forward to their glorious fulfilment:

> O felix culpa! o necessarium peccatum Ade!
> For thourgh that synne thi sone sent was to this erthe.

This solemnity of tone does not forbid a lightness of spirit. On the contrary, there is a joyful affirmation in the play upon words as Godhead takes to Itself man's nature in order to plead man's cause. The words *sute*—as in 'lawsuit' and 'suit' (of clothes, here human flesh) and *secte*—'set' or 'division', the human race, and also 'suit' in the two previous senses— are thus intertwined:

> And sith with thi self sone in owre *sute* deydest
> On godefryday for mannes sake at ful tyme of the daye,
> There thi-self ne thi sone no sorwe in deth feledest;
> But in owre *secte* was the sorwe and thi sone it ladde,
> Captiuam duxit captiuitatem . . .

The same play upon meanings is continued in the *sute* of the Risen Lord (human flesh and the 'set', or division, of mankind)—

> The thrydde daye after, thow 3edest in owre *sute*—

and the *armes* of mankind (in the double meaning of 'flesh' and 'armour') is the last English word in the mighty summing-up, so that the Latin echoes it with concluding and affirmative force:

> And al that Marke hath ymade, Mathew, Iohan, and Lucas,
> Of thyne dou3tiest dedes were don in owre *armes;* [8]
> Verbum caro factum est, et habitauit in nobis.

*gonne* began; *au3te* everything; *O felix* etc. 'O happy fault! O necessary sin of Adam' (in bringing about man's greater happiness), adapted from the Canticle *Exultet* sung on Easter Eve; *sith* then, subsequently; *thi self sone* Thy Son Himself; *ful tyme* high noon; *ladde* led (captive); *Captiuam* etc. 'he led captivity captive, (Eph. iv 8); *3edest* went; *ymade* composed, set down; *dou3tiest* most valiant; *Verbum* etc. 'The Word was made flesh, and dwelt among us' (John i 14).

The artistic significance of this joyful intertwining of man's cause and his mortal nature is clear if we attend to the lines that immediately follow. It builds a bridge between the high gravity of the earlier address to Deity and a quietly confident intimacy:

> And bi so moche, me semeth, the sikerere we mowe
> Bydde and biseche, if it be thi wille,
> That art owre fader and owre brother, be merciable to vs . . .

This stylistic development, which brings to the poem a wholly new tone—a reasoned simplicity, an intimate submission—is thus the exact equivalent of the doctrine which it expresses. The Incarnation, we may say, has brought the story down to our level. Man's kinship with God allows us to presume upon His patience ('bi so moche, me semeth'), and encourages us to speak plainly of the present need. The tone of Repentance's concluding two lines is that of tender intercession:

> And haue reuthe on thise ribaudes that repente hem here sore,
> That euere thei wratthed the in this worlde, in worde, thou3te,
> > or dedes.

With the ending of the sermon, we turn, as before in the course of this poem, from the single figure to a multitude, from quiet concentration of aim to energetic confusion and cross-purpose. This time it is a mighty throng; and at first it is wholly of one mind:

> A thousand of men tho thrungen togyderes;
> Criede vpward to Cryst and to his clene moder
> To haue grace to go with hem, Treuthe to seke.

Throughout this Passus we have had glances forward to a pilgrimage, in fulfilment of Reason's injunction

> 3e that seke seynte Iames and seintes of Rome,
> Seketh seynt treuthe, for he may saue 30w alle.

Thus, Greed, we remember, had forsworn crooked practices in trade; he would

> wenden to Walsyngham and my wyf als,
> And bidde the rode of Bromeholme brynge me oute of dette.

*sikerere* more surely; *mowe* may; *Bydde* pray; *ribaudes* rascals; *here* their; *sore* offence, annoyance; *wratthed* angered; *thrungen* thronged; *clene* pure; *Seketh* seek; *wenden* go; *Walsyngham* a celebrated shrine of Our Lady; *als* too, also; *rode of Bromeholme* fragments of the True Cross venerated at Bromholm, Norfolk; *brynge me* etc. by having his deceits forgiven he would be brought out of actual as well as spiritual debt.

So, too, the image of pilgrim-journeying had been sustained in Sloth's resolving that, after making restitution,

> with the residue and the remenaunt, bi the rode of
> Chestre!
> I shal seke treuthe arst, ar I se Rome!

Pilgrimage, we see, is the normal and natural action of the repentant. But this time it is not so simple. No man knows his way to their destination, the shrine of Saint Truth who can save them all. The penitents, in all the fervour of their new resolve,

> blustreden forth as bestes ouer bankes and hilles.

It is in this mindless and leaderless confusion that they come upon a figure who is the most ludicrous of all embodiments of the false which have appeared so far. Perhaps nothing less than the fatuous Palmer could adequately convey the poet's rooted contempt for mere show, the externals that give only a visible lie to the individual's real state. Certainly, nothing else could so forcibly express the plight of a whole society. None among the repentant can be found to guide, and the much-travelled Palmer is utterly ignorant of the Saint men seek. There is a deep irony in the description; he is 'Apparailled as a paynym'—a reference not merely to his outlandish dress, but, by implication, to his pagan state. And indeed the wholesale acquisition of phials, shells, crosses and keys speaks less of an excessive religiosity than of that un-relenting self-interest which was the foundation of Meed's rule over men. So we can understand the grim truth of Langland's laconic comment on these trophies of the chase which include, to make all plain, 'the vernicle' (the napkin bearing the imprint of the Saviour's features) 'bifore'

> for men shulde knowe,
> And se bi his signes whom he souȝte hadde.

It is echoed in the Palmer's own innocent assertion to the would-be pilgrims that they have only to look to see that he has journeyed in all weathers for his soul's health:

> ȝe may se bi my signes that sitten on myn hatte.

The implication is deadly. How else should men guess at his spiritual state? We are prepared for his puzzled reaction to the request:

*with* etc. using whatever is left. *rode of Chestre* a celebrated cross in Chester; *arst* first; *blustreden* blundered; *paynym* (pagan) Saracen; *bifore* in front.

Knowestow ouȝte a corseint that men calle Treuthe?
Coudestow auȝte wissen vs the weye where that wy dwelleth?

One feels that his complacency is really disturbed. Can it be that there is a Saint whom he has not—we may accurately say—reckoned with? But at least he can reply with assurance upon one point, and we need not doubt that he speaks the sad truth:

> I seygh neuere palmere with pike ne with scrippe
> Axen after hym er, til now in this place.

It is in this context, an entire emptiness of outward show, that the Plowman puts forth his head. The Plowman's claim to know truth is not uttered as any boast; he knows truth, he says, as 'naturally as a scholar knows his books'. His credentials are not in outward and visible tokens, but in his whole way of life:

> Conscience and kynde witte kenned me to his place,
> And deden me suren hym sikerly, to serue hym for euere.

They are the credentials established by Holy Church at the outset of the poem in her colloquy with the Dreamer. Conscience and natural understanding are the basis of our knowledge: they must exact from us faithful practice, continuance in well-doing. So the Plowman has followed Truth 'al this fifty wyntre'. As he is the type of honest labour—

> I dyke and I delue, I do that treuthe hoteth—

so he has his due reward:

> Ich haue myn huire of hym wel, and otherwhiles more.

There is a quick glance at the world the would-be pilgrims have come from—the world of Meed which, as we have seen, is a world of 'Th' oppressor's wrong' and 'the law's delay'—in the Plowman's assurance that Truth is

> the prestest payer that pore men knoweth.

It is thus strikingly appropriate that those he addresses, newly come from the venal world, immediately take the hint these words would

ouȝte (auȝte) anything, at all; corseint lit. holy body, Saint; wissen show; wy man, creature; seygh saw; pike staff; scrippe bag; Axen ask; er before; kynde witte natural understanding; kenned made known; suren (give security)undertake; sikerly (surely) firmly; dyke ditch; delue dig; hoteth bids; Ich haue myn huire of hym wel he pays me well; otherwhiles more sometimes extra; prestest readiest.

convey if spoken by one of Meed's servants. They offer him money to seal the bargain of leadership. But it is also the measure of the distance they must travel from that world that the Plowman immediately and absolutely refuses:

> 'Nay, bi my soules helth,' quod Pieres, and gan forto swere,
> 'I nolde fange a ferthynge, for seynt Thomas shryne!
> Treuthe wolde loue me the lasse a longe tyme there-after!'

His offer was to instruct them clearly ('I shal wisse ʒow witterly the weye to his place'). It is characteristic of the newly-penitent to attempt to secure not guidance but a guide. We should not, perhaps, judge them too hastily; in the long run, they may know their own need best. We remember Robert the robber's absolute appeal for help. But for the present Piers will have none of it. He will instruct them in the way; it is for them to make the journey:

> if ʒe wilneth to wende wel, this is the weye thider
> That I shal say to yow, and sette yow in the sothe.

The primary truth of this episode, and the counsel it leads to, is that the only payment for the services of a guide which has occurred to penitents and Plowman alike would be, in Langland's terminology, a *mede*. Truth, that 'prestest payer', would certainly love Piers less if he accepted a bargain in these terms. Piers therefore sets himself to instruct the pilgrims. We have advanced in our inquiry. Here is one who will tell us the whereabouts of the Shrine all must seek. But it remains to be seen whether instruction is adequate to man's need.

Pier's observations are truly categorized by the heading Skeat prints in his C Text: *Alta uia ad fidelitatem est obseruatio preceptorum.* Here, once again, is a statement of Law, cutting across the confusion and uncertainty of a crowded scene. This is the second 'signpost' allegory in the poem; it links with and extends that displayed in Passus IV. There, too, law was to be asserted (against Meed): and there, too, the application was to the 'wayfaring man', the Christian in his daily trials and opportunities. So the 'Puritan' concatenations in this passage ('Covet-not-men's cattle' etc.) echo those given before. But this time the echo is deepened. The signpost indicates, though yet far-off, a Promised Land where Law is superseded by Love and Grace:

*nolde* would not; *fange* take; *for* etc. for all the wealth of St Thomas's shrine; *lasse* less; *witterly* certainly, clearly; *wilneth* wish, purpose; *wende wel* go the right way; *thider* thither; *sothe* truth, true way; *Alta* etc. The high road to Christian obedience lies in keeping the Ten Commandments.

Thanne shaltow come to a courte as clere as the sonne,
The mote is of Mercy, the manere aboute . . .
And alle the houses ben hiled, halles and chambres,
With no lede, but with Loue and Lowe-speche-as-bretheren . . .
Grace hatte the gateward, a gode man for sothe . . .
And if Grace graunte the to go in in this wise,
Thow shalt see in thi-selue Treuthe sitte in thine herte,
In a cheyne of charyte, as thow a childe were,
To suffre hym and segge nou3te a3ein thi sires wille.

Such is the vision; the way is still unyielding. Contrition must be genuine, saying truly:

[I] am ful sori for my synnes, and so I shal euere
Whan I thinke there-on, *theighe I were a pope.*

The Plowman's eye is unsparingly upon the realities of the moral life, the good all men, highest and lowest alike, must do. So he concludes with the warning that the gates are portered by all the Seven Virtues; kinship with them is essential:

'And who is sibbe to this seuene, so me god helpe!
He is wonderliche welcome and faire vnderfongen.
And but-if 3e be syb to summe of thise seuene,
It is ful harde bi myne heued,' quod Peres, 'for any of 3ow
                                                              alle
To geten ingonge at any gate there, but grace be the more.'

God is thus a God of Righteousness; and while we see that Grace is available—for otherwise all would be nearly desperate—we do not know on what terms that Grace is accessible. The notion of kinship with virtue points the way; and it links with the *sute* and *secte* of which we had heard from Repentance—humanity's unchanging 'nature' and thus its all-but-impossible 'cause'. Hope is yet at hand; Grace may prevail. But how? For the moment, all stands in doubt. The standard is too high: men are dismayed, and the hubbub of self-excusing breaks out:

*courte* mansion; *clere* radiant; *mote* moat; *manere* manor-house; *hiled* roofed; *lede* (lead) metal; *Lowe* humble, uncontentious; *hatte* is called; *gateward* doorkeeper; *cheyne* chain; *segge* say; *a3ein* against, in opposition to; *theighe* though; *sibbe* related; *seuene* seven; *faire* handsomely; *vnderfongen* received; *but-if* unless; *summe* some, any; *ingonge* admission; *but grace be the more* unless mercy is specially given.

'Now, bi Cryst,' quod a cutpurs, 'I haue no kynne there!'
'Ne I,' quod an apewarde, 'bi auȝte that I knowe!'
'Wite god' quod a wafrestre, 'wist I this for sothe,
Shulde I neuere ferthere a fote, for no freres prechynge'.

Men are 'too quick despairers'. For the moment all threatens to relapse into confusion and defeat. It is the Plowman's first act of leadership to rally them. The poet brings this vividly before us in his phrase,

'ȝus,' quod Pieres the plowman, *and pukked hem alle to gode.*

The time for mere counsel is over; the penitents must be firmly heartened. The *pukked* of this line answers the *pukketh* of Wrath, the deadly enemy in the Plowman's own account, a few lines earlier—the wretch who

pukketh forth pruyde to prayse thi-seluen.

We are beginning to see goodness in action; the good counsellor comes a step nearer his actual listeners. But it is no false confidence he gives them. The kinship that is the essential link with virtue has been made possible—through Mercy:

Mercy is a maydene there hath myȝte ouer hem alle;
And she is syb to alle synful and her sone also;
And thoruȝe the helpe of hem two (hope thow none other),
Thow myȝte gete grace there, bi so thow go bityme.

It is a sound assurance: but the venal world of the *Visio* is not so easily persuaded to embark upon hypothetical gains. And, just as 'Wisdom' and 'Witty' had seen their advantage even in the hour of Meed's being summoned before the King (and they had been nearly right); so now, if the Pilgrims are left to themselves, there may be one more opportunity for fatal credulity and unashamed exploitation. A Pardoner is revealed. He will risk nothing without the signs (and tools) of his trade; and this represents a bid for leadership. A prostitute will keep company with the Pardoner; there is safety in numbers, and even more in mutual profits. Here is a leadership that will bring the company along all-too-familiar paths. It is the most dangerous situation we have yet encountered. Like

cutpurs cutpurse; *kynne* relative; *apewarde* an entertainer with a monkey; *Wite god!* Heaven help us!; *wafrestre* a woman selling confectionery; *wist I this* if this is to be believed; *ferthere* (go) further; *fote* step; *pukked* pushed, spurred on; *myȝte* power; *syb* related, kinswoman; *thoruȝe* through; *hope thow none other* be sure of this; *bi so* provided; *bityme* quickly, without delay.

the fatuous Palmer, the Pardoner is one of those who has no title in himself: his credentials are all visible and tangible. But, more dangerous by far than the Palmer, the Pardoner offers his tokens for sale. We come back to the venal, with its fatal power of attracting all men to itself. The good works long overdue from the penitents seem now least of all likely to materialize. It is time for goodness to turn from instruction to active leadership.

### III

*Passus VI*

'This were a wikked way but who-so hadde a gyde
That wolde folwen us eche a fote;' thus this folke hem
mened.

It is lamentable, but it is true. Nothing else will serve; every foot of the way they are liable to go wrong. The Plowman replies that he would both guide and teach them on their journey, if he had finished ploughing and sowing his half-acre. It is characteristic of Langland's ironic penetration that there is no offer of help from the would-be pilgrims: only peevish complaint—

'This were a longe lettynge', quod a lady in a sklayre,
'What sholde we wommen worche there-whiles?'

It is in reply to this largely rhetorical complaint ('But what are *we* to do?' rather than 'What are we to *do*?') that Piers says that they can help him—both directly in his trade (by sewing wheat-sacks to prevent loss) and indirectly by spinning and thus clothing the needy, whom it is Piers's duty to serve:

For I shal lene hem lyflode but ȝif the londe faille.

We thus come to an understanding of the Plowman's task as universal provider in society. He supplies rich and poor alike—

Flesshe and bred bothe, to riche and to pore—

throughout his life-time; and this service is given not as a duty but as an offering

*wikked* hard, difficult; *but* unless; *who-so* one; *gyde* guide; *folwen* accompany; *eche a fote* every step; *hem mened* made their complaint; *were* would be; *lettynge* delay; *sklayre* veil; *there-whiles* in the meantime; *lene* grant; *lyflode* sustenance; *but ȝif* unless; *the londe faille* the harvest fails.

for the lordes loue of heuene.

So it is in turn the duty of all members of society, who depend upon him, to help the labouring man to perform his allotted task:

> And alle manere of men, that thorw mete and drynke lybbeth,
> Helpith hym to worche wiȝtliche that wynneth ȝowre fode.

This help is to be given in various ways. Just as the 'louely ladyes' with their 'longe fyngres' could provide for Holy Church by sewing rich vestments for the Church, so the Knight will misunderstand his allotted role if he thinks of it as simple labouring:

> 'Bi Crist,' quod a knyȝte tho, 'he kenneth vs the best;
> Ac on the teme trewly tauȝte was I neuere.
> Ac kenne me,' quod the knyȝte, 'and, bi Cryst, I will assaye!'

The willingness is all. This free offer of the Knight's signalizes a new era, for the response it wins is given in love and admiration:

> 'Bi seynt Poule', quod Perkyn, 'ȝe profre ȝow so faire,
> That I shal swynke and swete and sowe for vs bothe,
> And other laboures do for thi loue al my lyf-tyme,
> In couenaunt that thow kepe holikirke and my-selue
> Fro wastoures and fro wykked men that this worlde struyeth.'

So the *couenaunt* is entered into, with the Knight pledging himself to fulfil his agreement even at risk of his life. The formality of the address on Piers's side (ȝe and ȝow) is nicely varied, as the relationship is entered into. On the Knight's side it is *thow* and *thi* all the time: but Piers employs the formal address in the opening phrases on each occasion, followed, for the most part, by the singular thereafter. Intimacy is gained, too, by Piers's interjection after the Knight has plighted his troth. It has the quality of eager co-operation in a new design:

> 'Ȝe, and ȝit a poynt,' quod Pieres, 'I preye ȝow of more . . .'

The ceremonious ȝe and ȝow of solemn agreement in this passage continues until we come to the powerful reminder of the domain of Lady Meed; then the *thi* and *thow* speak directly to the individual conscience:

*thorw* through; *lybbeth* live; *wiȝtliche* manfully; *wynneth* gains, provides; *tho* then; *kenneth* teaches; *teme* team of oxen (with perhaps a play on *teme* meaning Piers's theme, or 'text' of honest labour); *assaye* try; *swynke* toil; *holikirke* holy Church; *wastoures* wasters; *struyeth* destroy, ruin; *ȝit* yet, still.

Loke ȝe tene no tenaunt but Treuthe wil assent.
And thowgh ȝe mowe amercy hem, late Mercy be taxoure
And Mekenesse *thi* mayster, maugre Medes chekes—

a note which is heard almost uninterruptedly to the end: *I do the to
vnderstande.* But the Knight, we learn, well understands that mercy and
uprightness of life are required of any who would maintain law; and
in this the rule of Meed is at an end:

'I assente, bi seynt Iame', seyde the kniȝte thanne,
'Forto worche bi thi wordes the while my lyf dureth.'

With this agreement, the *mede* with which the Pilgrims would have mistakenly bribed Piers in their first entreaty has given way to *a mesurable
hire.*

It is therefore appropriate that Piers can now contemplate the pilgrimage. But the garb in which he proposes eventually to make the
journey is markedly different from the outlandish rig of the Palmer the
penitents had first encountered. There is to be nothing of the *paynym*
about this English ploughman. He will wear the garments of his hard
occupation:

My cokeres and my coffes for colde of my nailles,
And hange myn hoper at myn hals in stede of a scrippe;
A busshel of bredcorne brynge me ther-inne;
For I wil sowe it my-self, and sitthenes wil I wende
To pylgrymage as palmers don, pardoun forto haue.

There is no question for Piers that the pilgrimage is to take place, and
he to lead it. For him, as well as for his fellow-pilgrims, there is to be the
appropriate reward of pilgrimage—*pardoun for to haue.* Now the invitation is general: let all join in, and all shall share in the harvest—
save, of course, the traditional workshys and professional idlers. In
memorable words Piers declares his untroubled understanding of the
stage of life which he has now reached:

For now I am olde and hore and haue of myn owen,
To penaunce and to pilgrimage I wil passe with thise other.

*Loke ȝe* take care (not) to; *tene* annoy, injure; *but* unless (*i.e.* if punishment is
justified); *amercy* fine; *taxoure* assessor; *maugre Medes chekes* despite anything Meed
has to say; *cokeres* leggings; *coffes* mittens; *for* against, to prevent; *hoper* hopper;
*hals* neck; *scrippe* pilgrim's wallet; *bredcorne* grain (for making bread); *sitthenes*
afterwards; *don* do; *hore* grey-haired; *of myn owen* a sufficiency.

The life of honest labour has led to a self-sufficiency. It is therefore fitting that the Plowman should round off his career of toil by accompanying the penitents. As before, with Meed's marriage-contract, we have a document to establish a settlement. Here it is the ploughman's *biqueste*, the will of an honest labourer who can contemplate death with calm acceptance, for his life has been that of the

> pilgryme atte plow for pore mennes sake.

The work of the half-acre then begins. For the moment, all is well: we can look back over the road that has been travelled.

## IV

The stage reached has been long in coming. Everyone had desired to do right after Reason's moving sermon which, in its turn, had followed the sentence against Meed. We are dealing, of course, in collective terms: once, as a critic notes, 'all turn their backs' on Meed, 'she has vanished'.[9] So, too, we have seen a host of humanity in search of salvation, 'A thousand of men' who 'thronged together'. We therefore have an urgent problem, who can show the way?—and this, in the characteristic emphasis of Langland's poem, means, can anyone be found not merely to teach the Christian life but to exemplify it? This had been foreshadowed in the Dreamer's colloquy with Holy Church. He had wanted, before all else, to see for himself. He had however allowed himself to be too easily drawn aside into large questions, meriting the sharp rebuke to look in his own heart: and this is a Dreamer whom we shall meet again. But meanwhile another line of development leads up to the emergence of a good man, a helper at need. Repentance's moving appeal to the God who became *of flessh oure brother*[10] preludes the emergence of an earthly and human saviour. We may be reminded of Holy Church's characterization of the most part of the inhabitants of the Field of Folk—'Of other heaven than here they make no reckoning'. The truth, it appears, is to be made manifest to our understanding; God comes down to our level, to be revealed in our nature and for our cause. The Plowman, who is also 'our brother in the flesh', is sent to minister to man's need.

Something else that has been long foreshadowed—in fact from our first glimpse of the Field—is a sight of humanity at work. Holiday must at length give place to a working-day. Inseparably linked with work is the matter of 'reward' and 'payment', *mede* and *mercede*. The first of

*atte* at the.

the Dreamer's large questions addressed to Holy Church had been, To whom does the wealth of the world belong? We have learned, under Conscience's guidance, to regard as 'reward' only the disproportionate payment, thus bringing together the two great extremes of corrupt payment and the Divine reward to sinful man. All else falls within the scope of the *mesurable*, whether as *mercede* ('A maner dewe dette for the doying'[11]) or manifest *permutacioun* ('one pennyworth for another'). There is henceforward a double standard involved in all consideration of law and punishment, service and wage; and this parallels the dual aspect of service to God, which may be considered as obedience to law or as the response of love. Upon the horizon of all seeking there is placed that 'better' which Holy Church would not reveal to her impetuous inquirer at the outset of his journey, and which the light falls upon at different times and with varying effect. At this present stage, when the *mesurable* is to be sought, there rises the outline of something that goes beyond the *mesure* principle altogether. We have glimpsed it for a moment in the Plowman's simple allegiance; his service, we recall, is given not as a duty but 'for the Lord of heaven's love'. We have seen it, too, in the Plowman's signpost to the pilgrims, which pointed beyond Law. But for the present we are concerned not with the Plowman but with *The moste partie of this poeple that passeth on this erthe*, the 'thousand of men' who, left to themselves, 'blundered forward like beasts'. The road forward must lead through simple conformity to law. Good deeds are now to be required of men.

The stage is therefore set for the appearance of a good man who will both teach and exemplify conformity to Divine Law. The work long overdue is to be undertaken as a co-operative endeavour, so that society at large is apparently set to rights, as the King and his counsellors, Reason and Conscience, had hoped. The single figure of the good man thus introduced and taking the first step in leadership presents an effective contrast to the evil woman who had dominated the earlier part of the poem. Just as Lady Meed could claim, with some justice, to make the world go round, thwarting all right relationships within society, so now the honest Plowman sets his world to rights. It is typical of the small and painful beginnings of goodness that we exchange Lady Meed's domain, co-extensive with the King's realm, for the modest world of the half-acre. But we have at least made the essential step, in moving from the *mesurelees*, of one kind—the disproportion of bribery, corruption, 'Commodity, the bias of the world'—to the *mesurable*. All who share with Piers in the work of the half-acre will share in the harvest.

The question now before us is that which Reason had raised when the King, in his new-found resolve, was told that to rule justly would be difficult unless the *comune* assented thereto. Suppose some members of society do not take kindly to practical obedience? The theoretical structure, so readily assented to, is at once in jeopardy. And the question has another aspect; mere counsel must take second place to effective leadership. There is more to government than prescribing duties related to rewards. The Plowman has come to a cumulative solution of society's troubles—all the way from, first, his rallying the faint-hearted who had heard him with dismay; next, his firm retort upon the well-dressed lady who was impatient of delay; right up to his glad acceptance of the Knight's generous response. Indeed, anyone who wanted to make a strong case for Langland's inherently conservative bent might point to the whole solution—the social contract embodied in the work of the half-acre—as arising directly in response to the Knight's handsome offer to undertake manual labour. The important consideration is that step by step the Plowman has been drawn into the task of organizing and directing. All the time we have the continuing belief on his part that the work of the half-acre is an interlude—and that it ends his career:

> For now I am olde and hore and haue of myn owen,
> To penaunce and to pilgrimage I wil passe with thise other.

That even the best-laid plans go astray is perhaps the clearest argument for the existence of a Providence that shapes our ends. It is now for Piers to apprehend, in the task to which he has been called, the practical trials, and thus the needs, of anyone brought, however reluctantly, to exercise authority.

The simplicity of any merely theoretical arrangement disappears when the Plowman addresses himself to his first task as overseer:

> To ouersen hem hym-self; and who-so best wrouȝte
> He shulde be huyred ther-after, whan heruest-tyme come.

His reaction to the idlers—those who, we are ironically told,

> hulpen erie his half-acre with 'how! trolli-lolli!'—

is immediate and decisive:

> 'Now, bi the peril of my soule!', quod Piers al in pure tene,
> 'But ȝe arise the rather and rape ȝow to worche,

*ouersen* oversee; *wrouȝte* worked; *huyred* hired; *heruest* harvest; *hulpen* helped; *erie* plough; *'how'* etc. hey, nonny, nonny!; *quod* said; *tene* anger; *But* unless; *the rather* at once; *rape ȝow* make haste.

Shal no greyne that groweth glade ȝow at nede;
And though ȝe deye for dole, the deuel haue that reccheth!'

The *pure tene* of the Plowman springs from an entire simplicity of
nature, faithfully reflected in the remedy he now proposes: they
must work or starve. The reply is to pretend to be disqualified from
labour by sickness or disability. We hear the whining tone of the professional beggar, with his honorific address to the likely 'prospect' (the
'ye' and 'you' to round out 'his honour's' self-esteem), so very different
from the 'hey, nonny, nonny' of a moment before:

For we haue no lymes to laboure with, lorde, y-graced be ȝe!
Ac we preye for ȝow, Pieres, and for ȝowre plow bothe,
That god of his grace ȝowre grayne multiplye,
And ȝelde ȝow of ȝowre almesse that ȝe ȝiue vs here.

All the poet's contempt for bogus devotion burns in this savage little
parody of the beggar's art. Piers is not deceived; he is Truth's long
servant (his *olde hyne*) and knows them at once for the wasters they are.
But they have raised a real issue in a world of 'work or want'. Theoretical construction moves a step nearer to the real world when we see
that the genuinely disabled are provided for; they will have sustenance
as long as they need it. The loudly vocal wasters exemplify luxury and
sloth: it is only by God's Mercy that punishment does not overtake
them. The Plowman will support those religious who truly practise what
they profess:

For it is an vnresonable Religioun that hath riȝte nouȝte of
certeyne.

The theory of government has been made comprehensive. Now comes
the trial of strength, with 'a waster' and a 'braggart Frenchman' *(Brytonere)* openly defying Piers's terms with his work-people:

Wiltow or neltow, we wil haue owre wille,
Of thi flowre and of thi flessche fecche whan vs liketh,
And make vs murie ther-myde, maugre thi chekes!

*glade ȝow* rejoice your hearts; *at nede* when you need it; *dole* grief; *haue that
reccheth!* take anyone who cares!; *lymes* limbs; *lorde, y-graced be ȝe!* so please your
Honour!; *ȝelde* reward; *almesse* charity; *hath riȝte* etc. absolutely no support to
rely on; *Wiltow* etc. willy-nilly; *flowre* flour; *flessche* meat; *fecche* fetch, take;
*murie* merry; *ther-myde* therewith; *maugre thi chekes!* whatever you say about it!

This is the situation Piers had foreseen in his *forward* with the Knight. To him he accordingly turns:

> To kepe hym, as couenaunte was, fram cursed shrewes,
> And fro this wastoures wolueskynnes that maketh the worlde dere.

The Knight's warning to the wastrel is delivered with formal gravity:

> Curteisly the kny3te thanne, as his kynde wolde,
> Warned Wastoure and wissed hym bettere,
> 'Or thow shalt abugge by the lawe, by the ordre that I bere!'

But this 'fair speech', echoing the courtesy of the Knight's original plighting of troth with Piers, makes no impression. This 'waster'

> lete li3te of the lawe and lasse of the kny3te,
> And sette Pieres at a pees and his plow bothe.

It is time to invoke the ultimate sanction in a world of 'work or want'. The Plowman's great oath—heard for a second time—is a mark of its gravity:

> 'Now, by the peril of my soule!', quod Pieres, 'I shal apeyre
>                                                          3ow alle!'
> And houped after Hunger that herd hym atte firste:
> 'A-wreke me of thise wastoures,' quod he, 'that this worlde
>                                                          schendeth!'

It is a deadly power that is invoked. In the swift space of five lines, the once-arrogant rebels are brought to the brink of death; and, had the Plowman not intervened, then

> They hadde ben doluen bothe, ne deme thow non other.

The colloquial phrase—'make no mistake about it'—gives the truth an unmistakable warrant. As it is, the *Brytonere* will bear the marks of his punishment to the end of his days.

Now it seems that Piers has been wholly successful. Everyone sets to with a will—the better, it is clear, for the grim lesson. There is a sardonic humour in the brisk animation with which all now apply themselves:

*shrewes* rogues; *wolueskynnes* of wolfish kind; *that* etc. send up prices (by causing scarcity); *wissed* instructed; *abugge* abide (the penalty); *lete li3te of* set little store by; *pees* pea; *apeyre* harm, punish; *houped* hallooed; *atte firste* at once; *A-wreke* avenge; *schendeth* ruin; *doluen* (dead and) buried; *deme* judge, think.

> Faitoures for fere her-of flowen in-to bernes,
> And flapten on with flayles fram morwe til euen.

Even hermits—*an heep*, 'a pile', of them—turn to work:

> And wenten as werkemen with spades and with schoueles,
> And doluen and dykeden to dryue aweye hunger.

Necessity breeds a marvellous alacrity; and its curative powers are truly extraordinary:

> Blynde and bedreden were botened a thousande,
> That seten to begge syluer sone were thei heled.

There is no problem about exacting obedience:

> eche a pore man wel apayed to haue pesen for his huyre,
> And what Pieres preyed hem to do as prest as a sperhauke.

The law has been asserted—by invoking its sanction in self-interest, at the breaking-point of mere survival. Only on these terms do we at last see society in a fair way to prosper. Meed holds no sway; a *mesurable huyre* is the clear principle of this obedience:

> And there-of was Peres proude and put hem to werke,
> And ȝaf hem mete as he myȝte aforth and mesurable huyre.

The law is fulfilled in an exacted obedience. The Plowman has achieved the ends he had foreseen; the recalcitrant are brought to heel. But the practical lesson has led to a larger issue than obedience regarded as law-keeping. The first emotion is pity on the Plowman's part:

> Thanne hadde Peres pite and preyed Hunger to wende
> Home in-to his owne erde and holden hym there.

The next is the more prudent consideration that what has been achieved is only a temporary check to idleness and rapacity. Let Hunger tell Piers what to do before he goes:

> For myschief it maketh thei beth so meke nouthe,
> And for defaute of her fode this folke is at my wille.

---

*Faitoures* pretenders, impostors; *flowen* fled; *bernes* barns; *flapten on* struck, 'laid on'; *morwe* morn; *doluen* dug; *dykeden* ditched; *bedreden* bedridden; *botened* cured, made better; *That seten* Those who used to sit; *apayed* pleased; *pesen* peas; *huyre* wages; *prest* ready; *sperhauke* sparrow-hawk; *mete* food; *aforth* afford; *erde* dwelling, land; *holden hym* keep himself, stay; *myschief* (their present) hardship; *nouthe* now; *defaute* lack, shortage.

It is well for the moment: but it is not enough. There is a higher relationship than that of master and workman, and from it must come a new
basis of agreement, a *couenant* higher than that of *mesurable huyre*. For,
in the last resort, waster and honest workman are of one family:

'They are my blody bretheren,' quod Pieres, 'for god bou3te vs alle'.

So the bond cannot be that of law merely, but must be love:

> Treuthe tau3te me ones to louye hem vchone,
> And to helpen hem of alle thinge ay as hem nedeth.

The leader and teacher must himself be taught, if he is to achieve more
than temporary victories by *force majeure*. To Hunger, Piers says:

> now wolde I witen of the what were the best,
> And how I my3te amaistrien hem and make hem to worche.

Hunger replies with the practical counsel of plain fare for the sturdy,
with better things when they have been earned. Yet, he adds, there is
only one true rule, and it is of universal application—the 'law of
God' which 'teaches'

> *Alter alterius onera portate*
> And alle maner of men that thow my3te asspye
> That nedy ben and nau3ty, helpe hem with thi godis,
> Loue hem and lakke hem nou3te, late god take the veniaunce;
> Theigh thei done yuel, late thow god y-worthe:
> *Michi vindictam, et ego retribuam.*

The whole complexion of the argument is changing rapidly. He who
is set in temporary authority must know that it is still his duty to serve:
and this must lead to the further thought that we are to love and not
reprove the wayward. Judgement is the Divine Prerogative. Once this
is grasped, merely external considerations give way; for judgement
comes to bear on the just man himself, the leader and lawgiver. Hunger
concludes this first part of his reply with the direct counsel

> if thow wilt be graciouse to god, do as the gospel techeth,
> And bilow the amonges low men, so shaltow lacche grace.[12]

*blody* of one blood; *bou3te* bought; *vchone* each one; *ay* always, continually;
*witen* know; *amaistrien* control; *Alter* etc. 'Bear ye one another's burdens [and so
fulfil the law of Christ]' (Gal. vi 2); *asspye* see, discover; *nau3ty* having nothing;
*lakke* blame, reproach; *late* let; *veniaunce* vengeance, requital; *late thow god y-
worth* let God (*i.e.* God's prerogative) alone; *Michi* etc. 'Vengeance is mine;
I will repay, saith the Lord' (Rom. xii 19 etc.) *bilow* humble; *lacche* get.

It is the golden rule; and it immediately takes us beyond the *mesure* principle. The Plowman's reaction is to ask whether the hard treatment recommended for the idle is strictly acceptable by this standard:

'I wolde nouȝt greue god,' quod Piers, 'for al the good on
                                                    grounde;
Miȝte I synnelees do as thow seist?', seyde Pieres thanne.

Hunger's reply is firmly based in the realities of our common life. What is required of all is work; but it is work according to the best of our capacity—a lesson driven home by the Parable of the Talents. We thus return to a law acknowledged by all men, for it is written in their hearts:

Kynde witt wolde that eche a wyght wrouȝte
Or in dykynge or in deluynge or trauaillynge in preyeres,
Contemplatyf lyf or actyf lyf, Cryst wolde men wrouȝte.

The universal rule is work, whether that work be manual or spiritual; the uncompromising emphasis is upon *praxis*— 'Cryst wolde men wrouȝte'. This comprehends all men's activities: but, like Holy Church in her dealings with a Dreamer who also stood on the brink of new knowledge, Hunger gives this general truth its direct application to the questioner's present state. The life of honest labour rests under divine approval:

The sauter seyth in the psalme of *beati omnes*,
The freke that fedeth hym-self with his feythful laboure,
He is blessed by the boke in body and in soule:
        *Labores manuum tuarum, etc.*

The application is plain when we hear Piers ask Hunger for a remedy against stomach-ache. The simple Plowman is not without fault; the life of honest toil has its own temptation, over-indulgence in time of plenty. It calls for plain counsel; let Piers and those of his servants who are troubled in this way practise abstinence. Then there will be no need to ask advice from those who have even the humblest medical knowledge. On the contrary, physicians will be out of business:

Phisik shal his furred hodes for his fode selle,
And his cloke of Calabre, with alle the knappes of golde.

---

*grounde* earth; *synnelees* sinless; *Kynde witt* natural understanding; *wrouȝte* worked; *dykynge* ditching; *deluynge* digging; *trauaillynge* labouring; *sauter* Psalter; *beati omnes* 'Beati omnes qui timent Dominum, 'Blessed is every one that feareth the Lord; *freke* man; *Labores* etc. '. . . thou shalt eat the labour of thine hands' (Ps. cxxviii 1-2); *hodes* hoods; *Calabre* Calabrian (grey) fur; *knappes* buttons.

These are profitable words, the Plowman concludes; and Hunger may now leave. But it is typical of the poet to insist upon an ever-present reality. Hunger will not go until he is appeased; and near-desperate measures are taken until the approaching harvest-time allows over-indulgence once more:

Thanne was folke fayne and fedde hunger with the best,
With good ale, as Glotoun tauȝte, and gerte Hunger go slepe.

Now, once again, it is the hour of Waster's opportunity; and the simplest folk grow over-delicate in their tastes. We hear the mocking echo of affected tastes in the pretentious delicacy of

fresch flesch other fische fryed other bake,
And that *chaude* or *plus chaud* for chillyng of her mawe.[13]

And so anarchy rules again, with the workman bemoaning his lot and cursing King, Council and laws. We are back in the individualistic world of the Prologue. The long interlude from the first promise of right government, with the King going to Church, up to the resumption of work in the half-acre after Hunger's intervention, is apparently over.

whiles Hunger was her maister there wolde none of hem chyde,
Ne stryue aȝeines his statut, so sterneliche he loked.

It is the final comment on the over-simplicity of the régime 'work or want'; as it is, too, on the dangers of the life of active self-sufficiency. The cycle plenty-insubordination-famine will, it seems, never be broken. In this light, law with an effective sanction appears the only remedy for mankind—unless, as the poet concludes, with the second of his mad prophecies[14]

god of his goodnesse graunt vs a trewe.

It is the last thing we might expect: but *a trewe* is about to be granted.

## V

*Passus VII*

With the seventh Passus we reach that episode in the poem which has provoked most discussion—understandably so, for it is clearly a major turning-point in the whole design. When that episode is over, the

*fayne* glad, pleased; *gerte* made, caused; *other* or; *bake* baked; *for chillyng of her mawe* to prevent their stomachs taking a chill; *stryue* strive; *sterneliche* fiercely; *trewe* truce.

first part of the *Liber de Petro Plowman* ends. From what we have seen of the poet's methods so far, we can expect this last Passus to sum up what has gone before and to prepare for the next phase. Broadly, the poem so far has been concerned with law and man's blameworthiness in respect of it. The specific point of the indictment has been venality— in a corrupt society everything is for sale including exemption from law, both secular and Divine. The balance—in Langland's terminology, the *mesure*—of man's need for material things has been overset; Lady Meed has been the presiding goddess. We have seen the extent of her sway even when judgement has been about to go against her. Her vanishing from the King's court at Westminster has not precluded the idlers and im- postors of the half-acre from asserting, by force if need be, their right to live at the expense of others. Force is therefore met by force, and Hunger wins undisputed victory; but it is known to be no final solution. We must turn now, to round off the account, to the question of *mercede* for those who have faithfully performed the tasks allotted them. Repen- tant humanity has made some advance in the sphere of co-operative endeavour; and Truth must be no less faithful to his followers than Meed to hers. The opening lines of the Passus proclaim an end of one intention—the going on pilgrimage—in the absolute approval of what had been undertaken as an interim measure, the work in the half-acre.

> Treuthe herde telle her-of and to Peres he sent
> To taken his teme and tulyen the erthe,
> And purchaced hym a pardoun *a pena et a culpa*
> For hym and for his heires for euermore after.
> And bad hym holde hym at home and eryen his leyes,
> And alle that halpe hym to erie, to sette or to sowe,
> Or any other myster that my3te Pieres auaille,
> Pardoun with Pieres plowman treuthe hath ygraunted.

'Truth heard tell hereof . . .' These words are commonly taken to refer to the work under Piers's supervision in the half-acre.[15] Yet per- haps this is not altogether satisfactory: we might suppose that Truth is more directly in touch with the work of his *olde hyne*. It is more consis- tent with the immediacy of Langland's thought if we suppose that what

---

*teme* team (of plough-oxen); *tulyen* till; *pardoun* indulgence; *a pena et a culpa* '(remission) from punishment and from guilt' (An indulgence ordinarily remit- ted the temporal punishment, not the guilt, of sin. That this formula was in use by corrupt Pardoners is clear from Pope Clement V's reprobation of it early in the fourteenth century); *eryen* plough; *leyes* fields; *halpe* helped; *myster* occupa- tion, employment.

now reaches Truth is the cry for deliverance from the endless cycle
which will certainly produce yet another famine. Humanity's plight is
grim indeed if there is no more to look forward to than exchanging the
control of plague for that of Famine:

> Thanne shal Deth withdrawe and Derthe be iustice,
> And Dawe the dyker deye for hunger.

There can be no escape from this roughest of rough justices,

> But if god of his goodnesse graunt vs a trewe.

Truth's answer is simple and goes to the root of the matter. They are
to continue in the work of the half-acre under Piers's direction. Nothing
will be lost: the pardon he and they had looked for after pilgrimage will
be forthcoming—only it will be beyond their expectation. It is pardon
*a pena et a culpa*, an absolute remission, that is granted to Piers; and it
applies to all who succeed him in his task—

> For hym and for his heires for euermore after—

and all who help him, by whatever means—

> And alle that halpe hym to erie, to sette or to sowe,
> Or any other myster that my3te Pieres auaille.

This is the *trewe*, which is both the truce in an otherwise endless cycle,
and also the settled basis of relationship between Truth and mankind.[16]
The transition whereby one Passus ends on a note of near-despair
(*graunt vs a trewe*) immediately transmuted by the opening words of the
next (*Treuthe herde telle her-of*) is an arresting move; and the wordplay
involved (*trewe—treuthe*) is perhaps a preparation for certain enigmatic
utterances which are to come.

   For the moment, the truth is penetratingly simple, and goes deeper
than the direct application to honest labour producing good harvests.
The demands made upon all who would help Piers are moral demands:
if they are obeyed, we have not only a world of unhampered effort
and thus of adequate sustenance, but also a world where self-interest,
the essence of Meed's sway, is ended in a community of aim and endeavour. It is with this understanding that the pilgrimage can be abandoned.
No need to seek Saint Truth in pilgrimage, when his approval is given to the
simple well-doing of co-operative effort! The Passus continues by speci-
fying what is entailed in helping Piers and thus setting out the terms
of a social contract. At the top of society the secular ruler, if faithful to
his task, may look

*Derthe* famine; *Dawe* Davy; *dyker* ditcher; *deye* die.

With patriarkes and prophetes in paradise to be felawes.

So, too, with those Bishops who are faithful to their calling—they are *peres with the apostles*. But for the remaining ranks of society we find degrees of reservation. The venal taint goes too deep to allow merchants, those whose livelihood is buying and selling, pardon *a pena et a culpa*.[17] Their distinctive failing is one especially abhorrent to a poet who apprehends self-interest, particularly in terms of monetary reward, as mankind's besetting sin. It is to justify their transactions, which know no respite, by the plea of Divine necessity:

> for thei swere by her soule and 'so god moste hem helpe'
> Aȝein clene conscience, her catel to selle.

They are fittingly brought to order by being made to part with the proceeds of trade (buying what pleases them best) for charitable purposes. The special nature of this provision—*vnder his secret seel Treuthe sent hem a lettre*—suggests the separate state of the merchants, who in their incessant concern with money-making are sharply unlike the figure of honest toil; and relief at this undertaking by Truth equally suggests the perilous state of these prime servants of Meed:

> Thanne were marchauntz mery, many wepten for ioye
> And preyseden Pieres the plowman that purchaced this bulle

The lawyers, however, come in for the most guarded treatment of all. The very mention of them at once recalls the trial of Meed:

> Men of lawe lest pardoun hadde that pleteden for Mede.

Their trade in misfortune is seen at its worst when they prey upon the innocent, whom they should help and from whom they should expect no recompense:

> Pledoures shulde peynen hem to plede for such, an helpe,
> Princes and prelates shulde paye for her trauaille

The good lawyer—he who

> scheweth lawe for owre lordes loue, as he it hath lerned—

will be saved. The mere traffic in *witte*— purchasing another's intellect— is an enormity as great as the buying and selling of any of the elements.

---

*peres* peers, of equal station with; *by her soule* etc. 'By my soul' and 'God help me' are cited as common oaths (protesting innocence or honesty); *catel* merchandise; *seel* seal; *bulle* indulgence; *pleteden* pleaded (her case); *scheweth* declares, explains.

Intellect and elements alike, all are the common gift of God. The *wynde* here included in the elements perhaps springs from contempt for feed' eloquence:

> Ac to bugge water, ne wynde, ne witte, ne fyre the fierthe,
> Thise foure the fader of heuene made to this folde in comune.

The lawyer's skill, like the landowner's possessions, is held in trust; and, like the land, its flourishing or decline is subject to Divine ordinance:

> Thise ben treuthes tresores, trewe folke to helpe,
> That neuere shal wax ne wanye with-oute god hym-selue.

It is a solemn thought and leads naturally to the waning of vigour, the time when the lawyer, in his turn, must look for remission. Langland here uses the word *Indulgences*; and the contrast between the technical and official term and the plain reality, the *pardoun* that truly meets mortal need, is hardly to be thought of as accidental.[18] The followers of Meed must learn that for them, just as for their clients, the shadow not the substance is alone purchasable:

> Whan thei drawen on to deye and Indulgences wolde haue,
> Her pardoun is ful petit at her partyng hennes,
> That any mede of mene men for her motyng taketh.

With the mention of *mene men* we come to the last orders in society; and here the poet can be splendidly brief:

> Alle lybbyng laboreres that lyuen with her hondes,
> That trewlich taken and trewlich wynnen,
> And lyuen in loue and in lawe, for her lowe hertis
> Haueth the same absolucioun that sent was to Peres.

Langland concludes by probing further the problem which marks the limit of the world of 'work or want', the just treatment of the helpless. It had confronted Piers in the pretended incapacity of the idlers and it had prompted the awareness *alter alterius onera portate*. Here, too, there is no question that the pure impostor is excluded from Truth's provision. But now we see something further: by this light—a light not of law but of love—those who deceive the charitable are revealed as doubly guilty. A pretended need not only deceives the giver; it defrauds the needy. An apparent problem is thus revealed. 'Cato'

---

*Ac* But; *ne* nor; *folde* earth; *fierthe* fourth; *tresores* treasures; *wanye* wane; *petit* small, scanty; *hennes* hence; *mene* lowly; *motyng* advocacy, counsel; *lybbyng* living; *wynnen* earn; 'Cato' (See above, p. 35).

would have us consider carefully to whom alms should be given; and
Peter Comestor tells us plainly to withhold our alms until we are sure
the recipient is genuinely in need. Yet on the other hand, St. Gregory
bids us give freely to all who ask. But it is not a real problem. We are
to leave judgement to God; the guilt, if any there be, lies upon the recipient:

In hym that taketh is the treccherye, if any tresoun wawe.

Let the beggar beware of asking more than is his due: for him, also,
there is a problem of *mesure*:

He hath ynough that hath bred ynough, though he haue nou3t elles:
*Satis diues est, qui non indiget pane.*

We glance once more at the waywardness of humanity; the beggar who
would ask more than his measure of bread brings to mind the almost
endless resources of guile. The undeserving beggar's is a life that knows
neither of the two mighty powers, love and law:

For 3e lyue in no loue, ne no lawe holde.

The punishment it incurs is therefore unsparing:

thei that lyue thus here lyf mowe lothe the tyme
That euere he was man wrou3t, whan he shal hennes fare.

It is characteristic of this sharp observer that we end with positive
statement—lest the mere beholding of wickedness should deaden our
own awareness of duty. We are to remember that those who are truly
afflicted, and who suffer their affliction in humility, have the highest
place in Truth's estimation; they

Han as pleyne pardoun as the plowman hym-self;
For loue of her lowe hertis owre lorde hath hem graunted
Here penaunce and her purgatorie here on this erthe.

It is on this note of affirmation, *here on this erthe*, that Langland ends
his account of the pardon granted by Truth to the honest Plowman.
It is appropriate that the C Text at this point includes the moving and
graphic account of the sufferings of the poor—*the most needy* who in
fact *aren oure neighebores and we nyme good hede*—and follows it with

*Peter Comestor* (d. 1198) author of a paraphrase of the Bible; *treccherye* deceit; *wawe*
(lit. 'walks') is; *Satis diues* etc. 'He is rich enough who does not want for bread'
(St. Jerome) *wrou3t* made; *hennes* hence; *fare* go; *pleyne* full; *and* if; *nyme* take;
*hede* heed.

a searing account of the *lunatik lollares and leperes aboute*. Langland has an exact sense of proportion—it is his own *mesure*—in society. Who but he would have thought of Truth, in the Plowman's account, as the *prestest payer that pore men knoweth*? The disproportion of a greedy beggar or an impudent *lollere* brings to his mind the sufferings of those who lack the bare necessities of life. Famine and pestilence have bitten deep. With him we are never far from a society where scarcity is the ever-present threat, so that the rapacity of one section directly diminishes what should be available for all. Thus we have his praise of patient poverty; and thus, too, his symbol, for this part of the poem, of goodness in the person of the honest Plowman, a producer, one who contributes to the common stock, set over against the wasters whose one end is to consume.

Upon this one good man who has come forth in the hour of need and applied the true remedy for society's ills—though he knew it not until now—the focus of the poem now gathers. Just as Meed had stood alone before her judges, now the light falls upon the figure of the Plowman as a Priest comes forward to interpret the document that bears the full authority of Truth:

> 'Pieres,' quod a prest tho, 'thi pardoun most I rede,
> For I wil construe eche clause and kenne it the on Engliche.'

The poet makes a rare appearance, so that we shall have, as it were, an eye-witness account. Here he is no mere Dreamer, quick to seize an opportunity of discourse: it is for him to witness silently to what we are now to see. The grouping arrests the attention, in a way similar to the kneeling of Conscience at an earlier moment of crisis in the King's court. All expectancy has been played upon. The judicial tone of the pardon's provisions (including the stern admonition to the charitably disposed to leave judgement on man to God); its 'summing-up'—as we may very suitably term it—of the issues that had gone before (as, most notably, the scope of 'reward' and the treatment of those disqualified from labour); and the measured provisions appropriate to various estates in society—all befit a legal document of unusual comprehensiveness and complexity. Now it is to be opened, for the Priest's interpretation:

> And Pieres at his preyere the pardoun vnfoldeth,
> And I bihynde hem bothe bihelde al the bulle.

*lollares* vagabonds, idlers; *leperes aboute* wanderers to and fro; *construe* interpret; *kenne* tell.

The comprehensiveness of this document is revealed:

> Al in two lynes it lay and nou3t a leef more,
> And was writen ri3t thus, in witnesse of treuthe:
> *Et qui bona egerunt, ibunt in vitam eternam;*
> *Qui vero mala, in ignem eternum.*

This comes with something of a comic effect of surprise, in the disproportion between the lengthy preparation (and the solemn authority of the Pardon's source) on the one hand, over against its utter brevity and devastatingly familiar content. The Priest's *Peter! . . . I can no pardoun fynde* has a touch of jocularity, in the play upon the name 'Piers' which he had used a moment before. And the Priest is of course wholly right in saying that the document he holds is 'no pardon'. It is no Indulgence; it is a statement not of concession but of rigour. It records Law—Law without 'variableness' or 'shadow of turning': and it comes as an old, old story, a phrase from the *Quicunque vult* which echoes alike the earliest memories of each individual Christian, and the oldest moral experience of all humanity. It is no more than

> 'Dowel and haue wel and god shal haue thi sowle';

but it is also no less than

> 'do yuel and haue yuel, hope thow non other
> But after thi ded-day the deuel shal haue thi sowle!'

We have seen the Plowman act impetuously—*al in pure tene*—before. It was when only an utterly simple and final answer would serve: the wasters in the half-acre were either to work or starve. Now once again the Plowman acts with entire decision, spurred by sheer vexation:

> Pieres for pure tene pulled it atweyne,
> And seyde, '*si ambulauero in medio vmbre mortis, non*
> *timebo mala; quoniam tu mecum es.*'

Since the message of this 'pardon' is no more than the moral law—the law which, as Holy Church had reminded the Dreamer, is written in all men's hearts—then it needs no documentary embodiment. Moreover,

---

*Et qui* etc. 'And they that have done good shall go into life everlasting: and they that have done evil into everlasting fire' (from the Athanasian Creed: the Dominical authority for this pronouncement is in Matt. xxv 46); *Quicunque vult* (opening words of the Athanasian Creed) 'Whosoever will be saved . . .'; *ded-day* dying day; *atweyne* asunder; *si ambulauero* 'though I walk through the valley of the shadow of death, I will fear no evil: for thou art with me' (Ps. xxiii 4).

the same perception that had led Holy Church to rebuke the Dreamer for overlooking what lay nearest home, prompts the Plowman's awareness that a formulated law can become a merely externalized law. These are characteristic emphases of the earlier part of the poem. We should not miss the simpler point which, sounded strongly at the trial of Meed, was found again among the detailed provisions of Piers's Pardon— that ever-present willingness of the experts to make a living out of the interpretation of law which had led the poet to condemn the traffic in 'knowledge' as abuse of the common gifts of God. Piers's present document certainly does not require expert interpretation—a 'construing' which might lead us back by an all-too-familiar road to Meed's domain. No rarer endowment than natural knowledge, the *kynde knowyng* to which Holy Church had referred the Dreamer in his over-haste and perplexity, is needed to understand the message of this 'pardon'. And, if this were not enough, the Priest has made abundantly clear the limits of skilled interpretation. He is wholly correct in his interpretation of what the Pardon says: but he is, as we shall see, at a loss to understand the meaning it has for its recipient. So the document is destroyed, and with its destruction there go both the possibility of externalizing the law of conscience, and the near-certainty of merely technical wrangling— the two salient characteristics of an unhappy Christendom.

The words that Piers now speaks have the effect of revoking his earlier will, the *biqueste* by which he had disposed of his *owen*. A new covenant replaces the old; and the new, in full conformity with the Divine example, is brief and without reservation where the old was explicit and detailed. The Plowman has led his pilgrims by way of the Commandments, for, as a C scribe had noted, they are indeed the high road, *alta uia ad fidelitatem*. Now to their guide comes an injunction he had not foreseen. He had thought himself approaching an end, and adequately provided for:

> now I am olde and hore and haue of myn owen,
> To penaunce and to pilgrimage I wil passe with thise other.

But it is in fact a beginning to which he is summoned—a life new to him, yet one which he immediately apprehends:

> 'I shal cessen of my sowyng,' quod Pieres, 'and swynk nouȝt
>                                                         so harde,
> Ne about my bely-ioye[19] so bisi be namore!
> Of preyers and of penaunce my plow shal ben herafter,
> And wepen whan I shulde slepe, though whete-bred me faille.'

*swynk* toil; *bely-ioye* 'good cheer'; *whete-bred* wheat-bread (*i.e.* delicate fare).

He is going to be less *bisi*—a word which carries the association of anxious care, fretfulness[20]—he who a moment before had been the pivotal centre of a world newly reformed. The vision of a society provided for and sustained by the honest labourer is now superseded. In its place we have a Creation dependent upon God Who provides for all His creatures; *god fynt hem alle*. So the Plowman, on whom all in the half-acre had depended, in his turn seeks dependence—the blessedness of entire dependence upon God. Those readers of the poem are right who observe that Piers does not say he is now to abandon the life of honest toil. But it is not always understood that Piers's resolve 'to do less' is a positive aspiration. The real quantum of less and more is determined by reference to utter dependence—the creaturely dependence of the *foules on the felde*. Piers's *bisi*-ness—the concern with material and temporal goods which has been his whole sphere of activity up till now—has preoccupied him to the exclusion of other and better things. For, as the common gloss on Piers's text would remind some at least of the poet's audience, while man is not forbidden to exercise foresight, to the end of daily sustenance, he is certainly forbidden that preoccupation which unbalances the mind and entices him away from eternal considerations.[21] Piers has had things in a wrong proportion: and we should not fail to notice that this comes home to him as culpable. It is of prayers and penance that he speaks. We may recall the earlier suggestion of faults in the life of honest labour—its tendency to over-indulgence, in time of plenty; and the mere rough justice of its fundamental principle 'work or want', answering to the harsher pressures of hunger and death. Repentance accompanies and is inseparable from the vexation with which Piers tears up his 'indulgence'. Truth's 'pardon' lies all in two lines; and if its first line promises eternal reward for those who do well, its second grimly assures eternal punishment for those who do ill. Once we move away from the *mesure* principle two things are abundantly clear at one and the same time. They are the Righteousness of God, and His Mercy: for when we glimpse, if only for a moment, what the Law in all its rigour would demand, we can do no other but cast ourselves upon God's Mercy. Only thus can man say *non timebo mala*.

Piers, then, repents: and it is true to Langland's bent, his characteristic fidelity to fact, that the Plowman's vexation with himself, the fervour of a new resolve, and anger at another all come into one focus—upon the Priest. The anger with the Priest is disproportionate to its immediate occasion. Certainly, the Priest is jocular—perhaps heavily so; we saw

*foules on the felde* birds in the fields; *non timebo mala* 'I will fear no evil'.

the repetition of *Peter* in his first words to Piers. Equally, too, there is the note of condescension; who taught this Plowman his little learning? But this, of itself, hardly merits the fierce contempt which leaps out in Piers's reply:

> 'Abstinence the abbesse,' quod Pieres, 'myne a.b.c. me tau3te,
> And Conscience come afterward and kenned me moche more.'

It is a stinging retort, if over-charged for the immediate occasion. Piers plays upon the similarity of sound between *abesse* and *a.b.c.* to express his aversion from mere learning divorced from moral experience. But he gets, I think, the worse of it. The Priest is a ready dialectician, and neatly returns the shaft launched against him, his ignorance of the *a.b.c.* of the good life:

> 'Were thow a prest, Pieres,' quod he, 'thow mi3te preche where
>                                                           thow sholdest,
> As deuynour in deuynyte with *dixit insipiens* to thi teme.'

Piers's attempted wordplay rebounds on his own head. The priest's *insipiens*, as one critic has noted,[22] plays with *incipiens*—Piers is both foolish (as witness not only his present rudeness, but his ridiculous 'pardon' and his impatient destruction of it) and he is a beginner in an art he does not understand, insisting upon instructing others. Let *him* attend to his a.b.c. (to learning); in the end he might qualify to lecture anyone he chooses. Piers can only reply with abuse of mere learning and a defensive contempt for this light-hearted wordplay. For him it proclaims the priest a *derisor*, a mocker of sacred things and thus a cause of contentious debate:

> 'Lewed lorel!' quod Pieres, 'litel lokestow on the bible,
> On Salomones sawes selden thow biholdest,
> *Eice derisores et iurgia cum eis, ne crescant, &c.*'

He thus, as one critic observes,[23] foreshadows some large questions (the value of learning and its abuse) which lie in wait for any more extended inquiry. But we may best apprehend these questions—and also see the train that leads to Piers's explosion at this point—if we look back. The priest is the first authoritative human figure we meet after

---

*a.b.c.* the rudiments; *kenned* taught; *deuynour in deuynyte* interpreter of theological matters; *dixit insipiens* 'The fool hath said' (Ps. xiv 1, liii 1); *teme* theme, text; *insipiens* fool; *incipiens* beginner; *Lewd lorel!* ignorant good-for-nothing!; *Salomones sawes* Proverbs of Solomon; *Eice derisores* etc. 'Cast out the scorner, and contention shall go out; yea, strife and reproach shall cease' (Prov. xxii 10).

the Plowman; and he is, it seems, all too like those whose operations at large were to be seen in the world of the *Visio*. The formal qualifications of office are there, but his action is singularly unhelpful. His interpretation of the document in front of him is literally true: but he can go no further. So a new note of awareness begins to be heard at the same time as a new problem is posed. The authoritative persons who are qualified to guide their fellow-men do not lack either learning or acuteness: but what they say may have no relevance to their interlocutor's real need. The priest is quite right; Pier's document is no indulgence. He is woefully wrong in not perceiving the significance the 'pardon' has for its recipient. Langland draws a major truth of his poem out of the mouth of one technically qualified to help, and amusingly dexterous in repartee. The priest correctly sees that the 'pardon' is no indulgence: it has no relation at all to those who seek release from law. He fails to see that it is immediately significant to those whose desire is not to ask exemption, but to fulfil. It is nevertheless characteristic of Langland's realism to give the better performance in the game of wits to the priest. Honest inquiry is no match for practised dialectics; though that may be a realization which is slow in coming to the observer, the Dreamer. The present episode ends in fruitless wrangling—

> The prest and Perkyn apposeden eyther other,
> And I thorw here wordes a-woke and waited aboute.

It is in this way that the poet safeguards what we may begin to see as the central truth of the poem as it has developed up to this point—that practice, an actual not a theoretical conformity to the Will of God, is all. The angry tones of dispute are the last sounds we hear from the world of the *Visio*. The account of the honest Plowman, ending this whole division of the poem, leaves one insistent truth ringing in the Dreamer's ears. Indulgences are well enough—but the supreme consideration is what man *does*. All the questions of Law have hitherto been questions of exemption from Law, concessions to human frailty. The Pardon has ended that at a single stroke; eternal life is for those who have done well. It is the same with the related question of wealth and its abuses. In the Pardon man confronts not the *mede* which God grants in mercy, out of all proportion to human deserving, but the *mercede* which is our due. The rule of Lady Meed is defeated even on its own level of self-interest; for, purchase indulgences as he may, man must still come for judgement and meet his individual reckoning—

*Perkyn* Peterkin; *apposeden* etc. disputed with each other; *waited* looked.

> acountis to ȝelde,
> How thow laddest thi lyf here and his lawes keptest,
> And how thow dedest day bi day . . .

Any and every purchased exemption will be useless without having 'done well'. There is no pause to reflect further on what 'doing well' may mean. All past confusions have vanished: and in the relief from tension, the world of scheming, self-providing, *bisi* England, the venal world of the *Visio*, is revealed as comically absurd. No use to plead licensed exemption, however varied and comprehensive the forms of insurance, at Judgement Day:

> A poke-ful of pardoun there, ne prouinciales lettres,
> Theigh ȝe be founde in the fraternete of alle the foure ordres,
> And haue indulgences double-folde, but if Dowel ȝow help
> I sette ȝowre patentes and ȝowre pardounz at one pies hele!

We do not end in high spirits. The world of the *Visio* has been set to rights; we must 'do well'. But the reminder of God's Righteousness would be cause for despair did we not know of His Mercy. So, like the Plowman, the Dreamer turns to prayer. All leads to an ending—*fortissimo*, as one critic notes [24]—in which the words of veritable *doing* beat insistently against man's known helplessness. We must do well; but this of ourselves we cannot do:

> For-thi I conseille alle Cristene to crye god mercy,
> And Marie his moder be owre mene bitwene,
> That god gyue vs grace here, ar we gone hennes,
> Suche werkes to *werche* while we ben here,
> That after owre deth-day *Dowel* reherce,
> At the day of dome, we *dede* as he hiȝte.

It is therefore fitting that at the end the light falls on the solitary figure of the Dreamer, conforming in his turn to the Plowman's example in seeking the Mercy of God.

The Pardon-scene has been a decisive turning-point: if old problems are disposed of, an unknown terrain lies in view. What foretastes are there of what is still to come? Clearly, what has already been revealed

---

ȝelde yield, render; *poke-ful* sackful; *prouinciales lettres* letters of indulgence given by the Provincial (the head of each order in a given country); *fraternete* fraternity (by special admission); *alle the foure ordres* Franciscan, Dominican, Carmelite, Austin; *but if* unless; *patentes* letters patent; *hele* crust; *mene* intermediary; *ar* ere; *hennes* hence; *reherce* repeat, declare; *hiȝte* bade.

must be probed more deeply. But now most of these issues can be treated from a point of view exactly opposite to that predominating in the *Visio*. There, the good had been patiently sought, and at last established, against a background of predominating evil. Henceforward, goodness is to be examined in detail. Thus, patient poverty will be in the forefront of attention, contrasted with the abuse of riches; simple faith, over against mere learning; the fulfilment of law—the problems of the Just Man—as against evasion or exemption from it. These are all questions too complex for the single set of answers which the *Visio* had prompted, in the presentation of merely venal society set on the right path by its one good man. But two special and overriding considerations remain. The first applies to the Dreamer, with whom we end the *Visio*. His personality had been deftly sketched at the outset, in the colloquy with Holy Church:

> This I trowe be treuthe; who can teche the better,
> Loke thow suffre hym to sey and sithen lere it after.
> For thus witnesseth his worde, worche thow there-after. (I 143-4)

There is the Dreamer established for us—impetuous in asking, but slow to grasp that theoretical inquiry must give way to steadfast application. The vexation of Holy Church with this inquirer who overlooked the knowledge written ineffaceably in his own heart may remind us of the *pure tene* of the Plowman when realization broke upon him. Now the inquiry is to come home to this Dreamer; and we have some ground for expecting that knowledge and practice may be long in meeting in him.

The second consideration is closely allied to the first. The Dreamer is to set out on his own; Holy Church took her leave of him long before, entrusting him to the promptings of an uncorrupted conscience. But the repentant sinners, we remember, for all their zealousness, were in sad confusion before they found what they sought—a guide qualified by practice in the good life. Will the Dreamer be any more fortunate? Certainly, in the characterization already given us, he is not a man to be content with less than the highest. But now that the standard of that highest has been revealed, he can be satisfied, if he is to be satisfied at all, with nothing less than Perfection itself. The notion of the wholly just, the one who could confront Law unafraid, has been brought before us more than once. We heard it in the sentence *(clause)* that brought Meed's defence to the ground:

> *nullum malum* the man mette with *inpunitum*,
> And badde *nullum bonum* be *irremuneratum*. (IV 143-4)

It was heard again in another two lines, those of the 'pardon':

> *Et qui bona egerunt, ibunt in vitam eternam;*
> *Qui vero mala, in ignem eternum.*

But these are absolute statements, marking theoretical limits. Where in the world of suffering and sinful men and women is any to be found who can meet this final challenge? The Dreamer is awake—at least sufficiently awake to perceive that the doing well that is required of all men cannot be evaded. He has still to awaken to himself: and it is thus a long road that lies in view.

## Notes

1. For 'Wille' two A Text MSS (VH) have 'William'. On wordplay in the poem, see Chapter VI, and on the poet's 'personality', Chapter VII, below.
2. *Coleridge's Literary Criticism*, ed. Mackail, London, 1908, p. 138.
3. On the language of this passage, see p. 208 below.
4. *Macbeth* V 3 40-6.
5. On wordplay (here, *wordes-wortes*) see p. 265 ff., below.
6. C's reading is more graphic in its conclusion of the immediate action:

> And ich, Wrath, was war and wroth on hem both,
> Til aither cleped othere 'hore', and of with the clothes,
> Til bothe her heuedes were bar and blody here chekes.
>
> (C VII 148-50)

But we miss the brooding satisfaction of Wrath's knowledge:

> Hadde thei had knyues, bi Cryst, her eyther had killed other.

7. The names of the thieves are given in *The Gospel according to Nicodemus*. M. R. James points out that there is some evidence for supposing that Dysmas (Dumachus) was originally the bad thief, Gestas the penitent. 'But the view that Dysmas was the good one has prevailed' (*The Apocryphal New Testament*, Oxford, 1924, p. 104 n. 1).
8. For the connexions between the Crucifixion and a jousting (and thus certain chivalric ideals), see pp. 217-8, below.
9. Mitchell, *loc. cit.*, p. 21.
10. C VIII 144.
11. C IV 307.
12. Skeat here deserts his main source for the B Text, MS Laud 851, preferring the weaker *biloue* ('make thyself beloved'), presumably in aversion from the repetitive emphasis of '*bilow . . . low*'. A certain innocence in face of verbal ingenuity is sometimes evident in Skeat's notes; as, for example, in his comment on XI 52, *come aither* one.

*to good*, where, he assures us, the literal meaning 'acquire wealth' is to be understood, for '*Morally* speaking, it would be a "going to the bad"'. Langland presumably intends us to perceive the ironic connexion; *cf*. IX 158 *For goode shulde wedde goode though hij no good hadde*. On the general subject of wordplay in this poem, see Chapter VI, in particular pp. 265-74; and for its bearing on textual criticism, Appendix, pp. 325-8, below.

13. For the contrasts of language here and in similar instances, see pp. 216-9, below.

14. *Cf*. the end of Conscience's account of the rule of *kynde loue* and *conscience* (III 323-27).

15. So, for example, R.W. Chambers, *Man's Unconquerable Mind*, London, 1939, p. 117; T. P. Dunning '*Piers Plowman*': *an Interpretation of the A-Text*, Dublin, 1937, p. 141; and N. K. Coghill 'The Pardon of Piers Plowman', Gollancz Memorial Lecture, British Academy, London, 1945, p. 18. D. C. Fowler, in the Knott and Fowler edition of the A Text (Baltimore, 1952), takes *here-of* as referring to 'the warning issued by Saturn in the lines immediately preceding' (p. 164). This is a correct interpretation of the A Text, which does not have the concluding prophecy. But in both B and C the emphasis goes beyond the particular truth of approaching famine to the general plight of humanity it at once evidences and makes desperate—unless a 'truce' can be found.

16. For 'truce' as applying without limit of time, *cf*. NED *s.v.* TRUCE, *sb.*, 1 b, 1578 T. Norton, *Calvin's Inst*. . . . 'I will put my couenaunt betwene me and thee: and betwene thy seede after thee . . . by an euerlasting truce.' Passus XVIII 416 offers the same meaning, at the meeting of Peace and Truth in lasting concord: '*Trewes*', *quod Treuth*, '*thow tellest vs soth, bi Iesus!*' ('I give in!', cried Truth, 'What you say is perfectly true'). This example also illustrates the proximity of *trewe(s)* and *Treuth*—a proximity perhaps disguised from readers of Skeat's parallel-text edition, where Passus VII begins a new page.

17. It is perhaps worth pointing out that when he writes *Ac none* a pena et a culpa *the pope nolde hem graunte*, Langland is thinking of the literal source of Indulgences, the Head of the Church on earth, as he was in A VIII 8, *Part in that pardoun the pope hath i-graunted* (*hem grauntid*, Kane). He is not therefore implying that Truth, as granting Piers's unique Pardon, is to be simply equated with the Pope. There seems no real 'confusion' here, as Professor Coghill suggests (*loc. cit.*, pp. 18-19); but the process of revision is certainly away from any possible misunderstanding.

18. On similar contrasts of language, see note 13, above.

19. For a comparison with the A Text at this point, see Appendix, p. 326 below.

20. The 'Wycliffe' version of Matt. vi 25 and Luke xii 22 enjoins that we be not *bisi*. Similarly, Martha 'bisiede aboute the ofte seruyce', and was told 'thou art bysi, and art troubled aboute ful many thingis' (Luke x 40, 42). To miss the connotation of fruitless anxiety is to make poor sense of a good many passages in our older literature—as, for example, Criseyde's unhappy awareness, 'How *bisy*, if I love, ek most I be . . .' (*Troilus and Criseyde* ii 799).

21. '. . . non prohibet providentiam, per quam in sudore vultus panis praeparatur,

sed vetat sollicitudinem quae mentem perturbat et ab eternis revocat'. *Glossa Ordinaria* (Luke xii 22), *Patrologia Latina*, 114, col. 296.

22. Howard Meroney 'The Life and Death of Long Wille', *ELH*, XVII (1950), 1-35; 18-19. For a consideration of Professor Meroney's general view of *Piers Plowman*, see pp. 303-4, 313-4, below.

23. T. P. Dunning, *op. cit.*, p. 152, n. 76. Fr. Dunning, who does not appear to observe the wordplay *insipiens-incipiens*, prefers the priest's text in A (*Quoniam literaturam non cognoui*, 'For I have known no learning') for its 'ironical subtlety'. (This is perhaps a convenient point at which to remind the reader that the Vulgate numbering of Psalms differs from that of A.V.; and that those translations which are based upon the Vulgate—Douay, Challoner, Knox—differ at times from A.V. Here, for example, A. V. (Ps. lxxi 15; lxx 15, Vulg.) translates 'for I know not the numbers thereof'.)

24. R.W. Frank, Jr., 'The Pardon Scene in *Piers Plowman*', *Speculum*, XXVI 1951), 320-21.

CHAPTER III

# A Dreamer's Progress

## Passus VIII–XIV

Sed ad hominum studia reuertor, quorum animus etsi caligante memoria tamen bonum suum repetit, sed uelut ebrius domum quo tramite reuertatur ignorat.

Boethius, *Cons. Phill.* III, pr. ii.

But I retorne ayen to the studies of men, of whiche men the corage al-wey reherceth and seketh the sovereyne good, al be it so that it be with a dyrkyd memorie; but he not by which path, ryght as a dronke man not nat by which path he may retourne hom to his hous.

(Chaucer)

### I

The personality of the Dreamer is henceforward to be evident in a series of encounters with authoritative persons. With Holy Church, we remember, in Passus I, he was the impetuous inquirer, putting the large speculative questions while overlooking the knowledge granted inalienably to all men. So rebukes were appropriate; and, we may notice, for such an inquirer the mere hint will not be enough. We must pass from

> Holicherche I am . . . thow ouȝtest me to knowe, (I 75)

which left the Dreamer undeterred, to the scathing reproof:

> Thow doted daffe . . . dulle arne thi wittes! (*ibid.*, 138)

Truly, he is a Dreamer whose bent for the large-scale theoretical question takes him dangerously far from simple practice. It is as such that Holy Church counsels him, in any search for a truth 'better' than plain obedience, to listen attentively to what he is told, and to put it into practice:

> . . . who can teche the better,
> Loke thow suffre hym to sey and sithen lere it after. (*ibid.*, 143-4)

*corage* heart, mind; *dyrkyd* darkened; *not* (*ne* + *wot*) does not know; *doted daffe* stupid blockhead.

The search is now to begin. The Plowman cast himself utterly on the Mercy of God. The Dreamer must pursue the full significance of what he has seen; and he turns naturally enough to the learned, those whose role it is to *construe* the perplexing. The group of problems thus involved —simple faith as against doctrinal knowledge, faith contrasted with 'works', the uses and abuses of learning (which links itself inevitably with riches and temporal authority over against patient poverty)—all these lead, though by a long and even tortuous route, to the one great problem that the very personality of the Dreamer itself poses and, with each rebuff, makes ever-insistent—the unalterable difference between knowledge and realization, an apprehension of the truths so easily and ardently debated as bearing inescapably upon the self, and demanding fulfilment in practice. To bring about understanding of *that* problem, vision must supervene upon discourse. There must come to the Dreamer, as there had fallen upon the Plowman, an understanding which is immediate, surprising, and decisive; and for the Dreamer no less than the Plowman repentance is its necessary condition. The axis on which all pivots is Law. Law must exact fulfilment; and the fulfilment, as the 'pardon' implies, must be perfect if it is to have any validity at all. Our starting-point is what can be meant by the just—those who alone can hope to be approved at that final reckoning with which the *Visio* had ended. It is clear that we must work now, if we are ever to hear

> Dowel reherce
> At the day of dome we dede as he hiȝte. (VII 199-200)

## II

*Passus VIII*

At the outset of his journeying the poet meets with two Friars; and, like the would-be pilgrims of the *Visio* in their encounter with the much-travelled Palmer, he inquires of them as men who are best placed to know the answer from wide experience:

> For thei ben men on this molde that moste wyde walken,
> And knowen contrees, and courtes, and many kynnes places,
> Bothe prynces paleyses and pore mennes cotes,
> And Do-wel and Do-yuel, where thei dwelle bothe.

Their reply is without hesitation:

*molde* earth; *contrees* regions, districts; *cotes* cottages; *yuel* evil.

'Amonges vs,' quod the menours, 'that man is dwellynge,
And euere hath, as I hope, and euere shal here-after.'

It is a pertinent reply; no need to range widely for that which is to be found, if found at all, at home. But this brings at once into play the Dreamer's fatal facility in debate:

'*Contra*,' quod I as a clerke and comsed to disputen.

What the Dreamer seeks is immediately apparent. It is perfection, a whole and unvarying conformity to law which alone can have no cause to fear judgement. The Friars may have the merely just man dwelling amongst them: but that is not what the Dreamer seeks; for, he knows,

'*sepcies in die cadit iustus;*
Seuene sythes, seith the boke, synneth the ri3tful.
And who-so synneth,' I seyde, 'doth yuel, as me thinketh,
And Dowel and Do-yuel mow nou3t dwelle togideres.

The conclusion is clear; and it comes with the *ergo* of confident assertion:

*Ergo*, he nys nou3t alway amonge 30w freres;
He is otherwhile ellis-where to wisse the peple.

The Friars reply with the parable of the man in the storm-tossed boat. However roughly he is buffeted by wind and tide, provided he holds, so far as he is able, a true course, he is not blameworthy. They thus distinguish between sins of frailty and deliberate (mortal) sins. But no concession to frailty will serve for the Dreamer. He will be on his way:

'I haue no kynde knowyng,' quod I, 'to conceyue alle 30wre
                                                          wordes,
Ac if I may lyue and loke I shal go lerne bettere.'

It is an admission which echoes the colloquy with Holy Church. To her ample statement concerning Truth the Dreamer had replied:

3et have I no kynde knowyng . . . 3et mote 3e kenne me better,
By what craft in my corps it comseth and where. (I 136-7)

The reply richly earned Holy Church's rebuke. How stupid of him to say he does not know what is in fact written in all men's hearts!

*menours* (Friars) Minor; *as I hope* I am sure; *as a clerke* like a scholar, in the manner of scholastic debate; *comsed* commenced; *sepcies* etc. 'a just man falleth seven times' (Prov. xxiv 16) 'a day'; *ri3tful* righteous; *mow* can; *Ergo* therefore; *alway* always; *ellis-where* elsewhere; *wisse* teach, guide (the argument here is that since the Friars are sometimes at fault, at those times, if *Dowel* dwelt exclusively with them, humanity would be without a guide); *kynde knowyng* natural understanding; *conceyue* grasp; *Ac* but.

'It is a kynde knowyng,' quod he, 'that kenneth in thine herte
For to louye thi lorde leuer than thi-selue;
No dedly synne to do, dey thou3 thow sholdest . . .' (*ibid.*,
140-1)

The Friars are more gentle than Holy Church; and the parting blessing
fittingly[1] sends the enquirer on his way:

'I bikenne the Cryst,' quod he, 'that on the crosse deyde.'

It is time for the Dreamer to search the universe of discourse. We
therefore resume the dream-sequence, and encounter first of all Thought—

A moche man, as me thou3te, and lyke to my-selue.

Thought introduces a triple categorization, where before the distinction
had been simply between good and ill—

'Dowel and Dobet and Dobest the thridde,' quod he,
'Aren three faire vertues,—

and he adds the important consideration that they

'beth nau3te fer to fynde'.[2]

His explanation is in terms of right conduct, conceived in a social setting
—dutiful laity, virtuous and exemplary clergy, and spiritual potentates
(Dobest 'bears a bishop's crosier'). Indeed, it is so firmly social that it
can envisage the situation, puzzling in other terms, of conflict between
one of the lesser parties and the Dobest which is 'above both'. In such
a case

shal the kynge come and casten hem in yrens,
And but if Dobest bede for hem, thei to be there for euere.

The King is crowned by assent of these three, and must rule righteously,
doing nothing without their entire assent.

This explanation is not to the Dreamer's taste. True to his bent, he
must have examples from practice; as he says

I coueite to lerne
How Dowel, Dobet and Dobest don amonges the peple.[3]

He is accordingly directed to Wit. The long chase is on; and it is perhaps
an omen of its absorbing quality that Thought, accompanying the
Dreamer, is so deep in dispute that

*bikenne* commend (to); *moche* big, tall; *Dobet* Do-better; *fer* far; *yrens* irons,
fetters; *but if* unless; *bede* intercede; *don* do.

ar we were ywar with Witte gan we mete.

Unlike Thought—a *moche man*, we remember, and one resembling the Dreamer himself—'Wit' is 'long and lean' and *liche to none other*. The description is in no way arbitrary. Langland makes clear the 'faculty psychology' which he employs when he tells us that 'Wit', or Intelligence, has nothing to do with dialectic except in so far as Thought serves as intermediary:

> I dorste meue no matere to make hym to Iangle,
> But as I bad Thou3t tho be mene bitwene,
> And put forth somme purpos to prouen his wittes,
> What was Dowel fro Dobet, and Dobest fram hem bothe.

Wit is therefore of unassuming, almost neutral, appearance:

> Was no pruyde on his apparaille ne pouerte noyther,
> Sadde of his semblaunt and of soft chiere.

It is Thought who is ever-ready to turn the phrase (we see the significance of the word *Iangle*); and he does so in a way which arrests our attention:

> Here is Wille wolde ywyte yif Witte couthe teche hym.

His words are touched with the same kind of jocularity we encountered in the Priest of the Pardon-scene—a wordplay which penetrates deeper than the immediate occasion. How is Will, the principle of self-interest, to learn? How, indeed, is reflected in the ironical 'wolde *ywyte*—yif *Witte* couthe teche hym'. The implication is that if 'Wit' cannot teach the headstrong Dreamer, no-one can. We should note, too, that there is a similar air of the inherently absurd about putting forward a *purpos* to 'Wit' *to prouen his wittes*. Certainly, it is a *purpos* which is long in the answering. Perhaps the note of absurdity is still sounding in the penultimate line of the Passus, with its ironic repetitions of *man*:

> Whether he be man or no man, this man fayne wolde aspye.

Is the Dreamer not asking, unwittingly, to be taught how to use his eyes? Certainly that is what he may prove, in the long run, to need most

*ar* before; *ywar* aware; *gan* did; *liche* like; *meue* move, propose; *Iangle* dispute (with the implication, irresponsibly); *tho* then; *mene* intermediary; *purpos* proposition, topic; *hem* them; *pruyde* pride; *apparaille* dress; *Sadde* serious; *semblaunt* appearance; *soft chiere* mild expression; *ywyte* know; *couthe* could; *fayne wolde* would like; *aspye* discover.

of all. But put as baldly as Thought puts it, an inherent absurdity is apparent. However, Thought is true to his brief; it is examples from practice the Dreamer seeks—

> Where Dowel, Dobet and Dobest ben in londe—

as he has only one end in view—

> worchen as thei thre wolde, this is his entente.

The words echo those the Dreamer had used in excusing himself from further attendance upon the Friars, at the outset of the journey:

> if I may lyue and loke I shal go lerne bettere.

The Passus (a short one, as befits an introduction to the complex of problems on which the Dreamer has launched) ends, as did the *Visio*, in insistence upon action. But there is a difference. The last word here is not with act but with intention. There is much still to be said— and, more, experienced—before we can return to the entire simplicity of emphasis upon action with which the *Visio* ended.

### Passus IX

If the Dreamer is to set off, pilgrim-fashion, he will need directions. 'Wit' therefore offers one of those 'signpost' allegories which we have met on other occasions. His account of the 'Castle that Nature (*Kynde*) made' is clear enough, if mechanical. Anima, the soul, is the *châtelaine*, and she is guarded from her enemy, the Devil—

> A proude pryker of Fraunce, *prynceps huius mundi*—

by 'Inwit'.[4] The whole account is strongly ethical in its conception, and as such it adds little to the notion of *Dowel*, *Dobet* and *Dobest* beyond stressing the link that exists between them and 'Kind' (Nature)— a connexion first established for the Dreamer by Holy Church in Passus I. 'Kind' is now defined at some length. His castle, is *Caro*; Man is not mere spirit, and therefore must attend most closely to the promptings of 'Inwit:'

> Inwitte is in the hed and to the herte he loketh,
> What *Anima* is lief or loth, he lat hir at his wille;
> For after the grace of god the grettest is Inwitte.

*wolde* would (have him do); *pryker* cavalier; *prynceps* etc. 'The prince of this world' (John xii 31, xvi 11), the Devil; *Caro* Flesh; *loketh* watches over; *is lief or loth* wants either to do or to refrain from; *lat* lets, allows; *at his wille* in his discretion, as he decides.

This leads to a characteristic emphasis on the dangers of the Flesh; the world of the *Visio* with its overriding concern for creature-comforts is still not far behind the Dreamer. In its turn, this suggests the duties of one generation to the next (the instruction of the young), and of one section of the Christian family, the rich, towards the other, the poor. The emphasis in 'Wit's' discourse is upon the flesh all are heir to, with its ever-present snares of self-interest. His further definition of Dowel thus reaches the highest point of a merely ethical awareness:

> That dredeth god, he doth wel; that dredeth hym for loue
> And nouȝt for drede of veniaunce, doth ther-fore the bettere;
> He doth best, that with-draweth hym by day and bi nyȝte
> To spille any speche or any space of tyme ...

Intelligence, thoroughly applied, brings the argument to the same level as the Plowman's resolve to be less *bisi* about creature-comforts. The very phrase *bi day and bi nyȝte* echoes the text the Plowman had quoted

> *Fuerunt michi lacrime mee panes die ac nocte*

This constitutes no advance; but it serves to remind us that where conformity to Law is the primary question, all turns upon an absolute requirement. 'Wit's' emphasis upon the Flesh only makes clearer the unalterable fact

> *Qui offendit in vno, in omnibus est reus.*[5]

The character betokened on his entry, 'Grave in appearance, his expression mild', comes out in his counsel:

> Lesyng of tyme, treuthe wote the sothe,
> Is moste yhated vp erthe of hem that beth in heuene,
> And sitthe to spille speche, that spyre is of grace,
> And goddes gleman and a game of heuene.

His approval rests upon 'all honest, upright *(tidy)* men who are minded to work'. So he continues by praising Christian marriage, the foundation of Christian society, with fitting emphasis on the duties of parents.

---

*veniaunce* retribution; *To spille* from wasting; *Fuerunt* etc. 'My tears have been my meat day and night' (Ps. xlii 3); *Qui offendit* etc. 'Whosoever shall keep the whole law, and yet offend in one point, he is guilty of all' (Jas. ii 10); *Lesyng* wasting; *treuthe wote the sothe* lit. 'Truth knows this is true'; *vp erthe* on earth; *of hem* by those; *sitthe* then, next; *spyre* shoot (the image is perhaps suggested by the similarity of sound between *grace* and 'grass'); *gleman* minstrel.

It is all very sound, and all completely external—'all that observation can supply', to paraphrase Johnson on a different matter. The conclusion is exactly what follows from this ethical and social consideration of the good life:

> Dowel, my frende, is to don as lawe techeth,
> To loue thi frende and thi foo, leue me, that is Dobet.
> To ȝiuen and to ȝemen bothe ȝonge and olde,
> To helen and to helpen, is Dobest of alle.[6]

But perhaps there is a sting in the tail for the present listener, as we return to the wordplay upon *Wille* with which Thought had originally introduced the eager questioner. Now 'Wit' concludes:

> Dowel is to drede god, and Dobet to suffre,
> And so cometh Dobest of bothe, and bryngeth adoun the mody,
> And that is wikked Wille, that many werke shendeth,
> And dryueth away Dowel thorugh dedliche synnes.

'Wille' is the last enemy to be overcome.

### III

*Passus X*

At all events, the time of courteous attention to the Dreamer is over. 'Wit's' wife is *dame Studye*, and she has been waiting with unconcealed impatience for the end of her husband's discourse. The Dreamer has been rebuked before—though it is long before, in the colloquy with Holy Church. Then he had been careless and over-ambitious in the course of the discussion. But this is the first time that he has been denied a hearing. Study's attitude is simple enough. It is their actions which are the proof of men's real interests; the Dreamer's insistence on practice is turned back upon him:

> I sey it bi suche . . . that sheweth bi her werkes,
> That hem were leuer londe and lordship on erthe,
> Or ricchesse or rentis and reste at her wille,
> Than alle the sothe sawes that Salamon seyde euere.

The world of actuality is the world of the *Visio*, of whose inhabitants

ȝiuen (give) provide for; ȝemen take care of, protect; helen heal; adoun down; mody proud, stubborn; shendeth ruins, destroys; dedliche mortal; bi concerning; her their; hem were leuer they would rather have; reste at her wille leisure whenever they feel like it; sothe sawes wise sayings (the Proverbs).

Holy Church had said, 'They make no reckoning of any heaven but here'. Men pursue creature-comforts, taking empty amusement and selfish good-living for solid goods. It follows that knowledge of divine truth is best withheld: otherwise it will be impiously used, in a world where

> Leccherye, losengerye and loseles tales

are above all things preferred. For

> if thei carpen of Cryst, this clerkis and this lewed,
> Atte mete in her murthes whan mynstralles ben stille,
> Thanne telleth thei of the trinite a tale other tweyne,[7]
> And bringen forth a balled resoun, and taken Bernard to witnesse,
> And putten forth a presumpsioun to preue the sothe.

It is a passage which links the failings the *Visio* had brought to light with those which now lie in wait for the Dreamer. Material self-seeking and intellectual perversity are, we see, inseparable in those who

> dryuele at her deyse the deite to knowe,
> And gnawen god with the gorge whan her gutte is fulle.

The enormity of which Study complains does not cease with irreverent and even blasphemous discourse. While it goes on, the needy may wait in vain at the rich man's gate:

> Ac the careful may crye and carpen atte ȝate,
> Bothe afyngred and athurst and for chele quake.

These powerful men may be masters of divinity; but the evidence of their real state is clear:

> God is moche in the gorge of thise grete maystres,
> Ac amonges mene men his mercy and his werkis.

Study has proved the point about actions and beliefs, with which she opened fire. As this is the first occasion of outright attack upon the

*losengerye* flattery; *loseles tales* scurrilous stories; *clerkis* learned men; *lewed* laymen; *murthes* merry-making (pl.); *stille* silent; *other tweyne* or two; *balled* bald, barefaced; *Bernard* cf. the medieval proverb 'Bernard the monk didn't see everything', referred to by Chaucer, *Legend of Good Women*, Prologue (G) 16; *to witnesse* as their (pretended) authority; *presumpsioun* presupposition; *preue the sothe* as a clinching argument; *deyse* dais, high table; *gorge* throat; *Ac* but; *careful* wretched; *carpen* speak (ask for help); *afyngred and athurst* consumed with hunger and thirst; *chele* (bitter) cold; *quake* tremble; *mene* lowly.

Dreamer, so it is the first hard-and-fast distinction which his experience forces upon him. On the one side, learning and dialectical subtlety are associated with gluttony, misuse of wealth, and heartless indifference to the poor; on the other, righteousness, compassion, an active charity are to be found in *mene men*. These pairs lend themselves to familiar dichotomies, discourse as against action, eager eloquence (we remember 'Wit's' sober demeanour and his warning not *To spille any speche*) versus undemonstrative obedience:

> Clerkes and other kete men carpen of god faste,[8]
> And haue hym moche in the mouthe, ac mene men in herte.

It is in this light that we can understand Study's outright refusal to have anything to do with the Dreamer. We may be helped, too, if we recall, against this background of gross self-indulgence, the description of Study, who

> lene was of lere and of liche bothe.

She has no part in these gluttonous discourses; and her impatience at hearing 'Wit's' well-intentioned words to the Dreamer may be understood when we remember that she has had to listen too often to large speculations:

> I haue yherde heigh men, etyng atte table,
> Carpen as thei clerkes were of Cryste and of his miȝtes.

Such discourse can have only one ending: the disputants

> leyden fautes vppon the fader that fourmed vs alle,
> And carpen aȝeine clerkes crabbed wordes;—
> 'Whi wolde owre saueoure suffre suche a worme in his blisse,
> That bigyled the womman and the man after,
> Thorw whiche wyles and wordes thei wenten to helle,
> And al her sede for here synne the same deth suffred?

Theological perplexities, entered into in this captious spirit, can lead only to fruitless disputation. The disputants fall out with each other; while there remain the *mene men* who have God not 'much in the mouth' but in their hearts.

The whole of this first part of Passus X is pivotal to the poem's development. Study's attack both looks back to the world of the *Visio*

---

*kete* sharp, smart; *lere* features; *liche* body; *heigh* great, important; *Carpen* chatter; *as* as though; *miȝtes* powers; *leyden* laid; *worme* serpent; *blisse* Paradise; *wyles* wiles; *sede* offspring.

and forward to the train of barren speculations on which the Dreamer is embarking. He, too, will meet a 'Master' whose discursive zeal at table is equalled only by his absolute indifference to the needy who await his leavings. We should also note two things in the conclusion of Study's outburst. The first is a particular instance of the theological puzzles that will absorb the Dreamer, however soundly warned; and it renews the ever-present insistence on sin. How shall we understand the inherited guilt of Adam's sin as compatible with the law *Filius non portabit iniquitatem patris?* It is a problem real enough to engage any inquirer. The second thing is even more important. At the same time that she warns the Dreamer against profitless subtilizing (for it leads only to *mysbileue*) Study promises an eventual answer to his grand and all-embracing question. It is, as Skeat noted long ago, a striking, and unusually explicit, anticipation. The Dreamer is given hope; but he is directed, once again, to simple experience rather than extended speculation. His *purpos*, the topic put forward by Thought at the encounter with Wit, was simple enough:

> What was Dowel fro Dobet, and Dobest fram hem bothe.

He will receive an answer:

> Ymaginatyf her-afterward shal answere to ʒowre purpos.

Let him beware of going beyond his brief, and thus joining these 'masters' in their empty *glorie*. The great rule is

> Non plus sapere quam oportet.

Study can be concerned only with the facts of the human situation, which, reverently apprehended, are our starting-point:

> Al was as thow wolde, lorde, yworschiped be thow,
> And al worth as thow wolte, what so we dispute!

Practice is the only guide:

> And tho that vseth this hanelounes to blende mennes wittes,
> What is Dowel fro Dobet, now def mote he worthe,
> (Sitthe he wilneth to wyte whiche thei ben bothe),
> But if he lyue in the lyf that longeth to Dowel.

*Filius non portabit* etc. 'The son shall not bear the iniquity of the father' (Ezek. xviii 20); *mysbileue* unbelief; *fro* (as distinct) from; *Ymaginatyf* see p. 113, below; *Non plus sapere* etc. '(I say ... to every man that is among you), not to think of himself more highly than he ought to think' (Rom. xii 3): see p. 141, below.; *worth* will be; *what so* however; *hanelounes* wiles, devious tricks; *worthe* become; *longeth to* belongs to.

Without it no advance is possible; it is the entry, and the only entry, upon all the Dreamer would rashly know without further ado:

> For I dar ben his bolde borgh that *Dobet wil he neuere,*
> *Theigh Dobest drawe on hym day after other.*

It is a solemn warning; yet, as before, it is tinged with the humour of near-absurdity. Certainly, it ends the possibility of merely intellectual inquiry. 'Wit' is silenced; the Dreamer

> my3te gete no greyne of his grete wittis.

But it is with laughter that 'Wit' bids the Dreamer accept his fate. There has begun the wry comedy of cross-purpose in which an ardent seeker incurs the suspicion of authority, sadly experienced with the merely theoretical disputant. The Dreamer's submission is worth noting: it will be a long while before we see him again as a suppliant. Study's heart softens at this *mekenesse* and *mylde speche* on the part of one she had taken for a brash inquirer; and he is directed to 'Clergy' (Learning) and his wife Scripture:

> Thei two, as I hope, after my techyng,
> Shullen wissen the to Dowel, I dar it vndertake.

The directions to 'Clergy's' dwelling signpost, once more, an ethical terrain. It is the 'high way', the main road, again; though this time, as befits progressive understanding, a new emphasis is laid on certain perils:

> ryde forth by Ricchesse, ac rest thow nau3t therinne,
> For if thow couplest the ther-with to Clergye comestow neuere.
> And also the likerouse launde that Leccherye hatte,
> Leue hym on thi left halue a large myle or more.

This account, while once again stressing the part of duty, is the more valuable for Study's *apologia*. It is as though, having relented towards the Dreamer for his humble submission, she takes him into her confidence. The *sciences*, branches of knowledge, are reviewed, and Theology is especially noted as perplexing:

*bolde borgh* confident guarantor (I'll safely guarantee); *Theigh* though; *drawe* draw, drag; *day after other* day after day; *greyne* (grain) scrap; *wissen* guide; *ac* but; *likerouse* lecherous; *launde* meadow; *hatte* is called; *halue* side.

> Ac Theologie hath tened me ten score tymes,
> The more I muse there-inne the mistier it semeth,
> And the depper I deuyne the derker me it thinketh;
> It is no science for sothe forto sotyle inne.

But Study makes a most important connexion, which takes us back to Holy Church's counsel to the Dreamer, when she tells us why Theology is yet to be respected:

> A ful lethy thinge it were 3if that loue nere.
> Ac for it let best by Loue I loue it the bettre;
> For there that Loue is leder ne lacked neuere grace.
> Loke thow loue lelly 3if the lyketh Dowel;
> For Dobet and Dobest ben of Loues kynne.

The linked repetitions of the word *loue* sound joyfully.[9] We have touched in a moment the top of knowledge: from it we look down on a world of measure-for-measure, of strict retributive justice. Vengeance pertains to God, Who will discharge it. Man's duty is clear, and transcends all other considerations, including all branches of knowledge:

> For-thi loke thow louye as longe as thow durest,
> For is no science vnder sonne so souereyne for the soule.

It is a fitting end to the Dreamer's colloquy with Study. He learns from her, as from Holy Church, that the teaching of natural knowledge (*kynde knowynge*) is not, finally, law but love—the love that

> is triacle of heuene;
> May no synne be on him sene that vseth that spise.

Learning, as is to be expected, takes the Dreamer's question in terms, firstly, of the Christian Faith, right belief in the fundamental dogmas; such, from this standpoint, is Dowel:

> For had neuere freke fyne wytte the feyth to dispute,
> Ne man had no merite my3te it ben yproued:
> *Fides non habet meritum, vbi humana racio prebet experimentum.*

*tened* vexed, perplexed; *mistier* more obscure; *deuyne* search into, examine; *for sothe* truly, indeed; *sotyle inne* argue subtly about; *lethy* useless; *nere* (*ne* + *were*) were not; *Ac* but; *let best by* sets most store on; *there that* where; *ne lacked* there lacked no; *the lyketh* you like; *kynne* kin; *durest* last; *spise* (species) kind (of remedy); *freke* man; *fyne wytte* acute intelligence; *my3te* if it could (the argument is that faith would not be meritorious if Christian truth were capable of demonstration); *Fides non* etc. 'Faith has no merit where human reason provides a proof' (St. Gregory).

The next stage is to apply this to the individual life. Here Learning reinforces the earlier warnings on hypocrisy, discrepancy between profession and practice:

> be suche in thi soule as thow semest with-oute.

Dobet is thus seen as 'a suffering for the soul's health'. It follows that Dobest is the prerogative of the healthy; for only they can rightly reprove the guilty:

> Thanne is Dobest to be bolde to blame the gylty,
> Sithenes thow seest thi-self as in soule clene.

'Clergy' returns with emphasis to the crime of hypocrisy; it lies under God's displeasure:

> God in the gospel grymly repreueth
> Alle that lakken any lyf, and lakkes han hem-selue.

This leads to a full denunciation of clerical failings: for of the present age all that can be said is that

> now is Religioun a ryder, a rowmer bi stretes,
> A leder of louedayes and a londe-bugger,
> A priker on a palfray fro manere to manere . . .

It is the old, old complaint of the man of religion turned more worldly than the laity; and it rises to scathingly vivid condemnation. If 'Religion' in this guise reminds us of Chaucer's Monk, here, too, is the arrogant counterpart of his Prioress's over-delicate refinement:

> An heep of houndes at his ers, as he a lorde were.
> And but if his knaue knele that shal his cuppe brynge,
> He loureth on hym and lakketh, who lered hym curteisye?[10]

We are never far in this poem from vivid observation of the world as it is, for all the Dreamer's anxious scrutiny of far horizons. The *curteisye* insisted upon here may remind us of what Study had had to say of households barren of genuine hospitality:

*Sithenes* after; *repreueth* rebukes; *lakken any lyf* find fault with anyone else; *lakkes* faults; *han* have; *Religioun* the religious orders; *bi* through; *leder of louedayes* instigator of (or presiding figure at) days of settlement, when disputes had to be compounded (the implication being that there were appropriate pickings for any but the poor); *londe-bugger* land-buyer; *priker* horseman; *palfray* riding horse; *manere* manor; *loureth* scowls; *lakketh* asks reprovingly; *lered* taught.

Elyng is the halle, vche day in the wyke,
There the lord ne the lady liketh nouȝte to sytte.
Now hath vche riche a reule to eten bi hym-selue
In a pryue parloure, for pore mennes sake,
Or in a chambre with a chymneye, and leue the chief halle
That was made for meles, men to eten inne.

It is an accurate observation of the changing social scene; but the poet reaches a fundamental truth of human nature when the question is asked why it should be so. For while greed is certainly the cause, greed is yet curiously short-sighted. There can be no guarantee that the miser will live to spend what is saved; and certainly none that his heir will spend it wisely. It is therefore in vain

al to spare to spille that spende shal another.

Similarly, in 'Clergy's' present discourse, the cupidity of the rich has only one ending:

Litel had lordes to done to ȝyue londe fram her heires
To religious, that haue no reuthe though it reyne on here auteres!

There is in Langland, as we saw in the *Visio*, an acute understanding that evil involves its own undoing. Merely on the level of self-interest men deceive themselves. The salient characteristic of our failings is, from this standpoint, that they make us uncritical. It is a note sounded early in the poem:

Whan alle tresores ben ytryed treuthe is the beste.

As such it makes for and sustains the sardonic humour with which the world is surveyed; it is the ground of Langland's penetration, and is evident in the firmness of line with which he draws his satiric portraits. But it coexists with a profound sense of the judgement that waits inexorably—both upon individual man, in eternity, and upon mankind in this life. Each nourishes and is in turn sustained by his sense of Law, an awareness that payment though long deferred will surely be exacted. Man may therefore well seem ridiculous in his blind concern with lesser interests which overlook the greater. For it is not God who is mocked. The grim awareness of famine and pestilence as periodic checks upon

*Elyng* miserable; *vche* each; *reule* (rule) practice; *pryue* private; *for* against; *chymneye* fireplace; *meles* meals; *spare to spille* withhold from spending; *Litel . . . to done* They could have found something better to do; *reuthe* compunction; *auteres* altars.

man's idleness and self-seeking is matched with a prophetic assurance that time must have a stop; the heyday of monastic splendour will give place to desolation. We may be reminded of those terms of 'social contract' in which man naturally first conceives of *Dowel* (it was thus the first definition offered to the Dreamer, by Thought in Passus VII). If there is offence by any one party,

> Thanne shal the kynge come and casten hem in yrens.

So, in the day of temporal doom,

> there shal come a kyng and confesse 30w religiouses,
> And bete 30w, as the bible telleth, for brekynge of 30wre reule,
> And amende monyales, monkes and chanouns,
> And putten hem to her penaunce *ad pristinum statum ire*.

It will be an end of the rule of Meed in the cloister, when

> freres in here freitoure shal fynden a keye
> Of Costantynes coffres, in which is the catel
> That Gregories god-children han yuel dispended.

For, in that day, the mightiest will be laid low:

> And thanne shal the abbot of Abyndoun and alle his issu
>                                        for euere
> Haue a knokke of a kynge, and incurable the wounde.

The passage is, of course, remarkable for the accident of prophecy. But prophetic insight is entirely natural to Langland as one who sees in present corruption the unmistakable warnings of an apocalyptic ending. Hence both the energy of his protestation and the long range of its reference. For him, as for the greater Reformers of the sixteenth century, no single abuse exists of itself. All leads back to original offence, as it leads forward to a time, perhaps already at hand, when the final reckoning is to be made. There is in Langland an untiring vigilance to detect the terrible portents of that reign of Antichrist which must precede a new beginning:

*monyales* nuns; *ad pristinum* etc. to return to their original state (of obedience to monastic rule); *freres* friars; *freitoure* refectory; *Costantynes coffres* (alluding to) the wealth with which the Emperor Constantine endowed the Church; *catel* property, wealth; *Gregories god-children* monks (founded by St. Augustine in his mission appointed by Gregory the Great); *Abyndoun* Abingdon.

ar that kynge come, Cayme shal awake.

But the last victory is not with *Cayme*, for

Dowel shal dyngen hym adoune and destruyen his myȝte.

It is a passage in Langland's darkest vein—grim, measured, and utterly unsparing; the black cap is on and the sentence is irreversible.

Perhaps for that very reason—its utter finality—it is immediately followed by a lighter note. The Dreamer comes to a false conclusion; and his brief, eager phrase suggests that he has been attending less to the momentous things 'Clergy' has uttered than to the immediate implications for his own quest:

'Thann is Dowel and Dobet,' quod I, '*dominus* and kniȝthode.'

There is something of monomaniac intentness about the Dreamer as he is now revealed; and he is rightly rebuked by Scripture for his stupidity. It is the second rebuke of the *Vita*, and the third the Dreamer has encountered in his whole career. Yet we should not fail to note that the point on which Scripture takes him up is not entirely just. As Study had unfairly taxed him with mere curiosity, equating him with the voluble and uncharitable 'masters', so Scripture limits the application of the Dreamer's reply to the merely temporal status of King and knight:

Kynghod ne knyȝthod, by nauȝt I can awayte,
Helpeth nouȝt to heueneward one heres ende,
Ne ricchesse riȝt nouȝt, ne reaute of lordes.

It is rather less than fair, and it is certainly unfortunate for the immediate development of the poem. By one of those cyclic movements that the reader will by now begin to recognize as characteristic of the progress of the poet's argument, the whole discussion veers sharply around to the credibility of the rich gaining a heavenly reward. All moral witness— and here pagan antiquity is included, 'patriarchs and prophets, and poets, too'—

Wryten to wissen vs to wilne no ricchesse,
And preyseden pouerte with pacience . . .

Patient poverty is the only title to heaven, where

riche men no riȝte may clayme but of reuthe and grace.

Cayme 'Cain', here Antichrist; *dyngen* beat; *destruyen* destroy; *dominus* lordship, here kingship; *awayte* see, discover; *to heueneward* towards heaven; *heres ende* hair's breadth; *reaute* (royalty) pomp, state; *wissen* teach; *wilne* desire; *but* save, except.

This alas! is an opening which is irresistible to the Dreamer. Blown around, like the man in the *waggynge* boat, on to a fresh tack, the dialectician in him springs to the helm:

> '*Contra*,' quod I, 'bi Cryste, that can I repreue,
> And preue it, bi Peter and bi Poule bothe,
> That is baptized beth sauf, be he riche or pore'.

Scripture's reply is that although the heathen may be admitted on those terms, more is required of the Christian man. Her reply in fact brings the argument sharply back to its main bearings—the Law that must be fulfilled:

> For that Cryst for Cristen men deyde and confermed the lawe,
> That who-so wolde and wylneth with Cryste to aryse,
> > *Si cum Christo surrexistis, etc.*
> He shulde louye and leue and the law fulfille.

This Law is simple enough:

> That is—'loue thi lorde god leuest aboue alle,
> And after, alle Crystene creatures in comune, eche man other.'

This is the doing well that is required of all of us and in terms of which we must account at Judgement Day. With it goes the salutary reminder that this, though required of us, is not to be required by us from others. Once again, retribution is God's, and He will exact it. It is therefore a sufficient answer to the Dreamer—and, at that, surprisingly brief. Scripture has given in two dozen lines a comprehensive answer upon a wide and perplexing range of topics. It seems ungracious in the extreme for the Dreamer to reply

> This is a longe lessoun . . . and litel am I the wyser;
> Where Dowel is, or Dobet, derkelich ȝe shewen.

But several forces have acted upon him. There is the desire to find examples from practice which made him impatient of even the Friars' moderate and eminently practical counsel: he needs must see for himself. There is, too, the mistrust of mere learning which he had readily caught from Study (her equation of learning with self-interest, when set over against the example of patient poverty). Scripture's references both to the witness of pagan antiquity and to the salvation of Jews and Sara-

---

*repreue* disprove; *That* he who; *beth* is; *sauf* saved; *deyde* died; *wylneth* purposes, wishes; *Si cum* etc. 'If ye then be risen with Christ' (Col. iii 1); *leue* believe, have faith; *leuest* dearest; *derkelich* obscurely.

cens have awakened the recollection of Study's more personal message. Theology was *no science for sothe forto sotyle inne;* and Scripture now appears to be Theology's spokesman.

Many tales ʒe tellen that Theologye lerneth,

he begins, and no doubt included in Scripture's repertoire is the frightening 'tale' of Predestination:

> that I man made was and my name entred
> In the legende of lyf longe er I were,
> Or elles vnwriten for somme wikkednesse, as holywrit wytnesseth,
> *Nemo ascendit ad celum, nisi qui de celo descendit.*

The Dreamer is now well launched. The earlier silences and courteous acquiescences are far behind as the Dreamer deals in turn with the damnation of the Wise Ancients, Solomon[11] and Aristotle; the discrepancy between knowledge and practice, especially evident in the learned; and the precariousness of the 'clerk' in relation to salvation, when simple faith can save the Penitent Thief and such notable sinners as were the Magdalene, King David and the Apostle Paul, in their time. Only God knows whether love—and thus the sinner's righteous deeds— shall save him, or whether he will receive mere justice *(be allowed as he lyued so).* There is thus only one safe rule of conduct, and it applies with special force to clerics: 'Perform those acts which you see commended in your books'. Equally, there is only one wholly reliable thing to be said of the human condition in general:

> sothest worde that euere god seyde was tho he seyde, *nemo bonus.*

We have come to the same pass as that which concluded the *Visio*— an understanding that the Law is absolute; and thus that the Mercy of God is the only ground of hope. There is no confidence to be placed in learning; Our Lord did not commend it, and its dangers are manifest. But we can be certain of the simple faith that is found among

> . . . plowmen and pastoures and pore comune laboreres.
> Souteres and shepherdes, suche lewed Iottes
> Percen with a *pater-noster* the paleys of heuene,
> And passen purgatorie penaunceles at her hennes-partynge,

*lerneth* teaches; *y-entred* entered; *were* existed; *vnwriten* not written; *Nemo ascendit* etc. 'no man hath ascended up to heaven, but he that came down from heaven' (John iii 13); *sothest* truest; *nemo bonus* 'there is none that doeth good' (Ps. xiv 1; *cf.* Matt. xix 17); *souteres* cobblers; *lewed* unlearned, ignorant; *Iottes* peasants; *percen* (pierce) penetrate to; *penaunceles* without suffering; *hennes* hence.

> In-to the blisse of paradys, for her pure byleue,
> That inparfitly here knewe and eke lyued.

Knowledge and practice may alike fall short; simple faith will yet prevail. As we have seen, the jangling between Piers and the Priest at the end of the *Visio* prepares for this conclusion. The artistry with which it has been brought about deserves equal attention. After his simple persistence, and his courteous demurring to authority, the Dreamer who has now launched his broadside is one in whom a pent-up impatience with mere learning and a searing contempt for the pretensions of the rich has at last swept aside all reserve. Holy Church's warning *(Loke thow suffre hym to sey)* has been forgotten; so there disappears altogether the corollary to it, *worche thow there-after*. It remains to be seen whether the Dreamer has cut himself off from authoritative teaching; if not, then in due season we may turn to the application of that teaching.

### IV

*A Passus XII*[12]

Certainly, in the last Passus of the A Text, which now follows, the Dreamer has put himself beyond the pale. The charge Study had unfairly levelled on first encounter has now been abundantly proved:

> The were lef to lerne but loth for to stodie.

His motive is mere speculative curiosity:

> Thou woldest konne that I can and carpen hit after,
> Presumptuowsly, parauenture, apose so manye,
> That my3the turne me to tene and Theologie bothe.

As Study had predicted, without an attempt to practise *Dowel*—

> But if he lyue in the lyf that longeth to Dowel—(X 132)

the Dreamer will make no advance at all. So Learning withdraws his help—a help freely and fully given to any who genuinely seek practical truth:

> 3if I wiste witterly thou woldest don therafter,
> Al that thou askest asoylen I wolde.

Scripture concurs. The Dreamer

*inparfitly* imperfectly, inadequately; *here* here (on earth); *eke* also; *lef* willing, eager; *carpen* chatter (about); *parauenture* perhaps; *apose* debate with; *tene* anger, vexation; *But if* unless; *witterly* for sure; *asoylen* grant.

> cam not by cause to lerne to Dowel,
> But as he seyth, such I am, when he with me carpeth.[13]

Once again, humour supervenes. The Dreamer's plight is truly absurd; let him go to school to Experience itself. Natural understanding, Scripture's 'cousin',

> knowen is wel wide
> And his loggyng is with lyf that lord is of erthe.

The Dreamer is sent forth, a beginner once more; and his guide is no authoritative person, but

> a clerioun that
> Hy3t *omnia probate*, a pore thing withalle.

The text with which Conscience had satirized Lady Meed comes appropriately to hand to characterize the Dreamer. It is proverbial that it is fools who learn by experience: but, clearly, even this learning, 'a poor thing withal', is preferable to invincible ignorance. On this note, the A Text draws to its conclusion. Many things befall the Dreamer before he comes at last to *quod bonum est tenete;* and the precursor of Death, Fever, is the last witness to an inescapable truth. Man may not seek an end of moral effort; there can be only one counsel while man's *lyf and his lykhame lesten togedere :*

> do after Do-wel whil thi dayes duren.

*Passus XI*

In the B Text the end is not yet in sight. We open with the outright scorn which Scripture had held in restraint at the Dreamer's first ineptitude—the equation of *Dowel* and *Dobet* with 'kingship and knighthood'. After his long harangue, Scripture has one devastatingly brief comment:

> *multi multa sciunt, et seipsos nesciunt.*

It is a damning judgement; not only does it stamp the Dreamer as a self-convicted know-all, but it cuts across all the arguments about learning. The Dreamer is silenced; his chagrin is vividly conveyed:

> Tho wepte I for wo and wratth of her speche,
> And in a wynkyng worth til I was aslepe.[14]

*carpeth* talks, argues; *wel wide* far and wide; *loggyng* (lodging) dwelling; *clerioun* choir-boy, young scholar; *Hy3t* was called; *omnia probate* 'Prove all things' (I Thess. v 21); *lykhame* body; *lesten* last; *duren* continue; *multi multa* etc. 'many know much and know not themselves' (attributed to St. Bernard). *in a wynkyng worth* became drowsy;

He now looks back on his past life, and we learn that his youth was heedless. *Will* had the upper hand. His besetting sins were Lechery and 'Lust of the Eyes'; the latter, indeed,

> folwed me fourty wynter and a fyfte more,
> That of Dowel ne Dobet no deyntee me ne thou3te.

It may seem strange to his present audience; but it is true—

> I had no lykynge, leue me if the leste, of hem au3te to knowe.

This has the ring of the authentic in characterizing the Dreamer. The unsparing critic of the rule of Meed was for long her servant; and the relentless seeker after the perfection of Christian obedience—one who, as Clergy acidly observed, *coueyteth don betere than the boke telleth*—lived long in heedlessness of any such reckoning. How did the change occur? Here again mere experience played its part; with the onset of maturer years and the fact of poverty, recognition came that

> was Fortune my foo, for al hir faire biheste,
> And Pouerte pursued me and put me lowe.

The characterization here is, of course, that of the Dreamer. We must not unreservedly apply to Langland himself details which exemplify so well the developing truth of the poem.[15] It is, too, wholly characteristic of the poet's day that the first stirrings of concern with lasting truth arose from a dispute, a dispute, moreover, with the odious race of Friars, who turn out to be the Dreamer's fair-weather friends. He sees that their concern for the dying is for themselves as likely legatees; they are much less interested in souls coming into the world (the duty of baptizing infants). The Dreamer puts his first penetrating question to an actual cleric of his day. Is it not more meritorious to baptize?—for

> a barne with-oute bapteme may nou3t so be saued;
> *Nisi quis renatus fuerit ex aqua, &c;*
> Loke, 3e lettred men, whether I lye or do nou3te.

There is no answer. But the question leads to a larger issue for the Dreamer himself. Outspokenness in reproving others prompts the frightening thought that many are called but few are chosen. Now the

---

*fyfte more* fifth besides (*i.e.* fourty-five years in all); *That* so that; *no deyntee me ne thou3te* I set no value (on them); *leue* believe; *if the leste* if you like; *for* in spite of; *biheste* promise; *barne* child; *Nisi quis* etc. 'Except a man be born of water and of the Spirit, he cannot enter into the kingdom of God' (John iii 5).

dispute is all within. This text of Scripture drives the Dreamer back upon himself:

> Al for tene of her tyxte trembled myn herte,
> And in a were gan I waxe and with my-self to dispute,
> Whether I were chosen or nouȝt chosen . . .

This sudden and all-consuming fear is similar to that immediacy of realization which, also accompanied by *tene*, came upon the Plowman. But where the Plowman cast himself at once and entirely on the Mercy of God, the Dreamer looks for reassurance. He thus turns back in his thoughts to Holy Church, who had at the outset reminded him

> thow ouȝtest me to knowe,
> I vnderfonge the firste and the feyth tauȝte . . . (I 75-6)

Now the Dreamer gladly acknowledges the full significance of baptism—

> on Holicherche I thouȝte,
> That vnderfonge me atte fonte for one of goddis chosen—

and the argument at once widens to include all men, Christian and Pagan alike:

> For Cryste cleped vs alle come if we wolde,
> Sarasenes and scismatikes, and so he dyd the Iewes . . .

Christians may claim as of right their entrance upon God's work of salvation; and there is comfort in the thought that this cannot truly be renounced. The matter is put, with a characteristic emphasis, as a contractual truth. Whatever measure of punishment the errant Christian may merit, he cannot truly be lost; and, too, there may be remission of punishment.

For the moment, all is well. Scripture assents, on the simple and comprehensive ground that Mercy is above all other works of God. But with a suddenness that is utterly startling, a dissentient breaks in. Scripture speaks well from her books—but is that all?

> 'ȝee! baw for bokes!' quod one was broken oute of helle.

Trajan is come to prove from his own case that it was love of

---

*were* war; *vnderfonge* received (in baptism); *atte* at the; *Sarasenes* Saracens, pagans; *ȝee! baw for bokes* Bah! you can keep your books . . .; *Trajan* a reference to the common belief that the Emperor Trajan was spared the torments of hell through the prayers of St. Gregory the Great.

righteousness and consequent good works that led Gregory to pray for this pagan's salvation. Therefore,

> Loue and leute is a lele science.

It is, moreover, the only learning on which Divine approval rests: for this is the 'book' which God wrote *(with his on fynger)* in the Tables of the Law delivered to Moses. We see the great condition on which both right conduct and learning are acceptable:

> 'Lawe with-outen loue,' quod *Troianus*, 'leye there a bene,
> Or any science vnder sonne, the seuene artz and alle,
> But if thei ben lerned for owre lordes loue, loste is alle the tyme.'

His next words come home directly to the present situation of the Dreamer:

> For no cause to cacche *siluer* there-by, ne to be called a *mayster*.

It is characteristic of the poet's method that when, in the complex and even tortuous developments of the argument, a human example is set before us, light comes immediately; and it is light which is thrown back upon the past as well as upon the road that lies ahead. So here: the characteristic emphasis of the *Visio* was upon the mercenary motive; in the *Vita de Dowel* it is the sin of overweening. Each is subtle, pervasive, and absolutely corrupting. They are united in this one line, where *siluer* and *mayster* are equally abhorrent to the spirit in which man is to work—

> al for loue of owre lorde and the bet to loue the peple.

The theme of riches and poverty receives a new application when we reflect upon our kinship through the Redemption:

> For alle are we Crystes creatures and of his coffres riche,
> And bretheren as of o blode, as wel beggares as erles.

We are 'gentlefolk': it is the sounding of a new theme, a harmony among so many discords, which takes up the notes of *sute* and *secte*[16] which Repentance had confidently sounded in his appeal to a God Who had become *owre fader and owre brother* (V 495-513). But it is not

---

*leute* conformity to God's Law, practical obedience; *lele science* honest learning (as distinct from vainglorious wrangling); *on* own; *leye there a bene* don't give a rap for it; *seuene artz* the Seven Arts (of the medieval university curriculum); *But if* unless; *cacche* (catch) gain; *bet* better; *coffres* treasure-chests; *o* one; *erles* noblemen.

dwelt on here. We are recalled to the law that makes a reality of brother-hood; Piers had had to learn it in overseeing the work of the half-acre—*alter alterius onera portate*. Sharp reproofs are forbidden—'for there is none without fault'; and faith is to be commended above 'logic or law'. We are reminded once more what it is we are dealing with when we appeal to logic and law; they cannot finally be evaded or placated:

> *Eadem mensura qua mensi fueritis, remecietur vobis.*

The conclusion resolves at once any confusion between law and mercy (and between learning and understanding). We must learn 'the law of love', and it is a law that cannot be merely externalized:

> *Melius est scrutari scelera nostra, quam naturas rerum.*

The praise of patient poverty which follows is no digression, if we recall the practical point insisted on before—that learning encourages pretentiousness, and this leaves totally unregarded both our knowledge of the self and our real duties to our fellow-men. The consideration of poverty in its turn leads naturally to those professed dependants upon God's Providence, the clergy and thus, inevitably, to their many failings. The special point of indictment is their ignorance. Langland's unsleeping sense of law, more particularly the law of contract, prompts the sharp awareness that ignorance may endanger the validity of the rites:

> A chartre is chalengeable byfor a chief justice;
> If false Latyne be in the lettre the lawe it inpugneth

There can be nothing but contempt for the ignorant cleric—

> So is it a goky, by god, that in his gospel failleth
> Or in masse or in matynes maketh any defaute.

A heavy responsibility therefore lies upon the Bishop who

> crouneth suche goddes kniȝtes that conneth nouȝt *sapienter*
> Synge ne psalmes rede, ne segge a messe of the day.

But, as though mindful of his own counsel to look to oneself rather than reprove others, the speaker[17] apologises for this excursus and reiterates his central affirmation:

*alter alterius* etc. 'Bear ye one another's burdens' (Gal. vi 2); *Eadem mensura* etc. 'With what measure ye mete, it shall be measured to you again' (Matt. vii 2); *Melius est* etc. 'Better to search out our offences than the nature of things' (attributed to St. Gregory); *inpugneth* calls in question, finds fault with; *goky* clumsy idiot; *defaute* error; *crouneth* admits to the tonsure; *kniȝtes* knights, servants; *sapienter* 'with understanding' (presumably alluding to 'sing ye praises with understanding' Ps. xlvii 7); *messe* Mass.

This lokynge on lewed prestes hath don me lepe fram pouerte,
The whiche I preyse, there pacyence is, more parfyt than ricchesse.

New beginnings are apparent when the Dreamer is shown by Nature
('Kind') the natural world. The vision links back with the Field of Folk
when he is shown

how men token *mede* and mercy refused—

and it foreshadows things to come when the Dreamer perceives that
Reason rules all God's creatures save only man. It is an extended vision:
for once the Dreamer is momentarily silent. We become aware of an
enlargement of scope, and of an impending development away from
questioning to contemplation. But the interlude is brief; and the poet
marks the change as the Dreamer's fatal facility in dialectic re-asserts
itself:

Ac that moste moeued me *and my mode changed* . . .

What brings this about is, once more, the theoretical prospect of sinlessness; and this time the Dreamer must challenge Reason himself. Why
should not man be saved from his follies, as the animal creation is? The
point is put accusingly:

'I haue wonder of the,' quod I, 'that witty art holden,
Why thow ne suwest man and his make, that no mysfait hem
folwe?'

It is exactly the sort of question that Study had barred—the large
conjectures of those who

dryuele at her deyse the deite to knowe. (X 56)

To question the purposes of Almighty God is the ultimate attempt to
shift a responsibility which man would discard but cannot evade. It
is the Dreamer's last question of this kind: and it earns the most comprehensive rebuke to date—a rebuke which gathers up all that the Dreamer
should have learned, and thus underlines for the reader the intransigence
of mere speculative curiosity, its incapacity to learn by simple observation. Reason's reply runs: let the Dreamer first learn to rule his
tongue; then, before he blames others, let him ask if there is anything
praiseworthy in himself. It is God who created us, not we Him. The

---

*lepe* (leap) digress; *preyse* value; *parfyt* perfect; *mode* spirit, temper; *witty* clever,
wise; *holden* held, regarded; *suwest* follow, attend on; *mysfait* injury; *folwe* befall.

lesson of man's kinship with all God's creatures is twofold—firstly, whatever man may think of it, God approves His own Creation; second-ly, the simple truth about man's condition is that faultlessness is entirely out of the question. *Nemo sine crimine vivit*; Man is not pure spirit.

The shaft comes home directly to the Dreamer, the impossible perfectionist for whom God's Creation is too material. His search for the more-than-just man, the one who will be exempt from the common lot of sinning *seuene sythes* daily, is over in the moment that it is seen as foolish:

> Tho cauȝte I coloure anon and comsed to ben aschamed,
> And awaked ther-with.

But one thing at last is known, and known ruefully:

> 'Now I wote what Dowel is,' quod I, 'by dere god, as me
>                                                          thinketh!'

It is at the prompting of a newcomer upon the scene that this single piece of hard-won knowledge is revealed:

> 'To se moche and suffre more, certes,' quod I, 'is Dowel!'

He has realized, and his new interlocutor does not spare him the reali-zation, that he would have known more—had he kept his mouth shut:

> Ac for thine entermetyng here artow forsake;
> *Philosophus esses, si tacuisses.*

This tantalizing awareness—of having been several times on the brink of knowing—is very faithful to dream-experience recaptured in the first moments of waking. For the former Dreamer is awake now: his present companion has nothing to do with mere fiction. His name is *Ymagynatyf;* and the Dreamer's 'imagination' in this sense is his taking stock of past experience. It involves no flight of 'imagination' in the modern sense.[18] Sober realization, especially the realization of opportunities missed, is the key-note of what follows. If 'imagination' in the older sense has the primary meaning of bringing to mind that which is not present to the senses, it is yet not to be thought of merely as a mode of memory, but rather as the capacity to profit from experience. In

---

*Nemo* etc. 'No man can live without sinning' ('Cato', as before); *cauȝte I coloure* I blushed; *anon* at once; *comsed* began; *by dere god, as me thinketh!* my word, I should think so!; *certes* certainly; *entermetyng* meddling, interfering; *artow* art + thow: *Philosophus* etc. 'You would have been a philosopher if you had held your tongue' (adapted from Boethius).

this respect, man is released from mere dependence upon the succession of events; to be 'imaginative' is the outstanding characteristic of the intelligent.[19] The Dreamer had taxed Reason for a failure to control mankind. Now he is to find that man who will not make a right use of Reason will be the prisoner of mere experience. All this comes with a humbling effect; for the plight of the 'unimaginative' man in this sense—one who must be taught how to attend to simple experience—is very like that of the fool as Nashe describes him:

> A foole conceits no further then he sees,
> He hath no scense of aught but what he feeles.[20]

It is therefore appropriate that in these first waking moments Imagynatyf spares the Dreamer nothing of chagrin, as the authoritative figures of the dream begin to recede:

> 'Haddestow suffred,' he seyde, 'slepyng tho thow were,
> Thow sholdest haue knowen that Clergye can and conceiued
>                           more thorugh Resoun;
> For Resoun wolde haue reherced the riȝte as Clergye saide.'

It is all too late. But there is yet one avenue to the truth:

> Shal neuere chalangynge ne chydynge chaste a man so sone
> As shal Shame, and shenden hym and shape hym to amende.

It is not much; and certainly it is nothing to be dignified about. But the Dreamer receives accepts this guidance, with its crudely effective analogy of the *dronken daffe* fallen by the wayside and rescued by Need and Shame. It is a way back to the truth, and it is to be accepted; for, as Boethius observed, drunk men of themselves do not know the road home. So the Dreamer ruefully submits:

> 'Why ȝe wisse me thus . . . was for I rebuked Resoun'.

Ymagynatyf's reply is laconic. There is to be no dwelling on past mistakes. It is time to move on:

> 'Certes,' quod he, 'that is soth', and shope hym for to walken.

## Passus XII

In the brief Passus that follows, Ymagynatyf reveals himself for what

---

*Haddestow* haddest + thow; *reherced* declared, told; *chaste* chasten; *shenden* put to shame; *shape* cause, bring; *daffe* blockhead, fool; *wisse* instruct, counsel; *for* because; *Certes* quite right!; *shope hym* got ready.

he is. The time has come for the Dreamer to take stock; so *ymagynacioun* is set to work. There is an elegiac beauty in the disclosing of identity; the Dreamer comes face to face with his own experience, long known but not attended to, and bringing now the recognition that time is running out:

> how fele fernȝeres are faren and so fewe to come!

We begin to make sense of experience. Is it, after all, so difficult a thing to know the truth? The great Psalm often associated with contemplative life, which the Plowman had recited, is echoed, one stage further on in its affirmations. We see that it is suffering which both reveals and consoles:

> *Virga tua et baculus tuus, ipsa me consolata sunt.*

The Dreamer has been profitlessly employed—like his own errant clerics:

> thow medlest the with makynges and myȝtest go sey thi sauter,
> And bidde for hem that ȝiueth the bred . . .

We return to our starting-point in the *Vita de Dowel* with the reminder that there are many preaching Friars (in pairs, moreover) as well as books enough to *tell* men all about Dowel, Dobet and Dobest. It is penetratingly apt, and there is a vivid touch in the Dreamer's seeking to turn aside the uncomfortable truth:

> I seigh wel he sayde me soth, and *somwhat me to excuse*
> Seide . . .

What the Dreamer has to say shows him as very nearly incorrigible, for he is back at his concern with sinlessness once more. If only he could be finally satisfied ('*atte laste*' is his phrase) he would stay forever in Church

> And there bydde my bedes, but whan ich eet or slepe.

It is not to be. The Christian life is to be lived; and Faith, Hope and Love are the answer to his need. 'Love' means conformity to law in loving obedience:

> he doth wel, with-oute doute, that doth as lewte techeth.

*fele* many; *fernȝeres* 'old' years, past years; *faren* gone; *Virga tua* etc. 'thy rod and thy staff they comfort me' (Ps. xxiii 4); *makynges* verse-writing; *sauter* Psalter; *bidde* pray; *seigh* saw; *soth* truth; *bydde my bedes* say over my prayers; *but* save.

For all classes in the community, there can be no escape from the path of *obedyence, that heigh way is to heuene*. Once again, with painstaking care the Dreamer is taken over familiar ground. There is to be no discrepancy between what we profess and what we practise. The ground of 'Clergy' and 'Kind Wit' is natural knowledge and natural observation, *quod scimus* and *quod vidimus*. Grace is above all: and it is useless to ask its origins—it is a wind that blows where it will in the good purposes of God. 'Clergy' is defended, for Our Lord, releasing the woman taken in adultery, wrote in the dust the condemnation of her accusers. The preaching style that Ymagynatyf at one point adopts, '*Riȝt so goddes body, bretheren . . .*' is appropriate to a discourse in which things fall into place. Learning and Natural Knowledge, we now see, are intimately related (they are *cosynes*). The distinction between theory and practice cuts both ways; we are not to despise the doctrines of the Clergy because of the teachers' way of life. Natural knowledge of itself never saved anyone; and clerics were among those who first acknowledged Incarnate Deity at the stable in Bethlehem.

This discourse is vividly linked with the Dreamer's own experience. Ymagynatyf makes it clear that he has been present throughout and knows his man:

> I toke ful gode hede
> How thow contraryedest Clergye with crabbed wordes.

He takes up the matter of salvation where the Dreamer had earlier left it. The Dreamer had preferred the claim of the *lewed* to the *lettred*. Is that the right conclusion? Anyone who has been taught to swim will have a better chance in the Thames than the non-swimmer: and, again, 'benefit of clergy' has its uses—even if the 'clergy' goes no further than the 'neck-verse', the scrap of Latin that will none the less save a man's neck at Tyburn. Certainly, too, the Penitent Thief is saved; but his is a low place in the bliss of heaven. Above all, let the Dreamer remember that some questions are insoluble. Nature alone knows her own secrets. We can learn by observation of the natural order. For example, the birds can teach us the relative worth of outward show and true qualities (the gaudy but impotent peacock is contrasted with the lark in its beauty and swiftness). Aristotle is one of those who observed God's creatures; but, Ymagynatyf seems to imply, it rests with man to make a right application of knowledge. For of Aristotle, as of Socrates and Solomon, we cannot say that they have salvation. We may indeed

---

*quod scimus* 'that which we know'; *quod vidimus* 'that which we have seen'; *contraryedest* contradicted; *crabbed* cross, perverse.

hope for them, trusting in the Divine Grace, and in gratitude for their learning—

> For lettred men were lewed men ȝut, ne were lore of her bokes.

On this sensible and modest note Ymagynatyf's discourse ends. It has covered all the major issues with which the Dreamer has been vexed; and it has throughout been well related to Ymagynatyf's allegorical character. As an observer of things and of men, he has been able to speak for both 'Kind Wit' and 'Clergy'. His summing-up in the matter of learning, treated in terms of profit and loss to humanity at large, is soundly balanced.

Alas! the Dreamer must intervene. He is positive on a dogmatic point: there can be no question of salvation *with-outen Crystendome*. The debate is on once more, as Ymagynatyf replies sharply, in the manner of the schools, and with displeasure:

> '*Contra*,' quod Ymagynatyf tho, and comsed for to loure,
> And seyde, '*saluabitur vix iustus in die iudicij*.
> *Ergo saluabitur*'.

The mulish Dreamer is now opposed with an equal stubbornness; Ymagynatyf, we see, is an *alter ego*. His reply is that truth is not simple: in his obsessive concern with perfection the Dreamer might overlook the fact that all right conduct will have its reward. The first line of Piers's 'pardon', we may say, must not be forgotten:

> Ne wolde neuere trewe god but treuth were allowed.

There are other kinds of baptism than that known to the Dreamer. There can be baptism in martyrdom for truth, and baptism of desire to fulfil truth—if that truth is the highest known to man and is continued in to the end. It is an absolute check to the merely dogmatic notions with which the Dreamer has been wrestling. We return once again to the Psalm the Plowman had spoken aloud, and in the same stroke to renewed discussion of rewards which *(mede* and *mercede)* had preceded the emergence of the Plowman as the embodiment of simple obedience. In the *Vita* now, as in the *Visio* before, the true 'treasure' is revealed as

ȝut yet, still; *ne were* if it were not for; *with-outen Crystendome* without baptism; *tho* then; *comsed* began; *loure* frown; *saluabitur vix* etc. the righteous shall scarcely be saved in the Day of Judgement (adapted from I Peter iv 18; the meaning here is that 'scarcely' nevertheless implies that it will be so; *Ergo saluabitur*, therefore the righteous will be saved); *treuth* right conduct; *allowed* approved.

conformity to law at its highest and best; and this truth will sustain all society. The Priest, we remember, had been unable to *construe* the Plowman's 'pardon'. Now we learn the right interpretation *(glose)* of the Plowman's Psalm:

> The glose graunteth vpon that vers a gret mede to treuthe.

As in the Dreamer's waking thoughts at the end of the *Visio*, so now in Ymagynatyf's defence of the righteous ancients, it is obedience, conformity to the highest law man knows, that is decisive. And once again the Mercy of God, towards which, when Law was uppermost, the Plowman had turned, is the dominant note. Eternal life is now seen as the gift of God to His faithful followers. This *mede* is truly such, in the sense long ago established by Conscience before the King—it is a divinely disproportionate reward; as C has it, *cortesie more than couenant was*. Let the Dreamer with his painfully dogmatic notions attend as best he can. Ymagynatyf can do no more.

V

*Passus XIII*

This singularly thorough summing-up has ranged over the Dreamer's whole career and has come to rest at the starting-point, the paradox that man, at his best sinning 'seven times daily', need not fear a God Who yet is Righteousness. It is fitting that the next Passus opens by forging another strong link with what has gone before. The first twenty lines are an unusually simple and even prosaic epitome of progress to date. It is clear that we are shaping for a resolution of the problems with which the Dreamer has long been vexed. That he has been able to see the need for patience is the first step forward from theory to practice. Now he may progress if he attends to the moral virtues; for the example of the righteous ancients (Aristotle, Socrates, etc.) is one of conformity to moral law. So we next see the Dreamer accompanied by Conscience, and there is a return to the spirited manner of the *Visio* as, once more, a pilgrimage begins.

The Dreamer accepts an invitation to dine with Clergy, and there he meets one of those 'masters' of whom Study had earlier spoken. The episode constitutes in itself a proof that the argument is passing from theory to practice; and in a voluble but greedy theologian of the dinner-table we see a final discrepancy between theory and practice. The Dreamer's contempt grows until the time arrives to put the perennial question in terms this 'master' is qualified to understand:

'What is Dowel? sire doctour,' quod I, 'is Dowel any penaunce?'

The whole portrayal of the greedy Doctor is, as Whitaker long ago noted, a 'portrait of gluttony and hypocrisy combined . . . in Langland's best manner, strong and indignant'.[21] It is certainly a bold treatment of that unwitting discrepancy which, as we saw even in a repentant Sloth and Avarice (Passus V), is the lasting characteristic of the wicked—any awareness of failing is the last thing to be looked for. As such, this episode is a crowning-point in the poem's development. Here are combined in one figure those two vices which underlay all others in *Visio* and *Vita*—self-interest in the one, and heartless learning in the other. More, it is the apparent fulfilment of all the Dreamer had most feared (and thus had over-hastily repudiated) in the learned he had sought to interrogate. His insistence throughout had been upon examples from practice. Here, in the long run, is what confronts him— callous self-interest and bland theologizing. The end of one whole phase must be near (if indeed the whole journey is not to end) when evil remains massively complacent, apparently immovable. It remains only to note that the Dreamer has progressed in the essential virtue of patience. He accepts Patience's signal to be silent until the time comes; and, again, he holds his tongue, at Conscience's bidding, after firing his first broadside:

> 'By this day, sire doctour . . . thanne be ȝe nouȝt in Dowel;
> For ȝe han harmed vs two in that ȝe eten the puddyng,
> Mortrewes, and other mete, and we no morsel hade!'

Of the two 'definitions' of *Dowel* the Doctor gives, the first is purely negative (to do no ill to one's fellow-Christians), the second couched in terms of obedience and teaching (*Dowel* and *Dobet*, respectively). *Dobest*, in this second definition, combines both obedience and teaching— by practising what one teaches:

> Dobest doth hym-self so as he seith and precheth.

It is an emphasis that comes oddly, but not the less effectively, from this Doctor. We can well believe that the measure of the best is to conform doctrine and practice when we hear it in the mouth of this avidly self-interested creature, whose way of life is so evidently the opposite of his professionally glib preaching. But the real purpose of this bold demonstration is to make the break from all limited consider-

*penaunce* penance, mortification of the flesh; *Mortrewes* thick soups, stews; *mete* food.

ations of 'doing well'—to leave the low plane of habitual concern for the self, with its invariable dichotomy of doctrine and practice and thus the fatal implications of *mesure*. It is the great turning-point of the argument in the *Vita de Dowel*. There is heard once again the name 'Piers Plowman' and at one sweep we rise to the infinity of love, its immeasurable superiority over learning:

> one Pieres the Ploughman hath inpugned vs alle,
> And sette alle sciences at a soppe, saue loue one,
> And no tixte ne taketh to meyntene his cause
> But *dilige deum* and *domine, quis habitabit*, &c.
> And seith that Dowel and Dobet aren two infinites,
> Whiche infinites, with a feith, fynden oute Dobest,
> Which shal saue mannes soule: thus seith Piers the Ploughman.

We have at last outsoared the world of the *mesurable*, a retributive system that remains stubbornly within the region of the finite. In what follows, we hear the combined testimony of Learning, Conscience and Patience to the truth of Love and its unlimited power. In the moment that we have this affirmation we are also prepared for a further and final bearing of the argument. The Doctor contemptuously rejects this notion of Love's universal power as 'old stuff'. *It is but a* Dido . . . *a dysoures tale:* no power can reconcile

> the pope and his enemys,
> Ne bitwene two Cristene kynges can no wiȝte pees make.

It is a disillusioned insistence on the world that Christendom knows, as against the rule of universal love that Christendom might be. The sensible man, the Doctor seems to imply, will accept the actual situation and not be beguiled by millennial idealism. Let Learning and Conscience leave the fanatic Patience—for, as all sensible men know, *pilgrimes kunne wel lye*. But these persuasions are of no avail. Conscience will take leave of all others (Learning included) to go forth

> And be pilgryme with Patience til I haue proued more.[22]

The poet has made a set of unusually close connexions with the *Visio*. We have the pilgrimage, which as in the *Visio* follows upon aversion from self-interest when self-interest is at last stripped of all disguise.

*inpugned* called in question; *soppe* sop (morsel of bread, thing of no value); *one* alone; *tixte* text (of Scripture); *dilige deum* 'Thou shalt love . . . God'; (Matt. xxii 37) *domine quis* etc. 'Lord, who shall abide in thy tabernacle?'; (Ps. xv 1) *Dido* an old tale (alluding to the story of Dido and Aeneas); *dysoures* story-teller's; *wiȝte* man; *lye* lie.

This in its turn means that we leave aside the Old Law—which Learning would insist upon in its minuteness *(the leest poynte to knowe)*—as the Plowman had torn asunder his legal document and cast himself upon the Mercy of God. Learning, both here and in the dispute between Plowman and Priest, is seen to be a lesser thing than the practice of virtue. So, as before, repentance is the necessary pre-condition; but here we reach an end of merely external reflection on the Dreamer's part. Conscience speaks plainly of the force of example coming home to the observer:

> the wille of the wye and the wille of folke here
> Hath moeued my mode to mourne for my synnes;

and perhaps there is a reference to the Dreamer by name in the emphasis upon 'Wille' in these lines and those that immediately follow, proclaiming that in *Vita* as in *Visio* there must be an end of mercenary motive:

> The good wille of a wi3te was neure bou3te to the fulle;
> For there nys no tresore thereto, to a trewe wille.

The example of the Magdalene brings before us the true goal of Christian living. We are no longer to search amongst the learned; perfected patience is beyond all that 'Clergy' can offer:

> Me were leuer, by owre lorde, and I lyue shulde,
> Haue pacience perfitlich than half thy pakke of bokes!

It is a fine flourish; and it states an important truth. But still the whole truth is not finally as simple as it appears. There is great fidelity to the fact in Clergy's steady refusal to be parted from Conscience, his saying

> ful sobreliche, 'thow shalt se the tyme,
> Whan thow art wery for-walked, wilne me to consaille.'

It is on its own level one of the most graphic things in the poem, the more compelling for an unforced simplicity. 'You'll see the day ...'; it is spoken with complete certainty and without heat *(ful sobreliche)*. The long quarrel with learning is made up in this spirit of honourable terms of difference. For between them, if they are but patient with one another, they might achieve all things.

It is perhaps characteristic of Conscience—and worth noticing, for a quiet humour is certainly not one of the best known traits of this poet— that Conscience should pitch the claim very high indeed:

*wille* purpose; *wye* man (here, Patience); *therto* adequate (to it); *to* compared with; *and if*; *wery for-walked* worn out with walking; *wilne* desire, want; *consaille* advise (you).

> There nys wo in this worlde that we ne shulde amende,
> And confourmen kynges to pees, and al kynnes londes,
> Sarasenes and Surre and so forth alle the Iewes,
> Turne in-to the trewe feithe and in-til one byleue.

Social righteousness, millennial peace, and the universal sway of Christendom—these, linking back ultimately with Reason's exalted utterance in the *Visio*, are great prospects. But Clergy is slower to rise to them; and as he had spoken *ful sobreliche* before, so now he quietly replies

> That is soth . . . I se what thow menest.

He will bide his time, performing his appointed tasks until the pilgrim is finally tested and made perfect. There is a pleasant irony in the echo of Conscience's enthusiastic *confourmen kynges*:

> I shal dwelle as I do my deuore to shewen,
> And *conformen fauntekynes* and other folke ylered.[23]

It is wholly characteristic of Langland that there is no easy solution to apparent dilemmas. His *forte* is to perceive and communicate the real, the complexity of moral experience when man begins to inquire into it. So, here, the prospect of individual perfection, like that of millennial harmony among nations, is one thing, and has its own inspiration: but the tasks in hand remain. Martha and Mary, Clergy and Conscience-in-aspiration—each is necessary to the other. Certainly, the most enthusiastic will cool sooner or later. The mere eddying of human impulse has been with us long enough in the *Vita*; it is time the steady set of the tide began to be felt.

Now that the pilgrimage begins again, *Actiua vita*[24] comes forth, to tell the pilgrims of the simplicity and singleness of aim of the workaday world. And as though to authorize this statement of the good life on its simplest possible level we hear again the name 'Piers Plowman', whose servant 'Actyf' is. We are reminded, too, of Pardons, and of the emptiness of mere formalities. What mankind would ask is a respite from pestilence and disease; for a power of healing, besides the remission of sins, is a Divine legacy to the Church on earth. There is a marked irony in the implied contrast between the miracles wrought by apostolic poverty and the Church's present wealth but entire inability to heal. Yet the explanation is not to be found in a wicked Pontiff, but in general unworthiness:

*confourmen* establish; *al kynnes londes* all countries, nations; *Sarasenes* Saracens; *Surre* Syrians; *in-til* unto; *byleue* faith; *soth* truth.

Ac if miȝte of miracle hym faille it is for men ben nouȝt worthy
To haue the grace of god, and no gylte of the pope.

This echoes the firm protestation of faith in Papal authority, notwithstanding its abuses, which we had heard after the tearing of the 'pardon'
—*so I leue lelly (lordes forbode ellis!)*. There is, too, the same conviction
that experience is the only master to bring us, by a hard road, to true
repentance. We had met it in the *Visio*, where Hunger was seen in action,
restoring order in the half-acre when Piers's authority was insufficient.
So, here:

> may no blyssyng done vs bote but if we wil amende,
> Ne mannes masse make pees amonges Christene peple,
> Tyl pruyde be purelich fordo, and that thourgh payn defaute.

It is a reminder of the faults of active life as it is ordinarily encountered. Haukyn, the 'active man', is a wafer-seller, a purveyor of creature-
comforts. The way is open once more for that abuse of bodily appetite
which only the sharp lessons of hunger can limit. There had been a
clear hint in the *Visio* of the faults of the simple labouring life; but the
main emphasis there had necessarily been on its virtues, over against
the unashamed self-seeking that dominated the Field of Folk. Now for
the first time we may look critically at the life of active self-sufficiency;
for the Dreamer is no longer merely an observer—a vigilant Conscience is now his fellow-pilgrim:

> I toke gode kepe, by Cryst, and Conscience bothe,
> Of Haukyn the actyf man and how he was y-clothed.

The much-patched coat of Haukyn speaks eloquently enough of the
failings of 'active life', what passes for the practice of the Christian
religion in most men. But it is aptly related to the Dreamer, the sharp-
eyed observer of the faults of others. Haukyn, we learn, is a law unto
himself:

> Was none suche as hym-self ne none so pope-holy,
> Y-habited as an hermyte, an ordre by hym-selue.

The truth is out, and it is mercilessly pursued. To the obvious sins of
the world of the *Visio*—that of self-indulgence and thus all the ills of

*Ac* but; *miȝte of miracle* miraculous power; *faille* is lacking; *gylte* (guilt) fault;
*blyssyng* blessing; *bote* good; *but if* unless; *amende* grow better; *masse* Mass;
*purelich* entirely; *fordo* destroyed; *payn defaute* lack of bread, famine; *kepe* heed;
*pope-holy* holy as the Pope; *ordre* religious Order, sect.

the mercenary motive—are added those which the *Vita* has unfolded in
a Dreamer who has searched the world of discourse. There is an end of
the role of observer and facile judge of others when Haukyn is seen

> Lakkyng lettred men and lewed men bothe,
> In lykyng of lele lyf, and a lyer in soule . . .

The ringing antitheses are marshalled in a devastating characterization
of man as satiric insight reveals him. It is an indictment controlled and
directed to one end; man, we now see, exists in two worlds, those of
practice and profession:

> With inwit and with outwitt ymagenen and studye,
> As best for his body be to haue a badde name,
> And entermeten hym ouer-al ther he hath nou3t to done . . .

He desires a right reputation in the eyes of others:

> Wilnyng that men wende his witte were the best,
> Or for his crafty kunnynge, or of clerkes the wisest,
> Or strengest on stede, or styuest vnder gurdel,
> And louelokest to loken on and lelest of werkes,
> And non so holy as he ne of lif clennere . . .

A whole tradition of satiric insight, nurtured in a homiletic literature
shrewdly portraying the characteristic faults of communal life, lies
behind the figure of Haukyn. In the mirror Langland holds up we see
man as the unending prey of illusion, incapable of relating to his own
condition the faults easily remarked in others. This divided state can
lead only to one verdict: no man can serve two masters. It is one more
thrust of a two-edged sword; once again we are at a turning-point:

> *Si hominibus placerem, Christi seruus non essem;*
> *Et alibi: nemo potest duobus dominis seruire.*

*Lakkyng* reproving; *In lykyng* claiming to like (and thus to lead); *lele* righteous;
*inwit* (here) thought, reflective power; *outwitt* power of observation; *ymagenen*
(here) to conceive; *studye* meditate, calculate; *As* as is, that which is; *entermeten
hym* thrust himself in, interfere; *nou3t to done* no business; *Wilnyng* desiring,
wanting; *wende* should think; *crafty kunnynge* resourceful (natural) intelligence;
*strengest* most powerful; *on stede* on horseback; *styuest* (stiffest) sturdiest; *vnder
gurdel* in hip and thigh; *louelokest* handsomest; *loken* look; *clennere* purer, more
upright; *Si hominibus* etc. 'if I yet pleased men, I should not be the servant of
Christ' (Gal. i 10); *Et alibi: nemo* etc. and in another place (in the Scriptures):
'No man can serve two masters' (Matt. vi 24).

As with other affirmations of this order, the righteousness that is required of man is sharply divided from common and habitual accommodation to its demands, man's ready acceptance of anything less than the highest. We see at once how far man falls short—a knowledge which comes with the force of revelation, as similar understanding had come all in a moment to the Plowman. Haukyn's coat had seemed a poor thing; but now

> It was fouler by felefolde than it firste semed.

It is clear that those ancient enemies, the Seven Deadly Sins, have their full portion in Haukyn. As with the greedy Doctor, we seem to have progressed no further than the world of the *Visio* before its repentance. Indeed, the lengthy catalogue of Haukyn's misdeeds lays emphasis upon cupidity, the mercenary motive which had riddled the world of the *Visio*. Haukyn is no great sinner—only a steady and persistent one, who by petty shifts and stratagems lines his own pockets. It is an unrelenting portrayal of common humanity; and there can be no other conclusion than that man, in this state,

> Lyueth a3ein the bileue and no lawe holdeth.

Haukyn, we recall, is a wafer-seller; the trade suggests the Field of Folk, of whom Holy Church had truly said

> The moste partie of this poeple that passeth on this erthe,
> Haue thei worschip in this worlde thei wilne no better;
> Of other heuene than here holde thei no tale. (I 7-9)

The predicament of man is therefore shown as a nearly-incurable frivolousness:

> Vch day is haliday with hym, or an heigh ferye;
> And if he au3te wole here it is an harlotes tonge.

Yet entertainment offers a clue to man's real needs; since

> Clerkes and kni3tes welcometh kynges ministrales,
> And for loue of the lorde litheth hem at festes,

let the rich hospitably entertain those special minstrels who will bring present mirth and lasting happiness. The poor, the blind and the bed-ridden can awaken man from dangerous indifference:

*felefolde* many times over; *a3ein* against, contrary to; *bileue* (Christian) faith; *haliday* holiday; *heigh ferye* chief (high) festival; *au3te* anything; *litheth* listen to; *festes* feasts.

> Thise thre maner ministrales maketh a man to lawhe,
> And, in his deth-deyinge thei don him grete comforte.

It is a positive injunction; but the Passus ends on the note of continuing human failure. Why is it that Haukyn does not mend his ways? There is the stained coat; it must prompt the obvious question:

> Whi he ne hadde wasshen it or wyped it with a brusshe?

The question comes from Conscience, as is fitting; and it is put *in a curteise manere*. But it is of deadly import.

## VI

*Passus XIV*

All the imperfections of Active Life are seen most clearly in Haukyn's reply. The call to Perfection elicits the traditional response:

> *Vxorem duxy, et ideo non possum venire.*

Whatever his efforts, any sustained level of achievement is beyond him:

> couthe I neuere, by Cryste, kepen it clene an houre,
> That I ne soiled it with syȝte or sum ydel speche,
> Or thorugh werke or thorugh worde or wille of myn herte,
> That I ne flober it foule fro morwe tyl eue.

So hard experience confirms the large objection the Dreamer had put to the Friars at the outset—even the just man offends seven times daily. What then is to be done? Conscience has the answer: contrition, confession and restitution (here put forward as Dowel, Dobet and Dobest); These, energetically undertaken, are the remedy. Life lived in obedience to Conscience need fear no comparison. The humble minstrel will be transformed:

> Shall none heraude ne harpoure haue a fairere garnement
> Than Haukyn the actyf man, and thou do by my techyng.

But there is even more in prospect. Patience offers the greater good which the Plowman had been brought to perceive—that of simple

---

*maner* kinds of; *lawhe* laugh; *deth-deyinge* death-bed; *don* (do) bring; *wasshen* washed; *brusshe* brush; *Vxorem duxy* etc. 'I have married a wife, and therefore I cannot come' (Luke xiv 20); *That I* without my; *syȝte* (sight) covetous or lustful look; *ydel* frivolous, empty; *wille* desire, lust; *flober* dirty; *heraude* herald; *harpoure* harper; *garnement* garment.

dependence upon the Will of God—in words that repeat the Plowman's resolve:

> We shulde nouȝt be so busy a-bouten owre lyflode.

The proposition seems impossible to man in this world:

> Thanne laughed Haukyn a litel and liȝtly gan swerye,
> 'Who so leueth ȝow, by owre lorde, I leue nouȝte he be blissed!'

In his own fashion, the Dreamer, too, had been puzzled by the Plowman's immediate act. But Patience is true to his name, and in keeping with the truth already enunciated (and to be repeated)—*pacientes vincunt*—he labours to overcome Haukyn's disbelief. The lesson he teaches is that of the *Visio*; man shall not live by bread alone. All God's creatures are dependent upon His providing, from

> the wylde worme vnder weet erthe

to man himself. The true *lyflode* offered to the Christian is full acceptance of the Divine Order, *fiat voluntas tua*. Once again, the *mesure* principle is that by which man must govern his life. Truly applied, it would make an end of both scarcity and the ills that come from over-abundance:

> vnkyndnesse *caristia* maketh amonges Crystene peple,
> And ouer-plente maketh pruyde amonges pore and rich.

The means is indeed golden;

> mesure is so moche worth it may nouȝte be to dere.

It is also our protector against deadly sin, as is witnessed by the fate of the men of Sodom:

> For thei mesured nouȝt hem-self of that thei ete and dronke,
> Diden dedly synne that the deuel lyked . . .

We thus come back to the starting-point proposed by Conscience—contrition, confession and restitution:

*and* provided that; *busy* anxious, preoccupied; *lyflode* sustenance; *liȝtly* readily, easily; *gan* did; *swerye* (swear) protest; *leueth* believes, accepts; *blissed* (blessed) made happy; *pacientes vincunt* 'the patient conquer'; *weet* wet, damp; *fiat* etc, 'Thy will be done'; *vnkyndesse* uncharitableness, self-seeking; *caristia* dearth, scarcity; *pruyde* pride; *to* too; *mesured nouȝt hem-self* did not restrain themselves.

> For-thi mesure we vs wel and make owre faithe owre scheltroun,
> And thorw faith cometh contricioun, conscience wote wel,
> Whiche dryueth awey dedly synne and doth it to be venial.[25]

The firm repetitions of *mesure, mesured*[26] in this declaration reinforce the sense of finality. One main thread in the complex argument is being firmly tied. The faith which brings salvation is not merely theoretical; it is a faith issuing whenever occasion serves in the good works of confession and restitution. So, too, we reach an end of our questioning on the related topic of sin—

> shrifte of mouth sleeth synne, be it neuere so dedly;
> *Per confessionem* to a prest *peccata occiduntur,*
> There contricioun doth but dryueth it doun in-to a venial synne,
> As Dauid seith in the sauter *et quorum tecta sunt peccata.*
> Ac satisfaccioun seketh oute the rote and bothe sleeth and voideth,
> And, as it neuere had ybe, to nou3t bryngeth dedly synne,
> That it neuere eft is seen ne sore, but semeth a wounde yheled.

The simple categorization which the Friars had offered at the outset— between sins of deliberation and those of frailty—had been swept aside by a Dreamer intent on perfection. Now at last 'the wound is healed', by patient analysis of the complex act of repentance.

This definitive treatment of one problem is marked by the abruptness with which the next is raised. Without immediate preparation—for the preparation is in the whole nexus of problems from which, one by one, the separate strands are being teased out—Haukyn turns to the search for Charity:

> Where woneth Charite? . . . I wiste neuere in my lyue
> Man that with hym spake, as wyde as I haue passed!

The language is very similar to that of the incredulous Palmer of the *Visio;* and perhaps the question is put in a mood of disbelief. For Haukyn

---

*scheltroun* (strong) defence; *wote* knows; *dedly* mortal (as against *venial* sin, which does not involve the loss of grace; see note); *shrifte of mouth* oral confession *sleeth* slays, kills; *Per confessionem . . . peccata occiduntur* through confession . . . sins are slain; *sauter* Psalter; *et quorum* etc. '(Blessed is he whose . . .) sin is covered' (Ps. xxxii 1); *rote* root; *voideth* gets rid; *ybe* been; *eft* afterwards; *sore* sore, painful; *yheled* healed; *woneth* dwells; *wiste* knew; *wyde* far.

turns aside the brief but sufficient answer he is given ('wherever there is perfect truth and poverty of spirit with patient speech') to pluck from these phrases a dialectician's question:

'Whether paciente pouerte,' quod Haukyn, 'be more plesaunte
to owre driȝte
Than ricchesse riȝtfulliche ywonne and resonablelich yspended?'

It is a key-question, opening more doors than one. It sets the world of the *Visio*, with its painfully acquired lesson of the *mesurable*, over against the repeated insistence of the *Vita de Dowel* on patient poverty. This contrast, again, implies the whole ground of difference between the life lived in simple obedience to God as Lawgiver, and the life yielded in utter dependence upon God as Provider. Repentant humanity in the *Visio* had made their first entry upon the life of well-doing in terms of obedience to Divine Law. To their leader, the Plowman, there had been granted an awareness of the blessedness of dependence upon God, apprehended not as Judge but as merciful Father. The same hinge of the poem is about to turn once more. But before it can do so, repentance is necessary—the recognition of a Law ignored or contravened but never to be invalidated. Haukyn's merely intellectual eagerness, the comfortable self-possession with which man looks out upon a world incurring his moral judgements, must be shaken. Before truth can come, it must come home. Haukyn's question thus applies to the whole progress of the Dreamer, from his early patience, through his fatal propensity for wide-ranging speculation, up to his present rueful admission of failure. It is the last purely theoretical question we are to hear, the final attempt to reach by dialectic *the weyes of God almiȝti.*

The answer, when it comes, is so simple as to be startling. Before Patience will consider the question (and in this, too, his action suits his nature) he asks the simple question, 'Where will you *find* a right use of riches?'

'Ȝe, *quis est ille?*' quod Pacience, 'quik *laudabimus eum!*'

The 'problem' of the rich, no doubt, will always be with us ('right to the world's end'); but as to the problem Haukyn would pose, has anyone ever met *this* in reality?:

*plesaunte* pleasing; *driȝte* Lord; *ywonne* gained; *resonablelich yspended* properly, rightly (spent) used; *ȝe* True, but . . .; *quis est ille?* who is this (reasonable spender)?; *quik* quickly, at once; *laudabimus eum* we shall praise him.

I wiste neuere renke that riche was that when he rekne sholde,
Whan it drow to his deth-day, that he ne dred hym sore,
And that atte rekenyng in arrerage fel rather than oute of dette.

The facts on the other side are equally plain — the poor are always
'in arrears', where happiness is concerned; and the Judge who will
apportion all is just:

Ioye that neuere Ioye hadde of riȝtful Iugge he axeth.

Happiness is the due portion of all:

For to wrotherhele was he wrouȝte that neuere was Ioye shaped.

There is another plain fact which we may overlook. Like a just employer,
God will in some cases pay in advance:

Ac god is of a wonder wille, by that kynde witt sheweth,
To ȝiue many men his mercymonye ar he it haue deserued.
Riȝt so fareth god by some riche . . .

It is a grim reflection; once again, as when the Plowman's 'pardon' was
opened, all confusion dissolves before the unwavering Justice of God.
The *Visio* theme of rewards and deservings here receives its final statement. God may make advance payment to the rich: but assuredly the
account will be made up after death. It is the notion of *mercede*, of just
payment for services rendered, that is prominent here. But mercy is not
lacking; if the rich have compassion on the poor they need not fear that
their earthly prosperity will debar them from heavenly joys. For the
Divine generosity is certainly not less than that of any earthly employer:

as an hyne that hadde his hyre ar he bygonne,
And whan he hath done his deuor wel men doth hym other
                                                    bounte,
ȝyueth hym a cote aboue his couenaunte . . .

*renke* man; *rekne* give account; *drow* drew; *dred hym* was afraid; *atte* at the;
*rekenyng* accounting; *arrerage* debt; *that* he who; *riȝtful* just; *axeth* asks; *to wrotherhele* for a wretched state; *was he wrouȝte* was that man created; *that* for whom;
*shaped* made, prepared; *Ac* but; *a wonder wille* extraordinarily generous disposition; *by that* etc. according to, compared with, the teaching of natural
reason; *mercymonye* reward; *ar* before; *hyne* labourer; *hyre* wage; *deuor* duty,
task; *bounte* reward; *cote* cottage, dwelling-place (rather than 'coat', since the
parallel is with God's gift of *heuene*).

The gift beyond all agreement or conditions is, once more, a *mede*, a reward disproportionate to any man's deservings—as, in the unregenerate world of the *Visio*, bribes and favours were grossly irrelevant to merit.

The clarity and definitiveness of this treatment of an immemorial problem for the Dreamer are evident in a new thought. For the first time there is pity for the rich. Happiness as a payment in advance is a frightening thought:

> reuthe me it thinketh,
> For thei han her hyre here, an heuene as it were—

but there must be a terrible awakening. So the great quarrel between rich and poor is made up. The lines that beseech God for compassion on the poor in their earthly sufferings are deservedly praised:

> Ac pore peple, thi prisoneres, lorde, in the put of myschief,
> Conforte tho creatures that moche care suffren
> Thorw derth, thorw drouth, alle her dayes here,
> Wo in wynter tymes for wantyng of clothes,
> And in somer tyme selde soupen to the fulle;
> Comforte thi careful, Cryst, in thi ryche,
> For how thow confortest alle creatures clerkes bereth witnesse,
> *Conuertimini ad me, et salui eritis.*

Perhaps the great beauty of this appeal leads us to overlook the rare compassion of the lines that immediately precede it. For in fact this is the meeting-place of rich and poor: and the second half of this outpouring of pity complements the first, in which the rich are seen with an equal objectivity. Nowhere does Patience more clearly show himself obedient to his own precept, *fiat voluntas tua*:

> For alle my₃test thow haue made none mener than other,
> And yliche witty and wyse if the wel hadde lyked.

The rich are to be pitied in their dangerous situation:

> haue reuthe on thise riche men that rewarde nou₃te thi prisoneres;
> Of the good that thow hem gyuest *ingrati* ben manye;
> Ac, god, of thi goodnesse gyue hem grace to amende.

*reuthe* (pity) a sad state; *me it thinketh* as it seems to me; *hyre* payment; *put* pit; *myschief* misery; *tho* those; *care* trouble; *derth* famine; *drouth* drought; *selde* seldom, rarely; *soupen* (sup) eat; *careful* troubled, afflicted; *ryche* kingdom; *Conuertimini* etc. 'In returning and rest shall ye be saved' (Isa. xxx 15); *fiat voluntas tua* 'Thy will be done'; *my₃test* couldest; *mener* lower; *yliche* equally; *witty* clever; *the wel hadde lyked* it had pleased you; *ingrati* ungrateful; *amende* reform;

The picture is one of insulated content, a brief span of creature-comfort fatally guarded from that rough weather of the physical world which could awaken knowledge of man's dependence on God:

> For may no derth ben hem dere, drouth, ne weet,
> Ne noyther hete ne haille, haue thei here hele,
> Of that thei wilne and wolde wanteth hem nouȝt here.

We are certainly at a turning-point, when newness of understanding can reach so far. Now, too, the perplexities of salvation are cleared up, and with them goes the whole aching question of 'pardon'—on the one side our guilt, and our inescapable knowledge that what is required of us is right conduct; and, on the other, the formalities of religious observance, so easily susceptible of abuse—the parchment Pardons, the

> Pater-nostres and penaunce and pilgrimage to Rome—

all the world of the *Visio*, not forgetting the empty boasts visible in Friary windows. Patience merely affirms with the utmost simplicity what Conscience had already taught concerning contrition; that, following on our baptism,

> Confessioun, and knowlechyng, and crauyng thi mercy
> Shulde amende vs as many sithes as man wolde desire.

This is the answer to the over-tender conscience that would seek remission from the general human lot of sinning *seuene sythes* daily. Man has a sufficient surety:

> Ac if the pouke wolde plede here-aȝeine and punyssh vs in
> conscience,
> He shulde take the acquitance as quik and to the qued schewe it,
> *Pateat, &c, per passionem domini,*
> And putten of so the pouke and preuen vs vnder borwe.

There is re-affirmed as an unshakeable truth the intuitive certainty the Dreamer had clung to at the end of the *Visio*. At the Judgement Day, unless *Dowel* 'helps', then

*ben hem dere* injure them; *hete* heat; *haille* hail; *haue thei* so long as they have; *hele* health; *wanteth hem* they lack; *knowlechyng* acknowledging; *sithes* times; *Ac* but; *pouke* Devil; *here-aȝeine* against this; *as quik* at once; *qued* Evil One; *Pateat &c* (the usual opening of a document releasing or discharging from liability) 'Be it known to all . . .,; *per passionem domini* through the Passion of Our Lord; *putten of* put off, repel; *borwe* security (alluding to the Redemption).

I sette ȝowre patentes and ȝowre pardounz at one pies hele! (VII 194)
Man's title is sufficient and needs no documentary form. The *perchemyn*
on which it is inscribed must be that of *pure pacience and parfit bileue*.
More important, we are *vnder borwe*. This is a final check to mere aspiration, of ourselves, towards 'well-doing'—that insistence upon perfection of conduct which had both inspired and daunted the Dreamer.

Religious observance now falls into place; for all turns on the spirit
in which it is undertaken:

> But owre spences and spendynge sprynge of a trewe wille,
> Elles is al owre laboure loste.

We turn again to consider the Seven Deadly Sins—but this time they
serve to illustrate the advantages the poor have in the unending struggle.
Pride is the great adversary; but he has his special sphere of opportunity
with the rich. He has no power over patient poverty:

> in pouerte there pacyence is Pryde hath no myȝte,
> Ne none of the seuene synnes sitten ne mowe there longe,
> Ne haue powere in pouerte, if pacyence it folwe.

The same is true of all the Sins; and there is a characteristic freedom and
liveliness in the account of Avarice, *Coueitise*, in action:

> And if Coueitise wolde cacche the pore thei may nouȝt come
> togideres,
> And by the nekke namely her none may hente other.
> For men knoweth wel that Coueitise is of a kene wille,
> And hath hondes and armes of a longe lengthe.
> And pouerte nis but a petit thinge, appereth nouȝt to his
> nauele,
> And louely layke was it neuere bitwene the longe and the shorte.

There is evident here the sharp sense of the farcical which in Langland
keeps company with vigorous scorn and burning compassion. In the
*petit thinge* that poverty appears we seem to catch an echo of sporting
sentiment for the wily little man matched against a gigantic adversary.

---

*patentes* letters patent, certificates; *hele* crust; *But* unless; *spences* outlay; *Elles*
otherwise; *sitten* stay; *folwe* accompany; *cacche* wrestle with; *namely* particularly;
*her none* neither of them; *hente* seize, grasp; *kene wille* voracious appetite; *nis but*
is only; *appereth nouȝt* hardly reaches; *nauele* navel; *louely layke* satisfactory match.

The comic disproportion answers to the inherent impossibility of any real bout in these terms, conveying as perhaps nothing else could the absurdity of *Coueitise* contending with the poor.

The same spirit of irreverent fun lights up the frustration of Avarice:

> For pouerte hath but pokes to putten in his godis,
> There Auarice hath almaries and yren-bounde coffres . . .

and so on throughout this refutation of the Sins' power to inflict any hurt on poverty.[27] We are familiar enough with the licensed energy of the dance of the Seven Deadly Sins.[28] Here we have something like an anti-masque. For once, they are on the losing side; and their baffled movements are not less comic than their more usual assurance. The account ends with the slothful man discovering, willy-nilly, that in the ills of poverty

> God is his grettest helpe, and no gome elles.

It marks the linking of a further theme, stated first in Repentance's prayer for erring humanity (V 485 ff.)—Man's relationship to a God who prosecuted his cause by taking upon Himself man's nature. The playing upon *sute* and *secte* recalls the earlier appeal. In the present context we are especially reminded that it was not only in human flesh but in the garb (and, perhaps, the retinue or company) of the poor that God was made manifest. God is thus man's

> seruaunt, as he seith, and of his *sute* both.
> And where he be or be nou3te, he bereth the signe of pouerte,
> And in that *secte* owre saueoure saued al mankynde.

Patience's discourse ends with one more direct echo of a *Visio* that had come to its testing-place in the projected marriage of Meed, a maiden. Those are to be praised who for love of God leave worldly possessions,

> as a mayde for mannes loue her moder forsaketh,
> Hir fader and alle her frendes, and folweth hir make.

The analogy thus gathers into one focus the dominant issue in the *Visio*—the marriage with wealth that would solemnize the rule of the mercenary motive, the worship of the 'golden calf of Self-Love'—and the theme of patient poverty which the *Vita* has established:

*pokes* sacks; *almaries* cupboards, safes; *gome* man, creature; *elles* else, other; *sute* livery, clothing; *where he be or be nou3te* whether or not God helps (a particular man in this life); *secte* clothing (and division of mankind); *make* mate, husband.

Moche is suche a mayde to louie of man that such one taketh,[29]
More than a mayden is that is maried thorw brokage,
As bi assent of sondry partyes, and syluer to bote,
More for coueitise of good than kynde loue of bothe.

In these lines we have a single and sufficient truth for both parts of the
poem as it has developed up to this point. But, problems past, there is
the continuing truth that practice is all: and, in this context, we must
look to those who will lead and teach humanity. The last application
of patient poverty is to the clergy, who also must make a true marriage:

So it fareth bi eche a persone that possessioun forsaketh,
And put hym to be pacient and pouerte weddeth,
The which is sybbe to god hym-self and so to his seyntes.

The account of Poverty is complete. Now Haukyn has ceased to put
debating points: but no less spiritedly—though in wonder, not in argumentative zeal—he exclaims at the comprehensiveness of the praise
given to Poverty. What exactly *(proprely)* does it mean? It is a question
which, provoking a comprehensive Latin definition, leads to one more
request for skilled interpretation. The last link with the *Visio* is complete
when the simple man asserts:

I can nouȝt construe al this . . . ȝe moste kenne me this on Englisch.

Patience's interpretation, unlike that of the Priest in the 'pardon'
scene, is painstakingly thorough (and, we may add, is given only when
it is asked for). The mere divisions or aspects of poverty lay due stress
on its paradoxical nature (it is *possessio sine calumpnia, negocium sine
dampno, absque solicitudine felicitas*) and thus fittingly complete the riddling
course we have travelled, from the great paradox that had come home
to the Plowman all the way through lesser riddles to this present.
Haukyn's reaction is in the end the right one, as the Plowman's had been.

*to louie* to be loved; *of* by; *brokage* treaty by agents; *assent of* agreement between;
*syluer* money-settlement; *good* goods, property; *kynde* natural, proper; *persone*
person, individual (Skeat's note, that the sense 'parson' is meant, is surely mistaken; in fact the association between *persone* in that sense and *possessioneres*
'beneficed clergy' (V 144) may have suggested the deliberate disjunction, *persone
that possessioun forsaketh* 'the man who renounces wordly goods'); *sybbe* related,
akin to; *construe* interpret, translate; *kenne* instruct, tell; *possessio sine* etc.
ownership without deceiving (God), business without (eternal) loss, happiness
without fretful care;

We end in the tears of entire repentance; he

> weyled the tyme
> That euere he dede dede that dere god displesed.

The glimpse of developed Christian living has awakened that desire for
a better way which bitterly laments the mortal state. Haukyn regrets
that after his baptism he was not dead and buried:

> 'for Doweles sake—
> So harde it is,' quod Haukyn, 'to lyue and to do synne.
> Synne suweth vs euere'.

Only shame will serve as a covering for the flesh (*To keure my caroigne*).
The language echoes that of the Plowman's testament; for now, again,
man would take leave of life. The Passus ends a major division of the
poem with Haukyn's cry for mercy. All is prepared for the intervention
of a guide; or, at best, a saviour, someone who, like the Plowman,
being *of flessh oure brother*, can heal the conflict between man's sinful
nature and his desire for perfection.

The Dreamer has made the greatest single stride forward in the lessons
he has learnt from virtue-in-action, as against those merely speculative
issues in which he had been too long entangled. Patience had come first
as his own discovery—'*To se moche and suffre more, certes*,' *quod I*, '*is Dowel!*'
The Dreamer was thus fitted to learn from Patience himself those
severely practical lessons which have disposed, forever it is to be hoped,
of his large inquiries. The great lesson has been to confront reality. To
the eager impulse of the dialectician, quick to invoke the man of perfect
life—

> '*Contra*', quod I as a clerke, and comsed to disputen—

there is a steady answer:

> '3e, *quis est ille?*' quod Pacience, 'quik *laudabimus eum!*'

The problems that actually press upon us are thus seen to be very simple.
But they are also seen to be urgent: 'we would be at Jerusalem'. In
Haukyn's lament for the sinful flesh that impedes our travel we have,
isolated, the final problem that lies in man's path. Mercy is needed; how
shall it be brought to man? With repentance and the desire for a new
life the *Vita de Dowel*, like the *Visio*, comes to an end. Once again it is
time for the Dreamer to awake and ponder all he has seen.

*weyled* lamented ; *dede dede* did deed; *harde* hard lot; *suweth* follows, pursues;
*caroigne* carcase; *comsed* began; *quis est ille* who is he?; *quik* quickly; *laudabimus
eum*; we shall praise him.

# *Notes*

1. See p. 294 below.
2. For the play upon *faire* and *fer*, see p. 269 below.
3. A has *How dowel, dobet and dobest don on this erthe* (IX 104, Kane). C removes this emphasis altogether: 'Of Dowel and of Dobet, and he doth best of alle' (C XI 109, Russell).
4. See p. 44 n. 8, above.
5. A (X 87) carries a stage further the Psalm spoken by Piers, at the moment of his resolve, with the line, *Virga tua et baculus tuus ipsa me consolata sunt* ('Thy rod and Thy staff they comfort me', Ps. xxiii 4). In both versions, 'Wit's' discourse links back with the reality of guilt, and consequent punishment, which the 'pardon' had conveyed to the Plowman, when the second of its two lines struck home.
6. Donaldson suggests an attractive re-shaping of this passage:

> Dowel my frend is to doon as lawe techeth,
> To loue and to lowe thee and no lif to greue;
> Ac to loue and to lene, leue me that is Dobet;
> To ʒyuen and to ʒemen bothe ʒonge and olde,
> To helen and to helpen, is Dobest of alle.

This brings out admirably the comprehensiveness of *Dowel* and also the essential distinction between 'well' and 'better'. The advance beyond *Dowel* is made when the question is not the negative one of 'harming no man' but of a positive 'loving and giving'.

7. For *a tale other tweyne* Donaldson reads *how two slough the thridde* ('how two slew the third'). *Cf.* Appendix, p. 324, below.
8. *kete* is suggested by Donaldson for Skeat's *kynnes* '(of another) kind'.
9. See p. 220, below.
10. Donaldson, who suggests that *tauʒte* (printed by Skeat) is substituted for *lered* after the alliteration has been weakened (*asketh* substituted for *lakketh*).
11. The three Texts offer an interesting minor variation in treating of Solomon. B has *He demed wel and wysely, as holy writte telleth;* A, *Demde he not wel and wisly, as holy writ techith?* (XI 268, Kane). B thus moves the emphasis from righteous acts to right judgement. In C the emphasis is squarely upon the one great judicial act, the Judgement of Solomon: '*And demede wel and wislyche wommen bereth witnesse*' (C XII 215).
12. Text of A XII based on Kane throughout.
13. In his note on this line, Skeat oddly assigns it to 'Clergy', and refers to A XI 286, where the Dreamer asserts that *clergie* was not commended by Christ. It is, clearly, spoken by Scripture, who, having cited instances to show that truth is not something to be merely pried into, counter-attacks. The merely theoretical disputant (one who has come *not by cause to lerne to Dowel*) adapts Scripture to suit the purposes of his arguments. (Knott and Fowler (*op. cit.*, p. 170) suggest that there may be an allusion to Luke xxii 70 '. . . and he said unto them, "Ye say that I am".')

*lowe thee* humble thyself; *lene* give.

14. Donaldson. Skeat's repetition of *wratth* in the second line is dubious.

15. On the relations between Dreamer and poet, see Chapter VII, below.

16. See p. 52, above.

17. It is not clear who is speaking, but the whole tenor of the argument is more appropriate to *Leute* than Scripture. (In C, the speaker is *Rechelessnesse*, on whom see Donaldson, *op. cit.*, pp. 171-2.)

18. Readers of Chaucer's *House of Fame* may be reminded of the loquacious Eagle's preparation of his pupil for a set of practical examples which, however, their immediate situation in mid-air prevents his actually demonstrating. The Eagle must therefore draw upon the common stock of sense-experience to illustrate the principle of *kyndely enclynyng*:

> Now herkene wel, for-why I wille
> Tellen the a propre skille
> And a worthy demonstraction
> In myn *ymagynacion*.          (H.F. 725-8)

19. *Cf.* Berners: 'The kynge enclyned well therto, but the duke of Burgoyne who was sage and ymagynatyue wolde not agree therto' (NED *s.v.* IMAGINATIVE I), where the meaning is 'long-headed', 'far-sighted'.

20. *Summers Last Will and Testament* (*Works of Thomas Nashe*, ed. R. B. McKerrow, London, 1904-10, III 285-6).

21. *Visio Willi de Petro Plouhman* . . . London, 1813, Notes, p. 12.

22. For further consideration of this episode see pp. 210-12 and p. 263, below.

23. On the wordplay here, *cf.* p. 212 below.

24. For an account of 'Haukyn', *Actiua Vita*, which firmly grasps the tension between the speculative and the practical in the *Vita de Dowel*, see the article by Stella Maguire referred to at p. 43, n. 1, above

25. 'He who sins venially is retarded on his journey towards God, but, unlike a person in mortal sin who is averted from his last end, he remains on the way which leads to God and will eventually possess Him' (*The Teaching of the Catholic Church*, London, 1952, p. 947).

26. See pp. 220-22, below.

27. On the contrasts of language in these two passages, see pp. 208, 218, below.

28. 'The Gothic period saw an increasing dramatic and realistic quality [in the treatment of the Sins] which heralded the Renaissance. In *Piers Plowman* we catch this same dramatic and stylized quality better than in any other work in English Literature' (Morton W. Bloomfield, *The Seven Deadly Sins* (Michigan, 1952), p. 199).

29. I adopt Donaldson's suggestion *man*, for Skeat's *hym*.

*skille* reason; *kyndely enclynyng* natural turning, gravitation.

CHAPTER IV

# *Ascent and Return*

## Passus XV–XX

> Some also have wished that the next way to their Father's house were
> here, that they might be troubled no more with either Hills or
> Mountains to go over; but the way is the way, and there's an end.
>
> Bunyan

The remainder of the *Liber de Petro Plowman* can be told straight-
forwardly enough. The poem now develops clearly towards an end
long foreseen, and most effectively preluded in the first part of what
remains, the *Vita de Dobet* (XV–XVIII). There at last fulfilment of Law
is attained, a triumphant victory over Sin and Death. Then, in the
concluding section, the two Passus which constitute the *Vita de Dobest*,
there is a return to the state of the Church in the world of daily experience, where the Christian cause is to be affirmed against all odds. There
is thus much greater simplicity of design than before. But there is the
same fidelity to the fact, to the human condition as it is actually encountered, both in the burning questions we find when we look within,
and in the easy compliance with prudence and self-interest which,
looking out upon the world, we see may yet bring the Christian cause
to near-ruin. If the simplicity and certainty of vision must supplant a
merely ratiocinative ardour, that does not mean that, in the end, we
can leave the realities of the world we inhabit. The poet's awareness is
comprehensive; we see that the glory of Incarnate Deity is not lessened
but is enhanced by the unending waywardness of man. In every way,
these last five Passus are concerned with truth as unmistakable, made
manifest among men—if only man can be brought to see it.

I

*Passus XV*

We begin with a Passus where, firstly, a disclosure of identities takes
place. Passus XIV, the ending of the *Vita de Dowel*, had been a place of

*next* nearest.

problems solved; now we are to go beyond problems and their solution.
Identification, the reality behind varying names, is the first concern.
The authoritative figure whom the Dreamer now interrogates begins
by revealing the many forms under which he may be known:

> 'The whiles I quykke the corps,' quod he, 'called am I *Anima;*
> And whan I wilne and wolde *Animus* ich hatte;
> And for that I can and knowe, called am I *Mens;*
> And whan I make mone to god *Memoria* is my name;
> And whan I deme domes and do as treuthe techeth,
> Thanne is *Racio* my riȝt name, Resoun an Englisshe . . .'

—and so on, with the Inward Senses, Conscience, *Amor* and *Spiritus*
to complete the tale. There is a unity in apparent complexity, and this
the poem as a whole is now to declare. But our immediate link with
what has gone before is in the Dreamer's familiarity with this pheno-
menon—and what that familiarity implies:

> 'Ȝe ben as a bisshop,' quod I, al bourdynge that tyme,
> 'For bisshopes yblessed thei bereth many names,
> *Presul* and *pontifex* and *metropolitanus,*
> And other names an hepe, *episcopus* and *pastor,*

It is a reminder of the facility of the Dreamer in the *Vita de Dowel*, and
both the attitude underlying it (*al bourdynge*) and the colloquial manner of
expression (*other names an hepe*) recall the riddles the dialectician had
handled. But we are now to pursue the question of this debater's own
identity. It is with design that Anima echoes the Dreamer's name in
penetrating to his characteristic bent:

> now I se thi *wille!*
> Thow *woldest* knowe and kunne the cause of alle her names,
> And of myne, if thow myȝtest, me thinketh by thi speche!

The Dreamer at once, and courteously (it is the measure of the distance
he has travelled) admits the charge:

> Ȝe, syre . . . by so no man were greued,

quykke give life to; *corps* body; *Anima* spirit, soul; *Animus* purpose; *Mens* mind;
*deme domes* make judgements; *Racio* reason; *an* in; *Amor* love; *bourdynge* jesting;
*yblessed* consecrated; *Presul* Ordinary; *pontifex* Pontiff; *metropolitanus* Metropo-
litan; *an hepe* 'dozens'; *episcopus* Diocesan; *pastor* Pastor (as Bishop's title); *kunne*
learn, know; *by so* provided that; *greued* troubled, offended.

> Alle the sciences vnder sonne and alle the sotyle craftes
> I wolde I knewe and couth kyndely in myne herte!

It sounds harmless enough; but the reply is immediate and final:

> Thanne artow inparfit . . . and one of Prydes kny3tes.

This is the real point of departure for the next phase of the poem, which is to deal with the 'better' Holy Church had long ago touched upon. Now that Dowel is understood it is possible to advance—just as, in the *Visio*, once a good man was found it was then possible to ask the further question, how good was he? In each case a solution for one part of a problem—the only part that has presented itself up to this point— is not an end, but a fresh beginning for inquiry into the whole. The advance is by stages, but no one of those stages begins to emerge until that which precedes it has been found incomplete. The starting-point here, as always, is to concentrate on essentials; and the first essential is that the Dreamer should know his own characteristic failing. So the charge of Pride becomes explicit; and for the first time the Dreamer learns the positive harm of knowledge pursued without relation to practice:

> the more that a man of good mater hereth,
> But he do ther-after it doth hym double scathe.

The primal examples of Lucifer, Adam and Eve may remind the Dreamer that aspiration after mere knowledge can involve the loss of innocence through pride. He hears again the warning which Study (X 116) had first sounded:

> *non plus sapere quam oportet sapere.*

The connexion with the learned is apparent, and it is to clerical failings that Anima now explicitly limits himself:

> Of this matere I my3te make a longe bible,
> Ac of curatoures of crystene peple, as clerkes bereth witnesse,
> I shal tellen it for treuth sake, take hede who so lyketh!

*sciences* branches of learning; *sotyle craftes* skilled arts; *couth* understood; *kyndely* (naturally) fully; *artow* art + thow; *inparfit* imperfect, at fault; *But* unless; *ther-after* in accordance with it; *scathe* harm; *non plus* etc. 'not to think of himself more highly than he ought to think' (Rom. xii 3). The emphasis here, as in Study's citation (see p. 97, above) is rather on the inordinate pursuit of knowledge than self-esteem—though the connexion, in the Dreamer's case, is obvious enough; *Ac* but; *curatoures* those having the charge or 'cure' of souls.

The truth of his statement that inordinate curiosity brings a double damnation is abundantly clear in clerical corruption, which makes the Church itself the source of all evils:

> As holynesse and honeste oute of holicherche spredeth
> Thorw lele libbyng men that goddes lawe techen,
> Ri3t so out of holicherche alle yueles spredeth,
> There inparfyt presthod is, prechoures and techeres.

Once again, it is the poet's bent for the absolute that is apparent. What is *inparfyt* is not to be regarded as falling short of an attainable good, but as clean contrary to it. In Anima's discourse, as in the whole working of the poem up to this point, Langland's argumentative method is constant. Failure—here, in particular, an odious hypocrisy—must be scrutinized before we are free to contemplate fulfilment of *holynesse and honeste*. The disquisition on clerical failings prepares for all that follows to the end of the poem. It preludes firstly, and by contrast, the emergence of one who will show the Law as capable of fulfilment; and, secondly, the return, in the conclusion, to the Church men actually know.

In the long account of clerical shortcomings we see again the world of the *Visio*; but this time it is made more repugnant, and more deadly, by its fair appearance. The affectations and the ornaments of dress declare the evil within, the mercenary motive that taints all. It is the universal ill; and as such avarice meets its own undoing. Once again we see that evil is short-sighted; in their sins most of all are men neglectful of the ends they set themselves. The inheritance grudgingly and laboriously amassed falls to the thriftless; the legatee can gleefully say of his benefactor

> he was a nygarde that no good my3te aspare
> To frende ne to fremmed, the fende haue his soule!
> For a wrecched hous he helde al his lyf tyme;
> And that he spared and bispered spene we in murthe.

To neglect hospitality is, as Study had said, merely *to spare to spille that spende shal an other* (X 100). But the liberal man will be truly missed, and will have the charitable prayers of his beneficiaries. We thus reach the major question on which the next development of the poem turns—

---

*honeste* honourable dealing; *lele libbyng* living in conformity (to God's Law); *Ri3t so* equally; *inparfyt* (imperfect) corrupt; *nygarde* miser; *good* property, substance; *aspare* spare, afford; *fremmed* stranger; *spared* hoarded; *bispered* locked up; *spene we* let us spend.

What is Charity? The immediate answer fits very well with this stage of readiness to start again; men are to become as little children:

> 'a childissh thinge,' he seide;
> 'Nisi efficiamini sicut paruuli, non intrabitis in regnum celorum.'

It is fitting that the Dreamer, ready to set out in newness of heart, is given his 'baptismal' name. One might perhaps say the name given at his baptism of desire, a Long Will of continuing determination crossed with impetuousness, a Dreamer who will be brought to learn, as fools are said to learn, from his experience, his mere living *in londe*.[1] This Passus is, as we have seen, concerned to establish true identities beneath varying appearances. Here is the Dreamer, ready once more to go in search of the true exemplar, despite all experience to the contrary:

> 'I seigh neuere such a man, so me god helpe,
> That he ne wolde aske after his, and otherwhile coueyte
> Thinge that neded hym nou3t and nyme it if he my3te.'

Is this, perhaps, to be the final truth?—that perfection is one of the qualities we are never to see in this life? It is a revealing moment. For the first time this Dreamer, hitherto hot for certainties, is prepared to accept the mirror-image, not the substantial original. And indeed all the evidence seems on his side; like the much-travelled Palmer, he can give no other report on experience. But at the moment when even the Dreamer's ardour begins to flag, revelation is being prepared. It is movingly preluded in the very analogy the Dreamer sadly employs:

> Clerkis kenne me that Cryst is in alle places;
> Ac I seygh hym neuere sothly but as my-self in a miroure,
> Ita in enigmate, tunc facie ad faciem.

Yet the promise holds good. Christ is indeed to be made manifest in all places: and the lines that immediately follow point to a coming affir-mation while contrasting it with the world of habitual experience:

> And so I trowe trewly, by that men telleth of charite,
> It is nou3t champions fy3te ne chaffare, as I trowe.

*Nisi efficiamini* etc. 'Except ye be converted, and become as little children, ye shall not enter into the kingdom of heaven' (Matt. xviii 3); *seigh, seygh* saw; *his* his own; *otherwhile* another time; *neded hym nou3t* was unnecessary for him; *nyme* take; *kenne* teach; *Ita in enigmate* etc. 'For now we see through a glass, darkly; but then face to face' (I Cor. xiii 12); *trowe* believe; *championns fy3te* strife between (knightly) contenders; *chaffare* dealings in trade.

All the Dreamer's experience leads him to know Charity only by its opposite; and Anima is quick to point out that Charity *ne chaffareth nouȝte ne chalengeth*. There is no place here for the self-interest which taints men's common practice of 'charity':

> Men beth mercyable to mendynantz and to pore,
> And wolen lene there thei leue lelly to ben payed.

Yet the *champions fyȝte*, the tourneys of knighthood, in the real world are the faint images of the Jousting that is to come, and, too, of a courtesy which owes nothing to temporal rank; and even *chaffare*, the traffic of merchants, has its own relation to the idea of Redemption. For the moment, all that we are concerned with is Charity as Anima portrays him; and the portrait is of all that the Dreamer desires and has long sought. He can only cry, from the heart,

> By Cryst, I wolde that I knewe hym . . . no creature leuere!

The answer is direct and immediate, and marks the final reach of naming-and-identification which has developed steadily up to this point. Now all is ready for disclosure. Firstly, man must perceive his need for an exemplar:

> 'With-outen helpe of Piers Plowman,' quod he, 'his persone
> seestow neuere.'

Then, in answer to the question whether the learned know Charity (the climax of a long-standing debate), we make an end of knowledge without practice:

> Clerkis haue no knowyng . . . but by werkes and bi wordes.
> Ac Piers the Plowman parceyueth more depper
> What is the wille and wherfore that many wyȝte suffreth,
> *Et vidit deus cogitaciones eorum.*

This places in its true perspective a world of appearances, of which clerical hypocrisy is only one manifestation; and it is a salutary reminder that our judgement is fallible:

> There-fore by coloure ne by clergye knowe shaltow hym neuere,
> Noyther thorw wordes ne werkes, but thorw wille one.

*mercyable* kind; *mendynantz* beggars; *lene* give, lend; *there* where; *leue* think, expect; *lelly* faithfully, duly; *leuere* sooner, rather; *parceyueth* sees; *depper* deeper; *wille* intention, purpose; *wherfore* reason why; *Et vidit* etc. 'And Jesus knowing their thoughts . . .' (Matt. ix 4, etc.); *coloure* appearance, outward show; *clergye* learning; *shaltow* shalt + thow; *Noyther* neither; *one* alone.

It is a truth which is directly applicable to the ready observer of others' faults, the Will of the poem. As a final truth is being prepared, the poet draws us away from dependence on the Dreamer; we with him are being made ready for revelation. What is known to *no clerke ne creature in erthe* is known only to

Piers the Plowman: *Petrus, id est, Christus.*

The description of Charity that follows is of *goddis champioun*; thus, appropriately, the characteristics are those of the young Knight or Squire. Charity is

the meryest of mouth at mete where he sitteth.

The description is touched with an aristocratic quality which the poet can truly reverence:

The loue that lith in his herte maketh hym ly3te of speche,
And is companable and confortatyf...

For Christ bids His followers

*Nolite fieri sicut ypocrite, tristes, &c.*

It is the same quality, a profound courtesy, that comes home in such phrasing as that of Chaucer's Parson:

For soothly oure sweete Lord Jhesu Crist hath spared us so *debonairly* in our folies, that if he ne hadde pitee of mannes soule, a sory song we myghten alle synge.[2]

We are perhaps so much used to the notion of Langland as the poet of the poor and the inarticulate, the rigorous exponent of simple well-doing, that we may overlook his reverence for the ideal of knighthood. If so, we shall miss the special force the Incarnation has for him. That the Law has been fulfilled in man's 'suit', *humana natura*, is proof at once of the *gentrice* of God, the Divine nobility, and of the exalted kinship of all Christians, their true 'gentility'. It is a claim which does not invert social status, but cuts across it. Charity, the Dreamer learns, has been seen in silk as well as in homespun. He has been found in Courts:

*in* on; *Petrus, id est, Christus* 'Peter, that is, Christ'; *lith* lies; *ly3te* easy (not stiff or formal); *companable* agreeable; *confortatyf* encouraging; *Nolite* etc, 'be not, as the hypocrites, of a sad countenance...' (Matt. vi 16); *soothly* truly; *debonairly* graciously.

> Edmonde and Edwarde eyther were kynges,
> And seyntes ysette tyl charite hem folwed.

He was even a friar once—but

> it is ferre agoo, in seynt Fraunceys tyme;
> In that secte sitthe to selde hath he be knowen.

It is a reminder of the real world where, alas! Covetousness may be a member of the King's council; where the law-courts are scenes of brawling and backbiting, with suits long drawn-out for money's sake, and marriages made and unmade from the same motive. It is, we well know, the world where Meed reigns secure. Charity is no longer to be found in his former place, among the prelates of the Church, apportioning Christ's patrimony to the poor. Langland combines two trains of association—the Keys of St. Peter[3] and the keys of a money-chest—to reveal the true state of the Church in these latter days:

> Ac auerice hath the keyes now and kepeth for his kynnesmen,
> And for his seketoures and his seruants, and somme for here
>                                                    children.

It is Need's world of intertwined obligation, where 'commodity' is the universal consideration. But as it is seen from the present standpoint there is no ground for mere recrimination. Like Charity, man must 'suffer long'; let him not neglect his own duty, which is sufficiently clear:

> I ne lakke no lyf, but lorde, amende vs alle,
> And gyue vs grace, good god, charite to folwe!

On all occasions of anger Christians should call to mind

> That though thei suffred al this, god suffred for vs more,
> In ensample we shulde do so and take no veniaunce . . .

For clearly the Divine suffering, on any other principle, need not have taken place. We must then conclude that the Saviour's example is binding upon all His followers; and therein lies the assurance of final victory:

*eyther* (each) both; *ysette* considered, held to be; *tyl* according as; *folwed* accompanied; *ferre agoo* long ago; *sitthe* since then; *to selde* too seldom; *kepeth for* provides for; *seketoures* executors; *here* their; *lakke* reprove, blame; *no lyf* no one; *so* the same; *veniaunce* retribution.

he suffred in ensample that we shulde suffre also,
And seide to suche that suffre wolde that *pacientes vincunt*.

Anima's narrative can therefore turn away from the mercenary and
hypocritical clergy of actuality to the lives of the Hermits and Apostles.
These, living in the beatitude of simple dependence upon God, are the
archetypes of the clerical life; and being obedient to their own calling,
they show forth the true pattern of society:

religious, ry3tful men shulde fynde,
And lawful men to lyf-holy men lyflode brynge.

In these terms, there could be no problems of clerical avarice; and this
would have its own beneficial effect on the laity:

thanne wolde lordes and ladyes be loth to agulte,
And to take of her tenauntz more than treuth wolde,
Fonde thei that freres wolde forsake her almesses,
And bidden hem bere it there it was yborwed.

There runs throughout this whole passage the ideal which had flashed
upon the Plowman—*Ne solliciti sitis*, 'Take no thought'. It is a fitting
preparation for the emergence of a Saviour. But here our attention is
focused upon the enormity it reveals in the clergy of actuality—those,
above all, who profess obedience to a rule. Any who would give to a
clergy already sated with possessions[4] are like men adding water to the
Thames. There can be no occasion to diverge from plain Charity, the
simplest and most efficacious of our duties:

I conseille alle Christene to confourmen hem to charite;
For charite, with-oute chalengynge, vnchargeth the soule.

But the evil done by an avaricious Clergy extends beyond the obstacle
it makes to true Charity. Avarice prompts the thought of money, and
money, in turn, that of the metal of coinage, the base *lussheborwe* we
often meet, as against true 'sterling'. The 'alloy' of sin is similarly current
throughout the realm:

*pacientes vincunt* 'The patient conquer'; *ry3tful* upright; *fynde* provide for; *lawful*
just, righteous; *lyflode* sustenance, food; *agulte* offend, sin; *Fonde thei* if they found;
*forsake* refuse; *her* their; *almesses* alms; *bere* take; *yborwed* taken; *confourmen hem to*
comply with; *with-oute chalengynge* without contradiction, undoubtedly;
*vnchargeth* unburdens, frees; *lussheborwe* (Luxembourg) spurious coin.

> the metal, that is mannes soule, with synne is foule alayed;
> Bothe lettred and lewede beth allayed now with synne.[5]

Nor does the evil end there. All knowledge, from learning to simple observation itself, weather-lore, has waned:

> thorw werre and wykked werkes and wederes vnresonable,
> Wederwise shipmen and witti clerkes also
> Han no bilieue to the lifte ne to the lore of philosofres.

All is uncertain, including the knowledge being handed on to future generations, for

> Gramer, the grounde of al, bigyleth now children;
> For is none of this newe clerkes, who so nymeth hede,
> That can versifye faire ne formalich enditen . . .

It is, one feels, a characteristic emphasis when Langland's Anima scorns the weak dialectics of those who should be able to

> answere to argumentz and also to a *quodlibet,*
> (I dar nouȝt seggen it for shame) if suche weren apposed,
> Thei shulde faillen in her philosofye.

There is ground for fearing that this half-trained clergy skips in reciting the offices. But, however maimed the rite, the worshippers can have one great assurance:

> As clerkes in *Corpus-Christi* feste singen and reden,
> That *sola fides sufficit* to saue with lewed peple.

We thus come to yet another theme earlier debated and left unresolved. Here, in its proper place, under the treatment of 'Clergy', is the matter of universal salvation; for the sufficiency of faith applies to *Sarasenes ... scribes and Iewes,* no less than to Christians. The theme this time is placed in a true perspective. Although Christians may bitterly regret that

---

*foule* foully, badly; *allayed* alloyed, debased; *lewede* laymen; *werre* war; *wykked* wicked; *wederes vnresonable* unseasonable storms; *Wederwise* weatherwise; *witti clerkes* clever scholars; *to* in; *lifte* sky; *ne* nor; *lore* teaching; *philosofres* natural philosophers, scientists; *Gramer* (the teaching of) Grammar; *grounde* basis, foundation; *bigyleth* misleads; *nymeth* takes; *faire* correctly; *formalich enditen* properly compose a letter; *quodlibet* any question, freely put; *apposed* examined; *faillen* fail; *Corpus-Christi feste* Thursday after Trinity Sunday; *sola fides sufficit* 'Faith alone is sufficient (to save)' (from the hymn sung at vespers on that day); *lewed* ignorant.

their professions are not matched by practice, they are not the only ones; the Saracens, too, have had their false teacher, Mohammed himself, who was, we learn, a perverted Christian. The discrepancy seems, then, a universal condition of humanity. Mohammed's pretended authority brought the Saracens into their heresy; and this, of course, under Divine permission. It leads to the grim reflection that Mohammed and English clergy have something in common to answer for; *no man vseth treuth*. The more need, then, for the true witness of the Christian Faith in *parfit lyuynge*. It is a prospect which recalls the original triumph of the Apostles in bringing the world to Christianity:

> Elleuene holy men al the world torned
> In-to lele byleue.

St. Augustine's mission was triumphantly successful—but upon what conditions?:

> More thorw miracles than thorw moche prechynge,
> As well thorw his werkes as with his holy wordes.

The work accomplished by Augustine is a reminder of tasks still to be undertaken by the clergy, both at home (for the child unchristened is *hethene as to heueneward and helpeless to the soule*) and abroad in the countries that remain unconverted—while at home the shameful farce of titles *in partibus infidelium* is daily enacted:

> Allas! that men so longe on Makometh shulde byleue,
> So many prelates to preche as the pope maketh,
> Of Nazareth, of Nynyue, of Neptalim, and Damaske,
> That thei ne went as Cryst wisseth, sithen thei wilne a name,
> To be pastours and preche the passioun of Iesus,
> And as hym-self seyde so to lyue and deye;
> > *Bonus pastor animam suam ponit, &c.*

The pretentious titles are set in flat contrast to the one unequivocal duty of the 'pastor': *to lyue and deye*. It is a flash of the sardonic Langland of the *Visio*, ever-vigilant for the self-excusing propensity; and it unleashes energetic wordplay upon the Cross of Christ and the cross stamped upon coinage. As we have seen elsewhere in this poem, rapid wordplay can be

---

*torned* turned; *lele byleue* true faith; *thorw* through; *hethene* heathen; *as to* as regards, in the sight of; *Makometh* Mohammed; *So many* when there are so many; *Nynyue* Nineveh; *Neptalim* Naphtali; *Damaske* Damascus; *wisseth* directs; *name* title; *as hym-self seyde* in accordance with His teaching; *Bonus pastor* etc. 'the good shepherd giveth his life for the sheep' (John x 11).

a fitting accompaniment to the revelation of abuse—the handy-dandy game by which men profess one truth and conceal another.[6] We may notice, too, the characteristic vigour of the protest against acceptance of a world divided between Christendom and Paganism. If there is any warrant for the notion of Langland as a poet raising problems to which he does in fact know the answer[7] we may perhaps find it in such instances as these. Universal salvation, long worried over in the *Vita de Dowel* as a speculative issue, is now taken out of the region of pious (and perhaps fruitless) aspiration. The field awaits men's labours, and the command is unambiguous.

Clerical possession, from the donation of Constantine onwards, is the great foe to that 'perfect' priesthood which alone can set all things in the way to prosper, including the heathen world. The empty titles *of Bedleem and Babiloigne* remind the poet of the true title and thus the true practice of a cleric, as it is to be seen in the life of Our Lord. He, becoming 'man of a maid', established His ministry in Jerusalem, the Christian metropolis. The Saviour is therefore truly a *metropolitanus*. It is a neat retort upon the Dreamer's first jesting reference *(al bourdynge)* to bishops and their various titles. Now we know the real warrant of Christian leadership, in a Saviour who

> baptised and bishoped with the blode of his herte.

This links with the theme of *gentrice*, true honour as well as kinship, as opposed to the titles that are merely empty. The Saviour's is the example followed by the martyrs, whose witness is throughout the world. The empty titles *Bedleem and Babiloigne* of a moment before are reinvested with authority as the martyrs are recalled, those who

> Al for to enforme the faith in fele contreyes deyeden,
> In Ynde and in Alisaundre, in Ermonye and in Spayne.

Now the place-names resound like the battle-honours they are. The whole earth, we learn, is the setting for each single martyrdom. St. Thomas à Becket, done to death by Englishmen, is a martyr for the Faith and thus for all Christian countries:

> Amonges vn-kende Cristene for Cristes loue he deyede,
> And for the ri3t of al this reume, al reumes Cristene.[8]

The martyr puts to shame the merely titular bishops, those who, having

*bishoped* confirmed; *enforme* establish; *fele* many; *deyeden* died; *Ynde* India; *Alisaundre* Alexandria; *Ermonye* Armenia; *un-kende* wicked; *reume* realm, kingdom.

no cure of souls of their own, invade other men's territory. The very language alters as we are told that these rogues

> *hippe* aboute in Engelonde to halwe mennes auteres,
> And *crepe* amonges curatoures and confessen ageyne the lawe.

Once again, things are drawing to a head. The Passus that has dwelt long and unsparingly on the faults of the clergy concludes with a positive emphasis—the Saviour is shown as perfect Exemplar to the clergy. The Jews have their Law, a Law given by God. But they rejected the Messiah in their midst, even though by His miracles the title was proven. The Saviour is here seen as Lord of Life and Death; the great miracle is that of raising Lazarus—

> with styf voys hym called,
> *Lazare, veni foras.*

But in the end the divine victory is not through power, but through the patience that brings to naught all that the Jews would do to destroy the Saviour. He is thus the first and greatest to exemplify that truth towards which the *Vita* has steadily developed, *Pacientes vincunt.*

We end with a task still to be done, but to be done 'by little and little'. The starting-point in the wide world of heathendom, as in the little world of the *Visio*, is the same. First comes the law, since

> Pharesewes and Sarasenes, Scribes and Grekis
> Aren folke of on faith, the fader god thei honouren.

The rest will follow, given only a clergy fit to undertake it:

> sitthen that the Sarasenes and also the Iewes
> Konne the firste clause of owre bileue, *Credo in deum patrem*
> *omnipotentem,*
> Prelates of Crystene prouynces shulde preue, if thei my3te,
> Lere hem litlum and lytlum *et in Iesum Christum filium,*
> Tyl thei couthe speke and spelle *et in spiritum sanctum,*

*hippe* hop, skip; *curatoures* parish clergy; *confessen* hear (parishioners' confessions); *ageyne* against; *styf* loud; *Lazare* etc. 'Lazarus, come forth' (John xi 43); *Pacientes vincunt* 'the patient conquer'; *Pharesewes* Pharisees; *on* one; *fader* father; *Sitthen that* since; *Konne* know; *bileue* Creed; *Credo* etc. 'I believe in God the Father Almighty'; *Crystene* Christian; *preue* try; *lere* teach; *litlum and lytlum* by little and little; *et in Iesum* etc. 'and in Jesus Christ His (only) Son'; *couthe* could; *et in spiritum* etc. 'and in the Holy Ghost'.

And rendren it and recorden it, with *remissionem peccatorum,*
*Carnis resurreccionem, et vitam eternam. Amen.*

The process Anima speaks of is almost painfully simple, just as the
Dreamer's progress has been from confusion to the simplest of truths;
and it is cumulative, as the poem itself is now steadily cumulative. The
earthly Ministry of the Saviour is the unchanging pattern for his latter-
day followers. They, too, must learn that it is those who suffer who
achieve the victory. All this, and especially the great miracle of Lazarus
being raised from the dead, is the preparation for the clarity of full
demonstration that is to come. But it is perfectly in keeping with the
tone and temper of the poem as a whole that we end this Passus, in
which so much has been made plain, with the task of salvation still to
be accomplished in a world that abundantly needs the Christian ministry.

## II

*Passus XVI*

The Dreamer is now ready to consider that state of perfection from
which 'Clergy', truly considered, must ultimately derive. We thus take
up an old problem—indeed the very first with which the Dreamer had
contended: how shall we speak of a 'just' man when the best we know
is man sinning 'seven times daily'? It is time to advance beyond the
considerations which Haukyn's visit had made clear. To define the
limits then reached, we open with the Dreamer thanking Anima in
Haukyn's name for an unforgettable lesson:

'Now faire falle ȝow!' quod I tho, 'for ȝowre faire shewynge,
For Haukynnes loue the actyf man euere I shal ȝow louye.'

It is the end of one whole group of problems, centering upon an
apparent tension between the righteous works demanded by Law and
the full *mede* granted by Faith. Here, as before, repentance and the
remission of sins are the essential truths that resolve an apparent difficulty. But now we are to ask another question. Holy Church had
affirmed Love as the final truth. Recognition of the efficacy of Faith
prompts a question which is now revealed as the most important of all:

Ac ȝet I am in a were what charite is to mene.

*rendren* interpret, understand; *recorden* remember; *remissionem* etc. 'the forgiveness
of sins, the resurrection of the body, and the life everlasting. Amen'; *faire falle*
*ȝow!* may good fortune befall you; *tho* then; *faire* excellent; *shewynge* explanation;
*louye* love; *were* perplexity.

As, too, this is the next major stage in progress, it is fitting that the Plowman should once more come to the Dreamer's aid. The question is upon the meaning of Charity; it is glad news that it is a noble tree flourishing under Piers Plowman's tending:

> 'Piers the Plowman!' quod I tho, and al for pure ioye
> That I herde nempne his name anone I swouned after.

Now, for the Dreamer as for the Pilgrims of the *Visio*, there is real hope of reaching the goal; practical guidance is at hand.

We recall that the Dreamer had, at the outset of his journeying, refused the consolation offered by the Friars in the distinction between deliberate sins and sins of frailty (VIII 27-56). It is the more-than-*justus* he seeks, the one who will not sin seven times a day. The point is now put to him by Piers with a humour and lightness of touch which carry a note of affectionate remonstrance.[9] The tone is very different from the scathing rebukes incurred—and not always merited—at the hands, firstly, of Holy Church and, later, other authoritative interlocutors in the *Vita de Dowel*. For the Dreamer, as we have seen, has learned some degree of patience and humility. The Tree of Charity is underpinned by three *pyles* (*shoryeres*, 'props', C); and, in response to his question, the Dreamer is told why they are necessary:

> 'For wyndes, wiltow wyte,' quod he, 'to witen it fram fallynge,

—and so a new distinction is introduced—

> *Cum ceciderit iustus, non collidetur; quia Dominus*
> *supponit manum suam.*

We are thus reminded of what tends to drop out of sight in any extended concentration on the question 'What must I *do* to save my soul?'[10] Man is patient as well as agent: the ever-present Providence of God constitutes, so to speak, the permanent balance of power. One line of inquiry, the fruitless search for a mere human being who shall be exempt from the common lot of failure, is ended. At the same time the way is being prepared for the demonstration of an unchanging Power. It is entirely

---

*nempne* named (lit. I heard [one] name); *anone* at once; *swouned* fainted; *For* against; *wiltow wyte* don't you see?; *witen* guard, prevent; *Cum ceciderit* etc. 'Though he [the good man] fall, he shall not be utterly cast down: for the Lord upholdeth him with his hand' (Ps. xxxvii 24).

typical of the Dreamer that, with a new truth apprehended, he at once has questions clamouring for utterance:

> I have thou3tes a threve of this thre piles,
> In what wode thei woxen and where that thei growed . . .

but it is now noteworthy that he has penetrated to the central truth:

> to my mynde, as me thinketh, on o more thei growed,
> And of o gretnesse and grene of greyne thei semen.

The Dreamer, for once, forbears further questioning. Piers will discourse on the meaning of what he has seen—*egrelich he loked on me and ther-fore I spared*. The intent controversialist recognizes concentration of purpose in his interlocutor. And indeed it is time: for the Plowman's discourse, here as in the *Visio*, is simple and sequential; and it leads forward to a long-promised event. The power of the Adversary, we learn, is counteracted by a deeply-laid train of events; and now many related ideas are brought together:

> thanne spakke *Spiritus Sanctus* in Gabrieles mouthe,
> To a mayde that hi3te Marye, a meke thinge with-alle,
> 'That one Iesus, a Iustice sone, moste Iouke in her chambre,
> Tyl *plenitudo temporis* ful tyme ycomen were,
> That Pieres fruit floured and fel to be ripe.
> And thanne shulde Iesus Iuste there-fore, bi Iuggement of armes,
> Whether shulde fonge the fruit, the fende or hymselue.'

Here are assembled, and interacting, the ideas of Law and its fulfilment (Jesus as the *Iustice sone*); the fullness of time which brings seed to maturity and fruit to ripeness; and that jousting which *bi Iuggement of armes* is to decide justice, the right of possession.[11] If the *Visio* had shewn us a world whose motto was 'What I hold, I have', now we learn that the Divine title, too, is not only *de jure;* it is to be established *de facto*. The rare word *Iouke* underlines the high birth of the knightly contender; the language of falconry is appropriate to His high estate. Does it not, too, bespeak a true delicacy in the poet? The mystery of Incarnation is not to be invaded by any ordinary notion of 'sleep' or 'rest' which would

---

*threve* (bundle) number; *wode* wood; *woxen* grew, arose; *o more* one root; *gretnesse* size; *grene of greyne* green, fresh, in colour; *egrelich* keenly; *Spiritus Sanctus* The Holy Ghost; *hi3te* called; *Iustice sone* a Judge's son (alluding to Jesus's lineage); *Iouke* rest; *plenitudo temporis* 'the fulness of the time' (Gal. iv 4); *ful tyme ycomen* is Donaldson's suggestion, glossing *plenitudo temporis*, for Skeat's *fully comen were; Iuste* joust; *Whether* which of the two; *fonge* receive, take.

focus attention upon the unknowable. Perhaps, too, the sense of One come from on high is preserved in this term—a Hawk of heaven, as Francis Thompson's is a Hound of Heaven. A similar tenderness is apparent in the comment on the growth of the Child. He was in his Mother's womb

> Tyl he wex a faunt thorw her flesshe and *of fiȝtyng couthe*
> To haue y-fouȝte with the fende ar ful tyme come.

The image of any small boy, certain to fight sooner or later, is movingly submerged in that of the Child predestined to fight in the fullness of time. The poet makes a further link between the Champion and the Healer. Piers teaches Jesus

> lechecrafte his lyf for to saue,
> That thowgh he were wounded with his enemye to warisshe
> hym-self.

The Saviour is shown in an unusual light. His healing of the sick is done in obedience to the command to practise the art until perfection is attained, against the day of His own need:

> And did him assaye his surgerye on hem that syke were,
> Til he was parfit practisoure if any peril felle.

Perfection, *maistrye*, is reached when Lazarus is raised from the dead— the archetype of the victory which is to follow the Cross:

> Ofte he heled suche, he ne helde it for no maistrye,
> Saue tho he leched Lazar that hadde yleye in graue,
> *Quatriduanus* quelt; quykke did hym walke.

This then, was the goal achieved—power over death; and at one and the same time it was the occasion of Jewish hatred, bringing the Saviour to His own death:

> as he made the maistrye *mestus cepit esse*,
> And wepte water with his eyghen, ther seyen it manye.

The end is seen in the beginning; but the betrayal and death upon the Cross appear not as defeat but as victorious counter-attack. The Saviour

*wex* grew, became; *faunt* infant; *couthe* was capable of; *ar* before; *ful tyme* the appointed time; *lechecrafte* art of medicine, healing; *to warisshe* how to cure; *assaye* try, test; *hem* those; *parfit* fully accomplished; *felle* befell, came about; *leched* healed, cured; *yleye* lain; Quatriduanus *quelt* four days dead; *quykke* living; *did* caused, made; *mestus cepit esse* he began to be sorrowful (*cf.* John xi 33-5); *eyghen* eyes; *seyen* saw.

Iusted in Ierusalem a Ioye to vs alle.
On crosse vpon Caluarye Cryst toke the bataille
Aȝeines deth and the deuel, destruyed her botheres myȝtes,
Deyde, and deth fordid, and daye of nyȝte made.[12]

It is the momentous turning-point in Man's story. Now the Dreamer
is entirely drawn in. The fatal externalizing capacity which had made
doctrine—theological supposition and wide-ranging conjecture—so
attractive, and so barren, is stilled. Langland marks the change with a
most unobtrusive skill. With the raising of Lazarus the Saviour was
manifestly

> leche of lyf and lorde of heigh heuene.

But for Him there is the realization that His healing powers are now
fulfilled. Therefore,

> as he made the maistrye, *mestus cepit esse.*

Now the Dreamer awakes and he, too, wipes away tears. The Dreamer
is nearer his goal than he has been at any time in his journey. Now, too,
as all things have come to an appointed end, the fulfilment of long-
awaited promise, the narrative lays increased emphasis upon time,
particularizing the 'forty weeks' in the Womb; the *ful tyme* and the
*plenere tyme* of the Saviour's preparation; and finally the fatal dates
themselves—the *Thoresday in thesternesse* preceding the last Friday. Now,
as the Dreamer goes forth in search of Piers Plowman, the day is given.
It is on *a Mydlenten Sondaye* that he meets Abraham, the herald, Faith.
    The blazon Abraham is looking for at once identifies the Saviour,
establishing his kinship with the Trinity:

> Thre leodes in o lith non lenger than other,
> Of one mochel and myȝte in mesure and in lengthe;
> That one doth, alle doth, and eche doth by his one.

The mystery of the Trinity is well dealt with by Abraham. Here, for
once, is a man who can speak from direct experience of God. The
Dreamer had asked for examples drawn from practice; Abraham's
appearing is evidence that the Dreamer will get in full measure what he
has long sought. Perfection lies just below the horizon. Abraham's

---

*destruyed* destroyed; *her botheres myȝtes* the power of them both; *Deyde* died;
*fordid* undid, destroyed; *thesternesse* darkness; *Mydlenten* fourth Sunday in Lent;
*leodes* persons; *lith* (limb) body; *other* any other; *mochel and myȝte* size and strength;
*doth by his one* acts of his own accord.

calm assurance, looking back, preludes what is to come to the Dreamer in his turn: *Thus in a somer I hym seigh as I satte in my porche*. It is the language of quiet certainty. Similarly, Abraham's whole discourse is of what is appointed. The preaching of the Baptist and what he himself has heard, while dwelling among the *peple in derknesse*, are evidence that powerful deliverance is at hand—a gaol-delivery to fetch the virtuous dead *Oute of the poukes pondfolde*. The emphasis marks very well the whole steady shift of the poem from the agency of man, the earlier ratiocinative energy and ardour of the Dreamer, to man as the subject of Providence, awaiting an appointed revelation which is now at hand. We end with urgency, a swift movement to overtake time before it runs out. Another figure is seen running on the road already traversed, to overtake the Dreamer and his guide. And now question and answer are unhesitatingly exchanged. The day of long delays and circuitous advance towards the truth is behind us.

### III

*Passus XVII*

It is Hope who enters hastily upon the scene: and we are reminded vividly of time past in this poem when we are told that the warrant of Hope lies in obedience to Law *(a maundement vpon the mounte of Synay)* and that neither document nor seal is needed as evidence. When the warrant is sealed by Christ's Crucifixion, then *Lucyferes lordeship laste shal no lenger*. It is the truth of the 'pardon' scene once again. If we would know the Law, no long screed is necessary; and the material on which it is inscribed is more durable than parchment:

> Thanne plokked he forth a patent, a pece of an harde roche,
> Wher-on were writen two wordes, on this wyse y-glosed,
> > *Dilige deum et proximum tuum, &c.*

As on that earlier occasion, the Dreamer looks closely at the document: and as before there is no possibility of error. The text is brief but utterly comprehensive:

> This was the tixte trewly, I toke ful gode ʒeme;
> The glose was gloriousely writen with a gilte penne,
> > *In hijs duobus mandatis tota lex pendet et prophetia.*

*seigh* saw; *poukes pondfolde* Devil's pound; *maundement* commandment; *patent* letter patent, charter; *roche* rock; *wordes* precepts; *y-glosed* explained, interpreted; *Dilige* etc. 'Love God and love your neighbour'; *ʒeme* note; *In hijs* etc. 'On these two commandments hang all the law and the prophets' (Matt. xxii 40).

This time text and *glose* come together. They give a solemn assurance
that what is required of him who would do well will be rewarded:

> who so worcheth after this writte, I wil vndertaken,
> Shal neuere deuel hym dere ne deth in soul greue.

There the resemblances with the past end. The perfect naturalness of
Hope's modesty as he furnishes proof of this great claim is very unlike
the sophisticated retorts of some of the Dreamer's authoritative interlocutors, the Priest of the 'pardon' scene above all. '*For though I seye it
my-self*', Hope begins, disarmingly,

> I haue saued with this charme
> Of men and of wommen many score thousandes.[13]

Faith concurs, and points to

> Iosue and Iudith and Iudas Macabeus,
> 3e, and sexty thousande bisyde forth. . .

The Dreamer is moved to ask why man should have a new Covenant,
when the old, seen in all its excellence in Abraham, was sufficient *to
sauacioun and to blisse*. The Trinity had figured prominently in the first,
not at all in the second. Does not this make unnecessary complication?
Hard enough to practise Abraham's teaching, obedience to law; but
harder still to love the wicked! So, the Dreamer seems to imply doctrine
(here, the doctrine of the Trinity) can be accepted more readily than
practical duty (as, duty to our neighbour). The Dreamer rounds on Hope
as the unpractical idealist. Even if men learn his teaching they are hardly
likely to apply it:

> 'Go thi gate,' quod I to *Spes*, 'so me god helpe!
> Tho that lerneth thi lawe wil litel while vsen it!'

It is a striking reversal of roles; for once, the Dreamer can try on another
the charge so often levelled against himself. And there is a certain
appropriateness in the situation, as in the mild humour of his reproof.
The Dreamer is sufficiently travelled, and has suffered enough in the
process, for his words to have weight. But there is no parting of the
ways, as so often happened in the *Vita de Dowel*. The three go on
together, deep in discussion *(wordyng togyderes)*.

The exalted practice that the Dreamer is sceptical of is immediately
to hand, in the Samaritan, also hastening to the same destination—

---

*dere* injure, harm; *Iosue* Joshua; *bisyde forth* more besides; *litel while* not for long;
*vsen* practise, apply.

*To a Iustes in Iherusalem he chaced awey faste.* When a despoiled and naked wayfarer is seen, Faith and Hope come to their test: and there is all Langland's unsleeping awareness of the real in the sardonic observation that Faith, seeing the victim, *nolde nouȝt neighen hym by nyne londes lengthe.* So, too, though with a more open scorn, Hope is vividly characterized—Hope who, fleet-footed, had spoken with such assurance:

> Hope cam hippyng after, that hadde so ybosted
> How he with Moyses maundement hadde many men y-holpe;
> Ac whan he hadde siȝte of that segge, a-syde he gan hym drawe,
> Dredfully, by this day! as duk doth fram the faucoun.

In most moving contrast, the action of the Samaritan, also unhesitating, is to dismount and tend to the sick. The action is made the more arresting by the continuing note of urgency; he, too, has an appointment in Jerusalem. The inn-keeper is bidden to care for the sick man *til I come fro the Iustes;* and the Samaritan is away once more:

> 'For I may nouȝt lette,' quod that leode, and lyarde he bistrydeth,
> And raped hym to-Iherusalem-ward the riȝte waye to ryde.

Now all other considerations give way. The Dreamer, like the Pilgrims of the *Visio,* has at last found his exemplar; and he runs to offer his service:

> I soiourned nouȝte but shope me to renne,
> And suwed that Samaritan that was so ful of pite,
> And graunted hym to ben his grome; 'Gramercy,' he seyde,
> 'Ac thi frende and thi felawe,' quod he, 'thow fyndest me at
>                                                                            nede.'

Faith and Hope are to be forgiven: for there is only one cure for the mortally wounded man, *the blode of a barn borne of a mayde.* Then, too, he shall never be secure *Tyl he haue eten al the barn and his blode ydronke.* For no man ever went through the wilderness of this life without being despoiled—unless it were the Samaritan himself, or Faith and Hope, and those who, like the Dreamer now, conform themselves to this pattern— *such as suwen owre werkis.* The phrase may remind us of the Pardon

---

*Iustes* jousts, tournament; *chaced* hurried; *neighen* draw near; *nyne londes* (the width of) nine ridges (in a field), a wide berth; *hippyng* skipping; *y-holpe* helped; *segge* man; *gan* did; *Dredfully* terror-stricken; *lette* delay; *lyarde* horse; *raped hym* made haste; *riȝte* direct; *shope me to renne* (set myself to run) ran hard; *suwed* followed; *graunted* offered; *grome* servant; *Gramercy* Thank you; *felawe* companion, partner (as distinct from a master); *barn* child.

granted to Piers and all who were of his fellowship in the work of the half-acre. Now, however, the time of the despoilers is nearly up; and we return to the sense of urgency, ever-present in this part of the poem. Within another three days the reign of the Arch-Outlaw is to end:

> Ac ar this day thre dayes, I dar vndertaken,
> That he worth fettred, that feloune, fast with cheynes,
> And neure eft greue grome that goth this ilke gate;
> *O mors, ero mors tua, &c.*

The Child on whom all depends has been born in Bethlehem.

The Dreamer renews his question concerning the apparent difference between Faith's teaching and Hope's. How does the doctrine of the Trinity link with Hope's insistence on one God Who is to be loved above all things (and our neighbours, thereafter, as ourselves)? The question, we note, is put in polite submission, '*A! swete syre! . . .*' The Samaritan's reply is eminently practical. Faith's account is to be believed; and the Samaritan himself has demonstrated in practice what Hope taught. Let the Dreamer hold fast to the Samaritan's example, against any objections from Conscience or Natural Reason. It is consonant with this emphasis on example, the work of men's hands, that the Samaritan gives the Dreamer a similitude that need never leave him. The comparison of the Trinity to a hand—fist, fingers and palm—suggests that the most complex problems of theology are capable of the simplest application, and that without falsification:[14]

> Al is but an hande, how so I torne it.

The theme of sinlessness is glanced at in this discourse, under the possibility of injury to the palm. In such a case

> who so synneth in the seynt spirit assoilled worth he neure,
> Noither here ne elles-where, as I herde telle,
> *Qui peccat in spiritum sanctum, nunquam, &c.*
> For he prikketh god as in the paume that *peccat in spiritum sanctum.*

The analogy comes with compelling force after prolonged and frustrating debate. Now the document presents the plain realities of light

*worth* will be; *greue* trouble; *grome* man; *goth this ilke gate* passes this way; *O mors* etc. 'O death, I will be thy death' (Hosea xiii 14); *in* against; *seynt spirit* Holy Ghost; *assoilled* absolved; *here* in this life; *Qui peccat* etc. 'But he that shall blaspheme against the Holy Ghost hath never forgiveness, but is in danger of eternal damnation' (Mark iii 29); *paume* palm (of the hand); *peccat in spiritum sanctum* sins against the Holy Ghost.

and darkness, shivering cold and penetrating warmth. Langland's vivid and homely images are inseparable from a firm sense of inescapable Law. Failure in duty to one's fellow-men means eternal separation from happiness:

> To alle unkynde creatures Cryst hym-self witnesseth,
>> *Amen dico vobis, nescio vos, &c.*

Evil, once again, is self-defeating; and this thought, as always, is the occasion of high-spirited ridicule:

> Be vnkynde to thin euene-christene, and al that thow canst bidden,
> Delen and do penaunce, day and ny3te euere,
> And purchace al the pardoun of Pampiloun and Rome
> And indulgences ynowe, and be *ingratus* to thi kynde—
> The holy goste hereth the nou3t, ne helpe may the by resoun;
> For vnkyndenesse quencheth hym that he can nou3te shyne,
> Ne brenne ne blase clere, for blowynge of vnkyndenesse.

It is the same cadence, vigorous and denunciatory, as that with which the *Visio* had ended. The earlier insistence on *Dowel* is echoed in the iteration of *vnkynde, vnkyndenesse*—repeated with great skill a few lines further on:

> For thei that ben *vnkynde* to his, hope I none other,
> But thei dwelle there Diues is, dayes with-outen ende.
> Thus is *vnkyndenesse* the contrarie that quencheth, as it were,
> The grace of the holy gooste, goddes owne *kynde.*
> For that *kynde* dothe, *vnkynde* fordoth, as these cursed theues,
> *Vnkynde* cristene men, for coueityse and enuye
> Sleeth a man for his moebles, wyth mouth or wyth handes.

The passage, rich in paired opposites, comes to rest in a final image from the light-dark antithesis. It is Shakespearian in emphasis, though Langland's own in its reverential simplicity:

> For euery manere good man may be likned to a torche,
> Or elles to a tapre, to reuerence the trinitee;
> And who morthereth a good man, me thynketh, by myn inwyt,
> He fordoth the leuest ly3te that owre lorde loueth.

*Amen dico* etc. 'Verily I say unto you, I know you not' (Matt. xxv 12); *euene-cristene* fellow-Christians; *al that thow canst* as much as you can; *bidden* pray; *delen* give (alms); *euere* continually; *Pampiloun* Pamplona, capital of Navarre; *ingratus* ungrateful, disagreeable; *hereth* (will) hear; *that* so that; *brenne* burn; *blowynge* blowing, draught; *his* God's (people); *hope I* I am sure; *sleeth* kill; *moebles* goods; *mouth* tongue (by slander); *to reuerence* given to honour; *myn inwyt* my understanding; *fordoth* destroys; *leuest* dearest.

It is one thing, as Othello paused to consider, to put out the taper's light: another, to put out the light of God's creature. This is the sin against the Light itself, abolishing even Mercy, and marks the furthest reach of the whole conception of the *iustus*. In the Dreamer's search for the sinlessness that man may hope to attain he is brought up against the sin for which man will hardly obtain forgiveness—for in this instance Charity itself must demand requital. The Dreamer puts a question to test the principle involved. Is there truly a limitation on the Divine Mercy? The reply is based upon a notion, Augustinian in origin, which is central to Langland's thought—there can be no remission of sin unless there is restitution. The question posed is to be taken out of the region of mere theory. Those who live all their lives in sin may find, in the end, that dread and despair permit no entry for grace:

> Drede of desperacion dryueth a-weye thanne grace,
> That mercy in her mynde may nou3t thanne falle.

In such a case the indispensable condition, *His sorwe is satisfaccioun for hym that may not paye*, cannot be fulfilled. The fault is none of God's; Mercy remains above all His works. Once again the Dreamer confronts a Law which cannot be bribed or evaded.

The Passus ends with one more homely illustration of a central truth. As before, discomfort and darkness are dominant images. The shrewish wife, the leaking roof, and the smoking fire very well exemplify the common miseries of life. Man's duty is to endure the mortal condition and all its attendant ills in meekness. But the real danger is in the obstacles to spiritual health—

> the smoke and the smolder that smyt in owre eyghen,
> That is coueityse and vnkyndenesse, that quencheth goddes mercy.

It was a telling image that the poet had employed; for this sin brings damnation. The man caught in the smoke and thus blind to all else but his own predicament is an exact picture of spiritual darkness:

> blere-nyed or blynde and hors in the throte,
> Cougheth and curseth that Cryst gyf hem sorwe
> That sholde brynge in better wode, or blowe it til it brende.

We see that *unkyndenesse* is

*That* so that; *her* their; *falle* enter; *may* can; *blere-nyed* blear-eyed; *sholde* ought; *wode* wood; *brende* burned, caught up.

the contrarie of alkynnes resoun;
For there nys syke ne sori ne non so moche wrecche,
That he ne may louye, and hym lyke, and lene of his herte
Good wille and good worde, bothe wisshen and willen
Alle manere men mercy and forȝifnesse,
And louye hem liche hym-self and his lyf amende.

The lesson is at an end. But the Dreamer's journey is not. He had asked to behold Perfection; and it is to Jerusalem that the Samaritan is journeying. In a Passus where the 'wayfaring life' of the Christian, his unending daily tribulation, is simply and vividly set forth, there has been, too, a note of urgency, of all things coming to an appointed time. The end comes with one sudden and arresting phrase, *I may no lenger lette*. It repeats the Samaritan's earlier leave-taking. With the Dreamer, as with the wounded man, all that can be done to meet immediate need is concluded. There can be no more delay:

'I may no lenger lette,' quod he, and lyarde he pryked,
And went away as wynde; and there-with I awaked.

## IV

*Passus XVIII*

Relatively little need be said about a Passus which is familiar to many readers who have little other acquaintance with the poem. Here at last is the fulfilment of the Dreamer's hopes, in the second epiphany of Piers Plowman. So, as we noticed in the preceding Passus, exact indication of time (and place) is important. The season is Lent and we are at Jerusalem, a meeting-place for many—for the young Knight who now comes to his testing; for Faith, his *heraude of armes*; and, too, for the *olde Iuwes* of Jerusalem, who acclaim the long-promised Messiah. But we should not fail to notice the links with what has gone before, if we are to do justice to this concluding section of the *Vita de Dobet*.

The One who comes riding on the ass is not at first clearly identified. He is

One semblable to the Samaritan and some-del to Piers the
Plowman.

---

*alkynnes* of every sort; *nys* (is not) is no one; *sori* sorrowful; *so moche wrecche* in such misery; *louye* love; *and* if; *lene* give; *of* from; *wisshen and willen* desire and intend (towards); *liche* like; *lette* delay; *lyarde* (grey) horse; *semblable* like, resembling; *some-del* somewhat.

The Dreamer must ask his last major question, who is jousting?; and this
is addressed, as is fitting, to the herald, Faith. The answer links with all
that has gone before. It is Jesus, Who will

> fecche that the fende claymeth, Piers fruit the Plowman.

Yet the Dreamer's knowledge is incomplete, for he asks innocently if
Piers is in Jerusalem. It is his last check; and the moment is marked by
Faith's gazing intently upon the Dreamer as he reveals the final truth.
The Law that presses so hard upon man is to be fulfilled by One who
shares man's nature. This is the gentility of God, the principle of *noblesse
oblige*; and it links both the emphasis upon man's *suit, secte* (his
cause and his mortal nature) and the theme of kinship with Deity, the
*gentil* folk mankind have become by this great act of Adoption:

> 'Is Piers in this place?', quod I, and he preynte on me,
> 'This Iesus of his gentrice wole Iuste in Piers armes,
> In his helme and in his haberioun, *humana natura*;
> That Cryst be nou3t biknowe here for *consummatus deus*,
> In Piers paltok the Plowman this priker shal ryde;
> For no dynte shal hym dere as *in deitate patris*.'

One further question, and the Dreamer is done:

> 'Who shal Iuste with Iesus?', quod I, 'Iuwes or scribes?'

This, we now know, is no ordinary encounter; it is a trial *à outrance*,
and the defiances issued on either side are given:

> Deth seith he shal fordo and adown brynge
> Al that lyueth or loketh in londe or in watere.
> Lyf seyth that he likth and leyth his lif to wedde
> That for al that Deth can do, with-in thre dayes
> To walke and fecche fro the fende Piers fruite the Plowman
> And legge it there hym lyketh, and Lucifer bynde
> And forbete and adown brynge bale and deth for euere:
> O *mors, ero mors tua!*

*fecche* fetch, recover; *Piers fruit the Plowman* the fruit of Piers the Plowman;
*preynte* looked; *gentrice* nobility; *haberioun* coat of mail; *biknowe* known; *for* as;
*consummatus deus* Almighty God; *Piers paltok the Plowman* the jacket of Piers the
Plowman; *priker* knight; *dynte* blow; *dere* injure; *in deitate patris* in the Divine
Nature (as Son of God); *fordo* destroy; *adown* down; *loketh* 'sees the light'; *likth*
lies; *to wedde* as a pledge; *fecche* take; *legge* lay, place; *forbete* beat utterly; *bale*
sorrow, wrong; *O mors* 'O death, I will be thy death' (Hosea xiii 14).

This conception of knighthood, with all its implications, is sustained throughout the earlier part of the Passus. When 'Longeus', the *blynde bacheler*, has pierced Christ's body, the deed is shameful, entirely unknightly—*foule vyleynye*:

> To do the blynde bete hym ybounde, it was a boyes conseille.
> Cursed caytyue! kniȝthod was it neuere
> To mysdo a ded body, by day or by nyȝte.

It is in these terms that Faith unleashes his invective against the Jews, pronouncing upon them a curse which is in Langland's most darkly prophetic vein. It begins with fierce scorn—

> For ȝowre champioun chiualer, chief knyȝt of ȝow alle,
> Ȝelt hym recreaunt rennyng, riȝt at Iesus wille—

and it rises to the throbbing pronouncement of certain doom:

> For be this derkenesse ydo his deth worth avenged,
> And ȝe, lordeynes, han ylost, for Lyf shal haue the maistrye,
> And ȝowre fraunchise, that fre was, fallen is in thraldome,
> And ȝe, cherles, and ȝowre children, chieue shal ȝe neure.

The Jews present in Jerusalem are vividly linked with those of present time—a landless people, resorting to the abomination of usury. They have no

> lordship in londe ne no londe tylye,
> But al bareyne be and vsurye vsen,
> Which is lyf that owre lorde in alle lawes acurseth.

The ending is in the level tones of certainty:

> Now ȝowre good dayes ar done, as Danyel prophecyed,
> Whan Cryst cam, of her kyngdom the croune shulde cesse . . .

It is one of Langland's most notable gifts to look beyond the immediate point in time of his narrative. The prophetic manner—forth-telling rather than foretelling—is natural to him, and he assumes it with

---

*blynde bacheler* blind novice in arms (alluding to common tradition concerning the 'centurion' who pierced Christ's side: his blindness was cured by drops of the Sacred Blood); *to do . . . bete* to make a blind man strike; *ybounde* captive; *boyes conseille* knavish trick; *caytyue* wretch; *kniȝthod* worthy of a knight; *mysdo* ill-use; *chiualer* knight; *ȝelt hym* yields himself; *recreaunt rennyng* defeated in the course; *be . . . ydo* when this darkness is ended; *lordeynes* 'my lords' (ironic); *fraunchise* free estate, liberty; *fre* of high rank; *cherles* serfs; *chieue* thrive; *tylye* till.

authority. Fuller was merely complacent in calling him 'by *Prolepsis* . . .
a Protestant': but something of proleptic power is indissolubly part of
Langland's characteristic endowment.[15]

There is, again, no need to dwell on the Harrowing of Hell itself,
which follows the meeting between Mercy and Truth, Righteousness
and Peace. It is, of course, as has long been noted, a directly dramatic
account. But it is worth remarking the freedom and energy of the
dialogue which discusses what is to come. Mercy's notion is
coarsely ridiculed by Truth, *That thow tellest . . . is but a tale of Waltrot!* ;
and she is plainly and magisterially told to say no more:

> holde thi tonge, Mercy!
> It is but a trufle that thow tellest; I, Treuth, wote the sothe.

So, too, Peace is roughly rebuked by Righteousness—*What, rauestow? . . .
or thow art riȝt dronke!*—and blunt common-sense is pressed home with
colloquial certainty:

> . . . sustre, wene it neure!
> At the bygynnynge, god gaf the dome hym-selue,
> That Adam and Eue and alle that hem suwed
> Shulde deye doune riȝte . . .

Similarly 'downright' is her conclusion upon the whole matter:

> late hem chewe as thei chose and chyde we nouȝt, sustres . . .

But it is not all roughness and crude vigour. There is, too, an unforced
calm in Mercy's sure belief:

> That man shal man saue thorw a maydenes helpe,
> And that was tynt thorw tre, tree shal it wynne,
> And that deth doun brouȝte, deth shal releue—

and, over all, in her entire certainty that a new era has begun:

> Iesus Iusted wel, Ioye bygynneth dawe.

Where we find colloquial energy in this Passus it is well employed;
for it is the very voice of common-sense, of expectation born of habitual
experience. But now it is common-sense that, astonishingly, is defeated;
and no one can doubt the victory when plain speaking can find no more
to say.[16]

---

*Waltrot* nonsense; *trufle* absurdity; *sothe* truth ('. . . when I hear it'); *rauestow?* are
you delirious?; *wene it neure!* don't you believe it!; *dome* judgement, decree;
*suwed* followed, descended from; *doune riȝte* entirely, once and for all; *chewe*
(chew) suffer; *chyde* dispute; *tynt* lost; *tre* tree; *releue* raise up.

The answer to Righteousness, in her insistence on the rigour of Law, is an application of that principle of *mesure* which had earlier, in the *Visio*, resolved the problem of self-interest, the use of material 'goods'. Pain must have an ending, and woe turn to happiness; for who can truly know happiness who has not tasted misery? This principle is inherent in the Divine design for man and the universe he inhabits:

> If no ny3te ne were, no man, as I leue,
> Shulde wite witterly what day is to mene.
> Shulde neuere ri3te riche man that lyueth in reste and ese
> Wyte what wo is, ne were the deth of kynde.

So God has long purposed our happiness, and Himself tasted the bitterness of death—which is, too, the end of earthly troubles and beginning of peace:

> The which vnknitteth al kare and comsynge is of reste.

It follows that we have no title to speak of sufficiency until we know what the least is:

> For til *modicum* mete with vs, I may it wel avowe,
> Wote no wi3te, as I wene, what is ynough to mene.

The Divine plan is therefore long in maturing; and in its execution God has set us an example which goes beyond the *mesure* principle:

> god auntred hym-self and toke Adames kynde,
> To wyte what he hath suffred, in thre sondri places,
> Bothe in heuene, and in erthe, and now til helle he thynketh,
> To wite what al wo is that wote of al Ioye.

Langland's central doctrine is, very clearly, the Incarnation. That the Word was made flesh and dwelt among men is the ground of all persistence in well-doing; for it has been shewn, once for all, that fulfilment of the Law is possible. Repentance's appeal to the Saviour in the *Visio* preluded the appearance of the Plowman, the merely human figure who palpably is *of flessh oure brother*. In the present account, it is the Divine participation in man's nature which is to be made manifest to the Dreamer. God must in His own good purpose 'venture himself' to experience Adam's suffering. Identification with *Adames kynde* can

---

ny3te night; *wite witterly* know truly, really; *to mene* means; *deth of kynde* death in the natural order of things; *comsynge* beginning; *auntred* ventured; *kynde* nature; *wyte* know, learn; *thynketh* purposes; *that* He Who; *wote* knows.

do no less. Now the power of God is to be declared, and accordingly
the 'Book' of Holy Scripture[17] is cited to attest the Light dwelling
amongst men as an absolute power over the elements. Like Samson
bearing away the gates of Gaza, Jesus comes as a 'giant' not to be withstood, to carry off the spoils of victory. The Law is fulfilled: the Book,
needed no longer, will be destroyed. As we saw with the Pardon, the
poet's bent is for the immediate and decisive removal of what is no
longer necessary. Now the Jews, like the Plowman when the 'pardon'
was destroyed, must turn to the 'new law' unambiguously revealed;
but this time the alternative is utter loss.

There follows the Harrowing of Hell itself, beginning with the voice
coming out of the light, and Satan's immediate recognition that his
cause is lost. There is yet a last case to be made by the devil's party, but
its hopeless nature is emphasized in Lucifer's[18] opening word, '*Lyste-
neth* . . .' All are listening—but not to Lucifer; they listen for the nearer
approach of the Voice. The case is, like Lady Meed's, an impudent parody
of injured innocence. The coming event, he asserts, is a threatened theft;
for the infernal title to possession is valid by reason of Adam's Fall:

> If he reue my riȝte he robbeth me by maistrye.
> For by riȝt and bi resoun tho renkes that ben here
> Bodye and soule ben myne, bothe gode and ille.

It is the ultimate echo of that legalism which tainted the world of the
*Visio* and which is for Langland a leading characteristic of self-interested
man. But even in hell it is known as less than the whole truth. Deception,
we learn, was used in the first instance, and this will invalidate the devil's
title:

> I me sore drede,
> For thow gete hem with gyle and his gardyne breke . . .
> It is nouȝte graythely geten there gyle is the rote.

Satan's words are echoed by 'Gobelyn':

> god wil nouȝt be bigiled . . . ne bi-iaped;
> We haue no trewe title to hem, for thorwgh tresoun were thei
>                                                            dampned—

and this in fact is so, as the Saviour is later to declare:

*reue* deprive, take away; *my riȝte* what is mine; *maistrye* force; *renkes* men; *gete*
took; *breke* broke into; *graythely* duly; *rote* root, basis; *bigiled* deceived; *bi-iaped*
tricked, mocked; *thorwgh* through; *dampned* condemned.

> For the dede that thei dede, thi deceyte it made;
> With gyle thow hem gete agayne al resoun.

Satan is troubled, and the focus shifts to his past attempts to penetrate to a truth beyond his understanding. His baffled anxiety is vividly brought before us. To his questioning of the Saviour—*where he were god or goddes sone*—he received, he tells us, *shorte answere*. So he must warn Pilate's wife in her sleep 'what make of man' this is, *what dones man was Iesus*. It is a telling phrase, expressing in its entire simplicity the failure of all categorizing to denote this Man's making, and thus the wonder of the Incarnation. The impossible predicament of the Devil is revealed in the bold paradox that he would, if he could, have lengthened the Saviour's life—a desperate expedient to postpone inevitable defeat:

> I wolde haue lengthened his lyf, for I leued, ȝif he deyede,
> That his soule wolde suffre no synne in his syȝte.

The distinction between 'soul' and 'body' is between an adversary whose presence brings immediate realization of defeat, and one whom the Devil would, albeit desperately, keep at arm's length. Evil's one hope is to temporize; for its defeat is a question only of time. But now all temporizing must end:

> now I se where a soule cometh hiderward seyllynge
> With glorie and with grete liȝte—god it is, I wote wel.

It is the greatest single moment in the poem; and, characteristically, it gathers up much that has gone before. Firstly, the challenge—*What lorde artow?*—and the response, setting forth the titles of the Saviour, complete the honourable lineage of One first seen

> Barfote on an asse bakke, botelees . . .
> Wyth-oute spores other spere spakliche he loked,
> As is the kynde of a knyȝte that cometh to be dubbed.

The last and greatest title is achieved; now He is *Rex glorie:*

> And lorde of myȝte and of mayne and al manere vertues, *dominus*
> *virtutum,*
> . . . Cryst . . . the kynges sone of heuene.

*resoun* fair dealing; *where* whether; *leued* believed; *in his syȝte* in his presence; *seyllynge* sailing; *botelees* with bare feet; *spores* spurs; *other* or; *spere* lance; *spakliche* alert, vigorous; *myȝte and. . .mayne* power and might; *dominus virtutum* king of virtues.

Secondly, the fulfilment of Law is insisted upon, in all its rigour:

> *Dentem pro dente, et oculum pro oculo.*
> *Ergo*, soule shal soule quyte and synne to synne wende,
> And al that man hath mysdo, I, man, wyl amende.
> Membre for membre bi the olde lawe was amendes,
> And lyf for lyf also, and by that lawe I clayme it.

The demand that the world of the *Visio* had provoked, and thus the characteristic emphasis of the poem up to this point, is at last met. Equally, too, with the failure of Meed's case, the Devil's attempted self-justification is at an end:

> So leue it nou3te, Lucifer, a3eine the lawe I fecche hem,
> But bi ri3t and bi resoun raunceon here my lyges:
> *Non veni soluere legem, sed adimplere.*

Again, the hope of universal salvation, first heard in Conscience's discourse to the King in the *Visio*, and sounded more insistently in the *Vita de Dowel*, is asserted now. The present triumph is ground and foretaste of another, when the Saviour will

> come as a kynge crouned with angeles
> And han out of helle alle mennes soules.

Similarly, the Saviour's kinship with man, another theme long pursued, is linked with that of universal salvation. For this, too, is implicit in the Incarnation—that the Saviour as Judge should show mercy to all men, for they have become His kinsfolk:

> to be merciable to man thanne my kynde it asketh;
> For we beth bretheren of blode but nou3te in baptesme alle.

This fulfilment of Law establishes a Royal Prerogative; all lies in the King's grace:

> And 3if lawe wil I loke on hem, it lithe in my grace
> Whether thei deye or deye nou3te for that thei deden ille.

Certainly, there is no evasion of the law's demands; and here we meet once more the two clauses which had pronounced doom on Meed (IV 143-4):

Dentem etc. 'An eye for an eye, and a tooth for a tooth' (Matt. v 38); *quyte* quit, settle for; *wende* be exchanged for; *bi* according to; *leue* believe, think; *raunceon* ransom; *lyges* liegemen, subjects; *Non veni* etc. 'I am not come to destroy [the law], but to fulfil' (Matt. v 17); *han* have; *thanne* then; *in baptesme alle* all of one baptism; *lithe* lies; *deden* did.

*Nullum malum impunitum, et nullum bonum irremuneratum.*

Now it is seen that Purgatory is available for wrong-doers; and mercy will be shown by the Lord *to manye of my bretheren*:

> For blode may suffre blode bothe hungry and akale,
> Ac blode may nou3t se blode blede, but hym rewe.

It is the final assurance, and it brings home the truth the Dreamer had most recently learned from the Samaritan—the condemnation of *vnkyndenesse* between Christians that echoed and deepened the *Visio's* insistence upon conformity to law. Now there can be no question that Mercy is fully available to mankind, as God's own kindred. We end with music—with the song of the angels, and, from Peace, whose day this assuredly is, *of poysye a note*—and the kissing in reconciliation of the four sisters, dancing together *Tyl the daye dawed*.

As the dream fades, the imagined noises of the dream-world blend into the bells ringing in the real world. So, too, the united company of the dream gives place to the family on Cornhill:

> ri3t with that I waked,
> And called Kitte my wyf and Kalote my dou3ter—
> 'Ariseth and reuerenceth goddes resurrexioun,
> And crepeth to the crosse on knees and kisseth it for a Iuwel!'

The long night is past, and with it have gone the fears and ecstasies of the dream. But the Cross remains, to shed its light in every corner:

> for suche is the my3te,
> May no grysly gost glyde there it shadweth!

## V

*Passus XIX*

The life of Dobet is concluded; that is, we have been brought to know the highest sanction of that Law against which the folk of the *Visio* had offended and which came with such binding force to their leader, the Plowman, and, in his turn, to the Dreamer. The perfection the Dreamer sought, brushing aside in his impetuous fashion all proximate goods, has at last been revealed in Incarnate Deity; and we have ended with the

*blode* (blood) kinsfolk; *suffre* allow (to be); *akale* cold; *but hym rewe* without compassion; *poysye* poetry, verse; *Kalote* Nicolette; *reuerenceth* do honour to; *grysly* terrifying; *there it shadweth* where its shadow falls.

mighty implications of the Saviour's fulfilment of Law—implications which reach beyond Calvary and the Harrowing of Hell to the Day of Judgement, the end of recorded time. The Divine Plan is thus fully declared. We are now to seek its application in the long interim between the first Easter morning and the last Day. It is to the right ordering of the Church that the poet now turns.

It is therefore appropriate that the next vision comes to the Dreamer during the main service of the Church, *In myddes of the mass tho men ȝede to offrynge*. The completeness of what has been revealed in the previous vision is one thing. Now there must be a return to the real world, where the purposes of God are to be carried out in the enactments of the Church's ritual and in men's daily lives. After the joy of Easter Morning, the upsurge of wonder at the bells which proclaimed the perfected work of the Saviour, there is suddenly seen once more the bloodstained image of sacrifice. It seemed to the Dreamer

> That Pieres the Plowman was paynted al blody,
> And come in with a crosse bifor the comune peple,
> And riȝte lyke in alle lymes to owre lorde Iesu.

Who is this? It is time to return from visionary acceptance to the workaday world, where Conscience must guide us in our perplexities:

> Is this Iesus the Iuster . . . that Iuwes did to deth?
> Or it is Pieres the Plowman! Who paynted hym so rede?

Langland's unsleeping vigilance, his unwearied sense that the Christian life is to be lived, hourly and momently, against all-but-overwhelming opposition, is nowhere more sharply apparent than in this immediate return from triumph to continuing war. The solemnity of the occasion is marked, as has happened before, at Meed's examination (III 229), by Conscience's kneeling. The distinction he is to make is of vital consequence, and points the way forward in the poem.

> Quod Conscience, and kneled tho, 'Thise aren Pieres armes,
> His coloures and his cote-armure; ac he that cometh so blody
> Is Cryst with his crosse, conqueroure of Crystene.'

It is the point of departure for all that follows. We leave behind the Jesus of fulfilled promise, and turn to the Christ Whose work is yet to be done. The Dreamer's immediate question—*Why calle ȝe hym Cryst . . . sithenes Iuwes calle hym Iesus?*—is met by Conscience's chiding

ȝede went; riȝte exactly; *alle lymes* all appearances; *Crystene* Christians; *sithenes* since, whereas.

reply—*Thow knowest wel . . . and thow konne resoun*. We are back at the manner long familiar in the *Vita de Dowel*, where every inch of the ground had to be explored by the Dreamer.

Conscience's explanation takes us steadily away from the past of triumph into the continuing present of work to be done. Knight, King and Conqueror may all be titles applicable to one man; and there is special honour for the Conqueror,[19] as source of all other titles—a true 'fount of honour'. Once again, there is insistence on man's kinship— in fact, consanguinity—with God:

> to be conquerour called, that cometh of special grace,
> And of hardynesse of herte and of hendenesse bothe,
> To make lordes of laddes of londe that he wynneth,
> And fre men foule thralles that folweth nou3t his lawes.

The Jews, the former *gentil men*, are dispossessed; but those who accept Christian baptism

> Aren frankeleynes, fre men . . .
> And gentel-men with Iesu . . .

The Saviour therefore was both King in his earthly career, and, in his dying, Conqueror—a conqueror *of quikke and of ded*, and one who fitly rewards his liege-men with *Places in paradys at her partynge hennes*. But all this is in the past. His coming now bearing the 'cross of his passion' is to recall that for the present there is battle to be done. The Cross, overtopping all at the end of the *Vita de Dobet*, is brought into the orbit of daily life at the outset of this last stage in the journey. With the aid of the Cross men are to 'fight and guard themselves from falling into sin'. The lesson affirmed in Christ's Passion is the lesson to which all experience in the *Vita de Dowel*—including the hard knocks of the Dreamer's own erratic progress—had led. We are to

> se bi his sorwe that who so loueth Ioye,
> To penaunce and to pouerte he moste putten hym-seluen,
> And moche wo in this worlde willen and suffren.

'In this world . . .' The poem has travelled far, to return to its starting-point. The focus has shifted from a victorious climax to its preparation, the chief events of the Saviour's earthly career.

Conscience resumes the thread:

*hardynesse* valour; *hendenesse* courtesy; *laddes* young men; *of* from; *wynneth* conquers; *foule* low, abject; *folweth* follow, obey; *frankeleynes* freeholders; *hennes* hence; *willen* (be willing to) accept.

Ac to carpe more of Cryst and how he come to that name . . .

The Dreamer is told of the Saviour's Birth and the submission of the Kings, bringing their rich and symbolic gifts. But this alone does not make Christ the Conqueror:

> Ac for alle thise preciouse presentz, owre lorde prynce Iesus
> Was neyther kynge ne conquerour til he gan to wexe
> In the manere of a man, and that by moche sleight.

The title is to be won by hard experience; and it is this experience we are now to consider—inexhaustible in its range *(who so had tyme to telle it)* but here set forth under the three great categories the Dreamer had often met during the *Vita de Dowel*. Firstly, *Dowel*: it is at the outset of His ministry that the Saviour turns the water into wine, thus establishing His power and preparing for the next phase of public life. This is *Dobet*, manifest in the miracles of feeding and healing:

> Thus he conforted carful and cauȝte a gretter name,
> The whiche was Dobet.

The Saviour's title to rule over Israel is amply justified; and His death upon the Cross follows from the hostility of the would-be leaders of the Jews. But it is the Resurrection which earns the great title from Doubting Thomas, *Deus meus et dominus meus*. And this is the beginning of the third phase, the era of faith—*Beati qui non viderunt, et crediderunt* —and of forgiveness readily available to man on the condition of restitution, the very condition on which the Law had been fulfilled in the Saviour's perfect sacrifice. The Church is founded upon Peter the Apostle's commission, another but truer 'pardon',

> to assoille of alle manere synnes,
> In couenant that thei come and knowleche to paye,
> To Pieres pardon the Plowman, *redde quod debes*.

This is Dobest; and the Saviour Himself will return to deal in these terms with mankind, to

*carpe* speak; *wexe* grow; *in the manere of a man* to manhood; *sleight* skill, wisdom; *carful* troubled, wretched; *cauȝte* gained; *Deus meus* etc. 'My Lord and my God' (John xx 28); *Beati qui* etc. 'blessed are they that have not seen, and yet have believed' (*ibid.*, 29); *assoille* absolve, remit; *In couenant that* on condition that; *knowleche . . . to* acknowledge; *to paye* so as to please (God); *Pieres pardon the Plowman* the pardon of Piers the Plowman; *redde quod debes* 'Pay . . . that thou owest' (Matt. xviii 28).

> rewarde hym riȝte wil that *reddit quod debet*—
> Payeth parfitly as pure trewthe wolde.
> And what persone payeth it nouȝt, punysshen he thinketh,
> And demen hem at domes daye, bothe quikke and ded.

The two lines of Piers's 'pardon' are re-stated, for they still apply; Law has been confirmed, not set aside:

> The gode to the godhede and to grete Ioye,
> And wikke to wonye in wo with-outen ende.

So all is set in motion. The Paraclete descends, *Crystes messager . . . Grace is his name*, and the spiritual history of man this side of the Redemption begins:

> And thanne bigan Grace to go with Piers Plowman.

The poem has now, in its circular movement, reached a point that just precedes the world shown in the Prologue. The picture is of a society made up of individuals of differing gifts. Once again mention is made of that true *tresore* which the Dreamer in the first Passus had sought by question from Holy Church, finding it nowhere evident in men's lives. But now it is not only *Tresore to liue by to her lyues ende,* a sufficient grace for each individual. Much more—and once again an end is present in a beginning—it is a weapon for each to use in the day of final trial, when the whole of Christian society will be under attack:

> And wepne to fiȝte with whan Antecryst ȝow assailleth.

The social contract is re-stated, with due allowance for those who live a life retired from secular things. On 'active' and 'contemplative' alike there presses one great obligation:

> some he lered to lyue in longynge to ben hennes,
> In pouerte and in penaunce to preye for alle Crystene.
> And alle he lered to be lele and eche a crafte loue other,
> And forbad hem alle debate, that none were amonge hem.

There is to be unity in diversity, for all proceeds from Grace, who appoints the Plowman as his deputy:

> I make Pieres the Plowman my procuratour and my reve,
> And regystrere to receyue *redde quod debes.*

*pure* sincere; *thinketh* intends, purposes; *demen* judge, sentence; *to the godhede* to be with God; *wonye* dwell; *lele* obedient to God's Law; *crafte* occupation, activity; *procuratour* manager; *reve* steward; *regystrere* accountant, treasurer.

Thus, equipped with his teams for ploughing and harrowing, and furnished with the right seeds by Grace, Piers undertakes his labour of cultivation; and, at Grace's bidding, he builds a barn, *Vnite, holicherche on Englisshe*. The cart of Christendom, drawn by Contrition and Confession, under the supervision of Priesthood, will *carye Pieres sheues*. This time it is no half-acre that is to be worked. Grace goes forth

> As wyde as the worlde is, with Pieres to tulye treuthe.

The scene set—or re-set (as we last saw it in Passus VII)—the attack begins. Headed by Pride, the forces of dissension go to work; and we see once again the world of deceit and intrigue, tainted by venal interest, that we had met throughout the *Visio*. Now the emphasis is, suitably, upon it as a world where simplicity of doctrine has been totally obscured:

> ʒowre carte the Byleue
> Shal be coloured so queyntly and keuered vnder
> owre sophistrie,
> That Conscience shal nouʒte knowe by contricioun,
> Ne by confessioun, who is Cristene or hethen.

Conscience counsels withdrawal into Unity, and once again we have a picture of common effort, like the ploughing of the half-acre, as the work of fortifying Unity goes forward. Those who are of Meed's retinue—those who *for syluer were forswore*—are, of course, of the opposite party. But the rest work so manfully that all seems to augur well; and Conscience bids them to the Sacrament, with the provision that they first obey the injunction *redde quod debes*. It is alas! too much. The old, old motive, the habitual interest in the self, is too strong. There is surprise and even incredulity in the general reception of this summons:

> 'How?' quod al the comune, 'thow conseillest vs to ʒelde
> Al that we owen any wyʒte ar we go to housel?'

It is very like the sequence of the *Visio*, when, after the repentance of the Seven Deadly Sins, the 'thousand of men' anxious to make the first steps along the road to Truth had been set to work. The good deed is required; and the rot sets in. Here, too, we have a *brewere*, a purveyor of creature-comforts, who, like the *Bretoner* of Piers's half-acre, thinks it nonsense to set aside immediate good for a hypothetical future consideration. Conscience recognizes the threat for what it is; an end of the rule of *spiritus iusticie* is an end of any solid hope for society.

*sheues* sheaves; *tulye* cultivate; *the Byleue* the Faith; *queyntly* elaborately; *keuered* covered; *ʒelde* repay; *housel* Holy Communion; *spiritus iusticie* the spirit of Justice.

Confirmation comes at once; and it comes, characteristically, with the wordplay that can betoken sophistry, a too easy acceptance of the divided state of man.

Conscience's reference to the cardinal virtues is taken up by a *lewed vycory* who appeals to experience to show that Conscience and cardinal virtues are empty terms. Neither his parishioners nor he himself

knewe neure cardynal, that he ne cam fro the pope.

This in its turn leads to reflections upon the extravagance of Cardinals, and a bitter gibe at the motives for which they are found at both Avignon[20] and Rome. The prospect of a Christendom freed from these abuses seems remote. But who should set bounds to the possibilities if, as we heard after Meed's examination long before, Conscience were in the King's Court? The condition can now be added that Grace must be the guide of all clergy. Then men might see

Pieres with his newe plow and eke with his olde,
Emperour of al the worlde, that alle men were Cristene!

But the present state is far otherwise: the Plowman works honestly for rogues and worthy men, and one can only marvel at the patience of God. The Pope is in reality a despoiler of Holy Church and a destroyer of Christian lives. The state of the *comune* is as Holy Church had described it in Passus I: *Of other heuene than here holde thei no tale.* It is the same old story; men

counten ful litel
The conseille of Conscience or cardinale vertues,
But if thei seiȝe as by syȝte somwhat to wynnynge.[21]

This account is amply confirmed by the impudent assertion of 'a lord'. He holds it entirely fitting to recoup himself to the last penny from his stewards' accounts. Piers's grains, given by Grace, have been sadly misused: 'spiritus prudencie' *amonge the peple,* the parish priest had plainly said, *is gyle.* So for this landowner, when personal gain is in question, *spiritus intellectus* means acumen in searching out possible levies, and *spiritus fortitudinis* rigour in exacting them.

We have in the space of one Passus travelled all the way from the Triumph of Christ on Easter morning to the degenerate world of actuality. Will the secular authority help to save the Church from at

*lewed vycory* unlearned (unsophisticated) parish priest; *that . . . ne* who didn't; *seiȝe as by syȝte* see with their own eyes; *to wynnynge* for their (material) profit; *spiritus prudencie, intellectus, fortitudinis* the spirit of forethought, knowledge, firmness.

least the more flagrant abuses? We end with a King who asserts his
title to his revenues in return for his services as ruler of the *comune*
and defender of Holy Church—that is, we are forced back on *spiritus
iusticie*. Gone are the exalted hopes with which temporal society was
set on its way; it is now a matter of contractual bargaining. Once
again questions of *mesure*, of what is appropriate for services rendered
and allowable needs, are to the fore. Conscience tells the King that he
is to defend

> And rule thi rewme in resoun riȝt wel, and in treuth.
> Take thow may in resoun as thi lawe asketh;
> *Omnia tua sunt ad defendendum, set non ad depredandum!*

It is a far cry from the rule of Grace:

> alle he lered to be lele and eche a craft loue other,
> And forbad hem alle debate, that non were amonge hem.

The great advance in the *Vita de Dowel* had been to pass beyond the
*mesure* principle. Now we are, sadly, back where we were, and all the
talk must be of rights and duties; for we are in the prudential, self-
seeking world, where the highest reach of imagination is a bargain
upon mutuality of interest. Other parts of the poem portray with an
equal realism invincible folly or triumphant wickedness. But no one
Passus travels so far from the heights; none more faithfully records
the saddest of journeys homeward to what moral insight reveals as
habitual self.

# VI

*Passus XX*

It is with a heavy heart that the Dreamer goes on his way. Yet the
solution for the individual life is simple enough; and Need, or Necessity,
enunciating it, links together the two problems—of temporal power
and its abuses, and of the mesurable in creature-comforts: *spiritus
temperancie* is the one answer. Let each look to himself; if we must
accept a world of individuals, let us be sure that each begins with his
own account correctly estimated. It was the lesson the Dreamer of the
*Vita de Dowel* was slow to learn. In its light, we may see that *iusticia*
and *fortitudo* are unreliable criteria. *Mesure* is the key-conception; and

*Omnia tua* etc. 'All things are yours to protect, not to despoil'.

these will not readily observe *mesure*. Justice thus understood can be at best only a rough justice. As for *prudencia*, that, it seems, is least commendable: for

> Wenynge is no wysdome ne wyse ymagynacioun,
> *Homo proponit et deus disponit.*

*Wyse ymagynacioun* would offend against the principle of dependency upon God, the lesson which, above all, a materially-minded society must learn, and which had come home with such force to the good provider himself, the Plowman. The case seems desperate; but Need has the great Exemplar for model. Patient poverty, once again, is immune to all reproach:

> For-thi be nouȝte abasshed to bydde and to be nedy;
> Syth he that wrouȝte al the worlde was wilfullich nedy,
> Ne neuer none so nedy ne pouerere deyde.

The point is given full authority by placing in the mouth of the Crucified One the statement that the foxes and the birds have their dwelling-place but He has none. Skeat calls this a 'singular mistake'.[22] It is hardly to be thought of in these terms. Modern sensitivity to the literally accurate will not take us very far with older story-telling, whether secular or divine. Here the words spoken *on the selue rode* have the imaginative authority of an anachronism in Shakespeare rather than a textual slip. Friend or foe, who can doubt the truth of these words when they are spoken by the outcast, undergoing sentence of death? We may notice, too, that the sentiment comes full circle; the ending is in victory:

> There nede hath ynome me that I mote nede abyde,
> And suffre sorwes ful sowre that shal to Ioye tourne.

It is the last reminder we have of the Christ Who has made all things possible.

There now comes upon the scene Antichrist, incarnate too *(in mannes forme)*, and bringing devastation—

> al the croppe of treuthe
> Torned it vp so doune and ouertilte the rote.

*Wenynge* expectation; *wyse ymagynacioun* prudent supposition, careful forethought; *Homo proponit* etc. 'Man proposes, God disposes'; *bydde* beg; *wilfullich* of his own choice; *pouerere* poorer; *There* where; *ynome* taken, brought; *mote nede* needs must; *vp so doune* upside down; *ouertilte* overturned, tore up; *rote* root(s).

He is received with honour, by Friars foremost among the religious, and it is significant in the design of the poem that the bells are rung for him. We last heard the Easter Day peal of triumph in work perfected: now the welcome is for the one who will create havoc. The irony is completed in the contemptuous reckoning of those who refuse his leadership; they are 'fools'. Antichrist's host grows, and Conscience retires with his followers, the 'fools', into *Vnyte, holy-cherche*, there to withstand siege:

> And crye we to Kynde that he come and defende vs,
> Foles, fro this fendes lymes, for Piers loue the Plowman.

In 'unity', a community of purpose, lies their only hope:

> crye we to alle the comune that thei come to Vnite,
> And there abide and bikere a3ein Beliales children.

One of the dominant images of the poem has been the equation between truth and husbandry, the ploughman's work in the fields and the harvest of good deeds. It is Antichrist who has inverted this natural order, turning *vp so doune* 'all Truth's crop'. Nothing but famine, and in its train pestilence, can follow: at Conscience's appeal, Nature takes part, and down from above comes disease. It is the vividest expression of that relationship between work and health, both physical and spiritual, which is fundamental to the poet's imagination:

> Or in dykynge or in deluynge or trauaillynge in preyeres,
> Contemplatyf lyf or actyf lyf, Cryst wolde men wrou3te. (VI 250-1)

Such, we recall, was the counsel given by Hunger to the Plowman; and in the onset of pestilence we may be reminded of the sharp lesson Hunger had administered to the idlers in Piers's half-acre. Now, once more, authority is to be asserted:

> Kynd ... cam out of the planetes,
> And sent forth his foreioures, feures and fluxes,
> Coughes and cardiacles, crampes and tothaches ...

The casualties are many, high and low alike:

> Many a louely lady and lemmanes of knyghtes
> Swouned and swelted for sorwe of Dethes dyntes.

*Kynde* Nature; *Foles* 'fools'; *lymes* (limbs) agents; *bikere* fight; *foreioures* foragers, harbingers; *feures* fevers; *fluxes* flows (of blood); *cardiacles* heart-attacks; *lemmanes* mistresses; *swelted* died; *dyntes* blows.

Conscience obtains a respite for humanity; but all to no purpose. No sooner are they reprieved than they think themselves immune:

> Fortune gan flateren thenne tho fewe that were alyue,
> And byhight hem longe lyf . . .

The irony that links the paucity of their numbers with the false promise of long life is carried further when Lechery appears in the van. Against all evidence to the contrary—the toll death has taken of lovely ladies and *lemmanes of knyghtes*—Lechery can offer *a laughyng chiere*. But Avarice, too, is present; and once more, as in the *Visio*, we see the corruption of justice. Wordplay neatly underlines the ironical contrasts; Simony

> Iugged til a Iustice and Iusted in his ere,
> And ouertilte al his treuthe with 'take-this-vp-amendement'.

As Skeat notices, there is a play on his 'jogging towards' his easy prey, and his 'jogging' or nudging the somnolent judge. Full irony, too, marks the casual ease with which troth is broken. The phrase 'till death depart' is neatly parodied when the diocesan official is shown at work

> For a mantel of menyuere he made lele matrimonye
> Departen ar deth cam.

Avarice succeeds in his campaign to corrupt all society. Life takes Fortune for his paramour, and begets Sloth, who in his turn weds Despair. It is time to bring Age into battle with Life; and Life, ever subject to illusion, believes that his doctors can keep both Age and Death at bay for ever. Unhappily, a doctor dies: and Life has no further refuge in make-believe.

It is thus that the poet himself enters his poem. His *persona*, the Dreamer, has been one who has slowly learned from experience, from living long in land; such a one can bear witness at least to age's work, the trail of the passing years. As the time-scale of the poem now contracts, the figure of an ever-eager controversialist merges into that of an old man—bald, deaf, toothless, and suffering with gout. The blunt humour with which he describes a further physical weakness completes the picture of rueful old age; like some impudent misericord, it is a final comment on any dignified posturing. If we expect that this Dreamer

*byhight* promised; *chiere* countenance, expression; *Iugged* jogged; *til* towards; *Iusted* ran a tilt (at the justice's ear); *take-this-vp-amendement* take this in settlement; *mantel* mantle, cloak; *menyuere* ermine; *lele* true.

like some in courtly love-poetry, will be allowed a graceful *congé*, we mistake the whole truth of the poem. He himself, not unlike the Plowman proposing a final pilgrimage, may ask for release from effort— *for I wolde ben hennes*. The answer is that he too must enter Unity; and until he is sent for, let him learn some skill or occupation. There is no honourable discharge from an unending war. This is not the allegory of Love, where the Dreamer can be dismissed *por reposer*.[23] The return to reality, to a poet too old for dreaming, or indeed for any matter of concern save his approaching end, parallels the descent from the exalted beginnings of the Church to its actual and unlovely state. At this last hour in the enquiry it is time to re-emphasize the whole duty of man—in one simple statement:

'Lerne to loue,' quod Kynde, 'and leue of alle othre'.

There is an end of the Dreamer with his endless subtilizing. It is the 'better' knowledge which Holy Church would not reveal at the outset. And how shall man provide for his material needs? Once again, an act of faith is required, and all else will be added to him:

'And thow loue lelly,' quod he, 'lakke shal the neure
Mete ne worldly wede whil thi lyf lasteth'.

His questions at rest, the poet becomes a witness of the siege, where Antichrist stands at the head of his *seuene grete gyauntz*, the Deadly Sins. We are thus enabled to follow the closing action from within; here, as at the end of the *Visio*, the focus narrows into sharp detail.

Sloth makes the first major breach, and through it enter a host of proud priests, led by Covetousness. The Friars who would come to the rescue are dubious allies, only to be truly acceptable if obedient to Need's stern regimen. The very idea is enough to provoke laughter; but Conscience hospitably receives them,

зow shal no thyng faille,
With that зe leue logyk and lerneth for to louye.

Doing so, they will conform to the example of Dominic and Francis. As to any desire for clerical livings, here, too, a central lesson of the poem will suffice:

if зe coueyteth cure, Kynde wil зow teche,
That in *mesure* god made alle maner thynges.

*leue* leave off, lay aside; *lelly* steadfastly; *Mete* food; *wede* clothing; *зow . . . faille* all your needs will be met; *With that* provided that; *cure* cure of souls.

But this principle, literally applied, leads to the condemnation of the Friars themselves; for no man can measure their numbers. The conclusion is in bitter sarcasm:

It is wikked to wage ȝow, ȝe wexeth out of noumbre!
Heuene hath euene noumbre and helle is with-out noumbre.

The upshot is plain; the Friars are schooled by Envy in the notion that *alle thinges vnder heuene ouȝte to ben in comune.* How otherwise should their vast appetites be catered for? In practice, we find the Friars basing their whole economy upon the shame of the parishioner to confess his misdeeds to his own priest. Thus a mere traffic in men's souls is carried on; and it is Envy who in fact presides over the Friars' much-vaunted studies.

Conscience remains within his gates. But his regimen is not liked by all. For when wounds got in the skirmishes are to be treated, his insistence is always upon the old-fashioned remedy, *redde quod debes;* that is, contrition must precede the giving of absolution. It is the essential principle affirmed in the *Vita* as it has developed up to this point. The *Visio* had presented a world where all things were for sale, including justice, both secular and, as it appeared, divine. It had closed with the Plowman's 'pardon', which reaffirmed the undeviating rigour of the Law: no evasion was possible. In the long seeking of the *Vita* the Dreamer had been first prepared for and then granted a vision of Law perfectly fulfilled, so that Mercy was seen to be no evasion. For sinful mankind, living after the Saviour's fulfilment of Law, all turns upon the true act of repentance. But we see that in 'Unity' it is felt to be rigorous treatment; the weaker will seek a way out. And who readier to help than the Friar, Flatterer? Conscience objects: there is none better qualified than

persoun or parissh-prest, penytancere or bischop,
Saue Piers the Plowman, that hath powere ouer hem alle—

and even he, the Head of the Church, can grant no indulgence if the debt of contrition is unpaid. Mercy is not a mere benevolence, as the Christian religion is not 'morality touched by emotion'. As though to underline this truth, Conscience is seen fatally yielding to the anxiety of others, and the Friar is summoned.

We are now at the last stage of the Dreamer's long journey. It is part of the continuity of Langland's imagination that once more a document is to be produced, a certification, like that of the Pardoners, to practise a

*wikked* hard, difficult; *wage* pay; *wexeth out of noumbre* increase beyond reckoning; *penytancere* a specially-appointed confessor.

crooked trade. And the haste with which the Friar equips himself with this licence proclaims the energy and resolution which Avarice can give to his followers, recalling Conscience's rueful wish

> wolde Criste, of his grace
> That Coueityse were Cristene, that is so kene a fiȝter,
> And bolde and bidyng while his bagge lasteth!

Even yet, it is a near thing for evil. Peace will at first give no admission; and the name of the Friar once revealed—'sire' *Penetrans-domos*—leaves Peace more resolute yet. But, as with Contrition, so, too, with Courtesy—we give the benefit of the doubt and let in disaster.

The ironic simplicity of this final incident is complete. In the wheedling tones of the Friar, as he applies his own soothing remedy, we hear again the voice of the world where Meed is Empress. We had heard it in the false beggars of the half-acre, with their honorific address to the Plowman:

> For we haue no lymes to laboure with, *lorde, y-graced be ȝe*! (VI 126)

Their contribution would be to pray for Piers, and his plough, too—on condition of his being their benefactor. The Friar will with an equal smoothness of professional humility square accounts:

> I shal praye for ȝow,
> For all that ȝe ben holde to, al my lyf-tyme,
> And make ȝow, my lady, in masse and in matynes,
> As freres of owre fraternite—for a litel syluer.[24]

Thus Contrition is lulled asleep; and it is the opportunity for a fresh, and perhaps final, assault. The Church is betrayed from within. Contrition, who should come to the defence, cannot stir:

> 'He dremeth ydreynte', seyde Pees, 'and so do many other;[25]
> The frere with his phisik this folke hath enchaunted,
> And plastred hem so esyly thei drede no synne.'

It is the last comment on a world which has made a working reconciliation between irreconcilables. Those irreconcilables the poem has

*bolde* resolute; *bidyng* enduring; *bagge* purse; *Sir Penetrans-domos* Father Foot-in-the-door ('of this sort are they which creep into houses . . .' II Tim. iii 6); *lorde, y-graced be ȝe!* so please your Honour!; *that ȝe ben holde to* those to whom you are true, dear ones; *as freres* (alluding to a form of membership granted by 'letter of fraternity'—an offer Lady Meed had gladly accepted, III 63); *ydreynte* drowned (in sleep), drenched (with medicine); *plastred hem so esyly* given them such mild treatment (plasters).

presented as the human wish to insulate the self over against the Divine injunction to be of one family (the *Visio*); and (in the *Vita*) the desire to be left in our habitual follies—or to rationalize our acceptance of them—as opposed to the plain command to seek perfection. The great solvent at the beginning and end of the survey is money, the *lytel syluer* which makes all things possible—at the cost of blinding and deadening Conscience. There is only one thing left to do: and Conscience does it. In a world where all things are for sale he at least will not be bought. Conscience, abandoned by all, must leave the tottering structure of 'Unity' to seek, pilgrim-fashion, the one good man with whose aid he can begin again. It is entirely consistent with all we have learned that the poem ends on a note not of general hope but of unshaken individual resolution. It is consistent, too, that this resolution, faithfully pursued, opens up the widest prospects. 'Piers Plowman' in the conclusion is, like the Plowman of the *Visio*, individual man not given over to corruption. But also, with all the cumulative force the poem has developed, he might be the Church's head, a true Pope who would destroy Pride and set the Friars in order. If there is in the end no room for facile hope, there is equally none for despair. The individual's duty remains, and is paramount. Until his pilgrimage is achieved, while life lasts, Conscience must walk the wide earth.

## Notes

1. On the relations between poet and Dreamer, see Chapter VII, below.
2. *C. T.* I 315. For contrasts of language in Langland, see pp. 216-9, below.
3. They are seen in representations from at least the fifth century onwards. (G. McN. Rushforth, *Medieval Christian Imagery*, Oxford, 1936, p. 97).
4. The 'pore freres' of the B Text, alone conforming to the example *Dispersit, dedit pauperibus* ('He hath dispersed, he hath given to the poor', Ps. cxii 9), disappear in C, to make room for the counsel that charity begins at home—kith and kin are to be helped before *prestes other pardoneres other eny peuple elles* (C XVIII 59-61). Concentration of purpose leaves no room for any marginal qualification of the case against a mercenary-minded clergy.
5. For a discussion of the wordplay in this passage, see pp. 269-70, below.
6. See pp. 48-50, above.
7. See pp. 314 ff., below.
8. The passage commending the martyrs in general and St. Thomas in particular occurs in MS R of the B Text. On the acceptability of R and F readings see E. Talbot Donaldson, 'MSS R and F in the B-Tradition of *Piers Plowman*', *Transactions of the Connecticut Academy of Arts and Sciences*, XXXIX (1955), 177-212.

*other* or *peuple* people.

9. This lightness of touch is missing from the C Text, where Piers's explanation is made more abstract by immediate reference to the Trinity (C XIX 25-8).

10. On this point see, further, pp. 306-10, below.

11. On the wordplay 'just'-'joust', see pp. 272-3, below.

12. There is a very marked difference between the two texts here. C ends in the apparent defeat of the Saviour— *Thus Iewes to the Iustices Iesus thei ladden*—and proceeds at once to the Dreamer's awakening in utter confusion (*ner frentik*). C is thus, unusually, the more dramatic in its treatment (C XIX 179-80).

13. *Cf.* p. 213, below.

14. *Cf.* p. 216, below.

15. On this, see further pp. 224-7, and *cf.* p. 231, below.

16. *Cf.* pp. 212-3, below.

17. For a detailed examination, see R. E. Kaske, 'The Speech of "Book" in *Piers Plowman*', *Anglia*, LXXVII (1959), 650-54.

18. Satan and Lucifer, in accordance with a common tradition, are represented as two distinct devils. Langland differs, however, from the account given in *The Gospel of Nicodemus* by identifying Lucifer as the tempter both of Adam and Eve in Paradise and of Christ in the wilderness—thus, perhaps, emphasising the full circle of Divine Mercy in a single confutation of Hell's design.

19. As Skeat points out, 'Christ' is taken to signify 'conqueror'.

20. The Cardinals who in defiance of the Pope's authority remained at Avignon helped to precipitate the Great Schism (1378-1417).

21. Donaldson suggests *soune as by syȝte*, '(unless the "virtues") evidently tend to (material gain)'.

22. *op. cit.*, II 276.

23. See p. 229, 291 below.

24. *A litel siluer*, when used by Meed in scorn of Conscience's advice to the King (III 206), refers to three million gold crowns (of ransom-money).

25. Donaldson's suggestion, *dremeth ydreynte*, is attractive (as against Skeat's *lith and dremeth*).

# PART II

# *The Poetic Techniques*

. . . thow medlest the with makynges and myȝtest go
                                                sey thi sauter,
And bidde for hem that ȝiueth the bred; for there
                                                are bokes ynowe
To telle men what Dowel is, Dobet and Dobest bothe . . .
                                                XII 16—18

As we accumulate experience, we begin to perceive, sooner
or later, that every poem is an attempt to compose our
memories and to interpret this experience to our own satisfaction. We write in order to understand, not in order to be
understood; though, the more successfully a poem has interpreted to its writer the meaning of his own experience, the
more widely will it be 'understood' in the long run.

                                                C. DAY LEWIS

# CHAPTER V

# Rhythm, Speech and Argument

A modern writer is beset by what Rossetti called 'The soulless self-reflections of man's skill' . . . He may escape to the classics . . . or with much loss of self-control and coherence force language against its will into a powerful, artificial vividness.

W. B. Yeats

The previous chapters have dealt with the content of *Piers Plowman*, the nature and scope of its argument. I turn now to consider its form, the modes of expression at the poet's disposal and their suitability to his purpose. Here, above all, it is important to guard against giving an impression of subtle unity, a degree of highly-wrought purpose underlying apparent irregularity. The flexibility of Langland's instrument, the four-beat line, corresponds with a general freedom of structure; there is marked variation in Passus-length, and between major divisions of the work—the *Visio* and the *Vita*—as there is within those divisions; the *Vita de Dowel* is half as long again as the *Vita de Dobet*, and *Dobest* consists of two Passus only. A dominant characteristic of the argument as we have followed it in Part I of this study is thus paralleled in the expression—progress is unsystematic, less like thought in its ordered expression and more like thought in its actual context, the 'thinking' that with many digressions and some returns upon itself finds its own way forward. It is central to the poet's purpose that the Dreamer is one in whom a dialectical ardour is fatally matched with a capacity for over-looking the primary relevance of the truths so eagerly debated. When realization begins to come, it comes from the pressure of experience—the wry awareness that however high 'doing well' may aspire, it must begin at home. 'Do Well', the Dreamer learns, is 'to see much and suffer more'. The Dreamer's mistakes are thus at least as important as his affirmations —the problems which he cannot solve as well as the truths he can confidently pronounce. To this end, the loose four-beat line, and the corresponding freedom of Passus-length and structure, are not without a special relevance and adaptability. So, too, is the genre in which Langland works—that type of personification-allegory which, ordinarily used for the statement of literal truth at a prudent or piquant remove, is

especially suited to an argument in which dialectics must give way to
revelation before truth can prevail. In the next chapter, I consider the
suitability to Langland's purposes of the allegorical vision-type poem;
in this, the capacity of the poetic instrument itself, the four-beat alliterative line and its resources of diction and imagery. Here, it will first be
necessary to say something in general terms concerning the different
kinds of verse-making possible in English. We may thus approach the
question of fitness for poetic argument with least bias.

I

> In a somer seson whan soft was the sonne,
> I shope me in shroudes as I a shepe were,
> In habite as an heremite vnholy of werkes,
> Went wyde in this world wondres to here.

These opening lines will serve to illustrate the essential characteristics
of Langland's metrical instrument. It is a four-beat line, commonly
alliterating in three out of the four stressed words, and employing a
medial pause—not, it should be noted, a caesura, but a distinct break.
The half-line is the essential unit of the verse, and this half-line is not
an arbitrary division but a unit of speech, a clause complete in itself.
Such an instrument, while requiring varying degrees of pause at the
line-end, lends itself very readily to the 'run-on' of sense and to parall-
elism of statement. But the chief characteristic is the entire absence of
any tension between the demands of speech (and thus sense) on the one
hand, and a theoretically unvarying metrical pattern on the other. In
this it differs fundamentally from that kind of metrical organization
which from the greater Elizabethans to the early Georgians dominated English verse-making—an organization which turned upon the
possibility of intimate contrast between the run of speech and a measured
norm. Such versification may at any given moment enlarge or reduce
the contrast, as the musical communication of that whole meaning which
the words only in part express. The music of this sort of verse is not
to be thought of as an accompaniment to, but is an indivisible part of,
the entire meaning of the poem. In such verse alliteration and length of
syllable take their place among a variety of devices directed towards
one main end, never better expressed than in Pope's precept, 'The
sound must seem an echo to the sense.' So, for example, in Gray's lines:

*shope me* dressed myself; *shroudes* clothing; *shepe* sheep (rather than 'shepherd').

The boast of heraldry, the pomp of power,
And all that beauty, all that wealth e'er gave,
Await alike the inevitable hour:
The paths of glory lead but to the grave.

—the stress falling 'regularly' (that is, where the ideal rhythmic pattern
would require it) in the last line finalizes the whole sentiment. The
progress to the grave is ineluctable; and as such it puts a metrical period
to exaggerated hopes based in 'heraldry' 'pomp' 'beauty' and 'wealth'—
all of which are suitably forced out of the regular position of the stress-
accent (an effect best heard in the second line, where the pattern of each
half of the line is held in suspense until we come to 'beauty' and 'wealth').
Similarly, the stress falling on long syllables in 'boast' and 'power'
gives a temporary weight and solidity which is overmastered by the
undeviating course of a last line where 'glory' finds its muffled echo in
the 'grave'. In such a pattern, alliteration, too, is used to reinforce
meaning. The 'pomp of power' is finally subordinated to a 'glory'
brought to the 'grave', by way of a third line in which the alliteration of
initial vowel sounds seems to speak the moment of awakening uncertainty before irresistible fact drives to its conclusion. Such orchestration,
even in so small an example, may serve to remind us of the triumphs
of that system of metrical organization which generations of Englishmen
accepted without question as the essential condition of 'poetry'.

These are, however, triumphs of a peculiar kind; and if we are to
deal justly with another kind of English poetry the nature of that triumph
must be grasped. In the lines of Langland earlier quoted, each half-line,
it will be recalled, is a unit, and is incapable of further division. The unit
of metrical organization is thus the phrase, whole and indivisible—
'In a somer seson'; 'as I a shepe were'; 'wondres to here'. It is the phrase
which *is* the half-line; the two phrases, qualifying each other, or paral-
leling, together or separately, things said before, constitute the line.
There can be no question of discrepancy, whether delicate or strident,
between a theoretically unvaried scansion and the actual demand of
speech and sense—that discrepancy which some modern writers call
(loosely) counterpoint and for which the older term 'modulation' may
be preferred.[1] It is the possibility of 'modulation' which distinguishes
the one system from the other; and this possibility, with all its range of
subtle and ever-variable effect, must be forgone at the outset. The point
may be stressed, since it is not wholly apparent that all our older poets,
or some modern writers on prosody, have grasped it as an essential fact.
The distinction is not between a line having a regular number of syllables

and a line where number of syllables is *per se* unimportant. That is
a secondary consideration. The essential distinction is between a line
whose base is the 'foot', a regular unit of one stressed and one or two
unstressed syllables, and a line which knows nothing of the foot, whether
for conformity or departure.[2]

The point may be illustrated from the equal and opposite dangers
into which the foot-counted line may fall. If the demand of speech
predominates, then harshness will result, the metrical base being faintly
sustained or all-but overridden. This exclamatory quality is the real
foundation of Jonson's charge that Donne 'deserved hanging for not
keeping of the accent'. The protest is against one dominant range of
effect. It is perhaps unnecessary to add that precisely this tone of
impassioned speech, whether exclamatory or meditative, is essential to
the dramatic quality with which the lyric is reinvested at Donne's hands.
The truth of Jonson's description remains, even if we cannot accept it as
a hanging indictment. On the other hand, mere conformity to the
metrical norm will assuredly demand variation if 'ten low words' are
not to do their fatal work. As Tyrwhitt observed, tracing out familiar
ground in order to win a fair hearing for Chaucer,

> It is agreed, I believe, that, in our Heroic Metre, those Verses,
> considered singly, are the most harmonious, in which the Accents
> fall upon the even syllables; but it has never, that I know, been defined,
> how far a verse may vary from this its most perfect form, and yet
> remain a verse.[3]

There are no rules for this relationship of ideal pattern and actual speech,
save only the 'rule' that the partners must be neither merely at variance
nor merely in conformity. As with the two antithetical faculties of the
poet as earlier ages understood them, Fancy and Judgement, there must
be, in the well-worn metaphor, marriage not mutual strife: the relationship is a living one or it is nothing. The proper development of the foot-
counted line is thus towards an Augustan ideal, the achievement of a
subtle and ever-varying balance of apparent opposites. In this light,
Dryden was right to call the heroic couplet 'the noblest kind of modern
verse'.[4] It was indeed an instrument fittest for the poet—if his discourse
were to be a tide of argument that, like Denham's Thames, might flow

> Though deep, yet clear; though gentle, yet not dull;
> Strong without rage, without o'erflowing full.

Obvious enough as this may now be, it was not achieved without
much labour and many failures. If we sometimes marvel at the weighty

infelicities which good Elizabethan judgments approved, we should do well to remember that sonority, a sustained dignity of sound in the longer line, was the great prize sought by the Elizabethan. Hence those ugliest of measures, the fourteener and the 'poulter's' (alternately twelve and fourteen syllables, to make up a kind of baker's dozen); hence, too, the 'quantitative' experiments that an Ascham could approve and a Sidney excel in.[5] These consist of attempts to base the verse-line in a foot consisting of long and short syllables variously arranged, taking length (the duration of time in the utterance of the syllable) and not stress (the loudness with which the syllable is produced) as the fundamental principle. Such versification is of course best suited to languages where the stress, though evident and often strong, is not the dominant force it is in English. For this reason, would-be 'quantitative' verse in English is always liable to sound artificial.[6] Fine effects, indeed, are sometimes possible—though, it would seem, more often in single lines than in entire passages or poems. And it is very difficult to avoid an air of antiquarian virtuosity, even when direct transposition is apparently effortless:

Quid faciam? moriar? et Amyntam perdet Amyntas?
What shall I do? shall I die? shall Amyntas murder Amyntas?[7]

The common and widespread solution is to make stress stand for length, so that the essential principle of the foot consists in stressed and unstressed syllables, not longs and shorts (though long and short may of course play an important part in the developed harmony of the verse). But in the formative period of post-medieval English poetry, neither the would-be 'quantitative' experiments nor the wrestling with stressed or (as they are often called in opposition to 'quantitative') 'accentual' long lines, like the fourteener, constitute any real advance towards the syllabic foot-counted line. The mistake is to confuse mere length and weight of line, whether 'quantitative' or 'accentual' in pattern, with the possibilities of the modulated line, where discrepancy between ideal pattern and actual sound is the first requirement.

Perhaps our own apprehension of ancient metre does not much encourage us to make the distinction. The sonority that the Elizabethan would capture for English verse is to be heard in the Vergilian hexameter—if we will pass beyond merely mechanical notions of 'scansion'. Thus, we may learn from Dr. W. F. Jackson Knight to observe the changing texture in the opening lines of the *Aeneid*, as stress-accent now harmonizes with, now departs from, an unvarying regular beat, the *ictus* of the metrical norm. Only those which coincide— 'homodynes', as Dr. Knight terms them—are marked below (and totalled in the margin):

4   árma uirúmque cano, Troiae qui prímus ab óris
2   Italiam fato profugus Lauínaque uénit
4   lítora, múltum ille et terris iactátus et álto
3   úi superum, saeuae memorem Iunónis ob íram,
3   múlta quoque et bello passus, dum cónderet úrbem,
4   ínferrétque deos Latio, genus únde Latínum,
5   Álbaníque patres atque áltae moénia Rómae.

We see that the voice-stresses have the distinctive part in establishing a verse-texture which responds to the changing demands of the argument. After the steady and impressive opening we pass to the uncertainties of the voyage, and the balance of opposing forces, until 'the Trojans begin to prevail, and then prevail triumphantly'.[8]

Against this background, Elizabethan efforts to establish a stateliness of sound in the long line have omitted the one thing needful. Their efforts are either stress-treated-as-quantity or stress falling predominantly on long syllables. Either way, length and weight are no substitute for modulation, the delicate discrepancy between voice and metrical norm. In English, as Gilbert Murray once pointed out, 'A very strong stress generally devastates the values of all unstressed syllables in its immediate neighbourhood'[9]. The possibilities of subtle conflict, on which modulation entirely depends, are placed beyond reach where 'dignity' has become an emphasis ruthlessly hammered home. All experiments undertaken in the direction of conformity to pattern, whether the pattern is fetched from ancient quantitative or later European syllabic practice, are doomed to melodic failure in so far as they are 'metrically' successful. For such a notion of 'metre' is that against which Bentley contended; we are to measure the true music of verse 'not, like school-boys, by the beginning of each foot . . . but by the rhythm of the whole line'[10].

From this standpoint, the accidents of early experimentation may sometimes be more important than the achievements. Where so much is uncertain, it is hard to give judgement in particular cases. Professor C. S. Lewis has recently warned us against reading into some of Wyatt's longer lines subtleties which we hear 'against the background of an imagined norm'. Yet we may prefer the Egerton MS reading

Into a straunge fasshion of forsaking[11]

to Tottel's version

Into a bitter fashion of forsakyng,

and not think the preference wholly a latter-day sophistication. For

English ears in any period, whatever degree of favour might be accorded
to the effect, would recognize the naturalness of a line in which the run
of the voice breaks with the demand of the pattern. The test is not and
can never be the single word—'straunge' thrown into gaunt relief. It
is the phrase which is the essential and indivisible unit—here the 'straunge
fasshion', which achieves a powerful irony, whether or not it was for
some of its earlier hearers, and perhaps the poet himself, less than
consistent art. It is the phrase which in English speech is all-important and which sometimes, we may feel, comes to a plain utterance,
more like recitative and less like song, in those of Wyatt's longer lines
where language is not subdued to 'the ruthless accuracy of a metro-
nome'[12]. That his verse only rarely offers the great prize—the third
thing which is neither mere speech nor mere 'metre'—should not
deter us from recognizing the effects gained when speech breaks in
upon a set music. In this respect, of course, we reach differences in the
importance of stress between English, on the one side, and both the Latin
hexameter and French syllabic metres on the other; and since our verse-
writing has been decisively affected by admiration for models of excellence in both kinds, it may be as well to glance briefly at stress-accent
in French.

The fundamental vocal characteristic of English is the dominant part
played by stress—again, the loudness with which a syllable is produced.
We see at once the difficulties of Englishmen attempting to speak
French; and, less obvious, but more important, the misunderstandings
of French prosody that may result. The English tongue seeks naturally
in any given group of words for the syllable or syllables to be thrown
into decisive prominence. Hence the near-inaudibility to English ears
of the relatively light stress-accent in French; and so, in English pronunciation of French, the characteristic fault of hitting the final syllable
hard. Since the true stress-accent is hardly audible to the English ear,
the common practice is to preserve foreignness, a non-englishness of
speech, by putting a marked stress on final syllables, at whatever cost
to full articulation. So, too, in reading French verse, the English reader
trained to avoid the strong accentuation of his own language tends to
give a merely neutral, absence-of-stress, reading to lines in which stress,
though lighter than in English, has in fact a decisive contribution to
make to melodic delight. It is from this wary neutralism that there
has perhaps grown up the notion that in French verse stress-accent and
metrical *ictus* commonly coincide; and this makes a further justification
for monotonous sing-song. In fact, of course, a glance at the opening
lines of a classical French work should be sufficient to dispel the illusion:

Oui je viéns dans son témple adorér l'Eternél,
Je viéns selon l'uságe antíque et solennél.

Since the stress-accent is incomparably weaker than anything English
and German ears are accustomed to, it admits of a delicate variety of
placing, always provided that there is a stressed syllable immediately
before the caesura and at the end of the line. For this is a language in
which we are not given a broad choice of musical pattern—the extremes
of accentual freedom or syllabic control; the stress-accent, as Kästner
observes, 'is not sufficiently marked to sustain the cadence, being not
only much less intense than in the Germanic languages, but even less
so than in the other Romance languages'[13].

It will thus, I trust, be apparent that neither ancient quantitative nor
contemporary European 'syllabic' practice was wholly suited to English
verse-making in its most formative period. Gascoigne observed accurately that 'there is none other foote vsed but one; wherby our Poemes
may iustly be called Rithmes, and cannot by any right challenge the
name of a Verse'.[14] To 'rithme', the phrasal unit aptly placed, English
ears respond readily; it is the essence of English speech. 'Verse', the foot-
counted (and for Gascoigne especially the 'iambic') line, can have only
a precarious foothold until stress is allowed full play. But since that is
not the end but the beginning—for we then have all the possibilities
of 'modulation'—there is no cause for lament. Gascoigne was wise to
'take the forde as we find it'. What is required of any who would make
or hear English verse is, as Milton observed, 'An eare that could measure
a just cadence, and scan without articulating'.[15] The whole movement or
'fall' of the line, and hence of the poem in all its parts, is the essential
characteristic of English verse; and from this freedom proceeds that
liberty of interpretation which can, for example, give wholly different
but equally valid readings of a line as simple and apparently limited
as Gray's

The ploughman homeward plods his weary way.

'Homeward' and 'plods' are in the clearest opposition as strongly-
stressed syllables; but it is characteristic of English speech that they do
not *merely* balance each other. One must be dominant; and it makes a
world of difference which the speaker chooses. If 'homeward', then the
journey is long indeed: if 'plods', the motion itself is laboured and
'weary' comes into the strongest prominence. This is, of course, to say
nothing of an entire range of subordinate effect. Once more, it is understanding of the phrase, and thus the whole demand of speech and sense,

not in the line alone but in the stanza or verse-paragraph, which must shape each interpretation.

So much has been said of the capacity for 'modulation' in order to point the special triumphs of an English verse based upon a regular number of syllables. That a language in which stress plays the dominant part should find a working reconciliation with a structure eminently suited to lightness and flexibility of stress is perhaps one of the more striking meetings of form and medium in Western art. It remains to observe that the debtor side of this reconciliation is perhaps less obvious, though not less real. The foot-counted line can be a device for inflating sentiment—that 'dressing' of statement which lends itself readily to a notion of poetic diction; to an emphatic distinction between content and form; and thus to a heresy of paraphrase—for, labour as he will to 'echo' his 'sense', the poet may find his melody taken only as an incidental or accompanying music to a 'meaning' which his audience busily unravels. So, too, the classification of 'subjects' as poetical and unpoetical may move rejection of the prosaically real that is before us. 'Do not the lines cry out to be re-clothed in sesquipedalian iambics?' we ask of the great subject.[16] Perhaps; but it may be that insistence upon a region of great art, towering above the lesser, is, like undue insistence on the distinction between art and actuality, a heavy price to pay for the glories of a high-built poetic craft.

Certainly, the situation is rich in possibilities of satire and outright burlesque; and in them we may see the limits within which the poetics of the syllabic line must be confined. One kind of burlesque will dwell mercilessly on the rhetorical positioning which mere pattern, rigidly enforced, must require. For example, there is Chaucer's ogreish Sire Olifaunt uttering his terrifying threat to poor Thopas:

> Child, by Termagaunt!
> But if thou prike out of myn haunt,
> Anon I sle thy steede
> With mace.[17]

It is a comic effect possible only where regularity of form, answering to regularity of line-length, includes conscientious variation. The two last syllables which should crown the appalling threat limp in as absurdly late arrivals. Bathos can exist only where there is a truly grand manner. 'Those move easiest who have learn'd to dance'; and the satirist cruelly mimes the lumbering movement of those who would dance before

*Child* knight, warrior; *prike* ride; *sle* slay.

they can walk—both the inept versifier and the would-be hero of his tale.

Another and similar kind of burlesque is that which innocently discloses the kind of language which the simple equate with passionate speech. In doing so, it may make us think again about the grand manner. There is, for instance, Quince's strident emphasis on Pyramus's unhappy end:

> Whereat with blade, with bloody blameful blade,
> He bravely broach'd his boiling bloody breast.

Here is the urgency of nature overriding all other considerations—including that of remaining within the bounds of the natural in art. The mirror this self-appointed 'Prologue' holds up to nature reflects nothing; we see only its crazed surface. A specifically 'poetic' diction is, of course, not a special consequence of the foot-counted line. Alliterative poetry, as we shall see, is peculiarly liable to foster a language proudly distinct from that of ordinary life and thus capable of grotesque inappropriateness. But where the essential characteristic of the prosody is a dignified marshalling of the exigencies of speech against a solemn measure, Quince's blurted asseveration, flattening every other consideration, is doubly comic. The sound is all too faithful an echo to the sense. In the unrelieved succession of monosyllables we hear only a thrusting eagerness to convince at all costs.

This is not to say that in poetry, whatever its prosody, every plainness is either desirable or possible. Nor is it to suggest that the four-beat alliterative line is either all-inclusive as to subject or unvaryingly capable of directness and simplicity of appeal. It is, however, to suggest that the outstanding characteristic of Langland's verse-line is a profound capacity for truthfulness. It has neither a built language to maintain—though there is in the verse of the 'Alliterative Revival', as we shall see, a repository of language to touch upon as need arises; nor has it an internal principle of organization to temper the wide range of phrase and idiom. 'Elleuene holy men', 'Thow doted daffe!', 'A gobet of his grace'— these are the poetry of Langland, equally with 'Was neuere leef vpon lynde liȝter ther-after' and 'Dukes of this dym place, anon vndo this ȝates!' So far from requiring any adaptation, these phrases must come in all their life as speech if they are to be heard as verse, for it is the phrase which alone constitutes the principle of this verse-making. With this understanding, we may consider Langland's diction and imagery.

*leef* leaf; *lynde* linden, lime tree; *this* these.

## II

The time is long past, it is to be hoped, when mere plainness of statement, whether harrowing or sardonic, was thought of as Langland's
dominant characteristic. He is not the 'peasant's poet' that an earlier
tradition of criticism, making a direct and hasty contrast with the
sophisticated Chaucer, would have him. As Professor C. S. Lewis once
pointed out, it is hard to see the 'burel man' in any age making much
headway with lines such as these:

> 'The whiles I quykke the corps,' quod he, 'called am I *Anima;*
> And whan I wilne and wolde *Animus* ich hatte;
> And for that I can and knowe, called am I *Mens;*
> And whan I make mone to god *Memoria* is my name'.[18]

Nevertheless, the verve and directness of Langland's speech is, on the
whole, a true impression; and here again diction and metre are finally
inseparable. When syllabic, foot-counted verse declines it becomes that
'mere invertebrate flow' with which one modern writer thankfully
contrasts the alliterative line[19]. Such a 'flow', we may add, the writer of
foot-counted verse commonly hopes to check by an increased parade
of poetic language; so that the ordinary characteristic of bad verse is
not crawling ineptitude but staggering effrontery. Lines such as those
of Richard Kelsey, at the outset of his epic poem *Alfred of Wessex*, are
relatively rare:

> In fear, in trembling, in humility,
> Unnamed, unnoted, shrinking in myself,
> Feebly I sing . . .

—surely 'the most respectful exordium in all literature'[20]. The more
usual thing is the idiom imperfectly acquired, used as substitute for
direct apprehension:

> Come, flaming Hecla! on thy adure brow,
> Or near thy summit, Etna, let me stand;
> While fumid clouds obnoxious roll around,
> While streams of liquid fire in rage descend,
> Sulphureous vapours vex the ambient air,
> And showers of candent rocks informous fly
> On every side: on every side Despair,
> Tottering with phrenzy'd fear, shudders aghast
> At Nature's elemental warfare wild![21]

*burel* plain, homespun; *quykke* give life to; *corps* body; *Anima* spirit, soul;
*Animus* purpose; *Mens* mind.

One can well believe the poet's description of his work as 'the fruit of much miscellaneous reading, and some observation'. These are the exact proportions evident in the product. We should of course be on guard against the absurd critical procedure of extolling the virtues of one kind of poetry by decrying the failings of another. There is nothing here to give undeserved comfort to the apologists of the phrasal-unit line. As that line is sometimes practised in the fourteenth century, its badness may be thought an even worse thing. For then there is not even an invertebrate flow—only a series of stops and beginnings-again. A recent writer quotes with telling effect from *The Parlement of the Thre Ages*, a work nearly contemporary with *Piers Plowman*, the description of Youth:

> The firste was a ferse freke, fayrere than thies othire,
> A bolde beryn one a blonke bownne for to ryde,
> A hathelle on ane heghe horse with hauke appon hande.
> He was balghe in the breste and brode in the scholdirs.

It is a characteristic fault of poets of the 'Alliterative Revival' that 'They seem to rely on the intrinsic interest of the alliterative line and language to hold the audience's attention, as if, sometimes, the mere display of the words were enough'[22]. The commonplaces of a 'high style' *hathelle, blonke, balghe* (and of a 'poetic diction') *freke* and *beryn* are the substitute for any directness of feeling, as the wooden grouping in mere parallel runs of phrase marks the absence of any directness of purpose. It is the general characteristic of failure, whatever the prosody attempted. But it is the mark of a genuinely creative mind to draw unerringly upon this common stock for its own original purposes; and this Langland does—most often, as Mr. Burrow observes, in the mood of irony, as in Mede's deferential reception at Westminster, when 'myrthe and mynstralcye' and the sycophancy of the Justices towards this 'birde' (III 11-14) come with mocking force. In any age when an 'adulterated phraseology' is so generally accepted as 'poetic' that metre itself becomes 'a symbol or promise of this unusual language'[23], the remedy is either in an evident and arresting simplicity or in a provocative use of language designedly strange. So the Wordsworth-Coleridge combination was soundly conceived; and its masterpieces are evident both in the monosyllabic intentness of 'It is the first mild day of March' and the incantatory charm of *The Rime of the Ancyent Marinere*.

*ferse* fierce, warlike; *freke* man, warrior; *beryn* man, warrior; *one* on; *blonke* (white) horse; *bownne* ready; *hathelle* knight; *appon* upon; *balghe* deep(-chested); *birde* fair lady, sweetheart.

For Langland, there can be no question of a return to an imagined past, rich in association. That is, in a sense, the way of 'Alliterative Revival' verse, and it is fairly represented by the extract from *The Parlement of the Thre Ages* given above. There can however be a resort to a kind of 'augmentation' of the native language that will give a distinctive quality to some plain statements, where pretension and simplicity are deliberately brought together in one context. This we shall examine in a following section, and we must add it to the evidence of a poet drawing upon a mingled tradition of speech. But whatever the resources of diction, there can yet be an undeviating simplicity of *phrase*—so that even in the midst of technical argument a homely directness and insistence are brought to bear, and a graphic imagination presents not only tone of voice but movement and gesture. These qualities will be illustrated in detail, below. For the moment we may notice, with Mr. Burrow, that the phrases 'chiefly alliterative' which are the poetic diction of the 'Revival'[24] find little place in Langland. His achievement is a new thing. It is neither the built and near-hieratic language of Old English poetry, nor the weaker ornateness and elaboration of the 'Revival'; but a language which is fluent, varied in tone, resourceful in image and analogy, and everywhere vivid and insistent. Mr. Burrow would see this language as a response to the demands of a new situation—to the needs of 'an audience of hetero-geneous literary experience and expectations, reached not through oral recitation but through the dissemination of manuscripts'.[25] Certainly we may recognize a difference of appeal in Langland; he neither belongs to nor aims at the 'regional groups' for whom the manner of the 'Revival' poems may well have been appropriate. But it is the nature of his theme and his response to it which constitute the essential difference. Langland's originality of purpose makes direct comparison with other poetry of the period peculiarly difficult. *Sir Gawain and the Green Knight* or *Pearl* have so little in common with *Piers Plowman* that a judgement of relative worth in terms of vocabulary and versification is all but pro-fitless. His originality is in making of the lengthy argumentative poem (cast in the familiar dream-form of allegorical journey or *pèlerinage*) an instrument for establishing the interdependence of vision and argument. It is thus not only a matter of using 'ten visions, with a very definite structural function'—a use which 'cannot be paralleled elsewhere in medieval literature'[26]. It is his handling of the vision-poem to serve as the apt medium for a poetic argument in which reason and revelation have distinct yet finally indissoluble parts to play. We can therefore understand the unserviceability to his purpose of a mere poetic diction; as we can understand, too, his stripping the Prologue, as Mr. Burrow notes, to its 'bare essentials'. Both language and dream must be indeed functional. Mr. Burrow's essay is a valuable contribution to awareness of Langland's distinctive achievement; but the emphasis, I take it, is in the wrong place. It is not the audience for a poem that is the prior question for criticism; it is the poet's characteristic bent and the means of its communication.

What kinds of language do we in fact find in the poem? Langland's most characteristic manner may be illustrated from the picture of the poor man abed in Passus XIV:

> thou3 his glotonye be to gode ale he goth to cold beddynge,
> And his heued vn-heled vn-esiliche i-wrye;
> For whan he streyneth hym to streche the strawe is his schetes.
>
> (ll. 231-3)

It is vivid and laconic; the general truth—that the Deadly Sins can have little power over the poor—in this light needs no amplification. Here is uncomfortable poverty huddled on its straw mattress. A penetrating sense of the actual—Langland's 'power to communicate physical reality'[27]—is at one and the same time the source of outright comedy and profound compassion. The poor man, in this habitual plight,

> for his glotonie and his grete scleuthe . . . hath a greuous penaunce,
> That is welawo whan he waketh and wepeth for colde,
> And sum tyme for his synnes; so he is neuere murie
> Withoute mornynge amonge and mischief to bote. (ibid., 234-7)

The note is unforced, for the reality is unsentimentalized. Langland's is an unerring eye for woes that are actual; so his conception of truth (and justice) is firmly based. The same graphic power vivifies a traditional association in Passus XVII, where the gift of the Holy Ghost is to be asserted:

> as glowande gledes gladieth nou3te this werkmen,
> That worchen and waken in wyntres ni3tes,
> As doth a kex or a candel that cau3t hath fyre and blaseth,

his glotonye his characteristic failing; heued head; vn-heled uncovered; vn-esiliche i-wrye uncomfortably askew; schetes sheets (i.e. the sheet or blanket is too small to cover the body at full length); scleuthe sloth; welawo misery; mornynge grief; amonge at the same time; mischief misfortune, suffering; glowande glowing; gledes embers; kex rushlight; blaseth burns brightly.

Namore doth sire ne sone ne seynt spirit togyderes,
Graunteth no grace ne for3ifnesse of synnes,
Til the holi goste gynne to glowe and to blase. (ll. 217-22)

Who can doubt the truth of the doctrine, when common experience
is made so vivid? The demonstration comes with the unargued force
of a Gospel parable, for the experience is universal. The same exactness
of homely observation enables us to see vividly the state of the Penitent
Thief. Certainly he is admitted to heaven; but he sits

by hym-self as a soleyne and serued *on the erthe* (XII 205)

—'beyond the rushes', as Wells nicely renders it.[28] One recalls, too, the
unsparing realism that tells how far from intentness can be the thoughts
of the slothful at prayer—when only anger can focus them:

And 3if I bidde any bedes *but if it be in wrath*,
That I telle with my tonge is two myle fro myne herte. (V 407-8)

Or, again, the unappeasable quality of anger, in the Dreamer himself,
once rebuked:

Tho wepte I for wo and wratth of her speche,
And in a wynkyng worth til I was aslepe.[29] (XI 3-4)

There is, too, a simplicity of inference from divine pronouncement or
counsel that is on its own level unanswerable:

*Dixit et facta sunt, &c:*
*Ergo* throw his breth mowen men and bestes lyuen,
As holywrit witnesseth, whan men segge her graces,
*Aperis tu manum tuam et imples omne animal benediccione.* (XIV 60-3)

The *ergo* is complete, and brooks no reply. Since the words of creation
come from the mouth of God, all things are sustained by His Spirit;
the common grace before meals is reinvested with authority. The same
challenging simplicity is heard in Langland's insistence that the gifts of
God are to all men in common. The inclusion of 'wit' among these
gifts points a special warning against the mercenary motive in the
lawyer's occupation:

*sire. . . sone* Father . . . Son (in the Holy Trinity); *soleyne* solitary; *Dixit* etc.
'he commanded, and they were created' (Ps. cxlviii 5); *mowen* can; *segge* say;
*Aperis* etc. 'Thou openest thine hand, and satisfiest the desire of every living
thing' (Ps. cxlv 16).

Ac to bugge water, ne wynde, ne witte, ne fyre the fierthe,
Thise foure the fader of heuene made to this folde in comune;
(VII 52-3)

We see that intelligence is subject to the self-same law as other 'commodities':

Thise ben treuthes tresores, trewe folk to helpe,
That neuere shal wax ne wanye with-oute god hym-selue. (*ibid.*,
54-5)

This boldness in inference extends where necessary to outright transposition; as when the rich are advised to take counsel from the poor, those who can speak truly of life's sorrows. The image of entertainment dominates the whole:

For-thi I rede зow riche, reueles whan зe maketh
For to solace зoure soules, suche ministrales to haue;
The pore, for a fol sage syttynge at the heyз table,
And a lered man, to lere the what oure lorde suffred,
For to saue thi soule fram Sathan thin enemy,
And fithel the, with-out flaterynge, of gode Friday the storye;
And a blynd man for a bourdeoure, or a bedrede womman,
To crie a largesse by-for oure lorde, зoure gode loos to schewe!
(XIII 442-9)

The transposition from hapless poverty to a special minstrelsy is complete; and so, in consequence, is the happiness these entertainers bring. We end with sober relevance to the time of man's greatest need:

Thise thre maner ministrales maketh a man to lawhe,
And in his deth-deyinge thei don him grete comforte. (*ibid.*,
450-2)

Behind the animated foreground, as ever in Langland, there is the long perspective of eternity.

This power of direct reference to palpable experience, the life all men know because they share it, of course sustains Langland's most penetrating satiric effects. Of a hundred instances we might recall

*bugge* buy; *fierthe* fourth; *folde* earth; *wanye* wane, diminish; *rede* counsel; *reules* feasts, entertainments; *for* in place of; *fol sage* sage fool, shrewd jester; *fithel* (fiddle) recite; *bourdeoure* jester; *bedrede* bed-ridden; *largesse* alms, mercy; *gode loos* good report, praises; *lawhe* laugh.

the subservient, caught unforgettably in their arrogance towards their inferiors: they are

paciente of tonge

And boxome as of berynge to burgeys and to lordes,
And to pore peple han peper in the nose,
And as a lyoun he loketh there men lakketh his werkes.

(XV 195-8)

The one derisive phrase—'pepper in the nose'—lying between the two attitudes of servile conformity and studied contempt, pierces the empty shell of would-be *hauteur*. We are given for the moment a behind-the-scenes view of the creature turning from one audience to another. Similarly derisive and similarly revealing is the phrase that marks the defensive arrogance of Haukyn, the 'actyf man',

Was none suche as hym-self *ne none so pope-holy*,
Y-habited as an hermyte, an ordre by hym-selue ... (XIII 284-5)

There is the *noli-me-tangere* of 'active life', its readiness to reprove others equalled only by its power of exempting itself from judgement. This is indeed a contradiction in terms, fitly described as

Religioun sanz reule and resonable obedience. (*ibid.*, 286)

Those who are in this state—and it is the commonest of conditions—would have the best of both worlds,

In lykyng of lele lyf, and a lyer in soule. (*ibid.*, 288)

Langland's perception of paradox reaches from immediate awareness of ordinary hypocrisy to its ultimate implications. His is not the defect common to some satirists, that a vivid contempt or ready invective are accompanied by solemn protestations of the truth, the 'positives' the unsparing critic must affirm with altered voice. His sardonic observation is the foundation of all his building, for his is not a world in which mortal failing is an easily corrected condition; the satire reaches to the Dreamer himself. Equally, too, in Langland's understanding, Divine Purpose is not a high and awful truth beyond man's reach. The truth is one that is matched to man's imperfection; and error in man—his capacity above all for exempting himself, like Haukyn, from the judgement readily visited on others—is one and indivisible. Thus, no evil is unique or merely local. We may, for example, despise the incompetent clerk at work on legal documents:

*boxome* humble; *burgeys* citizens, burgesses; *lakketh* criticize, find fault with.
*lele* obedient (to God's Will).

The gome that gloseth so chartres for a goky is holden. (XI 299)

But let us be sure that we make the right connexion between this kind
of error and another:

> So is it a goky, by god, that in his gospel failleth! (*ibid.*, 300)

Langland's great capacity is to pursue the truth beyond its immediate
limits. It is thus that the whole first part of his design takes us beyond
castigation of man's acts to understanding of man's nature. His outright
comedy plays upon the façade which men make for their actions. As we
saw earlier, his gift is to show that the characteristic of sin is incompetence. We may recall Auaricia's slight error in the matter of 'restitucioun'—

> 'Repentedestow the euere . . . ne restitucioun madest?'
> '3us, ones I was herberwed . . . with an hep of chapmen,
> I roos whan thei were arest and yrifled here males' (V 232-4)

—and, too, Lady Meed's apparently innocent citation of the text,
*Omnia probate*. The comedy thus evoked is high-spirited; the Devil is
entirely mocked. We must not shrink from the full verve with which
error is confronted, or half-heartedness set to rout. Dame Study has
the right answer, albeit a vulgar one, to the contortions of those mortals
who move great speculations on Divine purpose:

> For alle that wilneth to wyte the weyes of god almi3ty,
> I wolde his eye were in his ers and his fynger after. (X 122-3)

We may compare the fine scorn with which an over-disputatious
Dreamer is sent on his way. Clergy, in the A Text, has no further time
to waste—he

> drow the dore after him and bad me go Dowel,
> Or wycke 3if I wolde, whether me lyked! (A XII 36-7)

The poet's language is plain and exact; any criterion of indelicacy is
wholly inapplicable, for there is 'nothing common or unclean' once
subjected to his dominant purpose. Wit speaks plainly of the dangers
of lust:

> leccherye in likyng is lyme3erde of helle. (IX 179)

*gome* man, fellow; *goky* fool; *holden* regarded; *gospel* (the Priest in reading the)
Gospel; *wycke* (do) wickedly; *whether me lyked* whichever I pleased; *lyme3erde*
lime-twig, snare.

His counsel can therefore be direct and unashamed:

> Whiles thow art ȝonge and thi wepne kene,
> Wreke the with wyuynge ȝif thow wilt ben excused. (*ibid.*, 180-1)

We may recall the rueful glance at the poet's own condition in old age (XX 192-7). But this is not to suggest that there is in him a kind of residual crudity. The graphic image of Avarice vainly trying to wrestle with Poverty shows the same sturdy sense that comic absurdity in the human condition is not the least evidence of design in all things: [30]

> if Coueitise wolde cacche the pore thei may nouȝt come togideres,
> And by the nekke namely her none may hente other.
> For men knoweth wel that Coueitise is of a kene wille,
> And hath hondes and armes of a longe lengthe.
> And pouerte nis but a petit thinge, appereth nouȝt to his nauele,
> And louely layke was it neuere bitwene the longe and the shorte.
>
> (XIV 238-43)

Langland is no moralist *in vacuo*. Inherent disproportion in the human situation points to final impossibility in the Divine purpose. Nothing he offers rests upon a merely argued foundation. His impatience with mere speculation may perhaps remind us of a Johnsonian sturdiness of conviction: 'Truth, Sir, is a cow that will yield such people no more milk, and so they are gone to milk the bull'.[31] It is the same sense of a comprehensive absurdity. But Langland's understanding of man and his goal is finally more assured than Johnson's. Man, with all other objects in the universe, is the creature of omnipotent and benevolent Deity—a Deity conceived finally not as a Lawgiver but as a God of Love. There is no shadow of the Despot whose commands are in themselves the justification of unquestioning obedience. What God commands, the Dreamer learned at Holy Church's hands, is written in men's hearts; and both natural reason and common moral experience are the Dreamer's faithful guides. Man's errors and absurdities are themselves part of the evidence of a divine dispensation which makes for our good: and, as we have seen in the first part of this book, the Dreamer's erratic progress itself constitutes a proof of that benevolent dispensation. In these terms, Langland is the first of our satirists to take into account all the evidence of man's nature, including the evidence of man's own sharp judgement, invariably turned outward upon others.

*cacche* wrestle with; *namely* in particular; *her none* neither of them; *hente* grasp; *kene wille* fierce craving; *appereth . . . nauel* doesn't come up to his navel; *louely layke* good match.

Langland's is a universe in which there is, finally, no accident; this is at once the source of some of the Dreamer's most intent questioning and the basis of the poem's whole working-method. If the Dreamer persists in seeking for comprehensive design it is nothing less that is found in the long run. Avarice and Poverty may not wrestle together— in any understanding. That Avarice 'hath hondes and armes of a longe lengthe' is not arbitrary—and so it is no more than just that he cannot have it all his own way on every occasion. Poverty 'nis but a petit thinge'; and in the comic grotesquerie of this village wrestling-match we have in little the great and predominating assurance that evil cannot always and everywhere prevail. Langland is thus not the exacerbated moralist that some hasty readers would have him (a figure doubtful enough in any effective satiric production). In fact, we see, not all the victories go to the wrong in this wicked world. Langland's is a true re-port on experience.

His realism can therefore be undeviating; and some of its best effects are gained by lively juxtapositions of language. So the 'petit thinge', with its note of humorous disproportion in the French term applied to the diminutive opponent, may remind us of the *diapenidion*, the sweet medicament which is useless against the mortal sickness of Envy:

> May no sugre ne swete thinge asswage my swellynge,
> Ne no *diapenidion* dryue it fro myne herte . . . (V 122-3)

There can thus be only one remedy; not sweet physic but plain surgery is required:

> Ne noyther schrifte ne shame, but ho-so schrape my mawe. (*ibid.*,
> 124

As with the *petit* of light mockery, so the technical word brings its own association (of soothing compromise)—only to show that no half-measures are in fact possible. This principle of contrast—the polyslylabic *diapenidion* that conflicts with the plain speaking of 'schrape' and 'mawe' —may remind us, in passing, of a kind of natural rhetoric in which Langland excels. There is, for example, the passage in Passus XV where the resounding titles of the Bishops-*in-partibus* conflict with the simpli-city of what is truly required of Christ's followers. We begin with

> So many prelates to preche as the pope maketh,
> Of *Nazareth*, of *Nynyue*, of *Neptalim* and *Damaske* . . . (XV 485-6)

*diapenidion* medicinal sweet; *but ho-so* unless someone; *schrape* scrape; *mawe* stomach.

They are mouth-filling names. But if these prelates do indeed 'wilne a name', let them do what is enjoined upon Christ's ministers,

> as hym-self seyde, so to *lyue* and *deye*. (*ibid.*, 489)

The simple words 'live and die' come home with unalterable force. This power of juxtaposition is inseparable from the poet's awareness of a mingled yarn, not of good and evil merely, but of misunderstanding and self-deception.

## III

In a long work which offers argument of an unusual kind—the varying pressures of doctrine and experience—a graphic treatment of human figures is all-important; and this must call into play a vivid sense of movement, gesture, turn of speech and timing. These are the readiest means to varying pace and emphasis in the conduct of the poem. We have seen the kneeling of Conscience as he makes his submission to the King when Lady Meed's case seems about to win the day (III 229). So, in the fullness of the design, he kneels again at the coming of a Saviour who is seen to resemble the Plowman:

> Quod Conscience, and kneled tho, 'thise aren Pieres armes,
> His coloures and his cote-armure . . .' (XIX 12-13)

The obeisance is appropriate, for it is One greater than the Plowman who is now at hand—

> he that cometh so blody
> Is Cryst with his crosse, conquerour of Crystene.

Similarly, we may recall the irruptions upon a settled course of argument, when nothing less forceful will serve to dispel long-established error or confusion. The Plowman first appears abruptly on the scene ('Peter!', quod a plowman, and put forth his hed'). Scripture, to emphasize the high matter of predestination, 'skipte an heigh and preched'—to be answered even more dramatically by Trajan:

> '3ee! baw for bokes!' quod one was broken oute of helle . . .

There is action in plenty to be recalled. One thinks of the door slammed by Scripture in the Dreamer's face; Haukyn's collapse into utter misery, the tears flowing; the joyful leap of the heart when the Plowman's name is heard once more, towards the end of the long search in the *Vita de Dowel;* Faith looking intently at a Dreamer who, at the hour of jousting in Jerusalem, asks 'Is Piers in this place?'; and so on. But the greatest single example of skill in this regard is the colloquy with the 'Doctor' in Passus XIII.

We start with the plain fare given to the humble—the sour loaf *agite penitenciam*, the drink *diu-perseuerans*, and so on—contrasted with the dishes at the high table:

> mortrewes and puddynges,
> Wombe-cloutes and wylde braune & egges yfryed with grece.
> (62-3)

Since Patience presides at the lower end of the hall we have a suitably contrasted audience for the voluble theologian. The creature's size and shape are next conveyed, as the Dreamer mutters his resolution:

> I shal Iangle to this Iurdan with his Iust wombe . . .[32]
> To telle me what penaunce is, of which he preched rather (83-4) —

and we are drawn into the conspiracy by Patience's reply:

> thow shalt se thus sone, whan he may no more,
> He shal haue a penaunce in his paunche and puffe at ech a
> worde . . .(86-7)

The satire is scathing and uninhibited. As before, once man embarks upon self-deception there can be no other issue than complete inversion of the truth:

> For now he hath dronken so depe he wil deuyne sone,
> And preuen it by her Pocalips and passioun of seynt Auereys,
> That neither bacoun ne braune, blancmangere ne mortrewes,
> Is noither fisshe ne flesshe but fode for a penaunte . . . (89-92)

The moment of debate is now prepared:

> sone this doctour,
> As rody as a rose, rubbed his chekes,
> Coughed and carped . . . (98-100)

It is time to attack, and there is a neat co-operation between Conscience and the Dreamer:

*agite penitenciam* do penance; *diu-perseuerans* long enduring (in tribulation); *mortrewes* thick soups, stews; *wombe-cloutes* tripe; *wylde braune* wild boar's flesh; *Iangle* to dispute with; *Iurdan* chamber-pot; *wombe* belly; *rather* lately; *deuyne* expound; *her Pocalips* the Apocalypse of the Gluttons (attributed Walter Map); *Auereys* perhaps referring to St. Avoya who was miraculously fed with delicate bread; *blancmangere* minced chicken; *rody* ruddy; *carped* began to speak.

> Conscience hym herde
And tolde hym of a trinite, and toward vs he loked.
'What is Dowel? sire doctour', quod I, 'is Dowel any penaunce?'
>> (100-102)

The whole scene is adroitly handled, as in the 'business' of the Doctor pondering the question while he takes a draught—

> 'Dowel?' quod this doctour, and toke the cuppe and dranke . . .
>> (103) [33]

When the Dreamer has made his scathing retort, the initiative passes to the thers:

> Thanne Conscience curteisliche a contenaunce he made,
> And preynte vpon Pacience to preie me to be stille,
> And seyde hym-self—

(the courtesy is effectively timed)—

> 'sire doctour, and it be ȝowre wille,
> What is Dowel and Dobet? ȝe deuynours knoweth'. (111-14)

We should note, too, the contrast between the Doctor's eloquence and the short thrusts that speak of Patience's utter certainty:

> bi hym that me made, miȝte neuere pouerte,
> Miseise ne myschief, ne man with his tonge,
> Colde ne care, ne compaignye of theues,
> Ne noither hete ne haille, ne non helle pouke,
> Ne noither fuire ne flode, ne fere of thine enemy
> Tene the eny tyme . . . (158-63)

The incantatory force, as of a spell, is in sharpest contrast to the Doctor's loquacity and his settled conviction that the actual is the only reality:

> 'It is but a *Dido*', quod this doctour, 'a dysoures tale
> Al the witt of this worlde and wiȝte mennes strengthe
> Can nouȝt confourmen a pees bytwene the pope and his
>> enemys,
> Ne bitwene two Cristene kynges can no wiȝte pees make,
> Profitable to ayther peple'. (172-6)

*a trinite* the threefold distinction (Dowel, Dobet, Dobest); *preynte* looked; *deuynours* expert commentators, theologians; *miseise* pain, affliction; *pouke* fiend; *fuire* fire; *tene* trouble; *Dido* an old tale (alluding to the story of Dido and Aeneas); *dysoures* story-teller's; *wiȝte* mighty; *confourmen* establish; *wiȝte* man.

The contrast is complete; and this complacent acceptance (of the world as it is) is marked by the speaker's action. With these words he 'put the table fro hym'. The question is disposed of as readily as the meal. Truly, this is one of the company Study foretold, those 'maisters' who

> dryuele at her deyse the deite to knowe,
> And gnawen god with the gorge whan her gutte is fulle. (X 56-7)

Langland's broad satirical effects are thus reinforced at need by a vivid and skilled dramatic sense, evident not only in the handling of individual figures—as, most notably, the Deadly Sins—but in his management of a whole scene. Less well known, perhaps, are those satiric effects which are mild, at times deceptively so—effects which depend not on any sweeping condemnation, but on subtle distinction. It is often distinction of a quietly humorous kind, where contrast of language serves to bespeak difference of attitude or purpose. In the present episode, as we saw in Chapter III,[34] when a rift between Conscience and Clergy is apparent, Conscience is all afire to be off on the great mission which he, unlike the Doctor, takes to be not only possible but a bounden duty. He will

> confourmen kynges to pees, and al kynnes londes,
> Sarasenes and Surre and so forth alle the Iewes,
> Turne in-to the trewe feithe and in-til one byleue. (XIII 208-10)

It is a boundless prospect; but Clergy's task is simpler. He will not seek to 'confourmen kynges' but to 'conformen fauntekynes'. What he must 'establish' lies nearer home—as does the salvation that Conscience would place upon a wide horizon. Patience is to make each man 'parfite'. The play upon 'confourmen' is prepared for by the entire simplicity with which he begins:

> 'That is soth', quod Clergy, 'I se what thow menest'.(211)

This plainness of word and phrase makes its quiet contrast not only with the more ambitious 'confourmen', but also with the resounding climax of Conscience's first assertion—'in-til one byleue'. Against the wide-ranging prospect which opens before Conscience—

> Sarasenes and Surre, and so forth alle the Iewes—

there is the steady demand upon the individual Christian

*al kynnes londes* all countries, nations; *Sarasenes* Saracens; *Surre* Syrians; *in-til* unto; *byleue* faith; *fauntekynes* infants; *soth* truth.

Tyl Pacience haue preued the and parfite the maked. (214)

Faith, like other virtues, and like Clergy's 'deuore' especially, is to begin at home. A similar simplicity of language, directed towards a like end, meets us in Spes, the bearer of an impressive commission,

> a maundement vpon the mounte of Synay,
> To reule alle rewmes with. (XVII 2-3)

But since the 'maundement' is no more—and no less—than 'a pece of an harde roche', Spes himself speaks with a disarming modesty which makes its own impression:

> For though I seye it my-self, I haue saued with this charme
> Of men and of wommen many score thousandes. (*ibid.*, 17-18)

It is perfectly credible because it is wholly unforced in tone. A Law from on high has become a touchstone of everyday life. In a similar vein are the exchanges between Mercy, Truth, Peace and Righteousness, as they await the Harrowing of Hell. Great words are to be spoken; but the prelude to them is an irrepressible scepticism. Mercy is plainly told to shut up:

> holde thi tonge, Mercy!
> It is but a trufle that thow tellest. (XVIII 146-7)

Peace, too, must be silenced—

> What, rauestow? . . . or thow art riȝt dronke! (*ibid.*, 186) —

and the language of experience is disillusioned and laconic: 'sustre, wene it neure!' The judgement on Adam and Eve is equally emphatic. They 'Shulde deye doune riȝte'; there is only one law— 'late hem chewe as thei chose'. It is against this background that the reversal of all ordinary expectation is to take place—in this setting of cynical and colloquial certainty that the words of miraculous liberation are to be heard.

This vein of realistic speech, whether quietly diffident or humorously blunt, is movingly heard in Langland's analogies from external nature:

> 'deere god', ich sayde,
> 'Wher hadden these wilde suche witt and at what scole?'
> (C XIV 169-70)

The eye that looks with a devastating candour upon the human scene

---

*deuore* duty, task; *maundement* commandment; *rewmes* realms; *trufle* (trifle) absurdity; *rauestow?* are you delirious?; *wene it neure!* don't you believe it!; *chewe* (chew) suffer; *wilde* wild creatures.

sees nothing to repudiate in the world of God's other creatures. It is the world of

> the wylde worme vnder weet erthe, (XIV 41)

a region of patient endurance, resembling that poverty which the poet honours:

> briddes and bestes that no blisse ne knoweth,
> And wilde wormes in wodes, thorw wyntres thow hem greuest...
> (*ibid.*, 111-12)

In due season happiness comes to these lowliest of creatures—

> after thow sendest hem somer, that is her souereigne Ioye
> And blisse to alle that ben bothe wilde and tame. (*ibid.*, 114-5)

There is a tenderness in this appraisal of God's Creation which itself exemplifies the truth asserted—that

> Kynde-wittede men han a cleregie by hem-selue;
> Of cloudes and of custumes thei contreuede meny thynges,
> And markede hit in here manere, and mused ther-on to knowe.
> (C XV 72-4)

Langland's own 'cleregie' in these terms, his awareness of the sky over his head and the natural world around him, is manifest at many turns. His is the eye that perceives the Mercy of God in the sun's rays on a winter's morning:

> as men may se in wyntre
> Ysekeles in eueses thorw hete of the sonne,
> Melteth in a mynut-while to myst and to watre ... (XVII 226-8)

This direct observation of God's Creation in one aspect is related immediately to another, for each is a demonstration of both the Power of God and His benevolence:

> So grace of the holygoste the grete my3te of the Trinite
> Melteth in-to mercy, to mercyable and to non other. (*ibid.*,
> 229-30)

Or, again, we understand the naturalness of growth in grace when we are reminded that, among the fruit of the apple-tree,

*cleregie* learning, knowledge; *contreuede* discovered; *ysekeles* icicles; *eueses* eaves; *mynut-while* moment (*grete my3te* is the object of *melteth*, the 'grace of the Holy Ghost' being likened to the sun); *mercyable* those who are merciful.

Tho that sitten in the sonne-syde sonner aren rype,
Swetter and saueriour and also more grettoure
Than tho that selde hauen the sonne ... (C XIX 64-6)[35]

The image of Divine radiance is as unforced as the growth it expresses. But indeed the concluding Passus of *Dowel*, where the argument has advanced from sinful man in society to the wider range of God's Creation, abounds in images of the natural order—of all that, in submission to the Divine Will 'is begotten, born, and dies'. The most moving, perhaps, is the picture of the beasts submitting to the primitive contemplatives:

there ne was lyoun ne leopart that on laundes wenten,
Noyther bere ne bor ne other best wilde,
That ne fel to her feet and fauned with the tailles. (XV 293-5)

There is a pleasing simplicity in these docile creatures; and it is fitting that the poet should find a voice for his dumb animals:

if thei couth han ycarped, by Cryst, as I trowe,
Thei wolde haue fedde that folke bifor wilde foules.
For alle the curteisie that bestes kunne thei kidde that folke ofte,
In likkyng and in lowynge there thei on laundes ȝede. (*ibid.*,
296-9)

The charm of the picture is inseparable from an innocent symbolism. Here, too, nothing is made in vain. It is the birds, and not the wild beasts, who are privileged to wait upon holiness—for a reason:

Ac god sent hem fode bi foules and by no fierse bestes,
In menynge that meke thinge mylde thinge shulde fede ... (*ibid.*,
300-1)

Langland has drawn his picture fully, down to its caption, the message implicit in the whole scene:

As who seith, religious ryȝtful men shulde fynde,
And lawful men to lyf-holy men lyflode brynge. (*ibid.*, 302-3)

## IV

This 'curteisie' of the beasts may serve to recall the poet's regard for

*sonner* sooner; *saueriour* more savoury, better-tasting; *selde* seldom; *laundes* wild (thickly wooded) country; *fauned with the tailles* wagged their tails (in their joy); *bifor wilde foules* even more willingly than the birds (fed them); *kidde* showed; *likkyng* licking; *lowynge* crouching; *ryȝtful* righteous, just; *fynde* provide for; *lyflode* sustenance.

true nobility, as we have seen it, above all, in the proud insistence upon man's kinship with Deity. Christians are gentlefolk, and the example set them is one of *gentrice*. There is thus ready to the poet's purpose a level of language which can convey refinement of feeling; and this may be employed in various ways. We have seen the *diapenidion* of useless medicament set over against the plain speaking of 'schrape' and 'mawe'. There can be no palliative physic for Envy; the only treatment is the knife. It is an exactly similar device that reveals the labouring-man grown over-delicate in time of plenty. We start with plain words for plain fare—

> May no peny-ale hem paye ne no pece of bakoun (VI 311)—

but an upstart delicacy will not be pleased unless

> it be fresch flesch other fische fryed other bake,
> And that *chaude* or *plus chaud*, for chillyng of her mawe. (*ibid.*,
> 312-3)

The finicking French words are juxtaposed with the contemptuous 'mawe'—the insensitive stomach which is the plain reality in this absurd refinement. The broad disproportion may remind us of Chaucer's parody, in his Tale of Thopas, of the *joculator* roaring his lungs out at the beginning of his 'Second Fit', to silence the hubbub which has broken out in his humble audience during the interval:

> Now holde youre mouth, *par charitee*,
> Bothe knyght and lady free . . .[36]

The absurd gentility of the foreign phrase and the plain monosyllables of 'Shut your mouth!' come together with richly comic effect; the 'knyght and lady fre' of the market-place are bullied into submission. A deadlier effect is produced when, as we saw,[37] the high-sounding foreign titles of Bishops *in partibus infidelium* are contrasted with the simple duty of all true servants of the Faith, 'to live and die'. But these satiric thrusts, very different in scope and effect as they are, are only one side of a principle of contrast which meets us at many turns.

There is the delicacy that chooses a word drawn from falconry to speak of the mystery of the Incarnation, in a passage which, in little, perfectly exemplifies a reverent courtesy. First, the note of humility is sounded in the simple monosyllables,

> a mayde that hiȝte Marye, a meke thinge with-alle. (XVI 91)

*peny-ale* common ale (at a penny a gallon); *other* or; *for* to prevent; *free* noble.

To her comes word from on high—and so an ampler language is heard:

> one Iesus, a Iustice sone, moste Iouke in her chambre,
> Tyl *plenitudo temporis* ful tyme ycomen were. (*ibid.*, 92-3)

'Iesus', 'Iustice' are titles of power; and 'Iouke' and 'chambre' are words of refinement—here, not a mere social delicacy but a nobility of spirit. The polysyllables of *plenitudo temporis* sound in confirmation of this title of true honour, completing a transformation scene from entire meekness to accepted destiny. A comparable feeling for true nobility, *gentrice*, meets us again in the young champion riding into Jerusalem. We start, as before, in unadorned simplicity; he is both like and unlike any ordinary knight:

> Barfote on an asse bakke, boteless . . .
> Wyth-oute spores other spere spakliche he loked,
> As is the kynde of a knyȝte that cometh to be dubbed,
> To geten hem gylte spores or galoches ycouped. (XVIII 11-14)

The differences are stressed not in order to set aside but to intensify awareness of a true knighthood, not to be found in externals. Faith can see beyond appearances, and therefore salutes the challenger:

> Thanne was Faith in a fenestre and cryde '*a! fili Dauid!*'
> As doth an heraude of armes whan auntrous cometh to iustes.
> (*ibid.*, 15-16)

It is a truly adventurous one who comes into the lists; and the theme of *gentrice* manifest in this work done for man, a 'condescension' in the old and honourable sense, is now affirmed:

> This Iesus of his gentrice wole Iuste in Piers armes,
> In his helm and in his haberioun, *humana natura;*
> That Cryst be nouȝt biknowe here for *consummatus deus,*
> In Piers paltok the Plowman this priker shall ryde. (*ibid.*, 22-5)

The language of knightly pursuits touches the whole passage like golden illumination. The truth is brought to a level the audience, with the poet, can directly apprehend. At the same time it loses nothing of sublimity; for here, recovered from the images of holiday and great folks' entertainment, is the primal image of chivalry itself, a code of *noblesse oblige*

---

*Iouke* rest; *plenitudo temporis* fullness of time (cf. Gal. iv 4) (For the reading here cf. p. 154, above); *spakliche* vigorous; *spores* spurs; *galoches ycouped* (elegantly) cut-away shoes; *fenestre* window; *fili Dauid* Son of David; *auntrous* challengers; *iustes* tournaments; *gentrice* nobility; *haberioun* mail-coat; *consummatus deus* Almighty God; *paltok* jacket; *priker* knight.

which, we now see, has ultimate sanction.We may recall the account of Charity given by Anima, when the identification of Plowman and Saviour had first been sounded with the words *Petrus, id est Christus*:

> charyte is goddis champioun and as a good chylde hende,
> And the meryest of mouth at mete where he sitteth.
> The loue that lith in his herte maketh hym lyȝte of speche,
> And is companable and confortatyf as Cryst bit hymselue . . .
>
> (XV 210-13)

The language here—'chylde', 'hende' is as traditional as could be ('chylde', we may note, in passing, is prompted by the 'childissh thinge' which is Anima's immediate reply to the question 'What is Charite?'); and the image of courtesy and lightness of heart at table is peculiarly that of courtly accomplishment. The longer syllables of 'companable' and 'confortatyf' fitly round out the account; for, we now see, there is nothing discordant in their being placed in apposition to the plain language of duty—to do 'as Cryst bit himselue'. The passage speaks, in Burke's phrase, 'the spirit of an exalted freedom'. Chivalry, in this understanding, bridges the common opposition of secular and divine. For once, there is no tension between plain speaking and refinement of feeling.

Langland's poetry thus draws upon a principle of contrast which, inherent in our language, is a resource of incalculable potentiality, if the writer can but employ it. Where words of native origin lie side by side with Romance adoptions there are many possibilities. The 'native' word will commonly carry the flavour of the authentic, the veritable here-and-now as against an imagined future, the real not the ideal, the particular and concrete as opposed to the abstract and the generalized. Thus, for example, it can give a sort of proverbial authority to such a statement as:

> pouerte hath but pokes to putten in his godis,
> There Auarice hath almaries and yren-bounde coffres. (XIV 245-6)

The contrast between the laconic 'pokes' and the resounding 'almaries and yren-bounde coffres' reinvests the truism. It is a technique which speaks directly to the English ear; one is reminded of Browne's being 'as content with six foot as the Moles of *Adrianus*'.[38] But in the present passage upon 'goddis champioun' we have, again, a reconciliation, an agreement upon essentials which reaches across inherent difference of

*chylde* noble youth; *hende* courteous; *lith* lies; *lyȝte* easy (not stiff or formal); *companable* agreeable; *confortatyf* encouraging; *bit* bids; *pokes* sacks; *almaries* cupboards, safes.

language. The point is important for more than one reason. Langland is
sometimes thought of as the sardonic moralist extolling the poor as against
their oppressors. One recalls Stubbs's notion of a 'strong, almost vindictive moral fervour ... the distinctive "note" of English religion;
that godliness, grim, earnest, and puritan, which was from henceforth
to exercise so deep an influence on the national character'[39]. Whatever
may be true of the national character, we see plainly that the virtue
Langland contends for is above all *amiable*. His patient poverty must
model itself on Charity, and Charity is

> As proude of a peny as of a pounde of golde,
> And is as gladde of a goune of a graye russet
> As of a tunicle of Tarse or of trye scarlet. (XV 161-3)

Similarly, Langland is sometimes thought of as the poet of a direct
and impassioned speech which owes little to sophistication. It is a point
which is of real importance to readers—and perhaps writers—of
poetry in our own day. The loose four-beat line will be misconceived
if it is thought to require a more-than-Wordsworthian plainness. The
famous lines on the Incarnation (I 146-58) exemplify the intricate but
natural relation of native and adopted word. The 'plant of Peace'

> whan it haued of this folde flesshe and blode taken,
> Was neuere leef vpon lynde li3ter ther-after,
> And portatyf and persant as the poynt of a nedle,
> That my3te non armure it lette, ne none hei3 walles.

The 'leef vpon lynde' is a natural image, expressed in native language;
but 'portatyf and persant' vary the pace and the mood. As the thought
turns from the natural and all-but-immaterial to the concrete and
particular, the work of man's hands, the language changes from native
monosyllable to adopted polysyllable. Each aspect of reality is subject to
the 'moste precious of vertues', and their co-existence, in language as in
meaning, communicates the marvellous nature of Love—a power
which neither courtly 'armure' nor the plain truth of 'hei3 walles' can
withstand.[40] There is nowhere in Langland that desire to 'augment'
plain language which R. W. Chambers rightly saw as an all-but dis-
abling characteristic of much late medieval prose-writing.[41] His poetic
speech is the direct expression of a wholeness of imagination: and in
such a mingled weave there is real hope of catching many-sided truth.
  One further characteristic of this poetic language calls for notice—

*russet* coarse woollen material; *Tarse* of Tartary (silk); *trye* finest; *folde* earth;
*lynde* lime-tree; *portatyf* light; *persant* piercing; *lette* withstand.

a power of repeated statement which comes into its own when a theme long pursued is brought to its climax. There is an interim instance in Passus X, where, though the time is not ripe for full affirmation, a distant prospect must be glimpsed before the rigours of the journey begin. Study, as though to make amends for her abrupt treatment of the Dreamer as a brash inquirer, takes him to some extent into her confidence. Theology, she says, is all but worthless; we begin to hear the repeated chime of something that lies beyond mere reasoning:

> A ful lethy thinge it were ȝif that *loue* nere.
> Ac for it let best by *Loue* I *loue* it the bettre;
> For there that *Loue* is leder ne lacked neuere grace.
> Loke thow *loue* lelly ȝif the lyketh Dowel;
> For Dobet and Dobest ben of *Loues* kynne. (X 184-8)

In these resounding lines, we reach for a moment beyond knowledge; but it is only a glimpse, at the start of a long and hard road. For a fully developed example, we may turn to those repetitions of *mesure* which in Passus XIV close the theme so long and doggedly pursued. The passage must be quoted in full:

> It is founden that fourty wynter folke lyued withouten tulyinge,
> And oute of the flynte spronge the flode that folke and bestes dronke.
> And in Elyes tyme heuene was yclosed,
> That no reyne ne rone; thus rede men in bokes,
> That many wyntres men lyueden and no mete ne tulyeden.
> Seuene slepe, as seith the boke, seuene hundreth wynter
> And lyueden with-oute lyflode, and atte laste thei woken.
> And if men lyued as *mesure* wolde, shulde neuere more be defaute
> Amonges Cristene creatures if Crystes wordes ben trewe.
> Ac vnkyndnesse *caristia* maketh amonges Crystene peple,
> And ouer-plente maketh pruyde amonges pore and riche;
> Ac *mesure* is so moche worth it may nouȝte be to dere,
> For the meschief and the meschaunce amonges men of Sodome
> Wex thorw plente of payn and of pure sleuthe;
> *Ociositas et habundancia panis peccatum turpissimum nutriuit.*
> For thei *mesured* nouȝt hem-self of that thei ete and dronke,

*lethy* empty, useless; *nere* ne + were; *let best* sets most store; *lelly* truly; *kynne* kindred, family; *founden* found (in the Scriptures); *folke* the Jews; *tulyinge* cultivating the soil; *flynte* rock; *Elyes* Elijah's; *rone* (rained) fell; *mete* food, crop; *the boke* the Golden Legend (Jacobus de Voragine); *lyflode* food; *defaute* lack; *vnkyndnesse* uncharitableness, self-seeking; *caristia* dearth, scarcity; *payn* bread, food; *sleuthe* sloth: *Ociositas* etc. 'fulness of bread, and abundance of idleness' (Ezek. xvi 49) fostered the vilest sins.

Diden dedly synne that the deuel lyked,
So vengeaunce fel vpon hem for her vyle synnes;
Thei sonken in-to helle tho citees vchone.
For-thi *mesure* we vs wel and make owre faithe owre scheltroun,
And thorw faith cometh contricioun, conscience wote wel,
Whiche dryueth awey dedly synne and doth it to be venial. (XIV
                                                        63-83)

In such a passage we reach from earth to heaven. Like some Perpendi-
cular tower it is rooted in the fields of daily labour but springs straight
and true to the sky; and the insistent *mesure* is perhaps like that richness
of the final stage which is the common characteristic of such architecture. Its function in the poem is comparable. However high we
aspire, the last reach of mind and eye returns us to homely things—
here to the undeviating sense that sin is to be wrestled with and overcome in the world we still inhabit. As such, it is both like and unlike
the ending of Chaucer's *Troilus and Criseyde*. There, in the first flight
of exaltation above middle earth the eye is directed downwards with
the repeated refrains—

> Swich *fyn* hath, lo, this Troilus for love!
> Swich *fyn* hath al his grete worthynesse! . . .

and so on, answered in its turn by the more solemn notes

> *Lo here*, of payens corsed olde rites,
> *Lo here*, what alle hire goddes may availle . . .

This order of construction, in Chaucer and Langland alike, may remind
us of late medieval architecture, especially perhaps in those terms which
one writer employs in praise of 'the finest tower of the Middle Ages',
as owing so much of its effect to 'the contrast between the richness of
its upper stage and the massive severity of its base'. The same principle,
he observes, is evident in 'every noble spire', where

> the crocketed shaft and fretted pinnacles and traceried flying
> buttresses spring from a tower that suggests the contrasting
> beauty of simple strength.[42]

Chaucer's is truly, in these terms, a spire. After the last look at earth,
our gaze begins to travel upward—from the figure-sculpture of

> that sothefast Crist, that starf on rode;

*tho* those; *vchone* each one; *scheltroun* strong defence; *Swich fyn* such an ending;
*corsed* accursed; *sothefast* true; *starf* died; *rode* Cross.

to the summit and beyond it, to be lost in the dizzying conception of
infinity:

> Thow oon, and two, and thre, eterne on lyve,
> That regnest ay in thre, and two, and oon,
> Uncircumscript, and al maist circumscrive...[43]

At the top of Langland's structure the repeated *mesure*, like some grouping
of identical pinnacles, closes the vista, returning us to a sense of the very
nature and function of the building. It is a tower which Langland has
reared, to speak of the strong-point which faith must be. We are to
'make owre faithe owre scheltroun'. Each poet builds well for his own
purpose. Chaucer must take us to a point far above the middle-earth of
man, for it is in that world and its brittle values that his story has been
placed from beginning to end. Langland's design is a meeting of earth
and heaven, alike in the perfected work of the Incarnation and in the
work still to be done in the life of each Christian. He must bring the
eye finally to rest upon the ground. His truth is not a subject for exalted
contemplation merely; and while it will most assuredly prevail in the
end, the hour of its triumph is not yet.

## V

What then are the great gifts of Langland? We shall go endlessly
astray if we conceive the vigour and directness of his speech as somehow
accidentally thrown up by his driving purpose, lacking the essential
characteristics of art. A very sound judge of medieval English verse
once spoke of *Piers Plowman*'s 'comparative lack of art'; and we may
gladly accept this characterization if by it is meant an absence of that
elaboration of diction and metrical pattern which, whether for better
(as in *Pearl* or *Sir Gawain*) or for worse (as in much of the 'Revival'
work) meet us elsewhere. But if we take this as evidence that the poem
'was intended for a public less literary and less critical than that for
which *Sir Gawain* was written'[44] then we are in danger of pre-judging
the worth of Langland's work. For this is to assume that 'the poetic'
is to be equated with the highly wrought, the work of 'polish' which,
as the critic noted, *Piers Plowman* evidently is not. In fact there remains
for our judgement the view that Langland's distinctive achievement is
to make poetry of speech, not by poeticizing but rather, one would
say, by *assembling* language—language considered not primarily for
its diction or its capacity for adept manipulation, but language as phrase,
and thus language in one way as unalterable as the fall of a phrase is

*on lyve* living; *Uncircumscript* unbounded.

unalterable. It is here we meet the real significance of the 'prosody' of the four-beat alliterative line. We are justified in speaking of the freedom and variety of Langland's poetical instrument; but in one way it is an instrument of strict limitation. There can be no juggling within the phrase, and thus no scope for those skills of inversion and transposition which can contribute markedly to our pleasure in the foot-counted line. This medieval poetry, least of any, can be fitted into a measured framework to yield the

> stretched metre of an antique song.

There is, we have seen, no question of that 'musical delight' which consists 'only in apt numbers, fit quantity of syllables, and the sense variously drawn out from one verse into another'.[45] We should note, too, that there is equally no question of single verbal effects of decisive importance, deftly positioned for the reader's delight,

> All the charm of all the Muses often flowering in a lonely word.

The 'prosody' of Langland does not allow patterned diction; but it is unalterably based in language as speech. This primacy of the phrase has implications for the editor in search of a true text, and these are touched upon in the Appendix.[46] Some of the poet's most striking turns of speech are considered in what follows.

Langland's is emphatically a poetry to be read aloud—and, at that, stated, not intoned—if the poet is to be given his own drive and emphasis. *Piers Plowman* is thus capable of effects which are hardly to be matched for sheer simplicity outside the later blank verse of Shakespeare. We have a Dreamer who can ask of the blood-stained Plowman, in Passus XIX, 'who paynted hym so rede?' He is the Dreamer whose thoughts clamour for utterance, 'thouȝtes a threve'; one who prompts the profound question concerning Incarnate Deity, 'What *dones* man was Iesus?'; who reports that the Magi were 'the hexte lettred oute'; who tells us, of God being born into a world of good and evil, 'Creatour wex creature to knowe what was bothe'; who comes upon us with no greater rhetoric than the opening, 'Why I move this mater is most for the pore'—this is the poet who, in Lowell's phrase, 'gets inside our guard with the home-thrust of a forthright word'.[47] But these are not isolated effects, 'salient lines', as Lowell would have it; they are the direct expression of a whole capacity for truth-telling. Where else do we find a steady refusal to accept all proximate solution, all easy distinction that promises finality but withholds the prospect of perfection? In the Dreamer's long search

*rede* red; *threve* bundle; *What dones* of what kind, make; *hexte* highest.

there is a full warrant for the elegiac beauty of Ymagynatyf's taking stock:

> how fele fernȝeres are faren and so fewe to come! (XII 5)

This is the kind of penetrating tenderness in which the native tradition of an unforced speech is unexcelled. The long line, complete in itself, owing nothing to end-rime or mere syntactical link with what precedes or follows, perfectly communicates at one and the same time the length of years and the absence of definitive purpose. Skeat thought Langland's line on sleep—

> The which vnknitteth al kare and comsyng is of reste(XVIII 213)—

superior to Macbeth's 'ravell'd sleeve of care'. There is little profit in comparing isolated lines; but it may be noted that the run up to the first stressed syllable ('The which vnknítteth ...') carries its own suggestion of continuing energy and unrest. The half-line that follows relaxes the tension; we are upon the threshold of sleep.

This characteristic structure of the line, in which the phrase is the indivisible unit, is well suited to the kind of argument Langland has to pursue, the movement between the twin courts of appeal, doctrine and practice; and this we may follow in detail in the next section. It is also peculiarly fitted to some of his characteristic preoccupations and turns of thought, the approaches he naturally makes to his subject and the distinctive vantage-points he adopts upon it. The rhythms of Langland's poem are responsive to the varying pace and intensity of his thought. Thus, Ymagynatyf's lament for the wasted years very well exemplifies the prophetic sense of time as indivisible. The fact that a day of reckoning cannot be indefinitely postponed takes us beyond an interim present. Any point in time may lead back to the original purposes of God and forward to their inevitable fulfilment—the long range, as I have called it, of Langland's mind.[48] It invests with grim authority his warning notes:

> Lo, lordes, lo, and ladies, taketh hede (C XIII 219, Russell)—

and the accents caught from the tradition of preaching

> Thise ben the braunches, beth war ...
> ȝe lordes and ladyes ... (XIII 421-2)—

which merge with a more personal and unwaveringly direct note as the message is brought home to his immediate audience: 'For-thi I rede

*fele* many; *fernȝeres* 'old' years, past years; *faren* gone.

ȝow riche . . .' (*ibid.*, 442). He has, too, an incantatory, spell-binding power at need:

> miȝte neuere pouerte,
> Miseise, ne myschief, ne man with his tonge,
> Colde, ne care, ne compaignye of theues,
> Ne noither hete, ne haille, ne non helle pouke,
> Ne noither fuire ne flode, ne fere of thin enemy
> Tene the eny tyme, and thow take it with the;
> *Caritas nichil timet.* (XIII 158-63)

Here the succession of measured phrases gives to each terror distinct shape; but all are made harmless in the last line, where we start with the stressed syllable ('Téne the . . .') to break the rhythm and undo the spell. A different rhythm of prophecy is heard in Conscience's wry comment on the remoteness of millennial peace:

> er this fortune falle, fynde men shal the worste,
> By syx sonnes and a schippe and half a shef of arwes;
> And the myddel of a mone shal make the Iewes to torne,
> And saracenes for that siȝte shulle synge *gloria in excelsis, &c.*,
> For Makomet and Mede myshappe shal that tyme;
> For, *melius est bonum nomen quam diuicie multe.* (III 323-7)

The 'scansion' is ostensibly similar, a recitative-pattern introduced in each line by two or more unstressed or lightly-stressed syllables ('ne noither héte' answering, by and large, to 'And the mýddel'). But the portents are made unreal, each dragged in by the heels ('and' . . . 'and' . . . 'and') so that there can be no conclusive last line, the succession of 'ands' being completed by the weak 'For'.

There is, again, a prophetic vein when the worldly ecclesiastic is brought into view. But this time it is a dark certainty that closes in upon the brief day granted to insolence. We start with the brilliant vignette of affronted dignity:

> A priker on a palfray fro manere to manere
> An heep of houndes at his ers as he a lorde were.
> And but if his knaue knele that shal his cuppe brynge,
> He loureth on hym and lakketh, who lered hym curteisye?
> (X 308-11)[49]

*miseise* affliction; *helle pouke* demon from hell; *fuire* fire; *Tene* distress; *and* provided that; *Caritas* etc. 'There is no fear in love' (I John iv 18); *the myddel of a mone* a full moon; *torne* be converted; *myshappe* come to grief; *melius est* etc. 'A good name is rather to be chosen than great riches' (Prov. xxii 1); *priker* horseman (perhaps with ironic overtone of 'knight'); *palfray* nag; *loureth* scowls; *lakketh* asks reprovingly.

It is the very face and voice of outraged *hauteur*. But the brief moment of humiliation is not all that is in store for arrogance. Those professed religious who do not care

> though it reyne on here auteres *(ibid.,* 313*)*

are seen against a background of reckoning: and here the verse is, like time itself, and the rain to come, regular, emphatic and unyielding. The initial 'And' of each line may be contrasted with the rhythm of Conscience's utterance. Now it is an itemising of each successive stroke, until it seems there is no end to the disasters. The 'wound' is, we may feel, 'incurable':

> Ac there shal come a kyng and confesse 30w religiouses,
> And bete 30w, as the bible telleth, for brekynge of 30wre reule,
> And amende monyales, monkes and chanouns,
> And putten hem to her penaunce *ad pristinum statum ire,*
> And barounes with erles, beten hem thorugh *beatus-virres*
>      techynge,
> That here barnes claymen and blame 30w foule:
>      *Hij in curribus et hij in equis; ipsi obligati sunt, &c.,*
> And thanne freres in here freitoure shal fynden a keye
> Of Costantynes coffres in which is the catel
> That Gregories god-children han yuel dispended.
> And thanne shal the abbot of Abyndoun and alle his issu for
>      euere
> Haue a knokke of a kynge, and incurable the wounde. (*ibid,*
>      317-27)

This most famous of prophetic passages has a measured finality un-equalled elsewhere in the poem. We may notice, too, the grim humour which accompanies the sentence of doom. The 'religious' are to be 'confessed' and put to 'penance' by this most drastic of means—for, the implication is clear, no other will serve. Here, as always in Langland, final truth is inseparable from a law which is to be obeyed whether man so chooses or not.

*auteres* altars; *monyales* nuns; *ad pristinum* etc. to return to their original state (of obedience to monastic rule); *beatus-virres techynge* the teaching of the First Psalm ('Blessed is the man . . .'); *barnes* children; *claymen* cry out; *blame . . . foule* revile; *Hii in curribus* etc. 'Some trust in chariots, and some in horses . . . They are brought down and fallen' (Ps. xx 7-8); *freres* friars; *freitoure* refectory; *Costantynes coffres* the endowment of Constantine; *catel* property, wealth; *Gregories god-children* monks (founded by St. Augustine in his mission appointed by Gregory the Great); *Abyndoun* Abingdon Abbey, outstandingly representative of monastic wealth and power.

Similarly emphatic and unyielding, but this time lengthened to accommodate extra stresses, are the lines that speak of the Crucified One's death:

The lorde of lyf and of liȝte tho leyed his eyen togideres.
The daye for drede with-drowe and derke bicam the sonne,
The wal wagged and clef and al the worlde quaued. (XVIII 59-61)

The regular balance of the clauses, each half-line beginning with a stress after an initial unstressed syllable, marks the solemnity of the occasion. Similarly weighted—that is, with three stresses—is the proud title of the Light that draws upon Lucifer with irresistible force. First, the challenge and brief reply—

'What lorde artow?' quod Lucifer, '*quis est iste?*'
'*Rex glorie*', the liȝte sone seide (*ibid.*, 314-5)—

then the full expansion of the title—

'And lorde of myȝte and of mayne and al manere vertues;
                    *dominus virtutum*'—

and so to the final word of authority:

'Dukes of this dym place anon vndo this ȝates,
That Cryst may come in, the kynges sone of heuene.'
And with that breth, helle brake with Beliales barres. (*ibid.*, 316-9)

Once again, the rise to the stressed syllable ('And with that bréth') momentarily suspends the action; then with redoubled speed, it seems, all is over. Langland's sense of certainty, the inevitability of final victory over evil, prompts both his prophetic power and his vivid scorn, in all its range from outright comedy to searing condemnation. It is Law that is his strongest awareness—Law as finally inviolable. The Law which, the Dreamer at last perceives, has been once and for all fulfilled, is not on that account to be set aside. On the Christian there presses not the lesser but the greater obligation. The range of Langland's creative imagining is therefore from full and explicit statement of the Divine Power and design to the sharply enigmatic and double-edged utterances that perplex man at every turn. Our last task in this chapter must be to seek the actual shape of Langland's discourse—his characteristic modes of inquiry and, above all, the kind of 'proof' his poem constitutes.

*leyed his eyen togideres* closed his eyes; *derke* dark; *wagged* rocked; *clef* split; *quaued* shook; *quis est* etc. adapted from 'Who is this King of glory? The Lord strong and mighty . . .' (Ps. xxiv 8); *sone* (soon) at once; *mayne* power.

## VI

Langland's is the great medieval subject—the relationship of *auc-toritee* and *pref*, what man must believe and what he may see and experience for himself. Against all considerations which the authoritative persons of the *Vita* would urge—and we see that they have reason for doing so, as we watch him become fatally engrossed in speculation—the Dreamer persists with his great question, Where will he *find* Dowel? To understand the tension between 'authority' and 'experience' in this poem we may glance briefly at Langland's contemporaries. The effect on the characterization of the Dreamer is discussed in the last chapter.[50]

We may recall the innocent-eyed scepticism of Chaucer in the Prologue to *The Legend of Good Women*. There are some things that we must believe upon authority, for there can be no direct experience of them in this life. It is so with heaven and hell; and, the implication runs, it may be so with the goodness of women:

> Wel oughte us thanne on olde bokes leve,
> There as there is non other assay by preve.[51]

Thus the God of Love's confidence in those authorities the errant poet should read is alas! ill-founded. The jest is not the simple one that the God is ignorant of the books he confidently lists—

> in alle thy bokes ne coudest thow nat fynde
> Som story of wemen that were goode and trewe? . . .
> What seith Valerye, Titus, or Claudyan?
> What seith Jerome agayns Jovynyan? . . .[52]

Certainly, knowledge of the titles rather than the contents is implied; and this is altogether, and happily, appropriate to the relation between man of affairs and poet dependent upon books. But the real irony is that the God of Love, like any other defender of women's reputation, has no choice but to use weapons which may be double-edged. Jerome can be used for examples of chastity, as in the Franklin's Tale; but he can also be found on the other side of the argument, as in the Wife of Bath's Prologue and the Merchant's Tale. So, too, 'Valerye'—whom I take to be Walter Map—admits the praise due to Penelope, Lucretia and the Sabine women; but he must continue with the wry theme, where will you find virtue nowadays? The *Romance of the Rose*, above all, we may remember, from one point of view Love's Bible, is from another indignantly repudiated by the God as 'an heresye ageyns my

*leve* believe; *assay* way of testing; *preve* direct experience.

lawe'. In sum, it is highly appropriate to Chaucer's design that the books cited in defence of female virtue should all agree that there is, or at least ought to be, such a thing—but that in some of them the authors should look in vain for virtue in the women of actuality. The authorities thus reveal, wittingly or not, a discrepancy between the real and the ideal. The poet's 'penance' is to write with the utmost skill in somewhat the same mode, so that a vein of polite incredulity is elaborately over-borne by deference to 'the books'.

What is smilingly conveyed at the outset of *The Legend of Good Women* is an unwillingness to believe upon authority what can be tested by experience. What is revealed in *Troilus and Criseyde* is the foundation of pity in a complementary scepticism. 'The books' tell us of Criseyde's guilt; and Pandarus will come to hate (it is his own word) Criseyde. But their creator does not find it so easy a matter to pronounce judgement:

> Ne me ne list this sely womman chyde
> Forther than the storye wol devyse.
> Hire name, allas! is punysshed so wide,
> That for hire gilt it oughte ynough suffise.[53]

I have elsewhere suggested that the humour of the Dreamer as a wholly doctrinaire servant of love, gravely counselling a Knight who has known and lost the heaven of fulfilled love, is the essential foundation of pathos in *The Book of the Duchess*.[54] We may remember, too, the remarkable ending of the *Confessio Amantis*, where reality breaks in upon the devout pupil, and knowing himself now too old for love he must make his way 'homward'.[55]

Langland's, then, is the common subject for discourse in fourteenth century vision-poetry; and in this need to set the opposing claims of doctrine and experience we have the main reason why the progress of his poem cannot be linear, consecutive, moving by cumulative steps of argument to a comprehensive solution. His Passus are not equal paces, nor is each necessarily a direct advance upon its predecessor. His progress is cyclic and repetitive, cumulative not by force of any steadily developing argument but by the increasing weight of experience, and this largely the experience of failure. The movement of the poet's mind is therefore more like the motion of his own man in the 'wagging' boat (VIII 50ff.) than the steady progress along a clearly-defined road which the Plowman confidently pointed out to the pilgrims of the *Visio* (V 568 ff.). In this Langland is suited not only by the flexibility of Passus-length,

*sely* 'poor'; *punysshed* reprobated; *gilt* guilt, offence.

where there is no external constraint to vary from as much or as little
as the immediate topic or episode warrants, but also by the nature of his
four-beat line, with its essential constituent of two half-lines complete
in themselves as to sense. Balance is almost posited by the form
itself, whether it be a balance of thesis and antithesis or of statement and
qualification. The line makes no compulsion to link thought with
thought in strictest sequence. Rather, it allows the poet to scan the
subject, turning from one aspect to another—each an aspect that will
not readily be subordinated to others; thus separately, and in little,
each is a 'finding'. Lest this be thought all nature and no art, we should
remind ourselves that the most marked characteristic—and decided
limitation—of the Middle English as against the Old English 'classical'
verse-line is that it is 'much more often self-contained, a single line
usually expressing a complete sense unit'.[56] The flexibility of Langland's
instrument is a distinctive achievement which cannot be readily paralleled.
The whole mode of inquiry, most strikingly evident in the *Vita de Dowel*,
is thus *toto caelo* different from Drydenian argument. It is not merely
that the progress of the 'thought' is unsystematic, digressive in the
highest degree, and finally inconclusive. In these terms, to be sure, there
is a primary distinction to be made between one kind of 'poet of ideas'
and another. Professor C. S. Lewis puts that distinction well in his
account of Daniel, a poet who

> actually thinks in verse: thinks deeply, arduously, and perhaps
> with some originality. This is something quite different from Dryden's
> power of neatly poetizing all the stock arguments for the side on
> which he is briefed. Dryden states: Daniel can doubt and wrestle.[57]

The distinction is radical; Langland, too, is one who can doubt and
wrestle. But we must go on to observe that though his intellectual
problems are not finally solved, the end of the Dreamer's search is not
a 'conclusion in which nothing is concluded'. In this kind of 'poetry
of ideas', authority and experience are so interlocked that not all the
argument in the world will answer man's deepest need. The Dreamer
must be brought to know himself; then—and not before then—can
revelation supervene on argument.

This is, perhaps, unpromising enough for any ordinary kind of
development. But there is yet another difference. *Piers Plowman* is
not merely an extended instance of argument failing and revelation
taking over to end the matter. We must above all notice that, in the
end, the question asked at the outset is put not with diminished but with
heightened force. What the argument demanded was what all experience

declared impossible—nothing less than perfect fulfilment of Law.
When this is in fact revealed, then we return to experience, to seek once
more the proof of religion in men's lives. That the Law has been fulfilled
means that no half-measures will serve. Thus there is condemned a
world of evasion and hypocrisy, with its 'pardons for pence', the realm
of Lady Meed. But the fulfilment of Law also means that, each according to his capacity, Christians must aspire to perfection: and this,
we finally see, is to be done in a world which has not abated its wicked
ways, for all the disapproval in which it has been progressively held.
We thus have a design in which circuitousness is an essential principle;
for all things here return to their beginning. It is a circuitousness which,
we may thankfully observe, owes nothing to the 'gratuitous poeticism'[58]
of 'Alliterative Revival' language. Langland is diffuse, sometimes
obscure, and not infrequently repetitive, because his matter is complex,
ambiguous, peculiarly unsusceptible to definition. From one point of
view, repetition, plain similarity of widely separated incident or significance, plays the largest part, We have the virtual identity of beginning
and end in a world of self-interested humanity. Even the 'Brytonere'
of Passus VI is evenly matched with the 'brewere' of Unity, as are
the wheedling tones of the Friar at the end with those of the beggars
in the half-acre. There is, again, the persistence of the world of 'active
life' as we see it at the beginning and end, revealed, too, in its confessed
inadequacies in the middle, Haukyn's account of his life (XIII 224 ff.).
Thus there is, at times, as we have seen, a striking 'proleptic' power in
the poet—as, for example, in Holy Church's counsel against over-ardent
inquiry delivered to a Dreamer who is, so far, patient, if fond of putting
over-large questions; in the warning by Study against those clerics who
'dryuele at her deyse the deite to knowe', delivered long before we meet
the greedy theologian of the dinner-table; and, too, in the assurance
given to a Dreamer that

Ymaginatyf her-afterward shal answere to ȝowre purpos. (X 115)

Less explicit, but not less moving in their effect, are those adumbra-
tions of theme which Professor Coghill has likened to musical composition, the skill

> to sound a theme or the fragment of a theme among the other
> music of his thoughts, and then, later, and after the reader has for-
> gotten it in other interests, to return to it in strength.[59]

In the whole traverse of the journey, the reader will both see, far off,

*purpos* proposition, question.

the land that awaits him; and he will at other times know that he stands
where he stood before. But at other times again, there are swift surprises.
The whole discussion veers sharply, there are striking irruptions and
apparent dead-ends, where no course is open but to retrace our steps.
These events when they occur come with an uncovenanted force;
and at two of the great turning-points, the end of Meed's trial and
Truth's approval of work in the half-acre, they come with a paradoxical
and riddling effect. In this they are wholly consonant with the tension
in which all is held—between Law and Mercy, between man as agent
of his salvation and man as patient of the Divine Will, between what is
contractually required of man and what is possible at the limit of his
capacity. The poet's strongest impulse is to be 'instant' in the apostle's
sense, unwearied in pressing the point of practice. What his Dreamer
must learn is that the first relevance of doctrine is to the individual
soul, the first movement towards true understanding that which issues
in right action. A world man readily condemns is a world he is in danger
of wholly removing from reference to himself. But the observer cannot
disclaim his part in the general scene.

There is thus a penetrating truth in the circuitous discourse of *Piers
Plowman*. Its origin as method is in that dialectic which is the natural
disposition of the medieval mind; but its implications are in no way
peculiar to one age. 'Nature', we are reminded in *King Lear*, 'needs
more than reason gives'. In Shakespeare's tragedy we see disaster proceeding from a rigid sense of covenant, the 'bond' between parent and
child interpreted strictly, as is 'reason's' way. Cordelia stands within, or
if we will, upon, her rights: filial duty will not reach out to Lear in
his unreason, his insistence upon going beyond the bounds of any right
or propriety. Does not a comparable theme—with whatever great
differences of execution—constitute the central imaginative authority of
*Piers Plowman*? We ask for the Law—on others; just as we seek, again
in others, nothing less than Perfection, our own state being wholly
immune from examination. And the way out of this *impasse* is something we must be brought to, for we are incapable of finding it ourselves.
In the end of both Shakespeare's tragedy and Langland's dream-poem,
when all illusion is put away, there is one thing to be done: a beginning
again. For if a heavenly perfection is glimpsed—a sacrifice on which
'The gods themselves throw incense'—an earthly society must still
continue on its way. In the medieval poem at all events there is for once
no palinode. The question with which the Dreamer began is the right
question. Authority has had its say; the Dreamer has learned much by

experience and much about himself, above all. But, the more clearly, the pursuit is still on.

In Langland's undertaking it is above all necessary that we should not have versified philosophy or theology, but that we should share in the very process by which his Dreamer is brought to know the truth. We need not, of course, suppose that what Langland recounts is necessarily the shape or sequence of his own progress towards understanding. But we can thankfully admit that where the general run of ratiocinative poetry may fail of application to our own lives by its very neatness, Langland's work is surer of entry. In this understanding we may apply to Langland Lowell's praise of Bunyan; it is truly 'the secret of his power' that

> while the representation of what *may* happen to all men comes home to none of us in particular, the story of any one man's real experience finds its startling parallel in that of every one of us.[60]

The Dreamer, however he may stand in relation to the author, is that one man whose experience we follow. Thus, the mere sequence of thought is not the whole truth; the Dreamer's failures and false conclusions, as we have seen, are no less important than his true inferences and unshakeable assertions. The heroic couplet, we may agree with Dryden,[61] is 'nearest Nature' if the highest expression of man's nature is the ratiocinative faculty. For a discourse which is directly and wholly ratiocinative, proceeding from axiom to conclusion, employing a fund of apt illustration and analogy, and pithily summing up successive stages of the argument—for this, Dryden chose well. But the greater fluidity of blank verse is essential to both a Thomson and a Wordsworth when the less predictable movements of imagination are to be spoken of. We may see that if the argument of a poem is to convey something of the limitations of argument itself, it must be a record of ideas impetuously caught up and points pursued beyond their immediate frame of reference. In that respect it will be more like the process of thinking, of following the argument whither it may lead, and less like thought in its logical sequence, which in a work of imagination may come to feel uncomfortably like wisdom after the event. For this purpose the loose four-beat alliterative line may be an instrument truer than any to the artist's hand, responsive not only to the varying play of thought (and a continuing sense of paradox), but also, and cumulatively, to the stubborn nature of experience if man would seek merely to argue his way to an entire and final truth.

## VII

In the twentieth century, the movement away from syllabic regularity has been towards re-establishing a prosody in which speech-rhythm is the all-important element and the phrase thus the essential unit of 'time'. There is of course no escaping 'form', of one kind or another; 'only a bad poet', as Eliot has said, 'could welcome free verse as a liberation from form'. In the modern situation, the study of music may help the poet; for 'the properties in which music concerns the poet most nearly are the sense of rhythm and the sense of structure'; and rhythm is of decisive importance:

> I know that a poem, or a passage of a poem, may tend to realize itself first as a particular rhythm before it reaches expression in words, and that this rhythm may bring to birth the idea and the image.[62]

Eliot added—surely rightly—that he did not believe that this was an experience peculiar to himself. This was said in 1942, the year in which *Four Quartets* was completed by the appearance of *Little Gidding*. It is a telling instance; for in *Four Quartets* 'rhythm' in the narrower sense, the constituent principle of the verse-line, is a speech-rhythm—whether meditative and withdrawn, suddenly passionate, or solemn and affirmatory—as rhythm in a wider meaning, the recurrence of certain themes, has become the 'sense of structure' which informs the whole work. From this characteristically modern poem we may conclude that where cumulative argument is not the poet's aim, what is wanted is not an instrument fitted for discourse in Dryden's sense but an instrument fittest for truth-telling, responsive before all else to the only 'law of nature'—'that poetry must not stray too far from the ordinary everyday language which we use and hear'.[63] Yeats put the same point differently when comparing poetry with that 'modern speech of the stage where only those words which affect the situation are important'. There can be no resting in the foot-counted line, however varied; for in syllabic verse, as Yeats went on to observe, 'all syllables are important'.[64] The traditional suitability of syllabic verse for extended argument is thus not superficial. By its nature it exemplifies the very qualities of steady exposition—the ordered progress of an argument sustained by wit or passion and varied in pace as in mood. By the same token, the line based in speech-rhythm is especially suited for unforced and individual communication of those truths which the poet must explore rather than affirm. Langland's four-beat line is a relatively simple instrument. But its range and variety will never be understood if it is approached with the prejudice that it is inherently limited, a distant and deservedly poor relation of the real thing. It is perhaps the deepest charge against a strongly ratiocinative poetry that it may win attention to its argument at the expense of a truly individual awareness on the reader's part. As the phenomenologists have re-discovered, 'when one is inside an event, one is not thinking of it. One can live or tell; not both at once.'[65] The account interposes between the reader and direct experience. In this sense, the feelings it arouses, whether of agreement or difference, may be artificial; and the real and lasting objection to a 'poetry which excites us to artificial feelings' is that it 'makes us callous to real ones'.[66]

Such poetry as Langland's is thus peculiarly hard to parallel. It is certainly unlike both bad 'Revival' work and those highly-wrought achievements in the alliterative tradition of which *Pearl* and *Sir Gawain* are the best examples: and this unlikeness pertains both to its characteristic modes of expression and to its major design. The design has, of course, this much in common with other medieval poetry of a non-lyric kind—its development is wholly distinct from that linear, consecutive progress which is the natural predisposition of the modern mind. If we are to do justice to *Piers Plowman*, as to any extended medieval poem, we must try to rid ourselves of the preconception which would give to the word 'digression' a merely pejorative flavour. With Chaucer as with Langland (as, too, in our approach to Gower, if we are to appreciate those qualities of *ordonnance* which constitute his originality) we must learn to respond to a design which can be concentric rather than linear. Here parallels from other art-forms may help—as, the common traditions of medieval tapestry, with its innocence of perspective and thus its criterion of nearness to the spectator as denoting relevance; or, more strikingly, the turning-point recorded for ever in Giotto's frescoes, where pictorial art makes its first fruitful encounter with a measured rhythm. The architectural harmony of the Upper Church of Assisi

> is not immaterial like that of the Sainte-Chapelle in Paris, with its heaven-aspiring rhythms and shimmering light; it unfolds itself in space, in depth. Its rhythm is measured, set by the wide bays whose orderly recession towards the haze of light at the far end of the church creates an evenly-distributed space.[67]

The contrast between Cimabue's thronging and apocalyptic figures and Giotto's spaced and balanced compositions marks the essential difference between two orders of artistic vision. On the one side, there stands the work of creative imagination as 'a thing made', having a beginning, middle and end, and thus in return for order demonstrating essential properties of relationship. Here we have pictorial and architectural works that offer themselves to every beholder, as we have a poetry of clear narrative or ratiocinative structure, responding to the measured rhythms, the 'evenly-distributed space', of the foot-counted line. On the other side, we have an insistent awareness of the real in all its intractable force; so that there may coexist in the work of art both a formidable simplicity of main design and a degree of minor graphic representation in which the eye loses itself in detail. It is to this kind that *Piers Plowman* belongs, and it is in this respect that Langland makes most demand (much more than Chaucer or Gower) upon our capacity for attending to the whole design. The critical tradition has been largely concerned with now this aspect of its detail, now another. But the fundamental characteristic of work of this kind is that it can make no *intermediate* offering of itself to the beholder. It has no narrative or ratiocinative content which, while confessedly less than the whole, is yet fairly representative of that whole. We must attend not merely to the sum of its arguments but to their varying force and distinctive quality in the Dreamer's experience. In the end, the poem will have entirely missed its mark unless we, with the Dreamer, are forced, in the words of a modern allegorist, 'not to propound, but to live through, a sort of ontological proof'.[68]

## Notes

1. *Cf.* 'The poets of Elizabeth had attained an art of modulation which was afterwards neglected or forgotten' (Life of Waller in Johnson's *Lives of the English Poets*). The sentence follows the praise of Waller as excelling 'in smoothness most of the writers who were living when his poetry commenced'. 'Modulation' is thus a principle of harmonious relation between speech and metrical base.
2. For a recent demonstration that 'The notion of the foot is essential to the full experiencing of the English ten-syllabled line as traditionally written and read', see M. Whiteley, 'Verse and its Feet', *Review of English Studies*, N.S. ix (1958), 268-79, and subsequent correspondence (*ibid.*, xxxx (1959), 292-3; xi(1960), 191-2; *ibid.*, 305).
3. 'An Essay on the Language and Versification of Chaucer', prefaced to *The Canterbury Tales of Chaucer*, Oxford, 1798, I 62, n. 73.
4. *Essays*, ed. W. P. Ker, Oxford, 1900, I 101.
5. They are to be seen at their best among Sidney's Arcadian poems (*cf.* C. S. Lewis, *English Literature in the Sixteenth Century*, Oxford, 1954, p. 327).

6. As Ascham remarks, to 'observe just number, and even feet' is not enough; unless the feet are 'distinct by true qualities of syllables' they will be useless—'feet without joints' ('Of Imitation', *Elizabethan Critical Essays*, ed. Gregory Smith, London, 1904, I 32).

7. Quoted by James Beattie, *Dissertations Moral and Critical*, London, 1783, p. 292.

8. *Accentual Symmetry in Vergil*, Oxford, 1950, pp. 19-20.

9. *The Classical Tradition in Poetry*, London, 1927, p. 84.

10 . . . *non, ut pueri in scholis, ad singulorum pedum initia . . . sed ad rhythmum totius uersus* (quoted in Jackson Knight, *op. cit.*, p. 88).

11. 'They fle from me that sometyme did me seke' (*Collected Poems of* Sir *Thomas Wyatt*, ed. Muir, London, 1949, p. 28).

12. *English Literature in the Sixteenth Century*, pp. 225-6.

13. *History of French Versification*, Oxford, 1903, p. 306.

14. 'Certayne Notes of Instruction' (*Elizabethan Critical Essays*, I 50).

15. *An Apology for Smectymnuus* (*Prose Works*, ed. St. John, London, 1848, III 140).

16. C. S. Lewis, *The Allegory of Love*, Oxford, 1936, p. 239.

17. *Canterbury Tales*, B 2000-3.

18. Lewis, *The Allegory of Love*, p. 159.

19. Derek Traversi, 'Langland's *Piers Plowman*' in *The Age of Chaucer*, London (Penguin Books) 1954, p. 134.

20. Peter Viereck, 'The Poet in the Machine Age', appended to *Strike through the Mask!*, New York, 1950.

21. W. Amphlett, *The Triumphs of War*, London, 1796.

22. J. A. Burrow, 'The Audience of *Piers Plowman*', *Anglia*, LXXV (1957), 373-84.

23. Appendix to *Lyrical Ballads* (1802) (*Wordsworth's Literary Criticism*, ed. Smith, London, 1925, p. 43).

24. As listed in J. P. Oakden, *Alliterative Poetry in Middle English*, Manchester, 1935, p. 175.

25. *loc. cit.*, 379. To the evidence of *Piers Plowman* circulating, along with short didactic treatises, among the clergy, may be added the bequest by Walter de Brugge to John Wormynton (1396) of 'a book called *Piers Plowman* and another book called *Pars Oculi*, with other tracts in one volume'. (Mr. E. St. John Brooks, in his interesting article on 'The *Piers Plowman* Manuscripts in Trinity College, Dublin', *The Library* VI, 3-4, Dec. 1951, points out that this MS cannot, as Mr Oscar Cargill believed, be that containing the famous memorandum on Langland's parentage—Trin. Coll. Dub. MS D. 4. 1; see p.    above.)

26. Burrow, *loc. cit.*, 383.

27. Elizabeth Suddaby, 'The poem *Piers Plowman*', *Journal of English and Germanic Philology*, LIV (1955), 95.

28. *The Vision of Piers Plowman newly rendered into modern English*, by Henry W. Wells, London, 1935, p. 158.

29. For the text here given, *cf.* p. 138 n. 14, above.

30. Cf. pp. 133-4, above.

31. *Boswell's Life of Johnson*, Birkbeck Hill-Powell, Oxford, 1934, I 444.

32. On '*Iust*', see p. 273, below.

33. For visual technique in this episode, see p. 263, below.

34. See p. 122, above. With the play upon 'conformen' in this passage compare the jingle *nolite conformari . . . sed reformamini* . . . (Rom. xii 2, rendered in A. V. 'be not conformed . . . but be ye transformed').

35. It is perhaps worth remarking that this passage and two of the preceding ('*deere god*', *ich sayde* . . . and *Kynde-wittede men han a cleregie by hem-selue*) are all from the C Text, as noted. We are certainly to heed Professor Donaldson's warning against concentration on 'one-line gems' (*Piers Plowman; the C-text and its Poet*, p. 72) ; but a notable proportion of such 'gems' in the C Text may put us on our guard against underrating its poetic worth.

36. *Canterbury Tales*, B 2081-2.

37. See pp. 149-50, above.

38. *Hydriotaphia*, Ch .V.

39. C.W. Stubbs, *The Christ of English Poetry*, London, 1906, pp. 75-6. This echoes, while it reverses, Lowell's verdict on Chaucer and Langland—'Both are kindly in their satire and have not (like too many reformers) that vindictive love of virtue which spreads the stool of repentance with thistle-burrs before they invite the erring to seat themselves therein' (*My Study Windows*, London, N. D., p. 236).

40. For a fuller discussion of the images in this passage, see pp. 328-9, below.

41. See *On the continuity of English Prose from Alfred to More and his School*, London, 1932.

42. E. A. Greening Lamborn, *The Rudiments of Criticism*, Oxford, 1923, p. 111.

43. *Troilus and Criseyde* v 1828-9; 1849-50; 1860; 1863-5.

44. Dorothy Everett, *Essays on Middle English Literature*, Oxford, 1955, p. 48.

45. Milton, prefatory note ('The Verse') to *Paradise Lost*.

46. Pp. 323-30, below.

47. *My Study Windows*, p. 236.

48. See p. 52, above.

49. For the text used, see p. 137, n. 10, above.

50. See especially pp. 285-95, below.

51. *The Legend of Good Women*, G 27-8.

52. *ibid.*, 271-2, 280-1.

53. *Troilus and Criseyde*, v 1093-50.

54. 'The Pattern of Consolation in *The Book of the Duchess*', *Speculum*, XXXI (1956), 626-48.

55. For a fuller treatment of the characterization of the protagonists in these episodes, see pp. 285-91, below.

56. Everett, *op cit.*, p. 27.

57. *English Literature in the Sixteenth Century*, Oxford, 1954, pp. 530-1.

58. Burrow, *loc. cit.*, p. 382.

59. *Visions from 'Piers Plowman'*, p. 134; see also 'The Pardon *of Piers Plowman*', p. 12. For an argument that such recurrences constitute 'thematic organization of the poem' (particularly as applied to the C Text), see A. C. Spearing, 'The Dev-

elopment of a Theme in *Piers Plowman*', *Review of English Studies*, N. S. xi (1960), 241-53.

60. *The English Poets*, London, N. D., p. 56.
61. *Essays*, I 101.
62. 'The Music of Poetry' (*On Poetry and Poets*, London, 1957, pp. 37-8).
63. *ibid.*, p. 29.
64. *The Oxford Book of Modern Verse*, Oxford, 1936, p. xxxix.
65. Iris Murdoch, *Sartre*, Cambridge, 1953, p. 11.
66. *Coleridge's Literary Criticism*, p. 3.
67. Cesare Gnudi in *Gothic Painting*, N. P. [Skira, Great Centuries of Painting], 1954, p. 55.
68. C. S. Lewis, *The Pilgrim's Regress*, London, 1943, p. 10.

CHAPTER VI

# Allegory, Similitude and Wordplay

The degree in which a poet's imagination dominates reality is, in the end, the exact measure of his importance and dignity.

Santayana

## I

A term so vast in its possible applications as 'allegory' may make us despair of finding any one acceptable set of definitions. Nevertheless, an attempt must be made, if we are not to abandon the term altogether; for the prospect of finding useful alternatives is hardly more encouraging. What then are we to mean by 'allegory'? It is, of course, not very profitable to ask the practitioners, the writers of allegory, themselves; for the writer giving an account of what he has done, or thinks he has done, appears to be in no better case than the critic approaching the work from without. As Dr. Tillyard observes:

> Most writers on rhetoric, classical, medieval and Renaissance alike, assume that poets make a poem as a conscientious housewife makes a pudding, by following the successive directions of a recipe. And the poets may have thought they worked that way. But we know that the best of them did not; and the right way to understand the allegorical method is to examine it in practice and not through the theories on which it is supposed to be based.[1]

Dr. Tillyard is here qualifying Professor C. S. Lewis's preliminary account of allegory as having 'a rigidity that may indeed be suggested by medieval theorists but which does not square with the best medieval practice or with some of his remarks later in the book'. However just this may be as a general criticism, we do in fact find Professor Lewis already recognizing the limitations of theoretical account, even when it is given by no less a poet than Dante and on a theme as potentially promising as that of multiple interpretation. Dante, as Professor Lewis observes, 'while parading four senses . . . makes singularly little use of them to explain his work'[2]. Clearly, it is necessary to walk warily in this matter. Let us begin by attempting a provisional definition and then see how it squares with allegory as we find it at various times.

Suppose we say that by 'allegory' we shall mean a work of imagination employing narrative elements which are coherent and interesting in their own right but from which transferred meanings naturally arise. This may, firstly, safeguard us from confusing allegorical fiction with allegorical interpretation of believed truth—as, notably, Holy Scripture. Whatever particular interpreters may make of the Bible, whether in its historical, prophetic or doctrinal parts, each such interpretation is the 'gloss' upon a text which remains separate from it and, as such, is susceptible of other or further interpretation. Secondly, and conversely, our definition insists upon the inseparability of text and gloss in the work of imagination: the 'story' is not there for the sake of the 'meaning', nor is the 'meaning' a *significacio* tacked on to that story. The transferred meanings, we have said, 'naturally arise'. However, we must meet a difficulty; what is the criterion of the natural? The meanings that occur to any given reader are certainly not to be admitted or excluded on the basis of the author's conscious intention. The work of art, we may thankfully admit, is susceptible of meanings which may be valid independently of the author's awareness of them. But to make the nature of allegory clear we must add that the presence of these further meanings is inseparable from the specific delight this kind offers. The 'specific' delight, be it noted; that order and quality of experience which allegory is uniquely fitted to effect, notwithstanding its possible occurrence in other forms of artistic expression. The qualification is important; for there is nothing to stop an unsophisticated reader from apprehending merely the part and mistaking it for the whole: and this in fact is a situation which can occur with allegory as with any other relatively complex art-form. It is not hard to find critics prepared to like allegory if it were not for its tiresome 'meanings'; just as there were, and are, those who could take to 'Metaphysical' poetry if it were not for its conceits—or, indeed, to any poetry, providing only they are allowed to re-write it. Perhaps the best of all comments on this 'if only' kind of criticism is that of Johnson, replying to Dryden's polite regret that Butler had not chosen to write *Hudibras* in heroic couplets:

When he wished to change the measure he probably would have been willing to change more. If he intended that, when the numbers were heroic, the diction should still remain vulgar, he planned a very heterogeneous and unnatural composition. If he preferred a general stateliness both of sound and words, he can be only understood to wish that Butler had undertaken a different work.[3]

'. . . a different work': there is the essential objection. The distinctive region of allegorical imagination is the interaction of 'meanings' ordinarily separate, to give at best a new understanding of meaning itself. The real problem is not one of definition, but of use. Coleridge once spoke of the impossibility of an Act of Uniformity against poets; the difficulties are as nothing compared with enforcing a similar statute against readers. It will be best to begin with a brief glance at the varying fortunes of allegorical writing.

## II

There is, we have said, nothing to stop the unsophisticated reader from detaching that part of allegory which he likes. The point is put, perhaps a shade loftily, in Spenser's letter to Raleigh 'expounding his whole intention' in *The Faerie Queene*. The 'historicall fiction' which is to render the moral purpose 'plausible and pleasing' is something 'the most part of men delight to read, rather for variety of matter, than for profite of the ensample'. Spenser thus has a ready defence against learned censure of the method he has chosen ('good discipline . . . clowdily enwrapped in Allegoricall deuises'). These critics are out of touch with the reading public:

> such, me seeme, should be satisfide with the vse of these dayes, seeing all things accounted by their showes, and nothing esteemed of, that is not delightfull and pleasing to commune sence.[4]

There is no mistaking the wry appeal, as between intellectual equals, over the heads of 'the most part of men'. The 'historicall fiction' is claimed as a groundbait; the learned can follow the poet's true intent without condescending to the simplicities of fairy-story. It is, of course, the characteristic note of the age, and on that account need not be taken too seriously. But it may serve to remind us that the sophisticated, too, can err in detaching that part of allegorical work they care for. And of these twin errors it is not easy to say which is the worse—to believe that the allegory may be left alone, since it will not bite you; or to affect to despise the poor 'literal' story as a concession to the vulgar. Fortunately, it is probable that no reader who has made any genuine entry upon allegorical work has ever been wholly under the sway of either notion. These common standpoints are, however, useful in putting us on guard against any over-simple expectations of our own. Whatever Spenser may say of 'a continued Allegory, or darke conceit', the modern reader must not expect a continuously interesting and coherent literal story to which the transferred meaning is an unbroken accompaniment. Professor C. S. Lewis points out that Spenser's statement that 'many . . .

aduentures are intermedled, but rather as Accidents, then intendments',
should warn us not to expect that 'everything in the poem is equally
allegorical, or even allegorical at all'.[5] Nothing, we may agree, could be
so readily fatal to the understanding of allegory as the determination
to seek out 'meaning' at every turn. Whatever the work of creative
imagination, we must follow it in its own distinctive workings and not
attribute to failure of purpose or incompetence whatever differs from
our expectation. With allegory in particular, we must not allow ourselves to be disappointed at what may remain obstinately 'literal' in
its appeal.

Spenser's account is instructive in another light. All story-telling that
goes beyond a fairly superficial level has some capacity to provoke
awareness of 'significance'. There is a sense in which a great part of
imaginative literature can be held to mean one thing by saying another,
and the ease with which such 'meanings' can be supplied witnesses to
the comprehensive power of the successful work of art. But the test here
must be our knowing these as alternative and incomplete statements
of a meaning which the poem, novel or play presents as a unity to the
imagination. The great characteristic of such work is to remake for the
imagination a world in which there may be 'a great many thoughts but
no such thing as a "truth" '—so that we see it is indeed man who makes
the 'truths',[6] and the artist who helps us to go beyond that making. We
must therefore beware of 'the false secondary power', in its insistent
drive to identify and assimilate to its own categories the truths which
are implicit in the work of art, allegory and non-allegory alike. The
example of *The Faerie Queene* may teach us that allegory is never less
likely to be grounded in story interesting in and for itself than at a
time when narrative art is seriously undervalued. Turn where we will
in Renaissance criticism, the sole aspect of extended fiction with which
men concern themselves is its 'moral' end. It is a climate less favourable
than any to interest in that kind of coherence and relevance which the
modern reader accepts—or has tended to accept—as indispensable to a
developed art of narrative. By contrast, the medieval standpoint is
readily discernible; the use of poetry is to instruct, and to instruct
agreeably. But this commonly means that 'profitable' and 'pleasing'
matter will lie side by side rather than achieve any degree of integration.
Thus, Gower's *Confessio Amantis* is set on its 'middel weie', offering

> Somwhat of lust, somewhat of lore,
> That of the lasse or of the more

*lust* entertaining matter; *lasse* less.

Som man mai lyke of that I wryte.[7]

It is natural that Chaucer's determinedly festive Host should insist on only one side of this dual obligation—he will have 'mirth', 'solas'; and disappointed in this, he must fall back on the alternatives of 'som murthe *or* som doctryne'. He thus unwittingly lands himself and the company with the uncompromisingly 'moral' and 'vertuous' tale of *Melibee*. This is Chaucer's turning to comic account a general recipe; and while we need not doubt that there is for him, as for his more sophisticated public, an inherent comedy in the recipe itself (the 'and' of the dutiful writer contrasted with the 'or' of the plain man's preferences), yet the common formula of medieval serious art remains—'profitable' matter diversified by arresting episode or telling illustration. Renaissance acceptance of poetry in these terms is characterized by a restriction in the range of the 'profitable'. Poetry teaches delightfully; but now the emphasis is upon that teaching in its ethico-political aspects—especially the intertwined themes of individual moral prowess and the art of governing one's fellow-men. It is against this background that an ambitious poet, Spenser or another, might seriously hope to 'overgo' his predecessors, ancient and modern, by dealing not only with more aspects of ethico-political truth than they—a purely quantitative success— but in portraying the great-souled man himself, that whole whereof the separate virtues are but parts. It is this tradition of agreement upon 'moral' significance, and its unremitting application in earlier work, which furnishes Spenser with characterization and incident already charged with significance, and thus makes inappropriate a mere coherence of narrative. The method of *The Faerie Queene* is soundly described by Professor Lewis: in each book there is 'an allegorical core, surrounded by a margin of what is called "romance of types", and relieved by episodes of pure fantasy'[8]. Spenser's is thus a complex and, we may find, sometimes confusing, method.

For our present purpose we must observe that *The Faerie Queene* is far from proceeding upon a groundwork of coherent story, continuously sustaining allegorical meaning. '*When it is allegorical at all*', writes Professor Lewis, 'it is radically and momentously allegorical'.[9] It is a remark which deserves careful consideration by all who would look closely into 'allegory' in the English tradition. Unfamiliarity should not betray the modern reader into thinking of all allegory as employing a method of consistent story-plus-significacio. Yet this is in fact the commonest assumption in discussion. It is perhaps reinforced by the exalted status

*solas* amusement.

which modern criticism accords to extended narrative. Where the novel has become the dominant literary form, we tend to be anxiously suspicious of narrative that has any reference beyond itself and to scrutinize it for a continual play of 'significance'. The freedom and variety of saying one thing and meaning another is not to be understood from within the simple alternatives of narrative in its own right or narrative-as-ubiquitous-groundwork. Nor, we may add, does narrative-as-symbol, as we find it in some modern work, most notably Kafka's, help us as much as we might hope. For here labyrinthine complexity of possible reference is liable to let the 'literal' drop out of sight altogether. In the good allegory, as in any other complex work of art, structure and meaning are finally inseparable. The element of story is not there simply as a means to an end, nor to develop interest through its own intricacy. It can afford free play to accepted type and symbol without therefore losing relevance; it can be discontinuous without being incoherent. It is thus a subtle and changing pattern, which challenges the reader's alertness. And this, we may feel, is wholly appropriate to the employment of allegory in both Langland and Spenser; for in each case the reader must be summoned beyond the appearances and acceptances of an immovably 'literal' world—the world of waking consciousness, which, we begin to see, means habitual inattention.

Allegory of this order directly proceeds from awareness of truth as many-sided and may rise to visionary intensity. But plain issues of conduct, conformity with a final rightness that is not less than 'Practical Reason' though it may, and indeed must, go beyond that, are the fundamental 'grammar of assent'. Not only vision and enchantment, but also sober discourse and patient endurance under trial play their interrelated parts in both *The Faerie Queene* and *Piers Plowman*. With the passing of this unforced absorption in conduct, approval of the good action as at once the evidence of and entry upon final reality, allegory dwindles immeasurably in potentiality. Where the standard of behaviour is an unargued conformity with 'good sense', then both satire and allegory come up against a decisive limitation of range. It is not for the writer to probe into the scheme of things, but to show departures from it in corrective satire or to trace its limits in decorative moralizing. The province of allegory thus sinks to the merely fanciful or the avowedly didactic; in the Vision of Mirzah and in *Rasselas* the allegorical standpoint confers no advantage beyond that of convenience—an agreed point of departure for sententious fiction. 'Allegory' of this kind merits no higher sentence than Johnson's own on the pastoral, with which it was not infrequently mingled; it is trite and hackneyed, making no real demand upon the reader—'easy, vulgar, and therefore disgusting'.

With the Romantic Revival we see something very like the converse of Elizabethan insistence on inevitable 'sentence' in extended story-telling. Now 'the fairy way of writing' is welcomed in and for itself. The *significacio* is so much museum-piece; the allegory can safely be left alone—it will not meddle with the reader. Hazlitt's confident assertion is well enough known. If we turn to Coleridge we can find an unexceptionable definition of allegory in general:

> The true sense is this,—the employment of one set of agents and images to convey in disguise a moral meaning, with a likeness to the imagination, but with a difference to the understanding,—those agents and images being so combined as to form a homogeneous whole.

But when, in its due place, after tribute to the 'indescribable sweetness' of his verse and 'scientific construction' of the metre, Coleridge comes to Spenser's allegorical achievement, there is no more to be offered than talk of the 'wondrous series of images', and the 'true imaginative absence of all particular space or time'. Our 'dreams' are the only counterpart; and it is in a dream that Spenser has placed his reader—in

> a charmed sleep, and you neither wish, nor have the power, to inquire where you are, or how you got there.

It does not sound very convincing; and so we need not be surprised at the endowment Coleridge credits the poet with—'fancy under the conditions of the imagination, as an ever present but *not always active* power'.[10] The essential working-method of allegory is to mediate between the external and an inner reality which is felt as all-but-inaccessible. A poetry which has as its distinctive subject moments of heightened awareness, when all is made plain, denies allegory its fundamental scope. Moreover, those moments are considered strictly as such. It is the central agony of the Romantic poet to know in the moment of full insight that the state is transitory. If inspiration is a wind that blows where it will, then the poet can neither contrive its coming nor delay its passing. Experience for the Romantic poet is sharply and painfully divided between the long periods of habitual awareness and the uncovenanted visitings of 'Imagination, awful Power'. The kind of poetry peculiarly appropriate to Romanticism is therefore the lyric, the short poem of intense awareness; and the aim and bent of poetry-making is to turn the objects of ordinary apprehension into objects of that imagination which 'dissolves, diffuses, dissipates in order to re-create'. The poem records in minute and faithful terms particular entries upon the 'One' as distinct from the Many, the perception of an 'essential beauty', glimpses of a world lit by 'the master-light of all our seeing'; and its common ending is in the fading of that intensity. However the individual poet may relate his insights to a theory of knowledge, all agree that to have seen the world with the eye of heightened awareness is to know the sad truth of habitual consciousness. The poet can cry, in the knowledge of an inspiration that keeps no covenant,

> I see them all so excellently fair,
> I see, not feel, how beautiful they are![11]

These are conditions absolutely fatal to the long poem which would steadily relate the objects of sense and the moral consciousness. The central understanding of the Romantic poet is man as patient, an Aeolian lyre that can only await the touch of inspiration. The allegorist's opportunity is when reality is not so sharply distinguished, and man's awareness is consequently more complex. The only theme which will sustain the long Romantic poem is an actual record of the insights that come to the poet. Wordsworth's *Prelude* faithfully records 'the growth of a Poet's mind'. It is the Romantic poem *par excellence*, succeeding in communicating both the entire dependence of the poet and his untiring vigilance to

> build up greatest things
> From least suggestions; ever on the watch,
> Willing to work and to be wrought upon.[12]

The subject of moral allegory, evident in Spenser and Langland alike, is the relation of sinful man to Divine Righteousness; and though man as agent is certainly not the whole truth it is yet for him to work out his own salvation. Successive episodes of individual combat or strenuous debate therefore constitute an essential part of the whole; truth is to be learned in act and not in vision merely. Allegory, both moral and courtly-erotic, witnesses, above all, to the Aristotelian truth that intellect of itself 'moves nothing'. But to the reader of Romantic poetry, alert only for the lightning-flashes that must come with all the force of the unpredictable, the long vistas are dusty indeed. So Coleridge's account of *The Faerie Queene* is perfunctory. All may be bright, with the 'exceeding vividness', perhaps, of dreams. But where the demand is for the lightning-stroke of 'imagination', Spenser's poem cannot but seem the work of 'fancy'. Dreams are well enough; but they come in 'a

charmed sleep': and Coleridge, for one, would have poetry call us into
more than wakefulness.

In the later nineteenth century, when the novel in a predominantly
naturalistic mode is the outstanding literary form, the fortunes of
allegory seem to revive slightly. W. P. Ker's criticism certainly does
not proceed from impatience, but, if I read him aright, from disappointment at an unfulfilled realism. 'With Bunyan', he says,

> You know where you are; and if ever the talk is abstract it is the
> talk of people who eat and drink and wear clothes—real men, as one
> is accustomed to call them.

Allegory conceived in these terms is perhaps in danger of becoming
an evolutionary stage in the development of the realistic novel. Thus
Ker regrets that although in *Piers Plowman* 'there is as much knowledge
of life as in Bunyan' this knowledge is imperfectly communicated;
'the visible world is seen only from time to time'. The objection is
clearly central. 'The form of thought', Ker complains,

> shifts in a baffling way from the pictorial to the abstract. It is tedious
> to be told of a brook named 'Be buxom of speech', and a croft called
> 'Covet not men's cattle nor their wives', when nothing is made of
> the brook or the croft by way of scenery . . .

It is evident that tolerance for allegory does not extend further than
for allegory as the relative simple statement of 'definite thought, never
lost or confused in the details'.[13] The obvious danger is an impatience
with the distinctive working of particular allegories, as against the simplicity and coherence of an imagined archetype. As we have observed,
narrative can be discontinuous without therefore being incoherent,
and a free play of common allusion and symbol is not to be ruled out of
order. We must beware of the recipe-and-pudding kind of thinking.
It is perhaps the most insidious form of that thinking which would make
all successful allegory a half-way house towards narrative realism.
For this is to offend against the great canon that allegory, if it is to exist
at all, must exist not to complicate but to reveal.

Against Ker's sturdy demand for narrative consistency and coherence
in 'the form of thought', some twentieth-century scholarship has insisted upon Langland's allegory as a mightily complex matter. It was
Professor N. K. Coghill who, in the Introduction to Wells's rendering
of *Piers Plowman*, brought into prominence 'four parallel lines of interpretation' common in medieval 'meditation on religious subjects'. 'All
these meanings', he affirmed

are to be found in *Piers Plowman*. They are sometimes simultaneous, sometimes interlinked, sometimes single; but on all four planes the poem is complete, and all understanding of it must move poetically among them all.[14]

It is unambiguous counsel against merely mechanical and over-simple interpretation. But it may perhaps blur the distinction between 'interpretation' and 'invention', between what can be derived from allegory and what is truly there as essential to our understanding—a distinction Professor Coghill puts well in a later work:

> To know that Holy Writ may have four meanings and to discern them is one thing, but to create a great work on this biblical scale is a feat of poetry almost above ambition[15]

It was not long before Langland's work was examined in this light. The method of the examination and some of its particular findings will concern us below. But for the moment we may consider the general conclusion reached:

> It is true that the architecture of the poem is not so obvious to the modern reader as that of the *Divine Comedy*, but when the principles governing that architecture are known it becomes clear that the English poem is no less perfect structurally than the Italian.[16]

There could hardly be a more marked shift from Ker's reminder to the reader to use common sense. The detail of the case remains to be considered; but even if its warrant as interpretation were granted, so resounding a conclusion must make us wonder whether we have not here a profound if not uncommon misconception. Scholarship can have much to tell us of 'the principles' of art. But, granted the principles, there remains the question of their application. The claim advanced above is to exhibit not the principles but the architecture itself. We must reply that it is one thing to teach us to use our eyes; quite another to tell us when they are open, and when shut.

Such 'historical criticism' as this is, of course, not peculiar to *Piers Plowman* studies, or to medieval studies in general: and it raises problems of the first importance. We are quite certainly not to allow the 'historian' to claim for his activity, as that activity is ordinarily understood, any special standing as 'criticism'[17]. For our present purposes, we may notice the striking counterpart it offers to Ker's approach. The status of naturalistic fiction led Ker to expectations of a realism and coherence which *Piers Plowman* cannot satisfy. Recent awareness of the non-rational in human behaviour may do more than merely rehabilitate older allegorical and symbolical usage. As Miss Helen Gardner has pointed out, 'it is not merely a wider dissemination of historical knowledge, a kind of antiquarianism, which has made scriptural symbolism congenial once more'.[18] Modern conviction upon the complex and ambiguous nature of mental-spiritual reality may blur the clear outlines and penetratingly simple positions of the medieval argument in its main bearings. We are in danger of replacing tolerant acceptance of limitations by a weight of praise greater than the work can sustain. And of these two kinds of injustice, it is open to question which is the worse. There is perhaps this to be said of some modern interpretation of *Piers Plowman* which, like that in other fields, notably the Shakespearian, stresses the complexity and allusiveness of late-medieval imagining. Such interpretation may at least win the reader from that tendency to mere paraphrase which in all the arts is the most natural resort of the reader, spectator or listener with too little time to give—and is surely the most deadly.

Against it, we may see from our brief survey, there can be no one remedy. But there are some attitudes towards allegorical work which are more helpful than others. Firstly, there must not be mere tolerance of allegory as a half-way house towards fully developed narrative art. Against this, allegory exists to make plain; it must be in that sense functional. Secondly, the reader must resist the temptation to extract meaning, to be half-way towards paraphrase in the very act of reading. The pressure and movement of the poet's imagining in its *wholeness* must be allowed its distinctive effect. Perhaps an example from later literature, where allusion or topical reference is in question, may help. On Pope's distinctive quality of 'delicacy' Mr. F. W. Bateson observes

> In the *Moral Essays* ... 'delicacy' resolves itself primarily into the nature and degree of personal allusion that is intended. The problem is not simply 'Who is Pope getting at here?' It is rather 'How far does the purely personal satire go?'[19]

It is the reader's essential business to perceive both the reference intended and its relation to the whole working of the poet's imagination. Only thus is he likely to share the poet's distinctive quality. Pope, we recall, thought 'delicacy' rarely apprehended; 'I scarce meet with anybody that understands delicacy'. We may well believe him; 'delicacy', like all other distinctive qualities of poetry, is easily overborne by any tendency in the reader to make direct and perpetual reference to local—in our sense 'literal'—meaning. The danger, present to some extent in all poetry, must be at its highest with work that involves any degree of 'transferred' sense. Here it is important not to misunderstand any advice, however authoritative, on 'stripping' allegory to arrive at its 'true intent'. For example, Dante declares it would be a cause of reproach

> if one should rime under the cloak of rhetorical metaphors, and, when asked, be unable to strip his words of this cloak and set them in a form that would make them clear.[20]

Dante is entering a *caveat* against arbitrary use of personification (here, the personification of Love), and that, moreover, at a decisive stage in his argument. Though there are many who 'rime ignorantly' *(rimano stoltamente)* he is not to be considered of their number.

Dante's words, rightly understood, may bring us to our last general consideration. All truly allegorical work, like the particular device, personification, Dante here treats of, is not ornament but instrument, not a manner of speaking arbitrarily *(senza ragione)* but a method of attaining to truth. In that sense, as we have seen, it is functional. But as we also saw, that function is not hindered but may in fact be aided by a free play of both the symbolic and the 'literal' as occasion demands. The whole design can give scope for a variety of effect which in some particular bearings may not be 'allegorical' at all. And this, so far from being exceptional, will rather be the usual case. For in the world of discourse shared by writer and reader nothing forbids but rather everything encourages a wide and varying set of responses. Not everything in our experience is apprehended in 'transferred' terms; and even those things that are generally understood as charged with significance may be capable of a strikingly 'literal' effect. Certainly, with a Langland or a Spenser no less an object is in view than man's whole nature and destiny; and the inquiry is into all the evidence accessible to man, including the varying shapes in which it presents and, it may be, disguises itself. We must not, in our newly-revived enthusiasm for the 'tropical', lose sight of the vividly literal; for it is by a plain realism that the older poet may mark those truths we would otherwise overlook. And of all the truths his poem offers, these may be the most important.

### III

A fourfold exegesis of Holy Scripture—distinguishing 'literal', 'allegorical', 'moral' and 'analogical' or 'anagogical' meanings—is familiar enough as a theory of interpretation. The relationships with Greek theories of the interpretation of poetry as well as with Hellenistic and other Jewish treatments of the Old Testament, coming to a 'climax of allegorization' in Clement of Alexandria and, above all, Origen, have been recently set forth with admirable clarity[21]. Similarly, Miss Gardner's stimulating treatment of the relations between the interpretation of Holy Scripture and the interpretation of poetry places the matter in the right context. Allegorical interpretation of Holy Scripture cannot usefully be isolated from the interpretation of literature, more generally considered. In the whole bulk of such figurative interpretation, beside all instances of the utterly eccentric or determinedly fantastic, there is no lack of interpretation, both of sacred and divine literature, which has *some* claim to attention. As Ker observed, 'All poetry has something of a representative character in it, and often it matters little for the result whether the composer has any definite symbolical intention or not'.[22] The problem for the critic is the rightness of any one interpretation, its relevance to the essential truth of the work under review. Where the question is of applying the fourfold categorization to *Piers Plowman* several considerations arise.

As we have seen in the first part of this book, *Piers Plowman*, though set in dream-form, is strikingly literal. In his dream, the Dreamer encounters for the most part an everyday reality, whether seen at a remove in the people of the Field of Folk, or met directly in the variously authoritative persons who are interrogated in the *Vita*. This reality, moreover, is not simply a background from which the figurative detaches itself. Whether in *Visio* or *Vita*, when personifications are encountered—as Holy Church and Lady Meed in the one, and Wit, Study, Scripture, and so on, in the other—the discourse is literal. It is not merely that Dreamer and interlocutor see and speak as they would in reality. Their talk is of particular aspects of Christian truth—of what man is to believe and how he is to act; and this is expressed as doctrine not mystery, fact not figure. Their discourse is not, for example, like that of Dreamer and daughter in *Pearl*, where what is literally true of the relation between bereaved father and daughter most skilfully conveys what is also true of Divine Purpose and 'in another country'—the Heavenly Jerusalem.

Again, in *Piers Plowman* allegorical persons come and go with real ones—as Lady Meed with the rascally 'sizours' and sheriffs, or the Minorite Friars and a greedy Doctor of Divinity side by side with Wit, Scripture, Patience, and so on. *Piers Plowman* belongs to that type of allegorical work which proceeds by way of personification of abstracts to the unravelling of problems which press upon man in this life. In such a design symbol and analogy will occur, as and when opportunity offers. But such figurative allusion, where it is not selected for patient explanation, will be largely of an established kind. The poet will not charge it with special significance—though he may well give it new force—for his concern is to make abundantly clear what is already complex enough. Nothing, again, in such a design forbids the entry of revelation upon a reason that has reached its limit. So, at the proper time, we hear of what Dante calls 'the supernal things of eternal glory'.[23] Only thus, we have seen, will all mysteries finally be made plain. But it is then, above all, that the Dreamer looks upon what is literally true; both the Jousting at Jerusalem and the Harrowing of Hell present themselves not as figure but as fact. At the centre of the poet's design, it is the literal, the mysterious made accessible to man, that resolves all confusion.

We may therefore avail ourselves of a useful distinction by following one critic in calling *Piers Plowman* 'personification-allegory'[24], provided we allow for the play of accepted symbol and figurative usage within this general framework. Whatever the case for application of a fourfold method of interpretation to other kinds of allegory, it is weakest for personification-allegory. As Dr Frank observes, 'its literal nature renders it an impossible medium for the fourfold method'[25]. The objection is not merely that any given personification stands in a direct and unambiguous relation to the argument, the developing truth about what man is to do in this life. This of itself precludes complexity of 'significance'. Much more, the meanings directly at work are sufficiently complex in their ordinary acceptance. The going is difficult not because implications of different orders are being drawn out, but because the meanings that are plainly there are profoundly difficult. But, most of all, a ready resort to interlocking planes of meaning—above all, the anagogical, showing forth the certainty that in the Divine Purpose all is ordered and harmonious—is in one way altogether to misconceive the decisive impact of a work in which the Dreamer can know no rest until all riddling is laid bare. His is the continuing desire to know, in Milton's phrase, 'nor seemingly ... nor in mist, the common gloss Of theologians'.[26] The poem is in detail literal[27] and moral, literal and anagogical, by turns, as the argument eddies to and fro: and this readily falls within that larger pattern which we have earlier seen—the shift of emphasis from intellectual faculties to moral virtue, as a Dreamer originally hot for dialectical certainty is brought to understand that the life about which he would know all is to be *lived*. The fourfold interpretation which some would have us apply in detail can do nothing but confuse. Comparison with Dante will do the English poet no service; there could hardly be greater dissimilarity of endowment, scope and method. More, we should observe that the very insistence upon applying a fourfold method to poetry (as in the Epistle to Can Grande) proceeds from the highly unusual nature of the undertaking. Dante is here, as Professor Bloomfield remarks, 'prophet rather than poet'[28].

If the fourfold method is considered solely as a method of interpreting Holy Scripture we still may not assume it as a natural and inevitable response. The system had its opponents as well as its adherents; and in the later Middle Ages the tendency appears to have been decisively away from figurative interpretation. As Miss Smalley has reminded us, the aim of St. Francis was 'to imitate Christ as "literally" as possible;' and the text that communicated God's will speaks of knowing mysteries — 'To you it is given to know the mysteries of the kingdom of Heaven ... but to them in parables' (Matt. xiii 11-13). Thus

> By a wonderful reversal, the *mystery* of the elect means to St. Francis not the mystical, but the strictest literal understanding of Scripture.

This is the ideal which 'gains ground in the thirteenth century ... What is evoked by the crib, the rosary, the crucifix, is the Gospel in its literal sense'[29]. To persist in re-clothing scriptural allusion in a determinedly 'spiritual' garb is to move against this tendency, nowhere more evident than in Langland's poem. Indeed, it may not be fanciful to suggest that we can use some modern scholarship in this field not so much to illustrate the truths the poem exhibits as to show the complexity of possible allusion with which the medieval poet must contend if he is to achieve clarity and urgency of appeal. Lastly, the case for a resolutely allegorical interpretation is not substantially altered if it is argued that these levels of meaning are to be understood as much more a habit of mind than a conscious handling of multiple reference[30]. Criticism of this order must always face the particular question, What on all the evidence is meant *here?*—and proceed cumulatively to a statement of the actual and essential meanings of the whole work, whatever its possible and marginal significances, its overtones and half-allusions. There is no escape from the ordinary task of showing that one interpretation is more plausible than another. Whatever the degree of complexity the critic takes as inhering in any one idea, the question of primacy of effect is paramount.[31] The fundamental objection to a theory of multiple reference, whether conscious or involuntary, is that it runs counter to the grain and joint of the work, 'the thing' that *Piers Plowman* is 'and no other'.

This is not to ask for a rigorously 'literal' reading of the poem. One or two instances may make the point clear. The 'second vision' of the poem is the scene of the ploughing in the half-acre. Here, if anywhere, it might be supposed, meaning is wholly unambiguous. A wicked world

is being set to rights, making the first steps along the road of that co-
operative endeavour which is the essential condition of human society,
if men are not merely to prey upon each other. Of course the situation
'stands for' something more than the actualities of helping a ploughman
who will in return lead a pilgrim company. But this something more
is not something other than the reality of social justice. Co-operative
endeavour, a duty of man to man, is not the whole truth of the poem as
it is to develop. But it is the whole truth accessible at this first stage of
'doing well'. We are to pass beyond a world of work or want; but we
must enter upon it first. Any attempt to give this scene a complex allegorical treatment does violence to the actual nature and method of the
poem's whole being. For the thorough-going allegorists, Piers is here
a type of priesthood: he works on the would-be pilgrims, implanting
virtue, as they work on the half-acre; the barley-bread and water of the
hard times that any slackening of effort will bring are equated with
'temporal rather than spiritual bread', and (we are told) 'water, the
opposite of the honey of sapientia, is "dulcedo hujus vitae" ' ; Hunger
is 'tropologically the lack of spiritual food'; and what Piers threatens
the wasters with is excommunication, thus succeeding 'where the secular
arm represented by the Knight failed'.[32] It is a method of criticism akin
to the omniscience of some modern 'mythographic' interpretation of the
novel. To assume that a multiplicity of meanings is continuously present to
the writer is to blur beyond recognition both the actual development of
the argument, and the distinction between foreground and background at
any given point in that development.

The essential proceeding of such a work as Langland's is to let us see
certain truths as it were in solution, so that we expect and attend to
their being precipitated. That 'precipitation', however, brings with it
awareness of other truths linked with those which have just come into
full clarity. The all-important device is the characterization of the
Dreamer[33]; the reader both explores with the Dreamer and, forewarned
of the Dreamer's limitations as a guide, begins to see for himself the
progress that must be made if truth is to be attained. There is no question
of direct and perpetual reference to man's spiritual state or divine purpose, 'tropologically' understood. In this present instance of the half-
acre, the poet keeps steadily before us the inescapable issues of plain duty.
This, of course, is set within a framework of belief about the sanctions
of that duty, the ultimate reach of Law; and the argument is to progress
by probing that framework. But there is no loss of depth or genuine
complexity in holding fast to the literal truth of this scene. As one
critic soundly remarks, 'The vision as a whole is something more than

a political poem, not because it has a second meaning, but because the poet talks of salvation'[34]. He talks of salvation because he knows no ultimate distinction between the political and religious. But it is to ultimates that the poet must contrive to bring his reader. The reader is not already there, through his acceptance of a set of symbols which are always and everywhere comprehensive. The poem is serial, not static; and the argument must go forward.

An emphasis on 'literal' meaning does not preclude the possibility of topical allusion where such allusion drives the poet's meaning home. The fable of the rats and mice against the cat (Prologue 146 ff.) stands in an obvious relation to contemporary situation—so obvious, indeed, that the poet excuses himself from making the application. He dare not, he says; which is a way of putting the reference beyond doubt for those that have ears to hear. The argument is upon effective government, and the particular issue of force comes to the audience with a direct and contemporary relevance. But this makes an entry for the whole topic; the poet has no wish to limit the application. The discussion comes to rest not in the local and temporary situation of change of rulers but in the permanent truth of division amongst men, a self-interest that without effective rule would know no bounds. Lady Meed's defence of her vocation is similar. She is very clearly that principle of payment-for-services-rendered which at her first flagrant appearance is easily seen as an abuse, and thus equated with all forms of disproportionate payment—from outright bribery to 'tickling commodity . . . the bias of the world'. But, as the argument deepens, 'mede' is seen to be even at its best no more than subject to *mesure*, and as such falling infinitely short of Divine example in matters of reward—that forgiveness of sinners which is richly disproportionate to their merits. As such, the primary and essential truth about Lady Meed is the same in all three versions of the poem. What she is does not depend at any point on topical allusion, 'made meaningful only by the identification of contemporary people at whom satire is being aimed'.[35] It would, indeed, be a cryptic piece of moralizing that was in fact wholly dependent upon allusion. But none the less the account in the B and C Texts of the inglorious events of the Norman campaign which ended in the Treaty of Bretigny brings the poet's audience a vivid and exact instance of the inseparability of efficacy and reward. As in the earlier fable of belling the cat, so here, the plain issues of government are brought home to all men; and—an important characteristic of the poem's whole method—the debate veers sharply from theoretical to firmly practical issues, from the faults readily detected in the present system of things to their bearing on effective rule (here, Meed's faults as counterbalancing her usefulness in sustaining a word of work and rewards). There is nothing finally to object to in the view that in Conscience, as Lady Meed sees him, there is a momentary glance at John of Gaunt, and in Meed herself, a King's comforter, a plain hint of Alice Perrers. What is to be rejected is either the belief that contemporary allusion is an immovable barrier to all other interpretation, or the high theological explanation that would show us in this passage 'the fallibility of Conscience, which, directed towards particulars, may err.'[36] The central truth is clear, and it is primary: Meed is not to be dismissed as mere bribery. Here again, as with the episode of the half-acre, the argument is progressive. If she is in some sense indispensable, what is to be done? This, since it leads to the *mesurable*, must ultimately lead beyond it. Meed's challenge is to ineffectual organization and timorous leadership—seen, of course, from her standpoint. But the challenge calls forth a reply that takes us beyond a world of rewards and punishments.[37]

What is true of particular episodes holds for the sequence of the argument and the interrelatedness of the main themes. Thus, as Dr. Frank points out, we are not to make a direct link between the sinfulness of Haukyn and the corruption of the church militant (the friars' complaisance in easy confession), as Robertson and Huppé would maintain[38]. The point is of some importance. Langland's Haukyn is the final comment on active self-sufficiency, the life of the wayfaring Christian. There can be no dwelling at the elementary stage he all too clearly exemplifies. The way leads forward from Haukyn to perfected obedience in the Christian's Saviour. To qualify Haukyn's state by suggesting that it is in some degree explicable and excusable is to lose the whole rigour of the demonstration. Certainly what is substituted for it is in some sense 'true'; but it is not the truth the poem at this point is dealing with. There is here no attack upon the Friars, and there are in fact references to the validity of confession, properly undertaken—just as when the necessity of 'doing well' is sounded uncompromisingly at the end of the *Visio*, the validity of the Papal forgiveness of sins is affirmed. We must learn to attend to the poet in his own sequence and with his own method of dwelling at different times on different aspects of the truths he probes.

Perhaps the gravest drawback of a method of determinedly 'spiritual' interpretation is found where not literal truth but symbolism is in question. In Passus XVI the Tree of Charity is shown to the Dreamer: and here, as is suitable at this stage of the poem, where the 'better' long promised is drawing near, many related ideas are brought together—

principally, on the one side, the predominantly ethical notions with
which the Dreamer has hitherto been concerned (his search for the more-
than-*justus*) and, on the other, the greater law of Love now to be revealed, and to which both Chastity and Charity are obviously related.
Langland's tree is, fittingly, a blending and adaptation of several sorts
of tree-image. The problem of their origins need not detain us here.
What deserves our notice is that Robertson and Huppé equate this
complex gathering of symbols with 'the *lignum vitae* of Scripture',
overlooking the composite nature of what, following Professor Bloomfield, we may call a 'Tree of Perfection'.[39] The reason is not far to seek.
Where a full complexity of meaning is thought to inhere in any one
image or conception there is little incentive to discriminate between
particular images. So here, 'the *lignum vitae* of Scripture'

> represents Christ or the Cross anagogically, the just allegorically,
> and the individual Christian tropologically.[40]

It is in little, applied at a critical point in the development of the poem,
an instance of the method at large. One kind of comprehensiveness is
purchased at the expense of any real exactness. It is hard to resist the
conclusion that what was held to be true of Conscience at Lady Meed's
examination may be applied to the method of interpretation itself. It,
too, when 'directed toward particulars, may err'. Perhaps the most
notable feature of the whole interpretation offered by Robertson and
Huppé is that notwithstanding what is said at the outset and in the conclusion of their survey, a fourfold meaning is in fact very seldom
exhibited for our view. We can, after a search as exhaustive as theirs,
conclude that though its origins may be celestial, it is not to be found on
earth: *Rara avis in terris nigroque simillima cygno.*

IV

What then are Langland's dominant characteristics as an allegorist?
There is, before all, the great graphic power which makes his truths
incarnate even as, in the Christian story, Truth itself became incarnate.
This I treat of in a later section. The range of devices at the service of
this graphic power is wide indeed, and interpretation need not go far
afield in search of them. Professor C. S. Lewis once counselled us to
look for the origins of *The Faerie Queene* not only 'in Renaissance
palaces and Platonic academies', but also nearer at hand, 'in the Lord
Mayor's show, the chap-book, the bedtime story, the family Bible, and
the village church'.[41] The influence on *Piers Plowman* of the preacher
with his stock of arresting images and vivid cautionary tales has been

remarked by Dr. Owst;[42] similarly, and by many editors and interpreters of the poem, the influence of the drama, notably in the Harrowing of Hell. There are signs, too, that some headway is being made with the iconography of the poem.[43] We need not doubt that the iconography of the church, from Jesse window and wall-painting to bench-end and misericord, played their part in stimulating Langland's imagination. The subject of *Piers Plowman* is universal; the poem draws upon homely image and familiar analogy as it does upon common proverb and down-right turn of speech. And just as this speech and imagery are heard along with echoes of skilled dispute and solemn tones of Holy Scripture, so too the greater images of Crucifixion and Triumph over Hell exist side by side with minor carving, both grotesque and emblematic. The ex-perience is not only of empty bellies and aching heads, but of visionary ardour and dialectical subtlety. This juxtaposition works upon us with all the force of the real. Langland's is a very English church; but the mode of its working is accurately conveyed in Lowell's words

> The moral of a poem should be suggested, as when in some medieval church we cast down our eyes to muse over a fresco of Giotto, and are reminded of the transitoriness of life by the mortuary tablets under our feet.[44]

As in its central affirmation, the awakening first of a Plowman, then of the Dreamer, to realization of the individual's own plight, so too in its particular stages, the truth of Langland's poem has the quality of coming upon the reader as something unpremeditated. To this end the familiarity of certain symbols directly contributes; what lies ready-made to Langland's hand is entirely suited to his purposes.

Simple moralizing—of the kind that incurred W. P. Ker's wrath— is from this point of view altogether appropriate to a Plowman who, speaking from within the world of limited experience, proclaims the way to Truth as by the brook 'Beth-buxum-of-speche'. It is idle to complain that 'nothing is made' of this 'by way of scenery'. Adherence to law is the Plowman's sole warrant for guiding humanity; and it is the measure of their need that no one more amply qualified can be found. To adapt Ker's phrase, if nothing is made by way of scenery, much is made by way of landscape—the bare co-ordinates of humanity's position are accurately plotted when no greater prospect can be offered than adherence to Truth-as-law. Such signpost 'allegories' have their own undeviating way to point: they are the high road to real, as against theoretical, understanding.[45] It is the same at the other end of the road, when, once again, humanity must build broad and deep. The 'allegory' of the team given by Grace—the 'foure gret oxen' and 'foure stottis', the two harrows, 'an olde and a newe', with the detail of the 'greynes' to be sown (XIX 257 ff.)—all this is not to be dismissed as mechanical or frigid. It is as simple and as unyielding as the Mosaic tables themselves. At such moments Langland's evident concern is to write the truth large and clear so that none need err. We may recall the patient explanation of each of the 'greynes' committed into Piers's charge, and the painstaking detail of the building of the barn, culminating in the title spelt out in both tongues—'Vnite, holicherche on Englisshe'. The truth about this type of allegorical writing seems to be that, so far from leaving matters to the reader's imagination, the poet's care is rather to particularize the intended significance.

We may see the same impulse in the explanation given of the analogy between the actual and spiritual dangers of rich and poor on life's highway (C XIV 65-100). The implication of this little parable of merchant and messenger is clear enough; and the poet openly says so ('3e wyten wel, 3e wyse men, what this is to mene'). But this does not deter him from a careful statement of the precise meaning he intends. This degree of patient exposition argues rather the necessity of channelling understanding than a willingness to touch off complexity of significance. No doubt the readiness of his audience to perceive 'sentence' is there: but the implication is that it needs careful direction. So, too, with the significances seen in the marriage-feast of Matt. xxii 4; the interpretation is painstakingly recounted (XV 454-77)[46]. There is nothing here of reliance on a meaning or group of meanings which the reader will readily supply; all is simple exposition—though the matter, of itself, is by no means complicated, certainly not even remotely approaching the complexity of some of the interpretations the exponents of fourfold significance would have us accept without demur.

Again, if we consider the explanation, requested by the Dreamer, of the Tree of Charity (Passus XVI), both the detail of the initial explanation (4-52) and the Dreamer's honest puzzlement—leading to further significance (67-72) and to demonstration (75-88)—hardly betoken reliance upon a habit of mind which moves at ease in multiplicity of reference. Rather there is in Langland a sturdy simplicity of explanation. He shows no particular aptitude or inclination to enliven what is merely normative, the statement of what man is to *do*. Similarly, he is not much concerned to dwell upon such traditional symbols as that of Samson carrying off the gates of Gaza, typifying the Saviour's

*stottis* bullocks; *wyten* know.

triumphant foray into Hell;[47] Christ is '*Gygas* the geaunt' (XVIII 250), without special implication or further reference. So, too, common kinds of medieval illustration or proof are caught up in the varying tides of his argument; but they are used with a distinct and limited relevance. We may recall the defence of clergy through Christ's writing in the dust (XII 59-94); or, on the other side of that debate, the fact that the shipwrights of Noah's Ark were not saved, for all their knowledge (X 399-413). It is not in complex symbol that Langland excels but in telling analogy or simple similitude: as, the true worth of clergy put beyond doubt in the example of the two men cast into the Thames (XII 161-9); the similitude of the man in the storm-tossed boat, giving the essential distinction between deliberate sins and those of mere frailty while it conveys vividly the unending plight of the sinner (VIII 30-7); or that great similitude of the hand which comprehends the truth of the Trinity with an exact homeliness of reference which makes doctrine and daily experience one (XVII 138-202). (The capacity of the good analogy to sustain detailed application is nowhere better illustrated than in the definition of the unforgivable offender—'he priketh god as in the paume that *peccat in spiritum sanctum*'.)

Langland does not hesitate to foreshorten his design to accommodate an established significance. Thus, in Passus XVI, Abraham, hitherto apprehended in terms of ordinary mortal existence, is brought into a different focus when we are to see in his keeping the great company that awaits release:

> I loked on his lappe, a lazar lay there-inne
> Amonges patriarkes and profetes pleyande togyderes. (255-6)

It is a bold and yet natural foreshortening; the onward drive of the argument brooks no great regard for consistency of representation. We may perhaps link it with that regard for dramatic truth which puts in the mouth of the Crucified One the sad awareness that the earth has no dwelling-place for Him (XX 42-6).[48] Langland's is a natural vigour of imagination, bound neither by consistent elaboration of significance nor by mere adherence to Scriptural sequence. We misconceive Langland if we attribute his power and comprehensiveness to any distinctive gift of complex allegorization or 'glossed' significance. Text and *glose*, indeed, in his poem are carefully distinguished; and when there is a question of glossing he is careful to point out the true gloss. How should

*geaunt* giant; *priketh* pierces, wounds; *paume* palm (of the hand); *peccat* etc. sins against the Holy Ghost (*cf.* Mark iii 29); *lazar* leper; *profetes* prophets; *pleyande* rejoicing; *togyderes* together.

it be otherwise, when the central purport of his poem is the truth we would variously hide from ourselves? His *Visio* develops to the unveiling of a truth in the Pardon; and the rest of the poem is to establish the true gloss on those unalterable lines, so that truth shall have its 'great meed.' It is not a marvellous complexity that is Langland's achievement; before all else, it is an arresting simplicity.

## V

No amount of attention to allegory must be allowed to obscure Langland's great 'literal' power, and the means by which the literal is made vivid and compelling. Firstly, in visual terms: to recall the decisive moments in *Piers Plowman* is to summon up two distinct sets of images. The one is of vigorous animation, whether crowd-scene or swiftly-successive action—as, the Field of Folk, the repentance of the Deadly Sins, or the Jousting at Jerusalem and the Harrowing of Hell; the other of single figures or incidents, etched in sharp relief—Meed turning to the King to make her defence ('I do it on the King'); the Palmer halted in astonishment at the unusual question put by the newly-repentant pilgrims; Haukyn's entire collapse into tears as the charges against him come unswervingly home; Faith's looking intently upon a Dreamer who asks, at Jerusalem, 'Is Piers in this place?'; the wheedling figure who stands upon the threshold at the end; and a hundred more. Langland's characteristic techniques here are well worth remarking as the means by which the literal, always in danger of being disregarded if we search for complexity of allusion, is made sharp and actual to the reader, just as the primary truth of his own need must come home to the Dreamer. Indeed, the parallel goes deep, so close-knit is the poet's imagining. We have seen in the *Visio* that single figures are thrown into focus by their following scenes of brisk activity—as the wedding cavalcade melts away, so the solitary figure of Meed detaches itself; Conscience kneels before the King when the balance of argument sways dangerously against him; and Repentance kneels to invoke God's Mercy on a vigorously self-seeking world, now grown silent. The light falls on these solitary figures as all ambiguities and distractions are momentarily put away. At the end of the *Visio* the single figure of the Dreamer has been brought into relief. He is wholly detached from the crowded and vigorous world of the *Visio;* for the implications of 'doing well' are to come home to the individual. He is the same Dreamer who, we had learned from Holy Church's characterization, readily externalizes the sense of moral failing. As the *Vita* develops, we see that it is the opportunities for debate so eagerly seized upon which stand between him and genuine awareness. So, in the *Vita* the technique seen in the *Visio* must be in one way decisively altered. Henceforward the relationships are between individuals, the Dreamer and the one or few interlocutors he deals with at any given point in his inquiry. But, given this difference, there is similarity in all else. At varying times the Dreamer must be confronted with an animated scene—as when he is shown the width and variety of God's creation; or brought back for a moment to the heedlessly self-seeking world of the Doctor of Divinity; or, most moving-ly of all, his awaking with the little company of Cornhill about him, to the sound of the Easter peal of triumph.

In this respect, at their crucial points *Visio* and *Vita* are alike. The most striking incident in the *Visio* is the unfolding of the Pardon. The crowded scene of the half-acre, with its disputes and hard lessons, fades as Plowman and Priest come into focus. We thus confront the reality directly—we see over their shoulders the Pardon; and we see it in unrelenting close-up —'all in two lines it lay'. A similar turning-point in the *Vita* is the ban-quet in Passus XIII, where, again, after the animation of the setting— the Doctor hard at trencher-work at the upper end of the hall, and the quick, ironic colloquy between the travellers at the far end—the scene comes into intentness of focus. The action sudenly changes tempo, as the Doctor repeats the word 'Dowel'; and his reaching thoughtfully for the cup brings the scene, again, into close-up:

'Dowel?' quod this doctour, and toke the cuppe and dranke . . .

A moment later and the revealingly negative answer is given ('Do non yuel'), and we are away headlong with the Dreamer's outburst.[49] The visual technique is cinematic in effect, and would, I believe, repay closer examination than is ventured on here. With such close-up work, we should compare the scenes of wide-angle vision, whether in richly varied detail, as in the Field of Folk, or of irresistible advance when the long-awaited light penetrates Hell's darkness. Hand and eye go together in the poet; for these alternating techniques answer perfectly to the argu-ment—that what is readily detected in crowded humanity must be refracted steadily upon the observer himself; and, equally, that it is this crowded world which is the unalterable setting of individual Chris-tian endeavour. Perhaps Langland's greatest single technical endowment is this sharp visual sense, springing from and never at variance with his deepest awarenesses.

Where then is the subtlety and complexity of this work?—for if it is, as we have seen, piercingly clear in its central issues, the perimeter is almost illimitable. There are clear affirmations enough—of the dangers of learning and wealth; of the virtues of patient poverty; the insistence upon *praxis* as against *theoria*, subtilizing set over against that doing well which, in whatever degree of proficiency, is required of all men as deed and not mere profession. But there are riddles and perplexities, problems that cannot be solved, as well as truths that are to be insistently affirmed. There may be a high-road to the truth—that *alta uia* of obedience to Law which the Plowman was qualified to assert. Yet it is not so directly that the Dreamer arrives at his destination, but by side-roads and even blind-alleys. There is thus one great central and continuing device of the poem we must not minimize or ignore, the character Will himself, the *persona* by which the poet manipulates his reader—a Dreamer whose characteristic failing of impetuous theorizing is established at the outset, and whose progress constitutes the clearest demonstration—a veritable *pref*, in the medieval sense—that man must in the end be brought to know the applicability to himself of the judgement he so readily visits on others. Since, too, the false paths the Dreamer takes are those of over-eager speculation and inconclusive debate, we have a second vital characteristic of Langland's art. The Dreamer is Will; but Will is ambiguous—there is the wish to know, but there is also, we quickly perceive, that self-interest which is blind to its own true needs and failings. So we have a Will who 'wolde ywyte—yif Witte couthe teche hym' (VIII 124); and the note of irony in Thought's words is unmistakable.[50] The truth can come home, in the end, only to a chastened Will: for, as the Dreamer had himself insisted at the outset of his journey, truth is to be known only through practice. Anima confirms it; the true is to be distinguished from the false

Noyther thorw wordes ne werkes but thorw wille one. (XV 204)

'Will' is thus not a simple irony; rather, it expresses an unchanging condition. The familiar opposition of Will and Wit is deepened by the lasting association of Will and 'Kind' (Nature); Will is a natural and therefore continuing desire. The Dreamer, we may remember, is one whose stubborn insistence on perfection is at last rewarded. Nothing less than the wholly Just will serve; so it is this which is granted as vision when all argument has exhausted itself. In this, too, the divine Providence meets man's deepest need; the Dreamer's search for perfection ends in no intermediate goal. We may be reminded of the Confessor's gentleness to his pupil in Gower's *Confessio Amantis*. In a context where Will and Hope are equated, against Wit and Reason, love—which we

*ywyte* know; *one* alone.

may see in Langland's poem as the continuing desire for perfection—excuses much:

> Thou dost, my Sone, ayein the riht;
> Bot love is of so gret a miht,
> His lawe mai noman refuse,
> So miht thou thee the betre excuse.

It yet cannot avert the final truth, to be won by experience:

> . . . natheles thou schalt be lerned
> That will scholde evere be governed
> Of reson more than of kinde.[51]

The link between Will and Hope is very relevant to all understanding of Langland's Dreamer; and these last three lines might serve as epigraph to the *Vita de Dowel*. No degree of preoccupation with a believed 'William Langland' should distract us from the presence and activity, organic to the whole design, of a Will who is both determination and, unwittingly, insentience, and whose credential for pursuing the enquiry is in his experience of men, his having lived long in land. Authority is thus questioned; all would be brought to the proof of direct experience. In the end, the Dreamer himself must be brought to knowledge; if it is fools who learn by experience, his persistence yet brings the highest reward. This Will-the-Dreamer is the true object of attention. In the last chapter I deal with the relation between him and those apparently biographical details which the poem also offers. The Dreamer's is a situation which, founded in an unalterable paradox of human nature, readily engenders verbal paradoxes. Wordplay is thus an unforced accompaniment to many an apparently plain passage; and it comes with dazzling force at some of the central crises, where many meanings are gathered into one focus of attention.

## VI

The treatment of wordplay in a notable essay by Bernard Huppé[52] will do much to promote awareness of this characteristic method of the poet. As Huppé observes, 'To play with the etymology or the sound of a word until it revealed an image, a symbol, or a moral, was to move on the high road to Truth'. Further, there is in the alliterative four-beat line itself a tendency towards wordplay—'the extension of the similarity in sound beyond the identity of individual letters'; and we have already

*ayein* against; *of reson* by reason; *kinde* nature, natural disposition.

seen in Part I of this study such conscious wordplay as that on 'cross', 'sute', 'secte', 'worts' ('words'), 'good(s)' (in both the material and moral sense), and especially the sharp exchanges between Plowman and Priest at the opening of the 'pardon'. There are, however, some distinctions we must make. Verbal 'play' of many different kinds is unforcedly present: it will be best to concentrate on the pun, the playing with two or more senses in the same word or its homonyms, to see what distinctive effects wordplay can secure.

We may omit from detailed consideration examples of mere verbal ingenuity, such as 'Wit's' adroit argument on the advantages to be drawn from wrong-doing:

> Bettere is that bote bale adoun brynge,
> Than bale be ybette, and bote neuere the bettere. (IV 92-3)

We omit, too, examples of quasi-cryptographic reference, as the *vix* (of *vix iustus saluabitur*) which alludes to the five wounds of Christ (C XVI 22-3); and we may similarly exclude such tricks of association as that apparent in IX 159-61:

> I am '*via et veritas*', seith Cryst, 'I may *auance* alle'.
> It is an *oncomely* couple, bi Cryst, as me thinketh,
> To gyuen a yonge wenche to a yolde feble.[53]

Here 'auance' may well have involuntarily suggested 'oncomely'; but there is no evidence that there is a double sense of 'oncomely'— displeasing, and not coming (to Christ)—for the parallel offered by Huppé—'Cloth that cometh from the weuyng is nouȝt comly to were' (XV 444)—is unconvincing. Similarly, we may rule out plain irony, as in the reply Repentance's insistence on 'Sorwe of synnes' receives from Envy:

> I am sori . . . I am but selde other. (V 126-7)

It is a jest which takes us no further than the distinct meanings of the word. Again, the recurrence of certain images does not necessarily, as Huppé believes, involve links between parts of the poem. Thus, the Castle of Truth, seen at the outset of the poem, is an image developed by Holy Church in Passus I to include the Castle of the flesh. The application is a familiar one; there is no real link with the same image as used by the Plowman in Passus V, by Wit in Passus IX, and as alluded

---

*Bettere is* etc. It is better that some recompense should be made, thus lessening the harm done, than that the offence be punished and no recompense made; *feble* weak, impotent; *weuyng* (directly from) weaving.

to by Clergy in Passus XIII. The recurrence of a common symbol has nothing of special significance to give to the poem. To claim, moreover, that it is this image which is 'transformed' into 'the figure of the Barn of Christendom' is to make unnecessary complication. The poet's conception throughout is of a militant Christianity and the image of the Castle comes ready-made to his hand; while that of the Barn, 'Vnite, holicherche on Englisshe' appears to be all his own. Similarly unreal is the claim that the presence of 'bidders and beggars' and 'pilgrims and palmers' at various points in his poem constitutes a distinctly 'thematic' repetition.[54] There is much to praise in the texture of Langland's poem; we must not press for complexity beyond that which is truly present in the whole design.

Of any given instance of functional wordplay—a designed activity of double meaning—we must ask first how far such meaning may have been present to the poet and his audience: then, the range of reference identified, so far as may be, we must ask with what effect it comes. Under the first head, we can identify meanings which are probable enough: as, 'queen'—'quean' (worthless woman); 'cosyn' (cousin and dupe); 'grace'—'grass' (where identity of pronunciation links entire difference of meaning); and others mentioned earlier in this section.[55] Such instances are entirely acceptable; but we must beware of reading into the text subtleties of our own invention. Thus, at XIV 220-1, in the lines

> For the pore is ay prest to plese the riche,
> And buxome at his biddyng for his broke loues

the meaning is clear; but Huppé would have us construe *prest* as a reference to 'priest' and 'loues' as echoing 'love'; so we have 'a metaphorical significance':

> the poor man is ever a priest who serves the rich and in his prayers serves the rich man so that he may obtain his broken love or favour.

The reader may find this over-ingenious: but it is not all. With the meaning 'petty' for *broke*, we have a further claim:

> the poor, oppressed by need, become like false priests who serve the rich so that they may partake of their worldly bread—

and so to a final reach of interpretation—

*prest* ready; *buxome* obedient; *broke loues* broken loaves, fragments of bread.

thus they turn their hearts from the *cibus spiritualis*, the bread of the spirit, the grace of God.[56]

Such interpretation is perilously near dispensing with all warrant in the text; the ingenuity of the exponent is all. Here, again, we must beware of that assumption of all-meaning-present-to-the-poet which we identified in the extraction of fourfold significance. Not only will it lead us to make extravagantly complex the simple; at the same time we may miss the tellingly obvious. Thus, Huppé makes much of Dame Study's warning on the dangers of Theology (X 180 ff.)—a pattern 'as complex as the subject about which she warns is difficult':

> Ac Theologie hath tened me ten score tymes . . .
> It is no science *for sothe* forto sotyle in . . .

But in all this parade of so-called 'puns' ('on *ten*, on *let* and *lethy*, *sothe* and *sotyle*'), the simple force of 'for sothe' is overlooked—the ordinary expletive 'forsooth', comes side by side with the literal sense 'for truth' (to 'sotyle inne'). Theology offers no foothold for the simplicity of truth. It is a kind of telling effect which is all Langland's own. We meet it again in Lady Meed's defence

> For kulled I neuere no kynge ne conseilled ther-after,
> Ne dede as thow demest, *I do it on the kynge*. (III 186-7)

It is well observed that in her answer Meed 'plays with the literal meaning of what Conscience has said: "she herself did not kill the king". His meaning she avoids'[57]. But we must not overlook the impudent equivocation with which she concludes. 'I do it on the kynge' means not only 'I assert before the King'; but it carries also the implication 'I practise my wiles on the King'. The threat to her opponents is made actual; for Meed's argument now turns back confidently on her present judge, by recalling a King's disastrous campaign. This impudent *bravura* is wholly in character. We may recollect a similar doubleness of meaning in her pretended submission to the King at the outset: 'But I be holely at ȝowre heste, lat hange me sone!' (111-12)—where ordinary asseveration ('hang me!') and ultimate penalty are defiantly linked.[58]

Any modern association of double meaning with mere duplicity—the play upon words as reflecting deviousness or outright deception—

---

*tened* vexed, perplexed; *sotyle in* argue subtly about; *kulled* killed; *But I be* if I am not; *heste* bidding, command.

must of course be carefully scrutinized. The altered fortunes of the 'pun' since medieval and Elizabethan times must not lure us into finding sophistries where there may be plain home-thrusts. Thus, we have from Thought a ready explanation of where Dowel is to be found:

'Dowel and Dobet and Dobest the thridde', quod he,
'Aren three *faire* vertues and beth nau3te *fer* to fynde ...'

(VIII 79-80)

But Thought's laconic observation does not necessarily mark a 'confidence in his knowledge of the life of perfection ... ironically pointed in the approximate rhyme of *faire* and *fer*'.[59] There is irony, certainly: but it is turned upon the Dreamer, not the speaker. It resides in the fact that the Dreamer need look no further than his own need and capacity —no further than his own 'tonge' and 'his two handes'. The irony is deepened for the reader, in that the Dreamer is re-established at the outset of his journey in the *Vita* in the same terms as those in which Holy Church had characterized him at the beginning of the *Visio*. Let him look in his own heart; and, above all, let him see that the truth is applied to himself—'worche thow there-after'. The irony is focused upon the Dreamer, and it is genial, though not the less penetrating on that account.

With these safeguards—of which an attention to the whole context of any one passage is the first, and a distinction between the conscious (and intended) as against the unconscious and associational the second— we may well respond to the fresh reading of the poem which awareness of wordplay may bring. Doubtful instances will of course remain. What for example, are we to say of the interpretation which Huppé gives of the wordplay at XV 342-55? Since it is offered as an illustration of 'structural word play' the whole passage may serve to introduce the question of function—in what circumstances may we expect any marked degree of wordplay, and with what characteristic effects?

Anima speaks of inward and outward in the Christian life:

As in Lussheborwes is a lyther alay, and 3et loketh he lyke a
sterlynge,
The merke of that mone is good ac the metal is fieble;
And so it fareth by some folke now, thei han a faire speche,
Croune and Crystendome, the kynges merke of heuene,

*faire* fair, noble; *fer* far, remote; *Lussheborwes* (Luxembourgs) spurious coins; *lyther* base; *alay* alloy; *fieble* (feeble) defective; *Croune* the tonsure; *Crystendome* baptism (these latter two alluding to the 'head' and 'tail' of contemporary coinage).

Ac the metal, that is mannes soule, with synne is foule alayed;
Bothe lettred and lewede beth allayed now with synne,
That no lyf loueth other, ne owre lorde, as it semeth.
For thorw werre and wykked werkes and wederes vnresonable,
Wederwise shipmen and witti clerkes also
Han no bilieue to the lifte ne to the lore of philosofres.
Astrymyanes alday in her arte faillen,
That whilum warned bifore what shulde falle after.
Shipmen and shepherdes that with shipp and shepe wenten,
Wisten by the walkene what shulde bityde.

It is suggested that there is here 'a pun on *mone*', in the two senses
'money' and 'moon', and thus, too, on '*sterlynge*, coin and star' and
'*mark*, sign and coin'. So there are several 'levels' of meaning: firstly,
'the image of man as God's coin'; secondly, 'the heavens as reflecting
man's loss of faith'. 'The transition is reinforced by a still further play:
as the sinner seems to *fare in faire speche* so shipmen and shepherds *wenten*,
*wisten* by the *walkene* (walk and welkin).' A footnote suggests that there
is yet another pun—'a play on *sterlynge*, the bird, reflected in *foule
alayed* (with pun on *foule*, foul, bird?)'.[60] Here are associations in plenty—
though how many of them can be said to be valid for the poet and his
audience is doubtful. What is beyond doubt is that the analogy of false
coin is followed through. The wickedness of man is seen as pervading
God's realm by a kind of Gresham's Law, so that the true coin of ordinary
portents becomes scarce. But it is hard to see how a sense 'moon' is
played upon in *mone*—particularly since the C Text has *moneye*, and yet
arrives at 'the sonne and the mone', which would suggest that any
association is unconscious. *Mark*, it is clear, is in the forefront of
consciousness; but *sterlynge* as 'star', with *foule* as 'bird' and *walkene* as
'walk', cannot be claimed with any certainty; and indeed the general
tenor of this passage, as of the poem in its entirety, seems to make
against multiplicity of allusion. Once again, we should not fail to notice
that concentration on complexity of meaning may lead to our overlooking a primary simplicity. Huppé, listing the evidences of 'God's
mark' on man, includes 'fair speech'. But the poet's 'faire speche' is
outward appearance, and implies contrast with the 'alloy' within.
It is hypocrisy that is being characterized (those 'That faire by-fore
folke prechen and techen', as C has it), not a divinely-given attribute.

*wederes vnresonable* unseasonable storms; *to* in; *lifte* heavens, sky; *philosofres* natural
philosophers, scientists; *Astrymyanes* astrologers; *alday* continually; *whilum* formerly; *falle* befall; *Wisten* used to know; *walkene* sky.

The trains of association Huppé is tracing may indeed exist (though our warrant for believing so requires some foundation in close study of comparable passages, as well as in general etymological principles). But the subterranean workings of the poet's imagination are one thing, the products of that imagination another. In this field, as in the study of Shakespearian wordplay,[61] we need to distinguish between the associations which may be present, in varying degree, in the writer's mind and the objects given for the audience's attention.

When that is said, the importance of this aspect of Langland's poem needs no further qualification. Wordplay is a primary device to bring before us the riddling complexities of a universe which both reveals and hides itself from the Dreamer—a Dreamer in whom, appropriately, there flourishes a strong argumentative zeal. There are thus certain points of development in the poem where we may look for concentration of wordplay—for example, as Huppé points out, in dramatic characterization, as in Meed's equivocation before the King. Above all, the wrangling of Piers and the Priest repays careful examination. As always, it is essential to study the whole context. Thus, Piers's thrust at the Priest—

'Abstinence the abbesse', quod Pieres, 'myne a.b.c. me tauȝte—'

does more than suggest 'the basic place of abstinence in the good life'. In the whole encounter between Plowman and Priest there is, as was suggested in an earlier chapter,[62] a manifest disproportion between the *tene* of the Plowman and its immediate occasion; and this disproportion implies a self-reproach in the Plowman venting itself on the object readiest to hand. So, too, the practised ease of the Priest in rejoinder shows very clearly that simple righteousness is no match for seasoned dialectic. There is indeed a gathering of meanings here; but they are not recondite allegorical or symbolical meanings. The Plowman's vexation is sharp and absolute; and the dialectical skill of the Priest warns us of a tension between knowledge and simple practice to come in the *Vita*, and which has the quality of permanency in human life.

The same rule of proceeding holds for all other occasions of sustained wordplay. Huppé offers us a major instance of meaning clustered upon meaning in the Harrowing of Hell, notably the mystery of God's grace revealed by Mercy (XVIII 134-60). But here, too, we should turn to the actual context; and there, as we saw, against the triumphant assertions of imminent fulfilment, there is the coarse language of incredulity ('a tale of Waltrot'; 'holde thi tonge, Mercy! It is but a trufle that thow tellest'). It is for this reason that affirmation gives way to argument—

Peace retraces the ground of the *mesure* principle as a preparation for the Saviour's victory (201-227). This in its turn is succeeded by debate, as Satan's last claim—to rightful possession—is disposed of. In Christ's speech to Satan (331-401) a pattern of 'identity in opposites', as Huppé rightly terms it, is contrasted, not only in its authoritative wordplay but also in its solemn tones of affirmation, with the colloquialisms of a shifty adversary who has prepared his last trick:

> 'Lysteneth', quod Lucifer, 'for I this lorde knowe'—

an assertion which he must immediately qualify—

> 'Bothe this lorde and this li3te, *is long ago* I knewe hym . . .'
>
> (*ibid.*, 270-71)

It is a fatal admission; and there is something of a time-worn feebleness in Satan's last piece of verbal juggling:

> If he reue me my ri3te he robbeth me by maistrye.
> For by ri3t and bi resoun tho renkes that ben here
> Bodye and soule ben myne, bothe gode and ille. (*ibid.*, 274-6)

It is against this equivocation the great affirmations are heard, proclaiming with level force

> *soule* shal *soule* quyte and *synne* to *synne* wende,
> And al that *man* hath mysdo, I, *man*, wyl *amende* . . . (*ibid.*, 338-9)

Law is once and for always triumphant; so life and death are affirmed as the final limits of Law's domain:

> Membre for membre bi the olde lawe was amendes,
> And lyf for lyf also, and by that lawe I clayme it . . .
> And that deth in hem fordid my deth shal releue. (*ibid.*, 340-1,
>
> 342)

In such a passage we may be confident in tracing the ringing changes of wordplay, for here all meanings are coming into one focus—the unalterable fact of a Law fulfilled comprehends and transcends all.

An aspect of wordplay which repays further attention is to be found in the related notions of 'jousting' and 'justice'. The figure of Christ's fulfilment of Law as a 'joust' links naturally with the 'justice' thus satisfied. In this light, we would do well to look at every instance of

*reue* deprives; *my ri3te* what is rightfully mine; *maistrye* superior force; *tho* those; *renkes* men, creatures; *quyte* requite; *wende* meet, counter; *mysdo* done amiss; *fordid* destroyed; *releue* restore.

*Iust* that the poem affords. The pattern of association in the poet's deepest imagination is, as we have said, not necessarily to be taken as a pointer to implied meaning in any given context. But acquaintance with the working imagination of the writer will be especially tested by the occurrence of a sense not found elsewhere in the poem. Thus, in the 'banquet-scene', looking upon the Doctor's great bulk set to the table, the Dreamer cries

I shal Iangle to this Iurdan with his *Iust* wombe! (XIII 83)

Skeat perceives that the word *Iust* here means a flagon, the big-bellied drinking vessel that perfectly represents the greedy Doctor of Divinity. And that is the only sense which the passage directly offers. But what threw this unusual word into prominence? We may recall the connexion between the 'jousting' that, in the Crucifixion, is to fulfil 'justice', and the mode in which it is to be made possible, the Incarnation:

Tyl *plenitudo temporis* ful tyme ycomen were,
That Pieres fruit floured and fel to be ripe.
And thanne shulde Iesus *Iuste* there-fore ... (XVI 93-5)

Here perhaps is an association which works by contraries. The matrix of Langland's imagining is dialectical—thesis and antithesis lie together in the deepest well of his mind. The *justa mensura* of the flagon, and the slow ripening of the fruit in due season, may be the wayward pattern of association which throws up the unusual word *Iust* for this entire antitype of 'a mayde ... a meke thinge with-alle'. Certainly, the last image of jousting, as Huppé points out, appears in Passus XX in the description of Couetise, who

Iugged til a Iustice and Iusted in his ere.

It has, as Huppé observes, 'magnificently ironic force' through the cumulative effect of all that has gone before.[63] We have only to add that the image is included in the next line

And *ouertilte* al his treuthe with 'take-this-vp-amendement'.

We are back at a world which, to all appearances, might never have known the great joust at Calvary, with its fulfilment of absolute demand. Now, once again, all is qualified and partial. This final jousting is truly, as Skeat called it, a 'mock-tournament'.[64]

*Iangle to* dispute with; *Iurdan* chamber-pot; *plenitudo temporis* 'the fulness of the time' (See p. 154); *justa mensura* right measure; *Iugged til* jogged (up) to; *Iusted* ran a tilt (at the justice's ear); *ouertilte* (tilted over) overturned; *take-this* etc. take this in settlement.

Of a similarly pervasive nature, and thus peculiarly resistant to any attribution of conscious and consistent wordplay, is that awareness of the threefold which runs like a golden thread from Holy Church's discourse upon '*tre*sore the *tri*est on erthe', through '*trust*' and '*tri*ennales' to the '*tre*wth that *tre*spassed neuere'; and so to a Tree of Charity which, as we have seen,[65] is a gathering-place of many meanings in a trinitarian fullness:

> '. . . a ful *trye tree*', quod he, '*trew*ly to telle . . .
> . . . the *Tri*nite it meneth.' (XVI 4, 63)

It is less a 'basic play upon three' than a deep-rooted characteristic of the poet's imagining. Here, as with the similitude of fingers, fist and palm, (XVII 138-202) the threefold is a natural framework of expression, rather than a form of wordplay. We must, however, surely count it a discovery on Huppé's part that there is a 'consistent use of wordplay in making the transitions from waking to sleeping (and the reverse)'.[66] As the images of dream recede, so insistent questioning begins: the *meteles* ('dream') provides food for thought to the *metelees* ('meatless') wanderer, his *metyng* ('dreaming') is of *metyng* ('meeting') with the authoritative, whose counsel he must heed before he falls victim to Old Age, whose threats, he well knows, will be fulfilled—'myȝt we euere *meten*'. This marked wordplay at the transitions between sleeping and waking is no accident. Truly awake or truly asleep, there is an intent simplicity in the Dreamer. The world of riddling conjecture is one we must pass through; it offers no dwelling-place. The verbal exchanges between Plowman and Priest, we saw, effect a transition from one whole mode of awareness to another. All that has been said of Langland's 'literal' power will be misunderstood if it is thought of as an untutored *naïveté*. Perception of subtlety in the handling of language will increase our awareness of the poet's capacity for a profound simplicity. Certainly, it is not a merely literal interpretation of truth which sustains hope in the Dreamer. The literal in that sense is evident in the Priest's interpretation of the Pardon; and of it Robertson and Huppé speak truly: 'he has the deadly literal-mindedness of which Paul spoke when he said, "The letter killeth" '.[67]

## VII

It is a comparable insensitivity to the many-sidedness of the poem that modern awareness of complex allegory and wordplay may make some claim to dispel. The day is long past when Skeat could count upon *trye* excellent.

ready agreement with his characterization of the simile of the hand as 'This supposed proof of the Trinity, from a fancied analogy with the fist, palm and fingers ... no doubt borrowed from an older source'; or notice as a mere misquotation of the Scriptural text the train of association that links *Piers* with *Christus*.[68] But, equally, if we persist in seeking allegory in terms of a fancied archetype, we shall be indifferent to the real nature of the poem's working and even, at times, as we have seen, to the very presence of wordplay. In all this we need to beware of an excess of minute interpretation. The things that are most important in this poem are those that are most accessible. Langland's is not, in truth, a poetry that has its 'true sense' hidden under a 'rich garment'. The common ways of medieval allegory may deepen our understanding of the issues he deals with, but they may mislead us as to his handling of them. Langland's originality is a very real thing; and it is this above all which may escape the scholar, ever-ready with his analogues and parallels, and his sense of the past as *difference*.

The poem offers us two great extremes meeting in a Dreamer, one who will strenuously argue the high theoretical point while steadily overlooking what lies nearest home. If we attend to the poem it has the power to raise with us the question, Are not these the extremes that meet in all men? It is himself man may leave out of the reckoning when he would pursue the great issues of 'doing well'; and thus, like the Dreamer, he may succeed only in externalizing them—as we in our turn may do in our reading of this poem. There is, then, every reason to oppose a 'historical criticism' which would prescribe the formal and elaborate patterns in which this, or any, poem is to be apprehended. If we respond to the poet in his own sequence, and at his own pace, we shall see that where he is most 'medieval' he is most lively and penetrating. Thus, the great image of chivalrous *noblesse* which invests the career of the Saviour is incapable of translation. There is no need to cast far afield for origins or subtle implications. No need; and it may be dangerous to do so, as taking us away from the full tide of imagination. We may understand not only the medieval but, much more, the modern if we start without either of two common expectations of the 'medieval' —either multiple allegorical-symbolical significance or minute and profitless debate. At least, we may then apprehend in *Piers Plowman* the vision which is prior to ratiocination and to which, in the end, ratiocination must yield. An unwearied zest in dialectic comes upon us at almost every turn; but, as in that Divinity School which is the chief glory of late medieval Oxford, the twin pulpits are put in their true perspective by windows which seem not so much an interruption of the walls as an unbroken reach from earth to heaven. We may call the design in this poem 'allegory' if we will; but we must not fail to perceive its multifariousness and above all its literal and graphic power. For in that literal power there meet not only vision and reason, but also adroit wordplay and comic stupidity. Will, the would-be know-all, is the one who must in the end be brought to the truth, a living example of all men's folly; *Multi multa sciunt, et seipsos nesciunt.*

Two central truths are never to be forgotten, as underlying the energy and drive of the whole. The first is comprehensive and pertains to the Will of continuing desire crossed with dialectical subtlety— 'In every good the Supreme Good is desired'.[69] There is the unending search for where the argument can come to rest. Pursuing it, men must meet the absolute demand—'Be ye perfect'; and thus despair threatens. But on the other side is a truth which is no less valid. The souls of men, we saw, 'albeit in a cloudy memory, yet seek back their good, but, like drunk men, know not the road home.'[70] This is the antidote to despair; we perceive that man must be brought to the truth, and that this, too, is implicit in a Providence which concerns itself with the Will of obstinate self-interest. So we have the apparently erratic progress, with its repetitions and digressions; but we have also the piercingly clear foretastes of a truth that will not be finally withheld.

In any movement away from the literalism of nineteenth century interest in medieval poetry we must not recapitulate the curve of eighteenth century attitude towards the 'Gothic' past, travelling all the way from polite indifference, or open contempt, via affectionate indulgence to a mere historical relativism. It was a great step forward to have established 'Gothic rules' as the criteria appropriate to 'Gothic art'. The peace-terms thus offered deserve our gratitude:

> The question is not which of the two is conducted in the simplest or truest taste; but whether there be not sense and design in both, when scrutinized by the laws on which each is projected.[71]

But they can be no more than peace-terms. A Ritson rises to proclaim the duty of preferring 'truth to hypothesis',[72] and the codification of Gothic laws has begun. The closed shop of scholars means, certainly, a purified text and a growing bulk of serviceable commentary. But equally it means a dangerous isolation of the work of art from the challenge of uninstructed interest. The commentary, we have seen more than once, will be accommodated to some arbitrary, if learned, notions

*Multi* etc. 'Many know much and know not of themselves' (attributed to St. Bernard).

concerning poetry. The right example is set by the medieval poet's counsel to his book at the outset of its journey:

> no makyng thow n'envie,
> But subgit be to alle poesye.[73]

It is perhaps the most important truth of all that the work of art must be exposed to the touch of life as men in every age encounter it, not as abstraction but as inescapable involvement. In the present the scholar meets a period which even he can hardly take as read. He may thus be enabled to see more clearly what it is in the past his own age may tend to overlook—and what, with an equal innocence, invent.

# Notes

1. *The English Epic and its Background*, London, 1954, p. 139.
2. *The Allegory of Love*, Oxford, 1936, p. 48 n.2
3. *Lives of the English Poets*, Life of Butler.
4. *Poetical Works*, ed. Smith, Oxford, 1909, II 485-6.
5. *The Allegory of Love*, p. 334.
6. Sherwood Anderson, *Winesburg, Ohio*, 'The Book of the Grotesque'.
7. Prologue to *Confessio Amantis*, 19-21.
8. *op. cit.*, p. 334.
9. *ibid.*, p. 298 (italics supplied).
10. *Coleridge's Literary Criticism*, pp. 137-8; 139; 140 (italics supplied).
11. Coleridge, *Dejection: An Ode*, 37-8.
12. *The Prelude*, ed. De Selincourt, Oxford, 1926, xiv 101-3 (1850).
13. *English Literature Medieval*, London, N. D., pp. 194-5.
14. *The Vision of Piers Plowman*, p. xvii.
15. 'The Pardon of Piers Plowman', p. 52
16. D. W. Robertson, Jr., and Bernard F. Huppé, *'Piers Plowman' and Scriptural Tradition*, Princeton, 1951, p. 247.
17. For a statement of the principles of 'historical criticism', see the contribution of that title by D. W. Robertson, Jr., in *English Institute Essays, 1950*, New York, 1951. An argument resisting some usual distinctions between the 'historical' and 'critical' activities is developed by the present writer in an essay 'On Historical Scholarship and the interpretation of Shakespeare', *Sewanee Review*, LXIV (1956), 186-206.
18. *The Limits of Literary Criticism*, London, 1956, p. 14.
19. *Epistles to Several Persons (Moral Essays)*, London, 1951, p. v.
20. *Vita Nuova*, xxv (tr. Ricci, *The New Life*, London, 1903, p. 131).
21. R. M. Grant, *The Letter and the Spirit*, London, 1957.

*subgit* subject.

22. *op. cit.*, p. 187.

23. *Convivio*, Second Treatise, Ch. I (tr. Wicksteed).

24. R. W. Frank, Jr., 'The Art of Reading Medieval Personification-Allegory', *ELH*, XX (1953), 237-50.

25. *ibid.*, p. 249.

26. *Paradise Lost* v 434-6.

27. It is soundly observed that a good deal of medieval understanding of the 'literal' differs from our own. 'Most of the Fathers considered the meaning behind a metaphor not a literal but a secondary sense' (R. E. Brown, *The 'Sensus Plenior' of Sacred Scripture*, Baltimore, 1955, p. 6, quoted by M. W. Bloomfield in his brief but challenging survey, 'Symbolism in Medieval Literature', *Modern Philology*, LVI, 1958, 73-81). Throughout, I use 'literal' in a modern acceptance—*i.e.* as including ordinary and unremarkable use of metaphor, image, or analogy, on which the poet may make distinctive variation constituting 'further' or 'allegorical' sense.

28. Bloomfield, *loc. cit.*, 79, n. 22. (C. G. Hardie argues against the traditional attribution to Dante in 'The Epistle to Cangrande again', *Deutsches Dante-Jahrbuch*, XXXVIII (1960), 51-74.)

29. *The Study of the Bible in the Middle Ages*, Oxford, 1952, pp. 284-5.

30. As in Professor Coghill's moderate view of the kind of allegory found in the *Roman de la Rose*—a 'rich way of multiple but simultaneous thought . . . by no means confined to poetry' (*The Poet Chaucer*, London, 1949, p. 13).

31. The point is well illustrated in E. T. Donaldson's 'opposition' paper 'Patristic Exegesis in the Criticism of Medieval Literature' (*Critical Approaches to Medieval Literature*, Selected Papers from the English Institute, 1958-59, N.Y., 1-26) where, rejecting Mortimer Donovan's 'patristic' reading of the *Nun's Priest's Tale*, Donaldson remarks acutely that 'the fruit of the *Nun's Priest's Tale* is its chaff'.

32. Robertson and Huppé, *op. cit.*, pp. 83-5.

33. This is treated more fully in Chapter VII, especially pp. 285-95, below.

34. R.W. Frank, Jr., *'Piers Plowman' and the Scheme of Salvation*, New Haven, 1957, p. 23.

35. Mitchell, 'Lady Meed and the Art of *Piers Plowman*', p. 7.

36. Robertson and Huppé, *op. cit.*, p. 61. They are, however, prepared to allow the 'historical suggestion' of Alice Perrers in Lady Meed (p. 51, n. 6).

37. Professor Mitchell, anxious to assert the poet's 'precision and vigour of thought' would reject topical allusion altogether; Meed is making no wild accusations' nor being 'simply abusive' (p. 8). Meed's accusations, we may agree, are far from being 'wild'; they are made cogent by telling allusion. She accuses John of Gaunt of being a robber, in pursuing his own interest. It is a charge that is uncomfortably difficult to shift: prudence in another's cause is not easily distinguished from self-interest. The poet's talent is for penetrating to the ultimate limits of a world governed by the *mesurable*; and the talent is evident here, in Meed's brilliant reversal of the obvious case against her.

38. Robertson and Huppé, pp. 169, 175-6; Frank, *Scheme of Salvation*, p. 76.

39. *'Piers Plowman* and the Three Grades of Chastity', *Anglia*, LXXV (1958),

227-53; 246.

40. Robertson and Huppé, p. 191.

41. *The Allegory of Love*, p. 312.

42. Dr. Owst's warning against taking as direct experience the vivid details the preacher could cull from his manuals is reinforced by W. O. Ross, *Middle English Sermons*, London, 1940, p. lx. Lively imagery is not necessarily drawn from the preacher's own first-hand experience; for some exceptions, however, see Owst, *The Destructorium Viciorum of Alexander Carpenter*, London, 1952, p. 24.

43. As in Bloomfield's essay, referred to at note 39, above. The whole subject awaits investigation in detail.

44. *Essays on the English Poets*, p. 55.

45. *Cf.* the heading Skeat prints at C VIII 204, *alta uia ad fidelitatem est obseruatio .x. preceptorum*, and Ymagynatyf's counsel to 'religious': *holde the vnder obedyence, that heigh wey is to heuene* (XII 38).

46. The explanation of what is to be understood by *the handefedde foules* (464-77) is found in MS R only. It is, however, not necessarily scribal, since the twin MS, F, has at this point a lacuna. The omission would therefore appear accidental.

47. For a charming representation of this common symbol, see M. D. Anderson, *The Imagery of British Churches*, London, 1955, pl. 5 (a misericord in Ripon Cathedreal, clearly copied from the *Biblia Pauperum*; *ibid.*, p. 97).

48. See p. 179, above.

49. For dramatic skill, the 'business' and timing of this episode, see pp. 210-12, above.

50. Robertson and Huppé point out that the faculty of will, as the source of moral action, is peculiarly fitted for instruction; but that the will 'can be good only in so far as it is guided by reason'. Their understanding of the role of Will is welcome; but it is unfortunate that they persist in relating the 'lessons' of the poem to the Church rather than the individual Christian (*op. cit.*, pp. 34-5).

51. *Confessio Amantis*, iii 1193-99.

52. '*Petrus id est Christus*: Word Play in *Piers Plowman*, the B Text', *ELH*, XVII (1950), 163-190.

53. I adopt Donaldson's suggested reading *yolde* ('spent') instead of the weaker *olde*; *cf.* '[He] with a yoldin yerd dois yolk me in armys', Dunbar, *Tretis of the Tua Mariit Wemen and the Wedo*, l.220.

54. Huppé, *loc. cit.*, 179.

55. See p. 266, above. Perhaps the most striking instances, to a modern taste, are those which occur in passages of great seriousness; as, of the Saviour at the raising of Lazarus, 'Ac as he made the *maistr*ye mest*us cepit esse*' (XVI 115); the giving of sight to 'Longeus', at the Crucifixion, 'The blode spronge down by the *spere* and vn*spered* the kni3tes eyen' (XVIII 86); and, most poignantly, the words of the Saviour on the Cross, 'There *nede* hath ynome me, that I mote *nede* abyde, And suffre *sorwes* full *sowre* . . . (XX 45-6). Skeat lists some twelve 'puns' (*op. cit.*, II

*maistrye* achievement; *mestus* etc. 'he grew sorrowful' (cf. John xi 35); *spere* spear, lance; *vnspered* unbarred, opened; *ynome* taken, brought; *mote* must; *nede* needs; *sorwes* (sorrows) pain.

482); for his attitude toward sverbal ingenuity, see p. 84, n. 12 above, and compare his comment on the line 'Suffreth my postles in *pays*, and in *pees* gange' (XVI 159): 'The repetition of the words is a defect in the line, but we must remember that the two clauses are quite distinct' (*ibid.*, II 239). *Cf.* Macbeth's 'Whom we, to gain our peace, have sent to peace' (III 2 20), where the F 2 reading 'gain our *place*'—which, as Muir remarks, 'ruins a nice point' (Arden edn., 1951, p. 85)— has sometimes been defended as repairing a similar 'defect.'

56. *loc. cit.*, 171.

57. *ibid.*, 177.

58. See p. 26, above.

59. Huppé, 165. (The point is not affected by Huppé's mistakenly attributing these words to 'the friar'.)

60. *ibid.*, 172-3.

61. The point is more fully treated in my 'Mind and Hand: some reflections on the study of Shakespeare's imagery' (*Shakespeare Quarterly*, VIII (1957), 179-193).

62. See pp. 79-81, above.

63. *loc. cit.*, 179.

64. *op. cit.*, II 279.

65. See pp. 257-8, above.

66. Huppé, 186.

67. *op. cit.*, p. 94.

68. *op. cit.*, II 244; 221.

69. *Cf.* St. Thomas Aquinas, *de Veritate*, q. 22, a. 3 (*Quaestiones Disputatae*, ed. Spiazzi, Rome, 1949, I 392).

70. Boethius, *de Consolatione Philosophiae*, III pr. ii. (For the Latin text and Chaucer's translation, see the epigraph to Ch. III, above; the translation given here is by C. S. Lewis, *The Pilgrim's Regress*, p. 19.)

71. Richard Hurd, *Letters on Chivalry and Romance*, ed. Morley, London, 1911, p. 118.

72. *Ancient Songs*, London, 1790, p. xxvi.

73. *Troilus and Criseyde*, v 1789-90.

*postles* apostles, disciples; *pays, pees* peace.

# Chapter VII

# The Poet and the Dreamer

... there yet remains a harder task ... that is, the maintaining the character of an author, which distinguishes him from all others, and makes him appear that individual poet whom you would interpret.
                                        Dryden, Preface to *Sylvae*

Langland's deepest awareness, we have seen, is of Law—a Law which cannot be evaded, though it is the common condition of humanity to seek evasion; and which must be absolute, though everywhere we see that perfect fulfilment is beyond humanity's reach. It is this certainty that God is not mocked which sustains both the great prophetic utterances, when law is triumphant, as in the Harrowing of Hell or Conscience's vision of milennial harmony (III 282-327), and also the satiric power of the poem, its characteristic *vis comica*. Evil is seen as comically *naïve*—in its own terms of self-interest, incompetent;[1] and the satiric power of the poet comes upon us at many turns and with a varying range of effect, from vivid scorn and impassioned rebuke to a quieter ironic humour[2]— with, ever-ready, the practised facility of the dialectician in crying the *Contra!* of swift objection. Yet the Dreamer himself is included within the range of the satire; and this very inclusion is the condition of our advancing at all in the argument of the poem. It is through a fallible guide that the poet manoeuvres his reader. We must therefore be especially wary when we come to identify both the poet himself—not 'William Langland' in a merely biographical sense but the author present in the whole work of *Piers Plowman*—and the doctrines which his Dreamer contemplates. It will be best to begin with the characterization of the Dreamer (and here comparison with Dreamers in Chaucer and Gower may help), and consider the nature of his progress, before we turn to those 'Lives' about which so much has been heard. In this light, it may be possible to ask whether the poem has an imaginative, and not a merely doctrinal, unity. Our starting-point is with the satire that meets us not only in the *Visio* but in the *Vita de Dowel, Dobet et Dobest*, and its bearing upon the characterization of the Dreamer.

## I

The satire abounding in the *Visio* is not always squarely faced by those who would elaborate a claim for the unity of *Piers Plowman*. True, there is general recognition that the perception of widespread wickedness prompts, by a natural reaction, the question 'How may I save my soul?' But the connexion between *Visio* and *Vita* may be thought to go deeper. Certainly, if we are to claim for *Piers Plowman* any unity of imagination, we must ask how the work of the satirist is related to the thinker's task of construction. Some critics may feel that the satire of the *Visio* is an involuntary concession to the age in which Langland wrote; and it is noticeable that as scholarship has attended closely to *Piers Plowman* it has become increasingly absorbed in the matter of the *Vita* in its three great divisions. We are so much concerned with the issues Langland unfolds that we may be in danger of neglecting the simplicity with which he begins. Professor C. S. Lewis states unambiguously what is implied by others when he invites us to consider Langland in these terms:

> He is writing a moral poem, such as Gower's *Miroir de l'homme* or Gower's Prologue to the *Confessio Amantis*, and throwing in, as any other medieval poet might have done, a good deal of satire on various 'estates'.[3]

This is a striking reaction from those earliest critics who, dwelling with satisfaction on the poet's more obvious satirical targets, hailed him as a great reformer—in Fuller's phrase, 'by *Prolepsis . . .* a Protestant'. But each side misses the mark; for Langland's satire is more radical than Professor Lewis allows and covers a wider range than Fuller perceived. What is central to Langland's whole design is the observed discrepancy between what we believe and what in fact we are. His poem has its focus in this aspect of the human condition. He therefore proceeds at the outset of the poem by way of external observation—the misdeeds of others—until he has amply shown the necessity of repentance. At this stage, he advances a step further in the whole inquiry by bringing forward the one good man the world of his poem can produce in its deepest need—only to humble him. In the realization that comes upon Piers we may see that we have not reached a final limit when goodness is found—for that goodness is now seen to be relative: the only absolute is Perfection. The Plowman who began by instructing others in the way of law (the stiff, signpost-like allegory of the Commandments in Passus V) has perceived that law condemns unless it is perfectly fulfilled. He therefore turns—or rather, he is turned—away from Justice to the Divine

Mercy; and his 'confession of evil works' is, in St. Augustine's phrase, 'the beginning of good works'.[4] For Piers there has opened a road to the Promised Land which leads beyond Sinai.

The satire of the *Visio* is emphatically not 'thrown in'. Langland indeed begins well within the customary usages of satire. But his genius is to carry the argument beyond those limits. If all men profess the truth and few or none can be found to practise it, we must pass from censure to inquiry; for this universal condition must make us ask what is man's capacity for the good life. It is in that light that we see the shortcomings of the best man the world of the *Visio* could produce, the Plowman whose Pardon brings an equal and undeviating assurance of both reward and punishment. And it is thus that we are prepared for the next appearance of 'Piers Plowman' before the Saviour's earthly career is recounted (Passus XVI); for it is the Redemption, perfectly fulfilling inexorable law, which allowed the Plowman of the half-acre to seek a Mercy which is not inconsistent with Justice. But the satiric intelligence has not done: what we have seen in the *Visio* is slow to yield its meaning to the Dreamer of the *Vita de Dowel*. In Langland imagination and logic are uniquely joined; his characteristic capacity is to imagine absolutely. The Pardon that is a 'pardon' only on condition that law can exact no punishment reveals the external world for what it is in the moment that we pass beyond it—a place of relative goods, where the highest attainment to be looked for is observance of the *mesurable*. If we are to look beyond that world, we must look within. There comes to the fore, after the Pardon scene, that Dreamer, hitherto the observer, on whom realization is yet to fall. How successful will he be? The Plowman, we remember, was ready for the knowledge which came to him, by reason of his long perseverance in simple well-doing. What of the Dreamer's qualifications? They are given at the outset of the whole work, after a Prologue in which we, with the Dreamer, have been shown a world whose law is self-interest. In the first Passus of the *Visio* Holy Church must explain. In doing so, as we have seen,[5] she encounters questions from the Dreamer which are inappropriate to his understanding; for the Dreamer, we observe, desires all-embracing answers, but his gaze is directed outwards. The colloquy deserves to be taken again in detail, for it is both a foretaste of that mode of inquiry which constitutes the *Vita* and at the same time is a clear indication of the inquirer's limited capacity to learn.

Holy Church, as yet unknown to the Dreamer, begins with the comprehensive statement that to do right is to live according to Truth's teaching, with the specific injunction to observe *mesure*. The Dreamer at once puts a large question—and this is to be characteristic of him: who owns the world's wealth? The answer is, as was Holy Church's first statement, that the individual is to look to himself: he is to render unto Caesar the things which are Caesar's. As she concludes her explanation of the Field of Folk, the Dreamer asks who she is; and her reply gives the first hint of a questioner who overlooks what is nearest home:

> 'Holicherche I am', quod she, 'Thow ouȝtest me to knowe,
> I vnderfonge the first and the feyth tauȝte'.

To the Dreamer's cry, 'How may I save my soul?' Holy Church again returns a sufficient answer. Those who do good and purpose no evil to their fellow-men shall have their reward. What she adds is very important for the implications that are later to come to the Dreamer of the *Vita de Dowel*—this 'answer' of hers is common knowledge to all men, Christian and Pagan alike: 'cristene and vncristne clameth it vchone'. This, again, points unmistakably to a questioner who must look within for answers to the problems he raises. It is fitting that Holy Church continues by emphasizing simple obedience to Truth; true faith is shown in actions. To this the Dreamer opposes another large question, How does Truth come to man?; and, to mark his folly, he avers that he has no natural knowledge to help him.

Now Holy Church roundly declares his stupidity. This is the first scolding the Dreamer receives, and the first of many that are to come in the *Vita de Dowel*. The over-ambitious question again reveals the fatal bent—to look without when the answer lies within:

> 'It is a kynde knowyng', quod he, 'That kenneth in thine herte
> For to louye thi lorde leuer than thi-selue;
> No dedly synne to do, dey thouȝ thow sholdest'.

It is simple, unambiguous and final. Speculation is exchanged for plain duty; and this is wholly sufficient for the Dreamer's present purposes:

> This I trowe be treuthe; who can teche the better,
> Loke thow suffre hym to sey and sithen lere it after.
> For thus witnesseth his worde, worche thow there-after

At one and the same time the poet establishes for us the character of his Dreamer and the central theme of the poem. The Dreamer is impetuous in asking (let him 'suffer' others 'to speak'); and this asking is dangerous, for it may turn him from simple practice to speculative

*vnderfonge* received (in baptism); *clameth* claim (to know the truth); *vchone* each; *kynde* natural; *he* she; *kenneth* tells, makes known; *leuer than* rather than; *sithen* then; *worche* work.

inquiry. The 'better' the Dreamer would seek is not denied but must for the present be withheld. The connexion between the problems man would raise and his capacity for apprehending them as realities is made indissoluble in the first Passus of the *Visio*. We are prepared for the last lesson the Dreamer of the *Vita de Dowel* is to grasp. Again, the vexation of Holy Church with one who would look further afield than the knowledge written in his own heart, may remind us of the 'pure tene' of the Plowman when realization breaks upon him. The focus of imaginative attention in *Piers Plowman* is upon our habitual incapacity to grasp that what we know as doctrine bears directly upon us, and hence our search for a truth which shall be comprehensive while in fact, and all unwittingly, we would exclude ourselves from the reckoning.

## II

The method of Langland's poem, as we saw earlier[6], is to present a Dreamer whose inexperience is matched only by his doctrinaire assurance, so that his coming to understanding constitutes at once the progressive argument of the poem and the lively demonstration of its central truth. In this, Langland's dream-poem offered comparisons with similar work in Chaucer and Gower. If we now examine the characterization of this Dreamer, the 'I' of *Piers Plowman*, we shall find a 'self-portrait' which is, again, not unlike those in Langland's contemporaries. With whatever differences of emphasis, the common tradition is one of humorous self-depreciation, ranging from mild self-mockery to rueful admission of stupidity. We here come upon the essential difference between a satire which remains external and that which includes the observer himself in its whole survey. Through the Dreamer the reader is brought into direct touch with the truths the poem affirms. But where so much is mediated through an 'I', that 'I' must itself be scrutinized, so that there is no final barrier to understanding. We must therefore be especially on our guard against identifying the *persona* thus established, and thus in the course of the poem corrected, with the writer in any narrowly biographical sense.[7] The temptation is perhaps not so strong where we have a number of short works from the same hand—so that varying 'self-portraiture' occurs—as it is in single sustained works like the *Confessio Amantis* or *Piers Plowman*, where one and the same Dreamer's progress is essential to the development of the whole. But in this we are inconsistent. What is common to Chaucer, Gower and Langland is the presentation of an 'I' who exhibits both eagerness to learn and a residual stubbornness, so that in the long run the central truth of the poem must be asserted at the expense of the Dreamer; and this assertion as we saw earlier, constitutes a *pref*, a demonstration that the *auctoritee* on which the Dreamer has originally relied is not, to be sure, mistaken, but inadequately applied to his own case. In the courtly tradition, this joins with and is sustained by the actual relationship of poet and audience. The civility of not presuming upon the audience's patience is worn naturally when the poet's place in the literary tradition is least because he is no more than the latest teller of common story. Thus his stock role is that of the inexperienced doctrinaire. His dependence upon his authorities is complete; and this is a stance especially capable of adroit effect where the poet's matter is of love. He is, he allows us to see, at the opposite pole from Alice, Wife of Bath, that wholly experienced authority upon 'love'. The poet's situation may be expressed by inverting the terms of her boldly challenging opening line:[8]

> *Auctoritee*, though noon experience
> Were in this world, is right ynogh for me...

This is the essential condition of the mere writer; and, what is worse, unlike his antitype, Alice, he does not at the outset know it. It is not merely a jest which has many possibilities. It is a mode of creative imagination which, properly handled, can move the poem away from statement to demonstration—to a cumulative effect which is not that of a merely argued progress observable in the Dreamer but of a conclusion the reader cannot avoid when the guide himself has been brought to newness of understanding. We shall understand Langland's work better if we glance at the varying characterizations of a Dreamer in Chaucer and Gower.

With Chaucer, the disproportions of doctrine and experience are mainly those proper to an erotic tradition. Thus, in *The Book of the Duchess*, a Dreamer who is love's doctrinaire, lacking all experience save that of unrequited love, must learn, all in a moment, both the happiness of requited love and the bitterness of its loss. Experience itself speaks in a sorrowing Knight whom

> deth hath mad al naked
> Of al the blysse that ever was maked.[9]

Similarly, but for wholly comic ends, the Dreamer of *The House of Fame* is one whose bookish service of love (a service rendered to Venus 'Withoute guerdon ever yit') will receive an appropriate reward. But this time, by a genial reversal of roles, it is the heavenly messenger, the *guerdon* recompense.

Eagle, who is loquaciously encyclopaedic, while the Dreamer, sailing helplessly far above the solid earth, must out of regard for his skin be monosyllabically brief. In the event, it is a disillusioned Dreamer who protests vigorously that what he has been shown is not what was promised. The energy of his protest, overflowing upon a well-intentioned inquirer, may perhaps remind us of Langland's Dreamer once the bit is between his teeth:

> '. . . these be no suche tydynges
> As I mene of'. 'Noo?' quod he.
> And I answered, 'Noo, parde!
> For wel y wiste ever yit,
> Sith that first y hadde wit,
> That somme folk . . .'[10]

The effect is wholly comic; no 'correction' of the Dreamer is implied— he has all our sympathy in his disappointment and irritation at a kindly indifference to his actual needs.

In *Troilus and Criseyde*, the master-achievement is to give doctrine-and-inexperience a separate existence. We have not a Dreamer but Pandarus, and he is at once high-priest and factotum to two innocents abroad. But here, too, in the end, it is doctrine that must, in effect, capitulate; for it reaches its furthest limit in pronouncing sentence upon apparent 'tresoun':

> I hate, ywys, Cryseyde;
> And, God woot, I wole hate hire evermore![11]

It is all doctrine can do, and its utter irrelevance is matched only by Pandarus's unfeigned misery in giving judgement. For now he must know himself for once as wholly inadequate. His 'evermore' is an empty thing beside Troilus's realization

> I ne kan nor may
> For al this world, withinne myn herte fynde
> To unloven yow a quarter of a day.[12]

To *unloven?*-the very word speaks the impossibility of the world of theory, with its unfailingly clear distinctions and its entire incapacity for direct understanding. Now we know that there has been a slow and steady growth of the real; the balance has shifted decisively against inexperience fortified by doctrine. We may recall how love had made its unspectacular way in Criseyde's timorous heart:

*wiste* knew; *woot* knows.

she gan enclyne
To like hym first, and I have told yow whi;
And after that, his manhod and his pyne
Made love withinne hire herte for to myne . . .[13]

Chaucer begins and ends the passage by emphasizing that hers is no
'sodeyn' love. This slow and delicate awakening is very different from
the onset of the 'sodeyn' Diomede. The love that 'tunnelled' within
Criseyde's heart is a natural growth; and so it is with Troilus. To end
it by an act of will is impossibility itself—even for 'a quarter of a day'.

Troilus and Criseyde is of course no dream-poem; when the author
speaks to us he does so in his own person—appropriately, as a narrator
who will deal justly with his text and not dilate upon it. But in the
Pandarus of crestfallen would-be wisdom there is the same truth that
is the mainspring of dream-poetry. It is a truth which irradiates the
whole of Troilus and Criseyde, giving the distinctive quality of innocence.
Inexperience has been taught to put on traditional guises—by a third
innocent, as it turns out. The Knight and the Lady is the fairy-tale that
Pandarus with childish joy and cleverness creates, schooling his two
pupils in their parts. When disaster comes, it is Troilus who must endure
and the doctrinaire Pandarus who knows no more than to end the
situation by canonical pronouncement. Chaucer's tragedie is no dream;
but Pandarus speaks in a bitter awaking from the dream in which perhaps all men would live—the illusion that doctrine will give a final
immunity from heartfelt experience. His hurt is deep; for his world is
at an end. This penetration into the human heart is all Chaucer's own.
But it may not be fanciful to suggest that his awareness of unspoilt
human nature, over against a world of confident assertion which in the
end is based upon no experience whatsoever—this is something which
the characteristic medieval emphasis upon auctoritee and experience
readily engenders and which the vision-poem is peculiarly fitted to
express. As in love, so in religion, it is the pure in heart who may be
most amenable to teaching; and who may in the end pass beyond its
limits.

Certainly, in The Legend of Good Women, as we saw earlier,[14] experience has to sing very small, for penance is to be done. The mood of
polite scepticism for auctoritee with which we open ('A thousand sythes
have I herd men telle . . .') is, however, deepened when we hear the God
of Love confidently citing his authorities. The Dreamer's part here is in
one respect an inversion of his ordinary role. He is usually one who must

pyne suffering, toil; mine mine, tunnel; sithes times.

truly learn his inadequacies; but this time the Dreamer makes a mock-rueful submission. Authority is all, and no man is to question it. It is a similar situation when the poet-pilgrim on his way to Canterbury is challenged by the Host; there is meek submission to authority.[15] The small, abstracted figure is brought into unmistakably comic contrast with the energetic Host. But here, too, there is a neat manipulation which ensures that robust insistence upon 'mirth' shall not have it all its own way. The parody of both the manner and the matter of the *joculator* proceeds from the pilgrim-figure Chaucer has drawn, a swift acceptance of the role of remote and ineffectual creature which the Host has jocosely thrust upon him. He can thus be so far removed from any conception of popular entertainment that there is no gainsaying his right to inflict upon them the other half of his disastrously limited reper-toire—the 'moral tale vertuous' of Meliboeus. Chaucer's device works with the reader as he intended it to work, serving a number of ends. The merely literary problem—what kind of tale to allot to the author himself—is solved in a pair of stories which preserves the tradition of humorous self-portraiture while showing the Host to be a figure of fun merely irresistible to Chaucer's own sophisticated audience—the plain man determined to enjoy himself.[16] Once again, in comic and realistic works, no less than in *tragedie* and vision-poem, the represen-tation of the author is functional, adapted to the purposes in hand, and commonly edged with mild self-depreciation. Even in *tragedie*, a humor-ous awareness of the impatient reader is not stilled; the slow growth of love in Criseyde must be emphasized against any too-ready cynic in the poet's audience:

> Now myghte som envious jangle thus:
> 'This was a sodeyn love; how myght it be
> That she so lightly loved Troilus,
> Right for the firste syghte, *ye, parde?*'[17]

In those concluding words we seem to hear an echo of the Duck in *The Parlement of Foules* coarsely refuting an ideal constancy in love—'*Ye quek!*'[18] So a misunderstanding which would be serious can be turned aside by a 'curse' light in tone, befitting mere churlishness: 'Now whoso seith so, mote he nevere ythe!'

The *Confessio Amantis* allows us to see this role of the author with a greater clarity; for here, as compared with Chaucer's *Canterbury Tales*, we have not only a prologue in which we meet the author, but also an

*jangle* argue (foolishly); *lightly* readily; *parde?* indeed?; *quek!* quack!; *mote* may; *ythe* thrive, prosper.

epilogue, where the holiday is over. We should note, too, that Gower's prologue tells us plainly of the poet's infirmity; but as we advance with the 'I' of the poem, the lover come to confession, we forget the darkness of the present—both the years and infirmity of the poet and the 'division' in human affairs which his prologue unsparingly conveys. Gower is true in more ways than one to his declared aim. His is a 'middel wei' not only between 'lust' and 'lore', but a middle flight of discourse, between present and future, earth and heaven:

> I may noght strecche up to the hevene
> Min hand, ne setten al in evene
> This world, which evere is in balance:
> It stant noght in my sufficance
> So grete thinges to compasse.[19]

In this he is wholly successful. We accept his simple assurance that he is one of Love's school, and that the experience he is about to relate happened 'not long ago', 'this enderday'. So, too, we can believe that on the May morning of fulfilled love his unhappiness is great. It is all in the tradition. Love, we have often enough heard, inflicts grievous wounds:

> ther may noman finde
> The rihte salve of such a Sor.[20]

It is with this understanding that we hear the despairing cry to Cupid and Venus:

> Now doth me pleinly live or dye,
> For certes such a maladie
> As I now have and longe have hadd,
> It myhte make a wisman madd,
> If that it scholde longe endure.[21]

In the dialogue with Venus that follows, the suppliant's real plight is skilfully hidden—from himself most of all. The point of departure is marked in his asking a boon—'Some wele after my longe wo'—and this, moreover, in terms of his deserving. For the reader there is an in-dication that the suit will not prosper in Venus's first unfriendly glance at her petitioner (there are many false claimants, we learn), and in the plea of merit. The lover who asks a return for his service falls well below the true standard—to serve without thought of reward; and perhaps in this there is already the implication of a merely bookish and therefore

*in evene* in equilibrium; *in balance* subject to uncertainty; *Sor* hurt, wound; *wele* happiness.

theoretical service. But it is Gower's artistry to hold his reader much as Chaucer does in *The Book of the Duchess*, through the deployment of a well-meaning but doctrinaire Dreamer. Knowing at the outset of the *Confessio Amantis* that the poet is old and infirm, we yet attend to the slow unfolding of his love-confession—'I woll than telle it on and on'; and in the telling do we not forget all else but the bright shapes of primal happiness, and accept this pupil come to confession as the ardent young lover? Certainly, the pupil's tale, unlike the Knight's in Chaucer's poem, is one of unfulfilled love. Yet in this respect, Chaucer-as-Dreamer and Gower-as-pupil are one: they are experienced in all but reality. Chaucer's sorrowing Knight knows that his part in love is at an end; whereas this is the knowledge that is to come to Confessor's pupil, as it came to the Knight's listener, with devastating effect. The device of the love-confession in Chaucer and Gower alike serves the same end; what is conveyed to the reader at the outset is wonderfully overborne in the telling. Here, again, the 'I' of the poem is one who must be brought to know a surprising truth. We, the privileged audience, are given a little more knowledge—and the artistry here is to give us so much as will place us in a position of vantage upon the 'I' of the poem, but not so much that his final discovery will fail to come upon us, as it comes upon him, with a whole effect of surprise. Thus it is in the end of the *Confessio Amantis*—an ending which, we may note, strongly resembles the last Passus of *Piers Plowman*. Here is the poet himself, revealed at last in the winter of his age; here, too, the company of middle-earth; the physician groping after the wound and a salve applied; and here, in the end, clarity of identification, a Dreamer and a poet made whole.[22] In its own right, Gower's ending is a masterpiece of undemonstrative skill. Now the pupil, knowing himself cured, knows also that love is a mystery inaccessible to him. Now Venus can smile; and the pupil, his sentence accepted, can smile, too. As in the close of Chaucer's *tragedie* of *Troilus and Criseyde*, we are directed 'home'. Love unfulfilled has yet an object, and there is happiness at our home-coming, the landfall of long voyaging.

### III

It is in this tradition that we should view the progress of the Dreamer of the *Vita de Dowel*. What deserves our notice at once is the series of rebuffs Langland's Dreamer receives from the authoritative persons he interrogates after his first colloquy, that with the Friars (VIII 8-61). From the Friars he has received practical counsel in the parable of the man in the storm-tossed boat—counsel which is designed to turn the inquirer away from the high theoretical question, How shall a man avoid sin? to the humbler recognition of common experience implied in the distinction between sins of frailty and deliberate sins. The Dreamer is not content, and seeks to know more. But we should note, in view of the scoldings he is to receive, that all he seeks to know is where he can find Dowel, so that, as he humbly says, he may learn of these high matters by direct observation:

> if I may lyue and loke I shal go lerne bettere. (VIII 58)

It is a sentiment which is repeated after Thought's 'explanation':

> I coueite to lerne
> How Dowel, Dobet and Dobest don amonges the peple.
> (*ibid.*, 108-9)

'Wit's' account of the matter is no more helpful to this Dreamer, insistent upon examples from practice. In the wooden allegory of Sir Dowel inhabiting the Castle of Kind, we may detect a similarity to the Plowman's account of the Ten Commandments, delivered to the Pilgrims of the *Visio*. In either case, the predicament of the listener is the same. Like the Pilgrims, the Dreamer seeks a living embodiment of the good, not mere discourse, however apt. It is therefore a striking irony that Dame Study, waiting with unconcealed impatience for the end of 'Wit's' discourse, should soundly berate the Dreamer as a seeker after mere knowledge. But the irony is deepened when we perceive that the Dreamer is eventually drawn into debate, so that Study's warning against high speculation, unfairly levelled at the Dreamer on first encounter, is later amply justified. Her very words

> *Non plus sapere quam oportet* (X 116)

are repeated at the end of the *Vita de Dowel* by Anima, rebuking a Dreamer who has sought to know all (XV 67). Similarly, Ymagynatyf was able to point, unopposed, the moral of the Dreamer's experience:

> for thine entermetyng here artow forsake,
> *Philosophus esses, si tacuisses.* (XI 406)

We see very readily that, in his being drawn into debate, the Dreamer has fulfilled Clergye's prediction:

*Non plus* etc. '(I say . . . to every man that is among you), not to think of himself more highly than he ought to think' (Rom. xii 3). *Cf.* p. 141, above; *entermetyng* meddling, interfering; *artow* art + thow; *Philosophus* etc. 'You would have been a philosopher if you had held your tongue' (adapted from Boethius).

The were lef to lerne but loth for to stodie.
Thou woldest konne that I can and carpen hit after,
Presumptuowsly, parauenture, apose so manye,
That my3the turne me to tene and Theologie bothe.[23]

But we should not fail to notice that before his meeting with the moral virtue in person, experience itself had already given the Dreamer a foretaste of patience. At his meeting with Ymagynatyf he could rue-fully contribute his own finding concerning 'Dowel':

'To se moche and suffre more, certes', quod I, 'is Dowel!'
(XI 402)

If we look back, we see that the Dreamer is one who has been drawn aside from his original purpose, from the question Where is Dowel? to discourse upon What is Dowel? He must therefore learn by expe-rience. But the situation in which he is placed, *vis-à-vis* Wit, Study, and the rest, is not simple; rather, it is one of cross-purpose. Just as his inter-locutors mistrust him, a seeker, as it appears, after mere knowledge, so the Dreamer mistrusts them, the learned and authoritative; for what, indeed, is learning beside the good life? In this, of course, Langland is echoing controversies of his own day[24]; but it is his achievement to communicate a universal sense of unchanging cross-purpose between entrenched authority and an eager inquirer. So we have a Dreamer who, meeting no direct answer to the over-simple question he proposes, finds himself involved in debate, to reach that point of ultimate weariness, foretold by Study, where all exercise of reason threatens to appear as profitless subtilizing:

The more I muse there-inne the mistier it semeth,
And the depper I deuyne the derker me it thinketh;
It is no science for sothe forto sotyle inne. (X 118-3)

He must learn to be constant to his own initial purpose, the search for a truth revealed in practice; but it is no easy matter. It is his final lesson, at the hands of Anima, that the search for knowledge may be not merely immoderate but even positively harmful; for

the more that a man of good mater hereth,
*But he do ther-after it doth hym double scathe.* (XV 57-8)

lef willing, eager; *carpen* chatter (about); *apose* debate with; *mistier* more obscure; *deuyne* search into, examine; *sotyle inne* argue subtly about; *But* unless; *scathe* harm.

In all this the Dreamer has been less fortunate than the repentant sinners
of the *Visio*. They found a guide, in the Plowman who was 'of flessh
oure brother'. The Dreamer's questioning will avail him little until, all
subtilizing exhausted, he is brought to contemplate Incarnate Deity,
the Saviour who

> wole Iuste in Piers armes,
> In his helme and in his haberioun, *humana natura*. (XVIII 72)

It is the last irony that those he had interrogated at the very outset of
his journey had, in the words of parting, given a sufficient answer to his
desire to find examples from practice:

> 'I have no kynde knowyng', quod I, 'to conceyue alle ȝowre
>                                                        wordes,
> Ac if I may lyue and loke I shal go lerne bettere'.
> 'I bikenne the Cryst', quod he, 'that on the crosse deyde'.
>                                                        (VIII 57-9)

The imaginative appeal of the *Vita* in its whole extent resides not in
any answer to the Dreamer's inquiries, though there is, as we have
seen, a decisive turn in the *Vita de Dowel* when the shift is made from
speculative to practical considerations. The essential appeal is in the very
failure of inquiry so long as the initiative is with the Dreamer. It is he,
at the outset insistent on the practice of the good life, who is in the end
brought to understand what his earlier interlocutors had doggedly
maintained as the ground of their reserve towards him—that practice
is all. Then, and only then, is he ready to apprehend as vision what has
consistently eluded him as discourse. The satiric intelligence penetrates
the defensive blindness of the reader when the Dreamer, in Langland no
less than in Gower and Chaucer, is one who must be brought to final
knowledge. It is a singularly complete survey that is thus made possible.
We speak often enough of medieval dialectic; and in the present study
we have more than once noted the opposition of theory and practice,
authority and experience, the doctrines long known and eagerly debated
over against the realization that comes progressively upon the Dreamer
as it had come all at once to a simple Plowman. But it is the characteristic of fourteenth-century imaginative literature as we have it in
Chaucer, Gower and Langland to give us in the end not a conclusion
so much as a turning away from the mutually antithetical positions on
which the debate has run. The argument may go on; but the individual's
course is at last clear. In this way, visionary insight and satiric humour

*kynde knowyng* natural knowledge; *conceyue* grasp; *bikenne* commend (to).

can coexist; for if it is fools who learn by the hither and thither of experience, it appears part of the Divine plan that it should be so. How otherwise, we see from a stubborn Dreamer's progress, should man learn at all?

## IV

The suitability of this imaginative method to the argument of the poem is worth further investigation, for both the connexion of *Visio* and *Vita*, and the emphasis laid in the *Vita* on 'three lives' are intimately related to the poet's deployment of the *persona* Will. I have suggested that the imaginative appeal, when the Dreamer comes to the fore, is in the sense of man as patient of Divine destiny; the focus is upon man as everywhere externalizing from himself the doctrines which press on him, and, in a vital sense, him alone. We saw that the vexation of Holy Church with the Dreamer is of the same order as the 'pure tene' of the Plowman when realization breaks upon him; Dreamer and Plowman alike overlook a knowledge written ineffaceably in the human heart. Langland's work thus offers a remarkable combination. His theme is of the greatest solemnity; man is a creature destined for regeneration. Hence vision must in the end show forth what remains hidden to discursive thinking. But it is the poet's genius to initiate and conduct the argument by showing man as determinedly ratiocinative, seeking the causes of all things and overlooking what lies nearest home. The argument of the poem is in one way certainly progressive; the advance from *Visio* to *Vita de Dowel* is an advance into complexity. But in another way it is towards a simplicity that has little to do with the riddles anxiously debated in *Dowel*. As the Incarnation draws near, all proximate considerations fall away: the overriding question is one of practice—a fulfilment that must be perfect before it can be in the least degree valid. To make this unmistakably relevant to the reader, we attend first, in the *Visio*, to the evidence of a wicked world as it presents itself to the Dreamer; then, progressively, to the evidence of the Dreamer's own condition. From that plane we can rise to the objective clarity of the *Vita de Dobet*, where all is made perfect. But lastly we must return with the Dreamer to the world shown at the outset, seen now with the simple understanding that no man is a spectator merely; in the search that remains, Conscience must go forth to seek Piers Plowman.

There are thus at work in the poem not so much a number of truths as two orders of truth. The first is that Law, so far from allowing any evasion, is absolute in its demands; the demands met, Love is seen to be greater than all. This is one region or order of truth; it is concerned

with absolutes, and it is objective and affirmatory. The other order of
truth concerns the nature of man; and here we see that he must be
brought to understanding, and that understanding consists in practice.
Here the tone is paradoxical and satirical; all remains error until understanding of the self is won. These two orders of truth are of course
entirely consonant one with the other; and the argument of the poem
may be said to move in parallel with them both. It is vital that interpretation at any point does not overlook this parallel movement. The
temptation to do so is the more insidious since each order of truth is
virtually complete in itself. In the poem no problem is simply abandoned;
for the ills he diagnoses in society, as in the heart of man, the poet can
offer singularly complete remedies. But his greatest skill, and the distinctive quality of his poem, lies in combining the two orders of truth;
and this we may too readily forget in any preoccupation with either
one of them.

Thus, within the sphere of Law, the *Visio* affords so complete an
indictment that the argument must move from man's duty to his nature.
In face of widespread failure, can we expect man to conform to any
standard other than that of self-interest? With this we cross a frontier;
and in the *Vita de Dowel* the question of the *justus* is pursued ardently
though fruitlessly. At the same time, a world needing correction is not
left without a standard appropriate to its present stage. The examination
of Lady Meed, and the conclusion reached, place the first step towards
the good life in the observance of *mesure*. We see the beginnings of new
life in the co-operative endeavour of the half-acre. At the same time, a
second level of understanding draws nearer, in the lessons the Plowman
must learn in administering his small world. We are pointed forward
from the inadequacy of a world of 'work-or-want' by the realization
which comes upon the best man a corrupt society can find at need. To
him there is granted the awareness that Law is absolute; so a world of
merely proportionate rewards and punishments recedes as the Plowman
casts himself upon the Divine Mercy. The poet, we have seen, had given
his reader a sufficient guide to this rule of Love—in Holy Church's
opening words to the Dreamer, and again in the vision of millennial
harmony which Conscience opposed to the merely *mesurable* world of a
regulated 'meed'. In this, as in his characterization of the Dreamer,
the artistry of the poet is to give the reader enough to prompt awareness
of ultimate design, while boldly underlining the immediate issues. For
example, Holy Church's first comprehensive statement is followed by
the Dreamer's large questionings; the portrait of the Dreamer thus falls
into place. Similarly, the day when Love shall be master and Law a

labourer is, in Reason's impassioned discourse (IV 113-48), yet a great way off: meanwhile there remains Meed, the enemy of Law itself. So, too, though the Dreamer at last beholds Love triumphantly fulfilling Law, that fulfilment is in the jousting at Jerusalem—placed in a past time, as millennial harmony is in a certain but remote future. The centre of attention, throughout, is where the poet means it to be—on a present in which the Christian cause is to be maintained against all-but-overwhelming odds.

The nature of the Dreamer and his progress in understanding—the other order of truth with which the poem deals—is thus not that of a lay-figure, one to be made wiser only. We reach a clear distinction from the role of Dreamer in Gower and Chaucer when, in the end of Langland's work, though all illusion is over, there is yet no resting-place. The poem does not end in disclosure and acceptance; it goes on from there to unwearied pursuit. In our search for the doctrinal coherence of the poem we must beware of overlooking this insight into human experience, which is wholly inseparable from Langland's understanding of the rigour of Law and the high mystery of Love. We must give sufficient weight to this: at the centre of the *Visio* is a Plowman who has had to be brought to awareness—firstly, of what is in fact required from his fellow-men, the Pilgrims whom he had set to work as an interim measure; and secondly, what is required of himself, the most proficient among them. The pilgrimage is cancelled not by the Plowman but by Truth; and in this we may see a central affirmation of the whole poem. The Plowman is one who is summoned to his task; the preparation is not the creature's but the Creator's. It is the same with the Dreamer, whose career we follow in the *Vita*—with one very important difference. What the Plowman saw in a moment, at the unfolding of the Pardon, the Dreamer must pursue long and confusedly. Here the relatedness of these two orders of truth is abundantly clear. The Plowman is qualified by his unremitting and faithful service; for the Dreamer, the simplicity of practical obedience is long in coming.

These truths of Langland's working imagination are essential to any understanding of the 'three Lives' of his poem. The salient considerations are: firstly, the distinction between the repentant sinners of the *Visio*, newly entered upon the good life, and the relative proficiency, in these terms, of their leader, the Plowman; and, secondly, the return in the last two Passus from exalted vision to firm appraisal of the actual. Langland's 'Dowel' is thus no invariable term; and we should beware of applying to the poem, without qualification, either of the groupings active, contemplative and 'mixed' lives, and purgative, illuminative and unitive ways, or setting these two up in mutual rivalry.[25] What is immediately necessary is that in all discussion we should be sure to stress the clarity with which 'Dowel' is invested. It is, we may say, the first syllable—the *do*-ing—which is of primary importance in 'Dowel, Dobet and Dobest'. Some modern criticism seems to recapitulate an error like the Dreamer's own in dwelling rather upon the 'well, better and best' than on the 'doing' which is prior to all. For, assuredly,

> Or in dykynge or in deluynge or trauaillynge in preyeres,
> Contemplatyf lyf or actyf lyf, Cryst wolde men wrou3te.
>
> (VI 250-1)

The tone of these lines suggests that they may be scribal; they nevertheless constitute a valuable reminder that 'active' and 'contemplative' can be misleading terms if they are set in mutual opposition. The tendency of the modern reader is to equate 'active life' with mere activity, action as opposed to contemplation. But as Wells long ago observed, and Fr. Dunning has reminded us, the 'good works' required in 'active life' are 'works of religion and devotion'.[26] There is thus room for the blending of the two traditional groupings of 'lives' and 'ways'. Indeed, so far from rejecting the one to provide for the other,[27] we must allow for their very interdependence if we are to do justice to the simplicity and comprehensiveness of 'doing well', and thus to advance with the Dreamer. But we shall best arrive at this truth not from without—the definitions of 'lives' and 'ways' hitherto put forward by interpreters of the poem—but from within *Piers Plowman*.

The hinge on which the poem turns is the Pardon, and it holds all in two lines the essential truth that links *Visio* and *Vita de Dowel, Dobet et Dobest*. The doing well that is required of all Christians is first shown to us in its ordinary and obvious aspect, obedience to law, right conduct in relation to an objective standard. This law must be the foundation of Christian society—hence the strength of the case against Meed's flagrant self-seeking. Once applied to the individual, it is seen to press with unremitting force; only repentance will serve. The way forward, the 'doing well' that is required at this stage, is conformity to the Law of God, expressed in the Mosaic Decalogue, to which the Plowman confidently refers his inquirers. But this truth is deepened and given the characteristic emphasis of practice by setting the pilgrims to work. In the co-operative labour of the half-acre, under the Plowman's agreement with the Knight, we see human society making its first essay in doing well. With that rudimentary and general beginning accomplished, the poet turns to the other extreme—the best individual the world of the *Visio* has yielded. The dialectical cast of mind now reaches from lowest to highest in the scale of human possibility, from palpable worst to conceivable best. In the Christian scheme of things the demand is from each individual; and that demand, the Pardon reveals, is absolute. Law, which had been the sufficient framework of the argument up till now, is seen as unyielding in its final requirement; so both reward and punishment are inseparable in the two lines of a 'pardon' which is the very antitype of any Indulgence granted to frailty.

The Pardon in fact opens a new region of possibility; to the Plowman there comes an awareness of Perfection. But it comes to him alone, for he is uniquely qualified by his long allegiance to Truth. That 'doing well' which has hitherto applied to all those we have met is now seen as the necessary condition of, and the preparation for, a further 'doing well' by the individual. As this further awareness comes only to the individual at the height of conformity to 'riȝtful reson', so it breaks the simplicity of mere injunction, the Law expressed in the Commandments. The good man of the *Visio* is now seen to be not the best that is possible; and a perception of positive, comparative and superlative is thus easily and naturally implanted in the Dreamer. But we should not fail to notice in this transition, firstly, the effect of surprise (for this communicates the all-important truth that we do not choose but are chosen): and, secondly, the terror in what is shown to Piers; for here we see the Divine Rod—*Virga tua*[28]—and learn that experience is a hard taskmaster. Langland's 'Dowel' is thus a singularly comprehensive term. As used at first it does indeed 'refer to the majority of Christians who have no special religious calling'[29]; but as the Dreamer, having witnessed the Plowman's submission, probes into 'doing well', the full range of possibility open to the individual Christian begins to declare itself. But it is less a 'doing' than a submission to the Divine Will; for even the just man, in universal experience, is culpable. Any but the least elementary account of 'doing well' must therefore include the 'doing well' of the spiritual life.

So much for the essential distinction between the two extremes of capacity for 'doing well' which Langland has presented in his pilgrims and their leader, the Plowman, in the first part of his poem. The second salient consideration in any discussion of 'lives' is the return, in the conclusion of the whole, from the high vision of fulfilment in *Dobet* to the actual and grievous state with which we had begun. No one grouping of 'lives' or 'ways' will help us here; nor will any supposed blending of the two survive close examination. For while a progression inherent in the terms 'well—better—best', however it may be qualified, cannot be finally gainsaid, the actual structure of Langland's *Vita de Dowel, Dobet et Dobest* is rather as under:—

I. *Vita de Dowel.* 'Doing well' in all its range of possibility for mortals—which may include but is not limited to 'Dobet' and 'Dobest' as various systematic conceptions of 'lives' and 'ways'. All this is presented in the course of debate, which the Dreamer is eventually brought to realize as profitless while it remains external to himself.

II. *Vita de Dobet.* 'Doing well' in its perfect fulfilment by Incarnate Deity, which includes and transcends all notions of 'Dobet' and 'Dobest' as derived from this perfect fulfilment and applicable to sinful humanity. This is apprehended as vision, and thus seen object-ively—a point of importance to which we shall return.

III. *Vita de Dobest.* 'Doing well' in a wicked world. The emphasis is on the government of Christian society: but we very soon see that this means the individual conscience as the only guide amidst the perpetual and all-but-successful assaults of evil, within and without the Church.

The *Vita de Dobet*, it will be seen, is affirmatory; there, all is perfected and made triumphant. It is therefore of a different order from the other two. What is common to the first section, the *Vita de Dowel*, and the last, the *Vita de Dobest*, is awareness of a law to be fulfilled; and in these two sections we have those two truths which are first and last in Lang-land's deepest understanding. In the insistent probing of the good life in *Dowel*, there is unyielding emphasis upon example: 'Cryst wolde men *wrouʒte*'. In the *Vita de Dobest*, with its faithful picture of a divided and disordered Christendom, there is renewed witness to the help that man constantly needs, an alert conscience:

> Inwyt is the [allie] that *anima* desirith;
> Aftir the grace of god [the grettest is Inwyt].[30]

There is no progression; on the contrary, there is very great consist-ency in both *Dowel* and *Dobest* in pressing the local and particular. The world of man is the central point of reference, notwithstanding *Dobet's* long reach into fulfilment. In this light we may see that it is not *Dowel* which, as is sometimes thought, is out of the line of development. It is *Dobet*, where for once questioning can be stilled, and the Dreamer beholds unalterable fact. But this is exactly the apex of the poem. The Saviour's perfect fulfilment of Law gives the co-ordinates of sinful man's position, his present situation and the prospects open to him. The devel-

opment of the whole is thus triangular rather than unilinear. All attempts
to bend one or both sets of 'definitions' of Dowel, etc. come up against
the grave difficulty that the parts of the poem are not truly progressive,
and they are not stages in any one order of experience. Certainly, there
is progress for the Dreamer—but it lies in achieving as vision what he
learns is denied to observation in the world around him. We shall understand this best if we hold fast to the nature of the Dreamer's progress—
his wayward stumbling to a goal. The *Vita de Dobet* can be thoroughly
objective in tone; for there the Dreamer is at last fit for instruction,
the disclosure of the perfection he had long sought. A failure to grasp
this non-sequential nature of the *Vita de Dowel, Dobet and Dobest* characterizes, in my judgement, the major attempts to interpret Langland's
'doing well'.

Thus, Fr. Dunning, perceiving the objectivity of *Dobet*, maintains
that this preludes a change in the tenor of the argument, so that in
*Dobest* we turn from stages of the spiritual life to the 'third objective
state, the life of prelates'. It is a suggestion which pays due regard to the
discontinuity of *Dobest* in any simple progression; but if the argument
is to have force it should be moved further back. It is *Dobet* that is anomalous if we are to speak of either threefold grouping. A Dreamer under
instruction in *Dobet* is more truly related to what has preceded this stage
in his progress—his preparation for instruction in both *Visio* and *Dowel*—
than to what follows in *Dobest*. Fr. Dunning rightly draws us away from
any single 'triadic' notion by emphasizing that, unlike Rolle and Hilton,
Tauler and Suso, 'Langland's concern is not with religious sisters but
with Christian Society'[31]. But let us emphasize, too, that this concern
manifests itself in the awaking to ultimate truth of a Dreamer who,
at last beholding the perfect exemplar, is not allowed to rest from conflict. Our attention throughout is not on any ordered system into which
problems aired in the poem are to be fitted, but upon the figure of a
Dreamer whose scrutiny ranges backwards and forwards in time, from
present corruption to past fulfilment of Law and to future harmony. But
past and ultimate future, it must be emphasized, are presented only in
visionary terms; it is upon the present of continuing struggle that the
focus is set.

Fr. Dunning has given us, in my judgement, the best account we have
yet had of the unity of doctrine in *Piers Plowman*, the awakening to
self-knowledge as the precondition of understanding the truths so long
accepted. This, I have suggested, constitutes the imaginative authority
of Langland's work, for it expresses a truth of the human predicament
which is not dependent on any one set of doctrines or convictions. The

poem offers an insistent probing of man's capacity for the good life. But the emphasis, as I understand the poem, falls not on any one conception of the good life, but on two things—the defensive blindness of the Dreamer; and the sphere of perfect fulfilment as that of Incarnate Deity. Once the Dreamer's blindness is penetrated, he can see Law as fulfilled. This seen, he must cease to be the observer of his fellow-men and 'learn to love, leaving all else aside' (XX 207). The objectivity of tone in *Dobet* marks the moment of poise, the highest reach of the design before it returns upon itself; it relates forward to the foundation of Christendom at the beginning of *Dobest*, before the rapid descent to a corrupt present, and back to the Dreamer of *Dowel* (and thus back to the Dreamer of the *Visio*, first characterized by Holy Church in Passus I). It thus seems to me that while the argument of the poem ranges widely and with marked differences of emphasis—including those varying 'definitions' we, with the Dreamer, may long ponder—the centre of our attention is always one man in his earnest scrutiny of truth; and the upshot of his inquiry is not a set of solutions, or a blending of solutions, but a clearer understanding of simple allegiance to God's Law and an unabated resolve to 'continue therein'. Fr. Dunning's notable contribution puts the emphasis exactly in the right place—the progress of the individual to understanding via practice; but that progress is in terms finally freer than any set of equivalences would allow. Langland's insight into the nature of experience, and thus the imaginative unity of his work, is a greater thing than the systems it draws upon and may variously combine. The 'definitions' we shall understand best when we see them in their dramatic contexts; and the final overarching significances that the terms 'Dowel, Dobet and Dobest' would give to the major divisions of the poem are dubious indeed if we allow them to suggest a progression of ideas which differs from the Dreamer's erratic progress.

Professor Donaldson's sensitive inquiry also suggests a blending—of active, contemplative and mixed lives, and purgative, illuminative and unitive states. It is a sound reaction away from mere one-for-one equivalence, towards the true nature of the poet's argument. Similarly, Professor Donaldson's immediate purpose, to demonstrate the C Text's distinctive emphasis upon 'Dowel' as the first step in spiritual awareness, gives due heed to the progress of a Dreamer as the central device. But here again the attempt to establish a degree of equivalence—this time with the grouping humility, charity and unity as dealt with by St. Bernard—runs up against the actual shape and non-sequential nature of the poem when considered as progression of thought. Professor

Donaldson would in the end persuade us that St. Bernard's 'humility' must be understood as the poet's 'patient poverty'; while *Dobest*, it is admitted, 'does not seem to contain much that is suggestive of the vision of God of St. Bernard'. This honesty of purpose is our best guide to the actual nature of the poem; and perhaps we see that nature best when we read, after the sentence just quoted,

> Nevertheless, in the section as it stands [*Dobest*] there are elements suggestive of the unitive condition of the soul, just as in B's Do-Well there is a good deal about patience and in B's Do-Bet the main theme is charity.[32]

... 'there are elements', 'a good deal about', 'the main theme'—these are accurate observations on the poem we are dealing with. Langland's 'doing well' has a fundamental simplicity that will not be confined to any lesser aspect of the truth than the absolute, the wholly valid. In its survey of all proximate meanings it touches with varying emphasis upon common connotations of the relatives 'better' and 'best'. For 'best' is, uniquely, a relative, when human is set against Divine. Perfection is revealed to the Dreamer not as figure but as accomplished fact; yet its place and hour are far off, in the past as in the future.

Once again, it is *Dobet* that stands in the path of all systematized equivalence. Nothing in the order of the poem, as nothing in the order of Divine Providence, can lead to or follow on its own plane the Saviour's fulfilment of Law. The Dreamer, we must insist, is here under instruction, brought to know as revelation what had long eluded him as discourse. This, above all, is the objection to any view that would take the three parts of the *Vita* as stages in the Dreamer's progress in the spiritual life. The mistakes the Dreamer makes are a condition of his going forward at all—in leaving the false path of purely intellectual ardour. Thus the view of Professor Howard Meroney seems to overlook what is quite central to understanding; it disregards the Dreamer as one who must be taught, and whose instruction consists in seeing as historic fact the work once and for all done on the Christian's behalf. The Dreamer certainly does not come 'to Vnite' in any sense which would support the 'unitive way'; and the descent of the Paraclete—giving 'each man a grace' (XIX 222)—is, again, something seen by the Dreamer historically, a once-for-all event following the perfect fulfilment of Law long sought, and not any stage in his own progress. Now we return to a Christian life to be lived—after the near-disintegration of a Christian Church which cries out for leadership. I take up in a later section[33] Professor Meroney's spirited perception of the *persona* 'Wille'. Here I would only

say that the Wille whom he sees—one 'hampered by a disdain for the
practical and the speculative'[34]—is certainly a fitter candidate for the
progress he outlines than the Will of the poem, whose consuming
desire is to behold the practical, the living embodiment of doing well,
but whose besetting weakness is his bent for the speculative.

Mr. Hussey's recent contribution to this matter of doctrinal equivalence
is sensibly empirical in its method. The poet's 'active life', it is seen,
includes 'much of what Langland's critics usually assign to Dobet'.[35]
It is the right start; but we are not therefore to assume that it is the
critics who are correct in their definitions of Dowel, Dobet and Dobest.
We have seen that 'doing well' is not to be thought of as opposed to
'contemplation', in that ordinary opposition of 'action' and 'contemplation' which is the predisposition of all modern thinking.[36] Langland's
emphasis is uncompromisingly where the central Western tradition of
spirituality puts it—upon the good works of the spiritual life. So much
may be said in correction of Mr. Hussey's standpoint; and it may be
added that Walter Hilton's conception of the 'Mixed' life is, on all the
evidence, influenced by particular purpose.[37] But Mr. Hussey's conclusion is sound:

> neither the triad active, contemplative and mixed lives, nor the
> triad purgative, illuminative and unitive states, nor a combination of
> the two is completely satisfactory as a definition of Dowel, Dobet
> and Dobest, and . . . the proposed equations break down especially
> in the case of the second elements, that is, that Dobet equals the con-
> templative life or the illuminative state.[38]

Yet, granted that no direct equivalence is to be found, what should we
do but try to trace out the real correspondences? Mr. Hussey's central
difficulty, having reached his conclusion, is that the simplicity which he
finds in Langland and with which he would like to invest the ideas of
Dowel, etc. does not square with 'the progression inherent in the
concepts of Dowel, Dobet and Dobest'. But this 'progression' is inherent
rather in the systematizations—whether of 'lives' or 'ways'—than in
the poem itself.

What the poem proclaims with the greatest simplicity is certainly,
as Mr. Hussey perceives, a truth applicable not to some few favoured
souls but to 'the majority of Christians who have no special religious
calling'. This is what is affirmed at the outset and in the ending; but in
the interim, the whole notion of 'doing well' has come up for rigorous
examination—and that on two counts. I should express them thus:

(i) If wickedness is all but universal, is man *really* expected to conform to 'riȝtful reson'? The *Visio* prompts the question, and the Pardon provides the answer. Man is required to meet an absolute standard, on pain of eternal punishment.

(ii) Granted that nothing less than perfect conformity is demanded, where shall we find that in practice? The Dreamer thus surveys the world of discourse—with its theoretical 'definitions' of lives and ways, good, better and best, and their less determinate connexions (as, secular organisation, etc.)—until he is brought to know himself. The practice that the Law demands is then seen—not here and now, but a great way off at Calvary, and a long time since in the austere beginnings of the Church. We return to seek the simple good of individual practice in this life.

A progression is there certainly, in the movement of the argument from tacit assumption—a law which is to be obeyed—to the question 'Can it be obeyed?'; and a progression, too, in the shift from the unquestioning observer, quick to condemn and, later, to dispute, to the wondering eye of faith at Calvary, and, in the end, the sober realization of a cause nearly overthrown. *Dobet* is indeed out of line with this progression. It towers above both beginning and end; all leads to it and away from it. In the grand design of the poem, as in all Christian understanding, it is the Incarnation which is central to and above all other truths. The argument, if we will put it so, is about Man's capacity for obedience. But once obedience is perfected in man's nature, all argument is stopped —to spur all endeavour.

Mr. Hussey is, I am sure, wholly right to stress the penetrating simplicity which invests Langland's term 'Dowel'. It is evident, above all, in that concern for the *practice* of the Christian life which is central to the whole design. But we shall be making an impossible demand if we insist that the Christian life, as the Dreamer begins to inquire into it in the *Vita*, must involve no complexities. Langland's concern is with right conduct, a 'doing well' which, first apprehended as the obedience to God's law required of all men, is deepened into awareness of the spiritual life—that life which may be expressed as conformity to God's will in the spirit of a son rather than a servant. As such, Langland's 'doing well' joins with and becomes indistinguishable from the 'doing well' of the spiritual life. But a 'better' in this sphere is in the end apprehended as vision; and we must return, last of all, from perfect beginnings to a corrupted present. Langland's poem has thus a design all its own: and we rightly reject those 'definitions' that would 'provide a ready-made guide' to his thought.[39] But we shall make no headway with Langland's thought until we grasp the connexion between the 'doing well' that is enjoined upon the folk of the *Visio* and the prospect of 'doing well' that is revealed to their leader, the Plowman. It is a prospect which, the Dreamer as would-be dialectician readily sees, reaches to infinity, the impossible ideal of the more-than-just—were it not that Heaven itself has stooped to us. All—well, better and best—has reached perfection in the Saviour; so that the verdict of 'Piers Plowman' is truly reported by 'Clergy':

> Dowel and Dobet aren two infinites,
> Which infinites with a feith fynden oute Dobest,
> Which shal saue mannes soule. (XIII 127-9)

In the end our understanding of Langland's poem will be sounder if we can concern ourselves less with the doctrines with which the Dreamer wrestles, and more with the nature of his progress towards his goal. The poem deals in mysteries, but the focus of attention is not upon man's ignorance of what is too dark for him; it is upon his insentience of what has been brought into the light of common day. Langland's poem thus succeeds in communicating not a cumulative effect of discursive thinking, but the very pressure of experience itself. It is the poet's greatest single achievement that at the turning-points we see that the preparation is not the creature's but the Creator's. Until the living example is set before the Dreamer, all inquiries serve only to mislead. So the Plowman, and after him the Saviour Himself, are sent to meet human need. It is entirely appropriate that Conscience goes forth at the end to seek a true exemplar. Langland's last and most individual stroke is in deepest conformity with his whole design. By it he draws that design conclusively away from a formal into a truly imaginative unity.

## V

It is this aspect, not of Christian truth merely, but of universal experience, which constitutes the specific appeal of *Piers Plowman*. The poem does indeed explore the whole conception of a good life, the possibilities of meeting a pre-existent standard. But its achievement is to bring into unmistakable prominence a truth which may be forgotten in any undue emphasis on the question 'What must I *do*?' If man is a creature whose capacity to know the truth as doctrine is proportionate to his capacity for hiding it from himself, then Providence must not so much furnish theoretical answers as bring the individual to confront practical demands pressing unequivocally upon him. To this end, as we have seen, Langland's creative imagination is nourished by an environment where authority and experience are the twin courts of appeal; and by a tradition of dream-poetry in which the mere opposition between these two is ended in the person of the Dreamer himself, a hapless figure touched with a mockery which is yet finally genial. Man acts— and, fortunately for him, is acted upon; this is the reality which is prior to all abstraction. Such poetry tends to the *eucatastrophe*, to use Professor Tolkien's term; there is a kind of happy ending which is no escape from but rather an affirmation of final reality.[40] This 'joyous turn' in the Dreamer's own fortunes marks the highest point of the poem; from it, as we have seen, we can only return to an everyday reality.

With this understanding we may reconsider a notion of the 'medieval' which, commonly held, is acutely put by Dr. Tillyard. Allegory, he says, should be thought of 'as allied to'

> The medieval impulse to stratify existence, not, like the classical Greeks, choosing a fixed position and approximating everything to it, but recognizing several positions and passing to and fro between them.[41]

This is well said in as far as it characterizes the essential method of Langland's poem—its passing to and fro between positions established now by doctrine and now by experience, so that the 'thought' in the *Vita de Dowel* is, as we have said, like thought in its living context, the activity of thinking in its mere, alogical, successiveness, its sudden leaps and returns upon itself. To this end, Langland's instrument, as we have seen, is well adapted; the two halves of the line are capable of passing to and fro between thesis and antithesis, and the whole fluidity of the Passus and the Part make for a truth-telling which is a record of observations as they are taken rather than in their ordered series. In this respect, the older tradition of English verse differs from that syllabic tradition which is well adapted to the *ordonnance* of consecutive thought. This difference is strikingly apparent if we compare English syllabic verse with a poetry very different in tradition and temper. Distinguishing Welsh poetry from that English poetry which is best known to the general reader, Mr. Gwyn Williams observes:

> English and most Western European creative activity has been conditioned by the inheritance from Greece and Rome of the notion of a central point of interest in a poem, a picture or a play, a nodal region to which everything leads and upon which everything depends.[42]

Welsh poetry, of course, as we may discover under Mr. Williams's skilful guidance, differs from both the older and the later English traditions; the older Welsh poets 'were not trying to write poems that would read like Greek temples or even Gothic cathedrals'. But perception of an essential difference between Welsh and the syllabic tradition in English may point to a characteristic of the alliterative line when properly handled. What Mr. Williams sees as the main characteristic of his poets is 'a collateral rather than a consecutive presentation' of experience: and this is certainly true of the Dreamer's whole career in the *Vita de Dowel* and, in a wider sense, of the poem as a whole. So, too, the devices employed in the Welsh poets offer a telling ground of comparison—for they include 'running parenthesis', 'purposeful reiteration', and 'the identity of end and beginning'.[43] Such a comparison may help us in assessing the characteristic movement of Langland's mind; and may, taken with Dr. Tillyard's observation, reinforce our sense that the 'positions' between which the poem passes are not to be merely identified, given the co-ordinates of 'lives' or 'states' in other and more systematic calculations of man's nature and destiny.

There is, however, a qualification to be made; and it will perhaps render this general characterization of 'medieval' as against 'Greek' finally less serviceable than it at first appears. Both the featureless landscape of the *Vita* and the crowded scene of the Field of Folk are set between Heaven and Hell. For the Dreamer, it is precisely because there is 'a fixed position', answering to these cosmological limits, that we have both the compulsion to search and the near-despair of finding the quarry. Langland's fixed position is the Incarnation. As we have seen, all leads to it, and all declines from it; and this rise and fall are sheer—on the plane of middle-earth, where the poem is decisively set, we can have at highest and best no more than the *mesurable*. The one good man who can be called beyond this is summoned away from our sight. The fixed position is clear, for it is absolute; nothing less than Perfection is in question—that we may know the truth of a 'doing well' which is required not of others merely but of ourselves. As such, *Piers Plowman* offers us an instance of medieval design which we may misconceive if we become engrossed in the positions by which the Dreamer's erratic course may be plotted. Langland's contribution to the poetry of Christian experience is only to be grasped if we follow the Dreamer's whole journey, experiencing it serially. The poet's undertaking must be not merely to state the apparent perplexities and nearly insoluble difficulties, but to communicate the very sense of weariness and apparent purposelessness than any stage of the journey may afford—if it is looked at neither from the end nor the beginning, but as it is encountered.

For this reason the charge of confusion and monotony in Langland,[44] a 'paradox of total greatness and local failures',[45] must be scrutinized in each instance against the background of continuing demonstration— that man, in the person of the Dreamer, is to be brought to understanding when all false paths have been explored. A criticism that makes much of 'Langland's repetitions and irrelevant moralizing'[46] may be refusing assent to the very principle of the poem's working. With Langland, such assent is much more than a frontier-courtesy. He is faithful to a central purpose, our blindness to what resists all our inquiry until we are brought to practise it; and for this fidelity we may be thankful. When penetrating clarity and largeness of vision are found side by side with the very taste of purposelessness we may feel that what is monotonous and confused is the necessary, but excessively rare, complement of those heights of intellectual imagination which thereby gain in authenticity and are saved from a merely willed austerity. If we are to grasp the method of proof which the poem offers, then, as R. W. Chambers remarked twenty years ago, when accepting Dr. Tillyard's first sketch of the essential qualities of epic, we must 'take the poem as a whole';[47] and this must include its fixed point of reference as well as the positions it surveys.

If we do so, we shall see clearly its distinctive contribution to the poetry of Christian experience. What must I do? is, naturally and insistently, the question which man puts; but it is one great function of art to show us what is done for man, the element of design in poem or picture thus answering to a central truth of the Christian revelation. The Plowman, we remember, took a decisive step away from self-sufficiency, casting himself upon the Divine Providence. This truth is deepened when we see the Dreamer unaware of his true need; for him there must be not the staff but the rod, and the *Vita de Dowel* records the long sequence of his correction. Langland's imaginative design is thus well adapted to the problems that pass before our eyes—the 'positions', in Dr. Tillyard's phrase—which we with the Dreamer must scan as the argument deepens from acceptance of an unarguable imperative to a baffled but persistent asking *how?* Fr. Dunning puts well the essential questions:

> ... how are we to distinguish the good from the bad, how can we judge the movements of the heart, how discern their provenance?[48]

Langland's answer is in effect twofold. Firstly, that we 'distinguish the good from the bad' all too easily—where others are concerned. This

is his *Visio*, where the reader, with the Dreamer, is the spectator of vice
and folly. But when we think we have found a good man, then the
standard that is at once in question must shake our habitual acceptances
and cause us to look within.

In this way, the poem makes its contribution not to Christian truth
only, but to all understanding of the human heart. Just as the long
passages of the *Vita de Dowel*, once the Dreamer becomes disputatious,
reflect a universal sense of cross-purpose between entrenched authority,
of whatever kind, and the impetuous inquirer, so the transition from
observer to rueful victim is, again, deeply consonant with all real experience. Langland appears to have solved a capital problem—how to
communicate in wholly imaginative and poetic terms the central riddle of
our experience. It is not only that we everywhere approve and seldom
practise the good: much more, it is that the realization of our own
predicament is the last discovery we make. The means by which this
is done are paralleled, I have suggested, in other dream-poetry of the
period, where a Dreamer is brought in the end to know his true plight.
But the power with which it is effected is equalled only, I believe, in
*Gulliver's Travels*. There, too, the standpoint of the observer and reporter,
Lemuel Gulliver, is decisively shifted. Dislodged from a comfortable
vantage-point, our guide, and thus we ourselves, must become involved,
no longer able to interpose between ourselves and reality that ready
satire which is indeed a 'sort of glass wherein beholders do generally
discover everybody's face but their own'.[49] But what draws upon
Gulliver as progressive understanding in a world of sober discourse
comes to the Dreamer all at once as action on the part of the Plowman—
an action which continues to perplex the Dreamer until action is perfected in the Crucifixion and made triumphant in the Harrowing of
Hell. The logical imagination of Langland can move easily from sardonic observation to exalted wonder. The quality of his poetry is an
unswerving fidelity to the facts of particular experience: for its centre
is in the hard fact that the human condition is to find self-knowledge
the all-but-impossible undertaking. Of this unusual order of poetry we
may be tempted to invert the old formula and say that the poet succeeds
by calling Reason to the aid of Imagination. Langland's poem propounds
an answer not to the simple, though profound, question, How do we
know ourselves? but to the question which lies closer to all real experience, How shall we be brought to know ourselves?

The kind of poem we are dealing with is thus not easily determined;
and we should be especially wary of a 'historical criticism' that would
pronounce definitively upon it by attending merely to its analogues and

apparent congeners. I have tried to show that the categorization 'moral poem energized and diversified by satire' is entirely inadequate, while drawing attention to the possibilities inherent in the figure of a Dreamer as we meet him in both Gower and Chaucer. To establish the kind of work *Piers Plowman* is we must look not only to the productions of its age. The prior condition of our knowing any work, save in the most superficial sense, is our allowing it to challenge us out of preconception; and as we saw when dealing with allegory in Chapter VI, of all preconceptions those of 'period' are hardest to dislodge. To turn to work in a later age may be the first step towards freeing ourselves from habitual assumption about the particular work or period which confronts us—and thus to put ourselves in a position to know by little and little what it is we must mean when we would refer to the 'medieval', or whatever the period in question. It is assuredly in this sense that we may accept Mr. Eliot's contention that past and present are inseparable for responsible poet and critic.[50] Comparison with *Gulliver's Travels* may show us the truly distinctive features in *Piers Plowman* which an examination of fourteenth century satire would hardly reveal save by striking contrast. On the one hand, *Piers Plowman* has a quality which has often been remarked and needs no foil. Its greatest things, 'sublimity' and 'largeness' of vision, come from the region of 'the "intellectual imagination".'[51] So, we may add, does its continuing energy, the play of a logical imagination in a predominantly satiric mode. But this introduces us to the other aspect in which the poem must be viewed. The satire is concerned with the truths we claim to know and yet do not apprehend: at the turning-points, as we have seen, vision must play the decisive part.

The poem thus appears to traverse two major kinds of imaginative creation to which we are accustomed—the radical satire[52] and the visionary search. For some modern readers great Romantic poetry may be the best entry upon the complexity of experience to which *Piers Plowman* is faithful—the penetrating simplicity of 'realization', and its uncovenanted nature; the sharpness of the sense of defeat (which at once redoubles awareness of what we seek while it falsifies all our contriving); and, rarely but most movingly, the exaltation of vision. Romantic poetry will especially help us to guard against classifying Langland's work with the poetry that expounds a system of beliefs. *Piers Plowman* is in its essentials more like that genuinely new imaginative kind for which the treatise poem or 'didactic epic' of the eighteenth century prepared a way—a poetry which is concerned not with the exposition of doctrine as a contribution to the reader's knowledge, but with the individual reader's apprehension of truth, his growing into awareness, as

the poem proceeds, of a path inescapably opening before him. These
different kinds may resemble each other at certain points; and we run
the risk of confusing them whenever we paraphrase for discussion their
content. It can hardly be otherwise, when there is no language to safeguard from misinterpretation the theme of 'Imagination'

Power so called
Through sad incompetence of human speech.

But there is yet a difference between *The Pleasures of Imagination* and
*The Prelude* which is not merely the difference between a greater poet
and a less. Some modern scholarship does well to recall us from an un-
reflecting acceptance of *Piers Plowman* as spiritual autobiography. But
we must not be diverted from the real centre of imaginative excitement,
the difference between knowledge and realization, between the doctrines
so long accepted and the significances at last apprehended. To this
essential character of the poem, always in danger of being overborne
by emphasis on the doctrinal implications of particular stages in the
Dreamer's course, Romantic poetry of a sustained kind may well direct
us. Yet in this correction of emphasis we must not let the really unusual
gifts of the poet drop out of sight. In Langland vision and pragmatic
temper are uniquely joined. His talent is for the absolutes—to seek, with
a Hobbesian insistence,[53] where the argument bottoms. In Langland a
penetration not inferior to Swift's is matched with a majestic tenderness.
We may perhaps think that something making for unity has gone out
of our tradition, in the later divorce between ruthless satire and tender
compassion, unsparing vigilance and visionary exaltation. It is possible
that a unity of apprehension grows more readily in a world where all
pertains to either of two categories—what must be believed and what
may be experienced. Mature awareness lies not in any dispute upon their
separate claims—though this is the common and natural expedient for
arousing attention—but in an acceptance of each in its true, not its
imagined, sphere. It is an acceptance which finally comes home to the
Dreamer as a *pref*, a prize won from experience, correcting an excess of
'knowledge' which is now seen to be merely a wisdom before the event.
The truth is thus never wholly simple, though realization itself can come
with devastating simplicity. This, it may be suggested, is a cornerstone
of Chaucer's art, the rare combination of objectivity and pity—fidelity
to the fact without either rancour or sentimentality; as, too, it underlies that quiet close in Gower's *Confessio Amantis* which is above all
praise, where we end with a humour which is gently rueful, and disappointment changes as we experience it to the sense of release.

Whatever the fundamental source of strength in others, in Langland, it is clear, the truth sustaining all is that theory and practice have been made one, not as figure but as fact, here upon earth, among the 'briars' of 'this working-day world'. The Christian truth is unalterably historical; the Saviour's victory was won for man and in man's condition. Here is the fixed position; in relation to it, nothing is impossible, and every one of the poet's faculties is called into play. Dialectical subtlety and vigorous realism find place side by side with visionary ardour and withering satire. If we are to speak of the personality the poem reveals, we must take into account the remarkable combination of gifts that in our later tradition are commonly found in isolation. We may try, if we choose, to identify the mind behind the Dreamer, manoeuvring the reader through his guide until vision becomes inescapable. But we should be very sure that we allow for the activity of the poem itself, bringing to the poet, in the act of telling, new relations and significances. Our criticism will be beside the mark if we do not see that the poem succeeds by communicating the mind, not behind, but in the poem.

## VII

The personality thus implicit in the poem is not always adequately distinguished from either supposedly autobiographical reference or the *persona* of the Dreamer. Professor Howard Meroney's lively protest against unfounded confidence in a 'William Langland' setting down his doctrinal message is suitably sceptical. But it is, in one way, not sceptical enough; for, substituting a spiritual progress for 'ways' and 'states' of life, Professor Meroney brushes aside any 'name-conscious' 'William Langland'; and, beginning with a determined misunderstanding of the opening of the poem and ignoring the objective standpoint of *Dobet*, he brings his 'Wille' to a 'Vnite' which is all of his own making. He has done no more than substitute one kind of unhappy systematization for another. Why, we may ask, in any event, should not a real William Langland be 'name-conscious'? Is there any inherent unlikelihood in the accident of the poet's name giving that very prompting to creative imagination from which a *persona* of 'Will Langland' might spring?—one agog to know but not very willing to apply knowledge to himself, and qualified, in the end, only by experience, his living 'long in lande'. Professor Meroney's perception of the spirited self-mockery of the 'I' of the poem is wholly welcome; but, failing to see its relation to the whole design by which truth comes to the Dreamer, he must read the poem as a record of spiritual progress on the part of the poet. It is indeed an odd interpretation which finds the Plowman exemplifying a 'tiresome righteousness', and can compare him in his insistence on ploughing the half-acre, before setting out on pilgrimage, with 'the boor who excused himself once by saying *Villam emi*'.[54] The great weakness of Professor Meroney's case is not its adapting particular parts of the evidence to its own ends. It is his disregarding the theme of man as patient, the plain fact that the Plowman and the Dreamer in his turn must be brought to know a truth that has eluded them; and that only then can there be an objective demonstration of the fulfilment accomplished for all men by a Saviour. It is this which before all else tells against Meroney's conception of a dexterous, allusive and humorous author—one who 'wrote *Piers Plowman* for pleasure, even if trivial, and not for business solely'.

Again, since the Dreamer is one brought to understanding by the pressure of experience, we should be especially wary of those interpreters who, rightly insisting upon a body of traditional teaching informing Langland's thought, seem at times to come very close to suggesting that he is a writer of clear purpose, involving his readers in perplexities that were for him only apparent, in order to win their better understanding. Thus, Fr. Dunning maintains that Langland 'largely takes for granted the traditional teaching on the spiritual life of the Christian'.[56] The question here is not one of degree—the mere extent, not covered by Fr. Dunning's 'largely', to which Langland might be thought *not* to take for granted traditional teaching—but rather of kind, the sort of activity we are to envisage in the writer. The matter of his name is in itself beside the point. Nothing forbids the assumption that it may in fact have been 'William Langland'—so long as we do not overlook the significances that 'Longe Wille' and his living 'in londe' have within the poem. Neither Manly's parallels (to show that 'I haue lyued in londe' had the quality of formula)[57] nor Meroney's rejection of 'a name-conscious "Wille Longelonde"'[58] are anything to the purpose against the existence of a William Langland as author of the poem. Rather, we have an equal warrant for supposing that such a name might prompt awareness of those significances which are central to the poem. Indeed, if the surname was not that of the sire[59]—for whatever reason— then awareness of name-significance might well extend from a surname known to be arbitrary, 'Langland', to the Christian name, 'Will'. Those who would guess at Langland's illegitimate birth[60] may perhaps find a special significance in the poet's emphasis upon *gentrice*, the noble blood-relationship of all Christians, which comes with fullest appeal in the poet's account of the Saviour's earthly ministry.

We have something more substantial in that account of the poet's livelihood in C VI, which, as Professor Donaldson observes, 'is both an apology and a prayer for grace'. It is tempting to relate to the emphasis upon *gentrice* (and, also, perhaps, his markedly contractual sense of law) the implications Professor Donaldson shrewdly observes in the poet's scorn for the beggar and the dishonest hermit:

> Naturally, he shows himself sensitive in speaking of these two types of parasite. But is not this acute sensitivity, evident in both B and C, a kind of proof of the truth of the autobiographical passage in which it receives its fullest expression?

The 'apologia' thus goes beyond its ostensible occasion and becomes 'a brilliant portrait of the personality of a man who knew himself well'.[61] We may add to this evidence, for what it is worth, the self-portrait at the end of the poem. The poet as victim of old age is the unflattering, all too life-like, portrait invested with rueful humour which Gower, also, as we have seen,[62] offers us in the close of his poem, when the mirror is held up to the would-be servant of Love. But realistic appraisal of this order, set as it is within a tradition of humorous self-depreciation, is not all the evidence that the poem offers concerning him who made it. The identity of the poet, the imagination inhabiting *Piers Plowman*, is not only realistic, riddling, and absolute in its pursuit of truth. Certainly, it is understandable that the poet should represent—and perhaps best know—himself in these terms; the step forward for Plowman and Dreamer alike is in the sharp realization of stupidity. Piers is vexed at a piece of capital foolishness: he has overlooked not merely something any Christian child might know, but something any Jew or Saracen could have told him. The Moral Law is universal: all men, Christian and Pagan alike, know that Justice at once exacts obedience and can never be satisfied. This is the one certain piece of knowledge which the poet can make the rock-like foundation of his building. The matter of the Righteous Heathen is nearer the true centre of the poem than criticism has always allowed. In the Plowman we have the plight of a good man, who in his earnest scrutiny of the map of knowledge has overlooked the largely printed name of a continent. The Law explicit in the Pardon needs no document; it is written in all men's hearts. The realization comes to Piers all in a moment: for the poet, who will care to say after how many years of anxious thought and with what stinging force?—'Fool! . . . look in thy heart and write.' Certainly, this is one aspect of the truth about the imagination at work in *Piers Plowman*. It constitutes the *vis comica* which binds together *Visio* and *Vita de Dowel*, and is suitably evident in the self-portraiture. But the satire of the poem, we remember, becomes radical. Where the first stroke had been to show a society that could produce at need only one good man, the second was to show how far short that good man falls of the standard enjoined upon all men—'Be ye perfect'. The Plowman turns out, in the long argument of the *Vita de Dowel*, to have been just this side of the frontier between the Christian and the virtuous Pagan. Of the Grace freely available to the Christian after Christ's perfect fulfilment of Law, Piers has made the least use; he thus stands upon the lowest level of potential Christian achievement. All this is examined—worried out— in the *Vita de Dowel*. But it is all implicit in the revelation that flashes upon the Plowman as he grasps the meaning of the Pardon and takes the irrevocable step of destroying it.

This perception of the crucial distinction between Law and Grace is that other aspect of the poet's personality which the tradition of self-portraiture he works in will not readily disclose, but which is fundamental to our understanding of Langland, the personality we grow to know as we read the poem. His contemporary, Julian of Norwich, has often been mentioned in connexion with the great and charitable hope of Universal Salvation which they appear to have in common. As Langland develops the argument of the *Vita de Dowel*, the resemblance between poet and mystic becomes more striking. The Dreamer's starting-point—the question, how shall a man avoid sin?—and the answer he receives from the Friars, may remind us of the 'soft drede' which was allayed for Julian by her Lord's answer, 'I kepe the ful sekirly'; for, she learned,

> in every soule that shal be savid is a godly wil that never assentid to synne ne never shal; ryth as there is a bestly will in the lower party that may willen no good, ryth so ther is a godly will in the heyer party, which will is so good that it may never willen yll but ever good.

Langland's conclusion is not that of Julian. Therefore, she says,

> we arn that He lovith, and endlessly we do that that Hym lykyt[h] . . . He lovith us now as wele, whil we arn here, as He shal don whan we arn there afore His blessid face, but for faylyng of love on our party therefore is al our travel.

Julian's are 'Revelations of Divine Love': pursuing the truth, like Langland in his fashion, seeking always the final bearings of the argu-

*party* part; *arn* are; *travel* trouble.

ment, testing what has been divinely revealed by resort to Scripture and
the authoritative teaching of the Church, Julian comes to a single and
all-embracing conclusion:

> And fro that time it was shewid I desired often times to witten
> what was Our Lords mening, and xv yer after and more I was ans-
> werid in gostly understonding seyand thus, Woldst thou wetten thi
> Lords mening in this thing?—wete it wele, Love was His mening.[63]

Langland's preoccupation is with Duty, with right conduct. His capacity for doubt and questioning is faithfully reflected, we may be sure
in the progress of his Dreamer. But, though the emphasis differs in
Langland and Julian, their starting-point is in a common awareness of the
Divine Perfection that at once makes almost negligible and at the same
time rewards all human striving after goodness—and understanding.

Their careers, too, are strikingly parallel, if we bear in mind that
Julian also has her 'A Text'.[64] Where almost all is unknown, no more
than a trial conjecture is possible. Yet the picture of Julian as Margery
Kempe shows her, late in life, giving good counsel from a developed
acquaintance with the Scriptures,[65] is very like what may be assumed of
the poet who devoted a lifetime to the elucidation of the truths implicit
in Piers Plowman's consummate act. To be sure, the differences in tem-
perament and approach could hardly be more divergent. On the one
side, there is patient contemplation of the Love of God; on the other,
impatience and even vexation, the very pulsing life of a man whom
Theology has 'tened' 'ten score tymes'. But neither can be content to
postpone the question, what does it mean?—how does it all fit with what
we may know of a God Who is good and still has dealings with sinful
men? Yet the *Vita de Dowel, Dobet et Dobest* is the work not of a meditative recluse but of a poet. His Dreamer is one who goes his way
through the world, passionately interrogating the learned and the
authoritative. In these terms it may be regarded as an account of 'the
growth of a poet's mind'—the record of a sense of purpose which may
have come to the poet with the sudden clarity and simplicity of vision,
but which remained to tease him out of thought. Of the Dreamer, as
of the young Wordsworth, it could later be said that he

> Sick, wearied out with contrarieties,
> Yielded up moral questions in despair.

And the abiding strength of Langland's poetry, as Wordsworth's, is in
a perception of Law which must 'preserve the stars from wrong'.

The hall-mark of Langland's work is a special authenticity, deriving

*gostly* spiritual; *seyand* saying.

from visionary power not at variance with but sustained by a penetrating realism. His poem, as we have seen, succeeds in communicating
the very pressure of experience itself. The arguments are there, and they
come with varying force—and relevance. But what is also there is the
sense that nothing less than the highest is at once required and made
possible. *Piers Plowman* is no merely didactic work, nor is it simply a
confession of faith. Its essential witness is to the whole need of man—
to make sense not merely of a scheme of things considered as external
to ourselves, but of the riddling and evasive heart of man himself.
Newman, we may recall, once said that he did not 'care to overcome'
the reason of his auditors 'without touching their hearts'. The stubbornness of the Dreamer, in the *Vita de Dowel* especially, demonstrates
a similar unwillingness to accept for truth what must be divorced from
the pressure and complexity of experience:

> Why am I to begin with taking up a position not my own, and
> unclothing my mind of that large outfit of existing thoughts, prin-
> ciples, likings, desires, and hopes which make me what I am?[66]

Just such an inseparability of doctrine and practice is fundamental
to any 'grammar of assent'. It is Langland's great gift; and his poem is
therefore peculiarly resistant to any attempts to abstract or simplify.

Poetry comparable with this is not readily come by in our tradition.
Perhaps, as was suggested in Chapter V, the weakening and virtual dis-
appearance of Langland's medium, the four-beat line and the loosely-
structured Passus and Part, made for an irretrievable loss. *Piers Plowman*
is the last major poem before the qualities of an evident clarity and
symmetry, in the line as in the stanza and canto, begin to make their
steady advance. Thus Langland's chance of fathering English poetry was
always slight; and his own singular qualities made that chance even more
remote. Yet who can say? It is after all a mysterious process by which
'the soul of Chaucer was transfused' and Spenser 'was begotten by him
two hundred years after his decease'.[67] It has recently been suggested
that there may be more than a general relation between Spenser and
Langland[68]. If the suggestion has substance then it is Langland who is in
part the progenitor of both Spenser and Milton. But Langland's direct
disciples are still to seek. Our own divided and uncertain age may find
fresh challenge in a vivid social sense that is utterly removed from cap-
tiousness, and an ironic penetration which is by turns sardonic and
exalted. Indeed, if one had to name that poet in our whole tradition
whom Langland most nearly resembles my own choice would be
W. H. Auden, with his vigilant moral sense, his ironic awareness of the

cash-nexus between man and man, and his unforced sublimities when
the figure of a Healer grows distinct, and we perceive not doctrine or
therapy but a power that men and women can invoke to make an end
of all separation:

> O Love, the interest itself in thoughtless Heaven,
> Make simpler daily the beating of man's heart; within,
> There in the ring where name and image meet.

Whatever Langland's following, they will have chosen a master
whose highly individual talent is least of all capable of becoming a
mere 'influence'. If we had lost the text of Chaucer, Spenser and Milton
what we should reconstruct from the work of their disciples would be
sadly less than the master-work; for it is the characteristic of disciple-
ship in every age to assimilate to itself certain single and simple aspects
of a master-work which has triumphed in holding many things in
balance. We should have an aureate Chaucer, a Spenser of gothic
fictions, a Milton given wholly either to an ever-musing melancholy
or to an aldermanic parody of the grand manner. The loss would be
grievous; yet something of the master-poet might be faintly discerned
beneath this crudely enthusiastic portraiture. But with Langland the
gift that awaits bestowal is not a manner, a style, or a standpoint, but an
individuality than can only bring the disciple to discover himself.
All that has been said of the poet of *Piers Plowman* will mislead if in
the end it is not plain that 'what most eludes description is not the
excellence of his gifts but the singularity of his essential being'.[69] From
this point of view, an undue curiosity about a real 'William Langland'
may obscure understanding. In the critical history of this poem unity
of authorship remains a liberating assumption; one man, we may
soundly suppose, 'made *Piers Plowman*'. But we must not identify
poet and Dreamer, lest we miss the nature of the Dreamer's progress,
and thus the distinctive quality of the poet's achievement. *Piers
Plowman* offers that rarest kind of argument which, to quote Newman
once more, 'is in different aspects both object and proof'; as it proceeds
upon, so it can elicit from the reader 'one complex act both of inference
and assent'.[70] The modern consciousness, we saw, is of a world which is
oppressively 'contingent'—'One can live or tell; not both at once'.[71] The
deployment of a Dreamer who is and who is not the author should therefore have a special interest and perhaps adaptability. It may suggest a way
of communicating 'the real lesson to be taught... that the human person is
precious and unique', without the cruel frustration of finding ourselves
'unable to set it forth except in terms of ideology and abstraction'.[72]

## Notes

1. See p. 206, above.
2. Cf. p. 212, above.
3. *The Allegory of Love*, p. 158.
4. *Tractat. xii in Joann. iii.*
5. See pp. 19-21, above.
6. See pp. 228-33, above.
7. Leo Spitzer writes acutely on the distinction between the 'poetic' and 'empirical' 'I' in *Traditio*, IV (1946), 414-22.
8. *Canterbury Tales* D 1-2.
9. *Book of the Duchess* 577-8.
10. *House of Fame* 1894-99.
11. *Troilus and Criseyde* v 1732-3.
12. *ibid.* 1696-8.
13. *ibid.* ii 674-7.
14. See pp. 228-9, above.
15. See E. Talbot Donaldson, 'Chaucer the Pilgrim', *Publications of the Modern Language Association of America*, LXIX (1954), 928-36; and, for an earlier treatment, H. Lüdeke, *Die Funktionen des Erzählers in Chaucers epischer Dichtung*, Halle an der Saale, 1928.
16. For the relation of this to the common formula, 'profit *and* delight', see p. 244, above.
17. *Troilus and Criseyde* ii 666-9.
18. *Parlement of Foules* 594.
19. *Confessio Amantis* i 1-5.
20. *ibid.* 32-33.
21. *ibid.* 127-131.
22. For the difference between the two endings, see p. 182, above.
23. A XII 6-8.
24. See W. A. Pantin, *The English Church in the Fourteenth Century*, Cambridge 1955, pp. 123-35.
25. For a sound examination of much previous discussion upon these 'triads', see S. S. Hussey, 'Langland, Hilton, and the Three Lives', *Review of English Studies*, N.S. VII (1956), 132-50.
26. H. W. Wells, 'The Construction of *Piers Plowman*', *Publications of the Modern Language Association of America*, XLIV (1929), 123-40; T. P. Dunning, 'The Structure of the B-Text of *Piers Plowman*', *Review of English Studies*, N. S. VII (1956), 225-37; 230.
27. A proceeding vigorously followed by Howard Meroney, who, insisting upon the spiritual life as the poet's dominant concern, finds it necessary to reject the triad of 'lives' as 'a false and mischievous analogy which has stultified *Piers Plowman* criticism for twenty years'. ('The Life and Death of Longe Wille', *ELH*, XVII (1950), 1-35.) For further discussion of this view, see pp. 303-4, below; and on Meroney's view of the character 'Wille', pp. 313-4, below.

28. *Virga tua et baculus tuus, ipsa me consolata sunt* 'Thy rod and Thy staff they comfort me' (Ps. xxiii 4). This is the continuation of the Psalm quoted by Piers, tearing the Pardon (VII 116-7).

29. Hussey, *loc. cit.*, 139.

30. A X 47-8 (Kane).

31. 'The structure of the B-text of *Piers Plowman*', 237.

32. '*Piers Plowman*' : *the C-Text and its Poet*, p. 197.

33. See pp. 313-4, below.

34. *loc. cit.*, 13.

35. Hussey, *loc. cit.*, 139.

36. *Cf.* Dunning, *loc. cit.*, 227-8.

37. 'Walter Hilton . . . will bring only confusion' (*ibid.*, 235).

38. *loc. cit.*, 146.

39. *ibid.*, 147.

40. 'On Fairy-Stories', in *Essays Presented to Charles Williams*, London, 1947, pp. 81-4.

41. *The English Epic and its Background*, London, 1954, p. 142.

42. *The Burning Tree*, London, 1956, p. 15.

43. *ibid.*, p. 16.

44. '. . . he is confused and monotonous, and hardly makes his poetry into a poem' (Lewis, *The Allegory of Love*, p. 161).

45. George Kane, *Middle English Literature*, London, 1951, p. 185.

46. Tillyard, *op. cit.*, p. 168.

47. 'Poets and their Critics: Langland and Milton', Warton Lecture, British Academy, London, 1941, p. 13.

48. *loc. cit.*, 226.

49. Swift, *The Battle of the Books*, The Preface of the Author.

50. 'Tradition and the Individual Talent' (*Selected Essays*, London, 1932, p. 15).

51. Lewis, *The Allegory of Love*, p. 160.

52. The capabilities of that satire which becomes 'radical' by including the observer in its scope are discussed in 'Radical Satire and the Realistic Novel', *Essays and Studies*, London, 1955, pp. 58-75.

53. The Dreamer of the earlier part of the *Vita de Dowel* has his share of the qualities which Mr. D. G. James sees in Hobbes, 'his sanguinity, his dash and his adroitness' (*The Life of Reason*, London, 1949, p. 17).

54. *loc. cit.*, 19, 17. The Scriptural reference is to Luke xiv 18.

55. *ibid.*, 6.

56. Dunning, *loc. cit.*, 225.

57. 'The authorship of *Piers Plowman*', *Modern Philology*, VII (1909), 97 n. 1.

58. *loc. cit.*, 3.

59. The C Text has a passage (IV 369-70) which discusses the circumstances in which it would be *noʒt reasonable ne rect* to refuse the sire's surname. Mr. E. St. John Brooks (in the article referred to at p. 237 n. 25, above) suggests that the reference is to suing for the father's livery, when the eldest son claimed his father's inheritance at the lord's court.

60. See p. 12, above.

61. 'Piers Plowman'; the C-Text and its Poet, pp. 224-6.

62. See p. 291, above.

63. British Museum MS Sloane 2499, ff. 24$^v$, 56$^r$-57$^v$.

64. Some reasons for supposing that British Museum MS Add. 37790 preserves Julian's 'A Text' are given in my 'Note on the Revelations of Julian of Norwich', Review of English Studies, N. S. II (1951), 255-8.

65. The Book of Margery Kempe, E. E. T. S., ed. Meech and Allen, London, 1940, I 42-3. There is a contrast here with the Revelations, as Dr Allen notes (ibid., 279), following Mr. T.W. Coleman (English Mystics of the Fourteenth Century, London, 1938, pp. 163-4). But it should not affect judgement of the reliability of Margery's account. On the contrary, this evidence of study is what we might expect of a Julian who had long meditated the relation between what was originally revealed and the received teaching of the Church.

66. Newman, An Essay in aid of a Grammar of Assent, London, 1887, p. 424.

67. Dryden, Essays, ed. Ker, II 247.

68. A. C. Hamilton, 'Spenser and Langland', Studies in Philology, LV (1958), 533-48.

69. A. E. Housman, Preface to Nine Essays by Arthur Platt, Cambridge, 1927, p.xi.

70. op. cit., p. 492.

71. Murdoch, Sartre, p. 11; cf. p. 235, above.

72. ibid., p. 76.

# Appendix

## Some Problems of a true text of Piers Plowman

It was suggested in Chapter V that we should be especially wary of any approach to *Piers Plowman* which would equate the 'poetic' with the work of 'finish'; for 'finished', in the all-important sense of concluded, given definitive shape, *Piers Plowman* never is. Professor Donaldson has tellingly commented on the separate versions we habitually deal with:

> I sometimes wonder whether the C Text, the B Text, and even the A Text are not merely historical accidents, haphazard milestones in the history of a poem that was begun but never finished, photographs that caught a static image of a living organism at a given but not necessarily significant moment of time.[1]

With the absence of 'finish' in this sense we must link 'finish' in its usual meaning of particular (at best, unique) verbal excellence, the one-and-only words which constitute an authentic text. We may unwittingly bring to *Piers Plowman* notions proper to the tradition of the syllabic, foot-counted line, where the word is all-important. The account given in Chapter V of the distinctive capacity and development of foot-counted as against phrasal line will have been in vain unless the reader has grasped that it is least of all in the word that the 'prosodic' principle of *Piers Plowman* resides, but in the phrase. The alliterative line is not to be understood as a kind of verse which operates upon a simpler rhythmic basis than the foot-counted line and is in all essential respects the same. Syllabic regularity necessarily means a decisive insistence upon the word, for it is the word which is thrown into prominence when speech-demand and metrical *ictus* are contending forces. If we are to establish the text of a poet whose prosodic system is based upon a regular number of syllables, it is to the word that we must primarily direct ourselves; and this will hold whether the measure be accentual or quantitative, ancient Classical or modern English (in the traditional foot-counted mode).

With such versification our understanding of an editor's primary role and working-method is beyond any doubt. It may be illustrated from the practice of an editor working upon a Latin text who furnishes an analogy from modern English. Housman illustrates the difficulties of emendation by citing Walter de la Mare's *Fare Well*:

> Oh, when this my dust surrenders
> Hand, foot, lip, to dust again,
> May these loved and loving faces
>         Please other men!
> May the rusting harvest hedgerow
> Still the Traveller's Joy entwine,
> And as happy children gather
>         Posies once mine.

Housman observes that if we were limited to a text that read *rustling* in the fifth line quoted above, the task of maintaining *rusting* as the true reading would indeed be a hard one, against that 'bulk of the reading public' who would certainly prefer *rustling* as 'exquisitely apt and poetical'.[2] The point illustrates very well the supreme importance of the word in any strictly metrical composition. But we should be careful to ask ourselves whether Langland's mode of verse is answerable to these criteria. Where the phrase is all-important, the individual word may be peculiarly hard to recover—and, dare one suggest, of less significance, in many instances, than an editor trained in a tradition of verbal exactitude may be able to bring himself to admit?

Certain gains may be clear enough;[3] thus, in the fable of the rats and the cat, a mouse sturdily opposes action against cat or kitten:

> And thou3 it had coste me catel, biknowen it I nolde,
> But suffre as hym-self wolde, to do as hym liketh,
> Coupled and vncoupled, to cacche what thei mowe. (Prol. 204-6)

The word *do* in the phrase 'to do as hym liketh' seems anomalous: and the alliterating reading *slen*, which one manuscript offers, can be accepted. What is the effect of such a reading? It brings out very clearly the note of round assertion; the mouse makes an end of all temporizing with the problem. We may take the reading *do* as a scribal weakening of an injudiciously strong statement, and relate the present passage to other instances of prudent interference (as, for example, the softening at B X 53 of the blasphemous conjecture that Study openly reports in both A and C Texts[4]). These are not spectacular, but they are solid gains; little by little we may begin to clarify Langland's characteristic tone and emphasis.

The major difficulty, however, of an editor of this poem remains. The grand alternatives which confront the editor of a strictly metrical com-

*catel* money; *biknowen* acknowledge; *nolde* ne + wolde; *hym liketh* pleases them (cat and kitten); *coupled and vncoupled* fettered or unfettered; *slen* slay, kill.

position are clear enough. However much or little he may succeed in conforming to the one and eschewing the other, the alternatives are The Poet Restored and The Poet Improved. But is it fanciful to suggest that in *Piers Plowman* this distinction is significantly reduced? The poem is so far oral in its essential mode of being that a true text is in some ways as artificial a conception as a true text of some of the ballads, or perhaps of certain lyrics of Wyatt. The impact of Langland's phrases, striking home upon the reader not with any effect of singular meaning in the word, but in the whole fall of the phrase, seems to make the poem peculiarly not any one speaker's property—so that an authentic, word-by-word text is to be distinguished from all variations—but the common possession of all who hear, and in their turn are moved to re-tell, it. In this respect, we may feel, Langland's work, unlike the clumsily elaborate verse of the 'Alliterative Revival', is truly *sui generis*, a poetry which in many respects genuinely allows freedom and variety of re-telling; and any undue insistence on the word may be opposed to that very principle of life and energy on which all depends.

What then can an editor hope to accomplish? Certainly, by grouping his manuscripts into 'traditions' he may make us aware of varying states of the poem, so that our tendency to ask for one definitive state, to which all others are in varying degrees inferior, is checked. Thus, Professor Donaldson's work on MSS R and F in the B-tradition points to 'a shape of the poem that is not precisely A or B or C', and this is a suggestion first made by so conservative a reader of the poem as Skeat[5]. Again, the work of scribes, moralizing or prudently paraphrasing, can be recognised for what it is; as, too, can that type of error which arises from a scribe's recollection of a MS of the poem in another tradition, thus giving rise to such apparent examples of *hysteron proteron* as C readings in A and B MSS, and so on. Here, too, we must be firmly on our guard against any notions of the copyist which derive from mass-multiplication of books by the printing-press. Where there is no 'true' state of the poem, there may be little feeling for a text to be preserved at all costs; and memorial powers unjaded by a world in which books are the commonest of commodities may reach a capacity we cannot easily imagine. For the rest, preference for one word over another must proceed under the safeguards already suggested.

There is, however, one type of context in which attention to the word is important and, one would suggest, may be especially rewarding. I refer to that wordplay which is treated more fully in Chapter VI.[6] A simple instance of wordplay, accessible not in Skeat's text but his variant readings, is the *bilow* which MS L offers against the *biloue* of MSS WCO:

> And if thow wilt be graciouse to god, do as the gospel techeth,
> And *bilow* the amonges *low* men, so shaltow lacche grace ...
>
> (B VI 229-30)

The wordplay *bilow-low* is entirely consonant with the poet's habit when practice of the truth is insisted upon. There is, I would suggest, a similar warrant for sustaining a variant reading in Piers's resolve to enter upon a new way of life:

> 'I shal cessen of my sowyng', quod Pieres, 'and swynk nouȝt so harde,
> Ne about my bely-ioye so bisi be namore!' (B VII 117-18)

The A text as printed by Skeat has

> Ne aboute my lyflode so bisi beo no more!

For *lyflode* (B, *bely-ioye*) Professor Kane, the latest editor of the A Text, reads *belyue*, on the ground that *belyue*, 'apparently not recorded after *Piers Plowman*, would seem to be the harder, and would not have been substituted for *liflode* by late fourteenth- or fifteenth-century scribes'.[7] We may venture to reinforce this view by another consideration; *belyue* in its primary sense 'livelihood' but with its second, punning sense 'belief', sounds the first note of the paradoxical wordplay which follows immediately between Plowman and Priest. The Plowman is not to be so *bisi* about his livelihood; for his *belyue*, understood as his creed, forbids anxious care while it demands the good works of faith. For a close connexion of *lyflode* and *byleue* we may compare Patience, displaying 'Vitailles of grete vertues' as he asserts, ' 'lo! here *lyflode* ynough if owre *byleue* be trewe!' '(XIV 37-8). It is a rueful and ironic awareness, echoed, in the present passage, by the play of words, two lines later, 'And beloure that I [be]louȝ' (where again Professor Kane adopts the harder reading, meaning 'smile upon, look with favour on'). The simplicity of a world of work-and-wages is beginning to dissolve for the Plowman, his task in the half-acre completed. These considerations may deepen our understanding of B's *bely-ioye*—a bitter irony, springing from the sense of wasted opportunity, to mark the contrast between man's spiritual and material sustenance.

*bilow the* humble yourself; *biloue the* make yourself beloved; *lacche* obtain; *swynk* toil; *bely-ioye* 'good cheer'; *lyflode* sustenance; *belyue* what one 'lives by', livelihood; *bisi* preoccupied (*cf.* p. 79, above).

One might argue in a similar vein for giving a different description to Avarice's wife from that which Skeat prints:

And my wyf at Westmunstre that wollene cloth made. (A V 129)
My wyf was a webbe and wollen cloth made. (B V 215)

Professor Kane reads (as do Knott and Fowler):

My wyf was a wynstere and wollene cloth made . . .

It is a peculiarly apt designation in a context where the various methods of 'winning', making money, are ironically elaborated. Recognition of this side of the poet's genius—his awareness of double meaning in the single word (perhaps reflected, too, as Professor Kane notes, in the variants *copiede*, *copide*, *coupide* at A VIII 44) may help us in considering the difficult imagery of that celebrated passage (A I 136 ff., B I 146 ff.) where 'loue' is

the leuest thing that oure lord askith,
And ek the plante of pes . . .

What the 'plant of peace' may be is hard to define; and Professor Kane, reflecting on the possibility of *plante* standing for an original *planete*, concludes, perhaps over-rigorously, that any appearance of certainty about the A Text at this point, 'as a glance at the critical apparatus might suggest', is unfounded.[8]

A connexion with 'planet' is certainly attractive; and Professor Kane records Morton Bloomfield's observation that the 'planet of Peace', Mercury, symbolizes Christ as the leader of souls (the 'psychopomp'), 'an idea perhaps reflected in B I 157, *leder of the lordes folke of heuene*'. This is of course to go beyond the evidence available within the version of the poem under review: *planete*, as Professor Kane notes, occurs in no A MS (it is found in one B MS as *planetes*). Moreover, in the parallel B passage it is possible that we have not a single, dominant meaning, but a gathering of meanings which includes both 'plant' and 'planet'. There may well be a meeting of plant and planet in the B poet's imagination; for it is the B version which exhibits this sort of intertwining of meaning more frequently, and on occasions more elaborately, than A. We must of course await the new edition of B before we can speak with confidence. But passages which are hardly in doubt and which suggest B's greater interest in wordplay are: when Priest and Plowman wrangle together, the replacement of A's single-minded jest *Quoniam literaturam*

*beloure* frown upon; *webbe* weaver; *leuest* dearest, most pleasing; *ek* also.

*non cognoui* by the ironic *dixit insipiens*, with its play upon *incipiens*, a foolish beginner who knows no more than his vaunted 'a b c'; the wordplay upon *secte*, *sute* and *armes* in Repentance's moving appeal for God's mercy; and the concluding lines of Saturn's prophecy, leading immediately from the appeal for a *trewe* ('truce') which ends one Passus on a note of near-despair, to the *Treuthe* who hears and sends a permanent truce.[9] And, to look beyond these alterations or additions within the scope of A, there is in B and C, as we have seen, the whole course of a Dreamer in whom a stubborn pragmatism and a dialectical facility are equally matched—a 'Wille' who 'wolde ywyte, yif Witte couthe teche hym' (VIII 124)—so that wordplay inheres in his characterization and role.[10] None of this is inconsistent with an undisturbed A reading of *plante* in the passage under review. The presumption from any comparison with B is not, of necessity, towards an original 'planet' in A. It is at least an equal possibility that a 'plant' in A started those trains of association which are in general more strongly developed in B than A, to give a 'planet', and perhaps a 'plenty', which do not displace 'plant' but coexist with it in a fullness of meaning appropriate to a meeting of earth and heaven in the mystery of Incarnation. The most scrupulous editor need not feel that the text of A is here 'seriously in doubt'.

It is perhaps worth while to trace out the detailed association of meanings in the B passage taken as a whole:

> For trewthe telleth that loue is triacle of heuene;
> May no synne be on him sene that vseth that spise,
> And alle his werkes he wrou3te with loue as him liste;
> And lered it Moises for the leuest thing, and moste like to heuene,
> And also the plente of pees, moste precious of vertues.
> For heuene my3te nou3te holden it, it was so heuy of hym-self,
> Tyl it hadde of the erthe yeten his fylle,
> And whan it haued of this folde flesshe and blode taken,
> Was neuere leef vpon lynde li3ter ther-after,
> And portatyf and persant as the poynt of a nedle,
> That my3te non armure it lette, ne none hei3 walles.

A 'plant' is perhaps suggested by the *triacle* (the sovereign remedy) and *spise* (the meaning 'kind, species', suggesting the meaning 'spice') of the preceding lines; the wonder-working properties of a herb are in

---

*Quoniam* etc. 'for I know no learning' (see p. 86, n. 23, above); *dixit insipiens* 'The fool hath said . . .' (Ps. xiv 1); *secte*, *sute*, *armes* (see p. 52, above); *ywyte* know; *yif* if; *yeten* eaten; *lette* hinder, obstruct.

the forefront of attention—as, too, though more faintly, is the place of a growing thing, between the earth in which it is rooted and the heaven to which it aspires. Perhaps, too, *plenitudo pacis*, on the analogy of *plenitudo temporis*, reinforces the sense of unique fulfilment as a coming to flower (*cf.* 'Tyl *plenitudo temporis* ful tyme ycomen were, That Pieres fruit floured and fel to be ripe', XVI 93-4).[11] But the heaven itself may have suggested those 'planets' which, too, exhibit wondrous properties. Certainly the passage as a meeting-point of apparent opposites expresses an irresistible power.[12] The linden (or lime) tree is both light and strong— hence its common use for shields. This in its turn suggests by contrast a force that penetrates the strongest 'shields'—the iron and masonry of 'armure' and 'heiȝ walles'. The lime tree as it grows, its leaves stirring in the wind, witnesses to that force as mysterious, coming out of heaven to touch earthly things. An editor may find the phrase *yeten his fille* yielding only a limited sense. He may instead offer us *yoten his sylue*, so that a meaning which draws upon the casting of metals may link the planet with earth, in a marvellous alchemy. For the 'planet' in question may well be thought of as Mercury, a metal both heavy and volatile; and the plant-imagery recalls *mercurialis*, the herb 'All good'. Gower can enlighten us, in his account of alchemical matters:

> to his part Mercurius
> Hath the quikselver, as it falleth,
> The which, after the bok it calleth,
> Is ferst of thilke fowre named
> Of Spiritz, whiche ben proclamed.

As G. C. Macaulay notes, comparing Gower's treatment of the seven bodies and four spirits of Alchemy with Chaucer's (*C.T.* G 819 ff.), Mercury is here reckoned both as a body and as a spirit[13]; it is thus a unique 'compound'.

Such considerations drawn from the immediate context may encourage an editor of the B Text to print *yoten his sylue*, whether or not he wishes to remove the 'plant' or 'plenty' of peace in favour of the 'planet' (however spelt). The first readers of the B Text need not be supposed incapable of making the transition from one train of images to another. We may add, going outside the immediate context, that just as here, in Passus I, a life-giving power comes down from the heaven to bring marvellous unity, so in Passus XX Kynde comes 'out of the planetes'

*plenitudo temporis* 'the fulness of the time' (Gal. iv 4); *yoten his selue* cast, fused itself.

With Deth that is dredful, to vndone vs alle!

Such an identity-in-difference of ultimate beginning and end is, like the varying play of association in the passage itself, wholly consonant with the poet's characteristic methods.

Close analysis makes the matter sound mightily complex. Yet it remains true that any reader of Langland's poem may take to himself for comfort and inspiration what Dr Sisam once said of Middle English texts in general—'Every blur is a challenge'.[14] We have seen that it is possible to search too diligently for the word in passages where emphasis upon particular verbal meaning has no place. As Sisam notes of the line

Mathew with mannes face mouthed thise wordis, (VI 240)

*mouthed* has no special significance; it fits the run of the alliterative line as *seyd* cannot.[15] But at those points where different meanings are gathered into one focus, whether in simple or complex associations, there is at once challenge and incitement for every reader. Although an editor may despair of presenting at every point the Poet Restored, a critical awareness of the poem as a whole, more particularly its characteristic modes of emphasis, will most help him, as all of us, to recognize that persistent intruder upon our attention, the Poet Improved.

## Notes

1. 'MSS R and F in the B-Tradition of *Piers Plowman*', 211.
2. *M. Manilii Astronomicon Liber Quintus*, Cambridge, 1937, pp. xxxv-vi. I notice that *rustling* appeared in the Everyman anthology *Poems of Our Time, 1900-1942* (London, 1945), subsequently corrected. It may be added that *Fare Well* is rendered *Farewell* in more than one printing of the poem, including, unhappily, the list of Contents in the *Collected Poems* (London, 1942, p. xi).
3. In what follows I am indebted to Professor Donaldson for stimulating conversation and subsequent correspondence.
4. *Cf.* p. 95, above.
5. Donaldson, *loc. cit.*, p. 211.
6. See pp. 265-74, above.
7. *op. cit.*, p. 450.
8. *ibid.*, p. 155.
9. On these instances see, respectively, pp. 80; 52; 72, above.
10. See pp. 264-5, above.
11. *Cf.* p. 154, footgloss, above.
12. For the contrasts of diction in this passage, see p. 219, above.
13. *Confessio Amantis*, iv 2474-8; *n. ad loc.*
14. *Fourteenth Century Verse and Prose*, Oxford, 1921, p. xliii.
15. *ibid.*, p. xxxix.

# Index

Abingdon, Abbey of 102, 226.

Abraham 156 - 7, 158, 261.

Actiua Vita
  *See* Haukyn.

*Aeneid, The* 193.

*Alfred of Wessex* 199.

Allen, H. E.
  ed. *Book of Margery Kempe* 322 *n.* 65.

Alliterative Revival, The
  characteristic language 198, 231, and how adapted 200-1; contrasts with *Piers Plowman* 235, 325.

Amphlett, W. 199.

Anderson, M. D.
  *The Imagery of British Churches* 279 *n. 47.*

Anderson, Sherwood 243.

'Anima'
  colloquy with Dreamer 140-52; account of Charity 218-9; insistence on practice 264, 269-70; rebuking Dreamer 292-3.

Antichrist
  coming foretold by 'Clergy' 102-3; by 'Grace' 175; his coming 179-80; the siege 182.

Aquinas, St. Thomas 276.

Aristotle 105, 118, 247.

Arnold, Matthew: quoted 183.

Ascham, Roger 193, 237 *n. 6.*

Athanasian Creed 77.

Auden, W. H. 7, 318-9.

'Auereys', St. 210.

Augustine, St. 102, 149, 162, 226, 283.

Bateson, F. W.
  ed. *Epistles to Several Persons (Moral Essays)* 250.

Beattie, James 237 *n. 7.*

Becket, St. Thomas à 150, 185 *n. 8.*

Bennett, J. A. W. 7.

Bentley, Richard 194.

Bernard, St. 107, 276, 302-3; (proverbial) 95.

*Biblia Pauperum* 279 *n. 47.*

Bishops *in partibus infidelium* 149-51, 208, 216.

Bloomfield, M. W.
  *The Seven Deadly Sins* 138 *n. 28*; article on symbolism in medieval literature 254, 278 *n. 27*; on the three grades of chastity 258, 279 *n. 43*; the 'psychopomp' 327.

Boethius 87, 113, 114, 276.

Boy Bishop, The 32.

Bretigny, Treaty of 27, 256.

Brooks, E. St. John
  article on MSS in Trinity College, Dublin 237 *n. 25*, 312 *n. 59.*

Brown, R. E.
  article on 'Sensus Plenior' of Scripture 278 *n. 27.*

Browne, Sir Thomas 218.

Bunyan, John 47, 139, 233, 248.

Burke, Edmund 218.

Burrow, J. A.
  article on audience 200-2, 231.

Butler, Samuel 241.

Can Grande, Epistle to:
  *see* Dante.

*Canterbury Tales, The*
  *see* Chaucer, Geoffrey.

Cargill, Oscar
  article on Langland 237 *n. 25.*

Carlyle, Thomas 17, quoted 134.

'Cato' 35, 74, 113.

'Cayme'
see Antichrist.
Challoner, Richard
(trans. Bible) 86 n. 23.
Chambers, R.W.
Man's Unconquerable Mind 85 n. 15;
On the continuity of English Prose
from Alfred to More and his School
219; 'Poets and their Critics: Lang-
land and Milton' 309.
Charity
Haukyn's question 128-9; expounded
by 'Anima' 143-7, 218-9; Tree of
Charity 153-4, 257-8, 260, 274.
Chaucer, Geoffrey
Book of the Duchess 229, 286, 291;
House of Fame 138 n. 18, 286-7;
Parliament of Fowls 289; Boece 87,
280 n. 70; Troilus and Criseyde 85 n.
20, 221-2, 229, 277, 287-8, 291;
Legend of Good Women 95, 228-9,
288-9; General Prologue of Canter-
bury Tales 9; Wife of Bath's Prologue 32-3, 228, 286; Merchant's
Tale 33, 228; Franklin's Tale 228;
Prioress 100; Sir Thopas 197, 216,
289; Melibee 244, 289; Monk 100;
Nun's Priest's Tale 278 n. 31; Can-
on's Yeoman's Tale 329; Parson's
Tale 33, 145; role of Host 244, 289;
Tyrwhitt on metre 192; comparison
with Langland 199, 238 n. 39, with
Langland and Gower 235-6; Dreamer
in Chaucer 281, compared with Langland and Gower 286-91, 294, 297,
311; Canterbury Tales compared with
Confessio Amantis 289; his art 312;
his influence 319-9.
Cimabue 235.
Clement of Alexandria 252.
Clement V, Pope 71.
'Clergy'
directions to his dwelling 98; colloquy with Dreamer 99-103; (A Text)
help withdrawn 106-7, 206, 293; on
perfectionism 108; his teaching wasted
114, 116; relation to 'Ymagynatyf'
117; invites Dreamer to dine 118;
episode of 'Doctor' 119-20; relation

to 'Conscience' 121-2, 212-3; em-
ploying image of Castle 267; re-
ports 'Piers Plowman' on Dowel
etc. 306.
Coghill, N. K.
Visions from Piers Plowman 43 n. 5,
231; article on Pardon 85 nn. 15, 17,
238 n. 59; introduction to Wells,
The Vision of Piers Plowman 248-9;
The Poet Chaucer 278 n. 30.
Coleman, T. W.
English Mystics of the Fourteenth
Century 322 n. 65.
Coleridge, S. T. 47, 200, 235, 242, 246-8.
Comestor, Peter 75.
Confessio Amantis
see Gower, John.
'Conscience'
at Lady Meed's examination 23-35,
186 n. 24, 257-8, 268; compared
with 'Reason' 38; foretelling mill-
enial state 39, 41, 85 n. 14, 170,
225-6, 281, 296; united with 'Reason'
and King 40, 63, echoed 177; distinguishing mesurelees from mesurable
41, 63, 118; differences in C Text
43 n. 7; his kneeling 76, 172, 209,
262; omnia probate applied to Dreamer
107; counsels silence 119, and co-
operates with Dreamer 210-11; he
testifies to power of Love 120; his
relation to 'Clergy' 121-2, 212-3;
fellow-pilgrim with Dreamer 123;
questions Haukyn 126; emphasis
on contrition, confession and restitution 127-8, reaffirmed by 'Patience'
132; explains to Dreamer at outset
of Dobest 172-5; counsels withdrawal
into Unity 176; his role in closing
stages 176-8, 180-5, 295, 306.
Constantine, Emperor 102, 150, 226.
Cornhill 13, 171, 263.
Covetousness
as instance of categorization 47; his
ignorance 49-50, 119, 206; resolved
on pilgrimage 53; no power over poverty 133-4, 208, 218; in assault on
Unity 181-2, 184, 273; his wife
described 327.

Daniel, Samuel 230.

Dante

*Vita Nuova* 251, 275; *Convivio* 240, 253; *Ep. Can Grande* 253-4, 278 *n. 28*; *Inferno* 33; *Divine Comedy* compared with *Piers Plowman* 249.

de Brugge, Walter 237 *n. 25.*

*de Contemptu Mundi* 39.

de la Mare, Walter 7, 323-4.

de Rokayle, Eustace 12.

de Voragine, Jacobus 220.

Denham, Sir John 192.

Despenser, Lord 12.

*Divine Comedy, The*
see Dante.

Dominic, St. 182.

Donaldson, E. Talbot
'*Piers Plowman*': *the C-Text and its Poet* 44 *n. 9*, 138 *n. 17*, 238 *n. 35*, 302-3, 315; article on MSS R and F in B-tradition 185 *n. 8*, 323, 325; article on patristic exegesis and literary criticism 278 *n. 31*; article on Chaucer the pilgrim 320 *n. 15*; suggested readings 7, 43 *n. 2*, 44 *nn. 15, 17, 21*, 137 *nn. 6, 7, 8, 10*, 138 *nn. 14, 29*, 154, 186 *nn. 21, 25*, 279 *n. 53*; 330 *n. 3.*

Donne, John 192.

Donovan, Mortimer
article on Chaucer's Nun's Priest's Tale 278 *n. 31.*

Douay (translation of Bible) 86 *n. 23.*

*Dowel*, etc.
how treated 10; divisions of poem 12-14; 'doing well' as Dreamer's conclusion upon *Visio* 82, 161; question put to Friars 88; *Dowel* opposed to *Do-yuel* 89; defined by 'Thought' 90, 269, 292; by 'Wit' 92-4, 292; 'Study's' emphasis upon practice 96-8, 106; defined by 'Clergy' 99-100, 102; destroying *Cayme* 103; identified with temporal power 103, 107; defined by 'Scripture' 104; Dreamer's realization 'to see much and to suffer more' 113, 293; defined negatively 119; in terms of obedience and teaching 119; considered as *infinites* 120, 306; as contrition, con-

fession and restitution 126; fulfilment in Saviour's career 174; Dreamer's progress from 'where?' to 'what?' 293; relation to 'lives' and 'ways' 297-8; applied to Plowman as against his followers 299, 306; as comprehensive term 299; relation to spiritual awareness (C Text) 302-3; 'doing well' as absolute 303; not 'action' as opposed to 'contemplation' 298, 304; 'doing well' examined on two counts 304-5.

Dreamer, The
colloquy with Holy Church 19-21, 175, 283-5; over-ambitious 40-3, 62, 189, 271; practice required 36, 69, 83, 178, 205, 269; natural knowledge a sound guide 78, 207; perfection to be sought 83-4, 223, 228; his character and progress, Ch. III *passim*; admits his characteristic bent 140-1; revelation being prepared 143-5; Tree of Charity expounded 152-4, 257-8, 260; meets with forerunners of Saviour 156-60; Law reaffirmed 162-3; last questions answered by 'Faith' 164; 'Conscience' explains lessons of Christ's victory 171-3; Dreamer at last stage 181-3; nature of his progress 207-8, 230-3, 236, 252-3, 255, 259, 262-3, 274-6, 312, 319, 321 *n. 53*, 328; relation to 'Will' and Hope 264-5; compared with 'I'-representations in Chaucer and Gower 285-91; Dreamer's progress reviewed 291-5; related to 'lives' 295 ff; Meroney's view of Dreamer 303-4, 313-4; 'autobiographical' reference 313-6.
see also 'Will'.

Dryden, John 192, 230, 233-4, 241, 281, 318; quoted 246.

Dunbar, William 279 *n. 53.*

Dunning, T. P.
'*Piers Plowman*'; *an Interpretation of the A-Text* 85 *n. 15*, 86 *n. 23*; article on structure of B Text 298, 301-2, 309, 314.

Dysmas (Dumachus) 84 *n. 7*, 116, 203.

Eliot, T. S. 234, 311.
*Envy*
  his *naïveté* 48, 266; his mortal sickness 48, 208, 216; presides over
  Friars 183.
*eucatastrophe* 307.
Everett, Dorothy
  *Essays on Middle English Literature*
  222, 230.

*Faerie Queene, The* 242-7, 258.
'Faith'
  in Passus XVII, 158-60; Passus
  XVIII, 163-4, 209, 217, 262.
Fescennine licence 32.
Field of Folk
  in Prologue 17-19; referred to by
  Holy Church 21, 62, 284; precedes
  emergence of Deadly Sins 47; related
  to Haukyn 123, 125; as objective
  presentation 252; animated scene
  262-3; set between Heaven and Hell
  308.
'fourteener' 193.
Fowler, David C.
  with Thomas A. Knott, '*Piers the
  Plowman': a Critical Edition of the
  A-Version* 85 *n. 15*, 137 *n. 13*, 327.
Francis, St. 146, 182, 254.
Frank, R. W., Jr.
  article on Pardon scene 86 *n. 24*;
  article on personification-allegory
  253; '*Piers Plowman' and the Scheme
  of Salvation* 255-6, 257.
Friars
  shelter 'Falsehood' 24; shrift given
  Lady Meed 25-6, 27; stimulated by
  Wrath 49; their four orders 82;
  fair-weather friends of Dreamer
  108; plentiful 115, 183; Charity once
  of their number 146; receive Antichrist 180; dubious allies of 'Cons-
  science' 182; presided over by Envy
  183; *Sir Penetrans-domos* 184, 231;
  to be set in order by a true Pope 185;
  'pore freres' 184*n. 4*; laxity in confessions 257.
  (Minorite Friars in Passus VIII) colloquy with Dreamer 88-90, 291-2;

his impatience 104; his large objection
126, 128, 153; Friars not abstractions
252; mistaken attribution 280 *n. 59*;
irony of valediction 294; comparison
with Julian of Norwich 316.
Fuller, Thomas 166, 282.

Gardner, Helen
  *The Limits of Literary Criticism* 250,
  252.
Gascoigne, George 196.
Gaunt, John of 257, 278 *n. 37*.
*gentrice*
  reflected in 'Charity' 45; opposed to
  empty dignities 150; linked with
  *suit-secte* 164, 314, and with universal
  salvation 170; Jews as *gentil men* dispossessed 173; bearing on language
  216-7; related to 'self-portrait' 315.
Gestas 84 *n. 7*.
Giotto 235, 259.
*Gluttony*
  in the ale-house 50.
Gnudi, Cesare 239 *n. 67*.
Gower, John
  ending of *Confessio Amantis* 182, 229,
  291, 312; art of *Confessio Amantis*
  235, 236, 243-4, 282, 291; pupil
  compared with Langland's Dreamer
  264-5, 281, 285-6, 289-91, 294, 297,
  311; 'self-portrait' 315; on alchemy
  329; *Miroir de l'homme* 282.
Grant, R. M.
  *The Letter and the Spirit* 277 *n. 21*.
Gray, Thomas 190-1, 196.
Gregory, St. 75, 99, 102, 109-110,
  111.
*Gulliver's Travels* 310-11.

Hamilton, A. C.
  article on Spenser and Langland
  322 *n. 68*.
Hardie, C. G.
  article on Dante 278 *n. 28*.
Harrowing of Hell 13, 168-72; language 213, 271-2; how presented 253,
  262, 263, 281, 310.
Haukyn
  article by Stella Maguire 43 *n. 1*;

his role considered 123-36; thanks given on his behalf 152; his defensive arrogance 205; his tears 209, 262; his confession of failure 231; his sinfulness not to be linked with corruption of Church 257.

Hazlitt, William 246.

Hilton, Walter 301, 304.

Hobbes, Thomas 312.

Holy Church
in Passus I, 19-21, 283-5; contrasted with Lady Meed 22; admonishes Dreamer in terms of natural knowledge 30, 77-8, 89, 207, and necessity of practice 46, 55, 62-3, 69, 94; *lewte* her lover 31; as isolated figure 42; Dreamer's aptitude for her instruction 43 *n. 1*; vexation compared with Plowman's *tene* 83, 295; establishing character of Dreamer 87, 106, 153, 231, 262, 269; her verdict on humanity at large 95, 125, 177; her lesson compared with that of 'Hunger' 69, 'Study' 99; her lesson remembered 109; the 'better' originally withheld 141, 182; Love as the final truth 152, 296; as personification 252; on Castle of Flesh 266; on *tresore* 274.

'Hope'
in Passus XVII, 157-60; association with Will in Gower 264.

Housman, A. E. 319, 323-4.

'Hunger'
answers Plowman's call 66-7, 123, 180; counsels him 68-9; unappeasable 70; no final solution 71; an interpretation rejected 255.

Huppé, Bernard F.
(with D. W. Robertson, Jr.) '*Piers Plowman*' *and Scriptural Tradition* 249, 255, 257-8, 274, 279 *n. 50*; article on wordplay 265-74, 280 *n. 59*.

Hurd, Richard 276.

Hussey, S. S.
article on 'three lives' 299, 304-6, 320 *n. 25*.

Indulgences 74, 77, 81, 85 *n. 17*.

Innocent III, Pope 39.

'Inwit'
defined 44 *n. 8*; in Castle of *Caro* 92 (A Text, 300).

James, D. G.
*The Life of Reason* 321 *n. 53*.

James, M. R.
ed. *The Apocryphal New Testament* 84 *n. 7*.

James, St. (the Great) 38, 46, 53.

Jerome, St. 75, 228.

John of Gaunt 257.

Johnson, Dr. 94, 207, 236 *n. 1*, 241, 245-6.

Jonson, Ben 47, 192.

Julian of Norwich 316-7, 322 *n. 65*.

*Justus*, the just man conceived as fulfilment of law 83; immunity to punishment 88; exemption from common failure 113, 126, 132-3, 152-3, 162, 258, 296; insistence finally rewarded 264; relation to 'doing well' of spiritual life 299, 306.

Kafka, Franz 245.

Kane, George
*Piers Plowman: The A Version* 7, 85 *n. 17*, 137 *nn. 3, 11, 12*, 326-8; *Middle English Literature* 309.

Kaske, R. E.
article on 'Book' 186 *n. 17*.

Kästner, L. E.
*History of French Versification* 196.

Kelsey, Richard 199.

Kempe, Margery 317.

Ker, W. P.
*English Literature: Medieval* 248-9, 252, 259.

Knight, W. F. Jackson
*Accentual Symmetry in Vergil* 193-4.

Knott, Thomas A.
see Fowler, David C.

Knox, Ronald
(trans. Bible) 44 *n. 16*, 45, 86 *n. 23*.

*Kynd*
how treated 10; kynde witt 30, 44 *n. 8*, 'Scripture's' cousin 107, related to 'Clergy' 116-7; kynde knowyng 78, 89-90, 99; kynde loue 85 *n. 14*; Castle of Kind 92, 292; 'Kind' and the

Dreamer 112; comes at 'Conscience's' call 180, 329; counsels love 182; association with 'Will' 264.

Lamborn, E. A. Greening
The Rudiments of Critcism 221.
Lawlor, John
article on Book of the Duchess 229; on historical scholarship and literary criticism 277 n. 17; on Shakespeare's imagery 280 n. 61; on 'radical' satire 321 n. 52; on Julian of Norwich 322 n. 64.
Lechery
in Chaucer's Parson's Tale 33; in assault on Unity 181.
Lewis, C. Day 187.
Lewis, C. S.
The Allegory of Love 197, 199, 240, 242-4, 258, 282, 309, 311; English Literature in the Sixteenth Century 194-5, 230, 236 n. 5; The Pilgrim's Regress 236, 280 n. 70.
Lord of Misrule 32.
Lowell, J. R.
My Study Windows 223, 238 n. 39; The English Poets 233, 259.
Lüdeke, H.
Die Funktionen des Erzählers in Chaucers epischer Dichtung 320 n. 15.

Macaulay, G. C.
ed. Confessio Amantis 329.
Maguire, Stella
article on Haukyn 43 n. 1, 138 n. 24.
Malvern, Great 12.
Malvern hills 39.
Manly, J. M.
article on authorship 314.
Manuscripts
Dublin D.4.1, 12, 237 n. 25; Huntington Lib. Hm 128 (formerly Ashburnham 130), 12; Laud 851, 84 n. 12; L and WCO, 326; R and F in relation to B-tradition 185 n. 8, 325, 279 n. 46; instances of hysteron proteron 325; MSS and nature of audience 210, 237 n. 25.
Map, Walter 210, 228.

mede
distinguished from mesurable hire 29, 61, 67; from mercede 30, 41, 44 n. 7, 62-3, 81, 117-8, 130-1; granted by Faith 152.
see also Lady Meed.
Meed, Lady
in Passus II-IV, 21-42, 43 n. 4, 44 n. 20; escaping punishment 45; misappropriating wealth 48; her ignorance significant 50, 107, 168, 170, 206; extent of her rule 54-6, 58, 78, 134, 146, 184, 231; her rule ended in Knight's forward with Plowman 60-3, in measurable huyre 67, in co-operative endeavour 71-4, 176, at Judgement Day 81-2, in cloister 102; as isolated figure 76, 262; her defence overthrown 'all in two lines' 83-4, 232; the Dreamer her servant turned critic 108; presence of 'Conscience' at her examination 172, 177, 186 n. 24, 209, 257-8, 268; deference shown her at Westminster 200; as personification 252; significance not dependent on topical allusion 256-7, 278 n. 36; impudent equivocation 268, 271; accusations cogent 278 n. 37; relation to mesure and to 'doing well' 296-8.
see also mede.
'Mercy'
(at Harrowing of Hell) ridiculed by 'Truth' 166, 213; declaration of God's Grace 27.
Mercury 327, 329.
Meroney, Howard
article on 'Long Wille' 86 n. 22, 303-4, 313-4, 320 n. 27.
mesure
principle of mesure, the mesurable 39, 63, 69, 71, 75-6, 79, 120, 127, 129, 167, 178-9, 257, 278 n. 37, 283, 296, 308; mede mesurelees and mesurable hire 29-30, 41, 67-9; mesure reaffirmed by 'Patience' 128, 220-2, and by 'Peace' 272; justa mensura 273.
'Metaphysical' poetry 241.
Milton, John 33, 196, 223, 253, 318-9.

Mitchell, A. G.
    article on Lady Meed 27, 32, 62, 256, 278 *n. 37*; C Text 8.
'modulation' 191.
Mohammed 32, 149.
More, Sir Thomas 34.
Muir, Kenneth
    ed. *Macbeth* 280 *n. 55*.
Murdoch, Iris
    *Sartre* 235, 319.
Murray, Gilbert
    *The Classical Tradition in Poetry* 194.

Nashe, Thomas 114, 138 *n. 20*.
Newman, J. H. 318, 319.
*Nicodemus, Gospel of* 84 *n. 7*, 186 *n. 18*.

Oakden, J. P.
    *Alliterative Poetry in Middle English* 237 *n. 24*.
Origen 252.
Owst, G. R.
    *Literature and Pulpit in Medieval England* 258-9; *The Destructorium Viciorum of Alexander Carpenter* 279 *n. 42*.

Pantin, W. A.
    *The English Church in the Fourteenth Century* 320 *n. 24*.
Pardon of Piers Plowman
    as link between *Visio* and *Vita* 11, 82, 283, 298-9; Pardon scene 71-82, paralleled in 157-8 and 263; *a pena et a culpa* 72, 73; contrasted with 'Indulgences' 74, 77, 81; as statement of moral law 77-9, 88, 183, 283, 299, 315; Priest unable to *construe* 118; significance of tearing 121, 168, 316; emptiness of formal 'pardons' 122, 132; ending confusion 130; uniting leader and followers 159-60; reaffirmed in Apostle Peter's commission 174-5.
    *see also* Piers Plowman; Priest (of Pardon scene).
Pardoners
    in Field of Folk 18; witnessing marriage-contract 22; succouring

'Liar' 24; among pilgrims 58-9; compared with Friar entering Unity 183.
*Parlement of the Thre Ages* 200-1.
*Pars Oculi* 237 *n. 25*.
'Patience'
    in Passus XIII, 119-20; echoes Plowman's resolve 126-7; answers Haukyn 129-32; praises poverty 133-5; patience as Dreamer's discovery 136; at banquet scene 210-11; as personification 252; wordplay 326.
'Peace'
    (at Harrowing of Hell) rebuked by 'Righteousness' 166, 213; retraces *mesure* principle 167, 272; sings 171; reconciled with 'Truth' 85 *n. 16*; present in Unity 184.
*Pearl* 201, 222, 235, 252.
Perrers, Alice, 257, 278 *n. 36*.
Peter, St.
    Pope his successor 17; his Keys 146; his commission 174.
Piers Plowman
    type of honest labour 13, 55-6, 62-3, 76, 177; advice to the pilgrims 56-7, 229, 259, 292, 298, and this issuing in practice 296, 298; leader 58-9, 64, 78; universal provider 59-60; his will 61-2, 78, 136, 182; beggars of half-acre 65, 180, 184, 231; 'Truth's' servant 65, 71; helped and counselled by 'Hunger' 66-70, 180; dependent on God 79, 179, 297, 314; repentant 79, 135, 137 *n. 5*, 282-3, 296, 309; his vexation 79-80, 83, 109, 285, 295, 315; immediacy of understanding (in Pardon scene) 125, 147, 168, 259, 295, 297, 299, 315-6; dispute with Priest 77-81, 263, 266, 271, 274, 327-8; his *belyue* 326; kinship with man preluding Saviour 167, 294.
    second appearance prepared 144, 283; identified with Christ 145, 209, 218, 275; expounds Tree of Charity 153-5; jousts in Jerusalem 163-4.
    third appearance 172; deputy to Grace 175; work of building and

cultivating 176-7, 260; Head of the Church 183, 185; to be sought by 'Conscience' 185, 295, 306.
*see also* Pardon of Piers Plowman.
*Pilgrim's Progress, The* 47; quoted 139.
*Pleasures of Imagination, The* 312.
Pope, Alexander 190, 250; quoted 197.
'poulter's measure' 193.
*Prelude, The* 247, 312.
Pride
no power over poverty 133; to be destroyed 185.
Priest (of Pardon scene)
the scene 76-81; significance of dispute 106, 158, 274; true *glose* of Pardon 118; how presented 263; wordplay 266, 271, 327-8.

Quirk, Randolph
article on *Kind Wit* and *Inwit* 44 *n. 8.*

Racine
quoted 196.
Raleigh, Sir Walter 242.
*Rasselas* 245.
'Reason'
sent for 35; present at Lady Meed's examination 36-40; enthroned with King and 'Conscience' 42, 63; preaches before King 45, 62, 297; followed by 'Repentance' 46; challenged by Dreamer 112-4; Reason (and Wit) in Gower 264.
*Rechelessnesse* 138 *n. 17.*
'Repentance'
in Passus V, 46, 50-3; appeal to God made man 62, 110, 134, 167, 328; as solitary figure 262; receives ironic reply 266.
'Righteousness'
(at Harrowing of Hell) rebukes 'Peace' 166-7, 213.
*Rime of the Ancyent Marinere, The* 200.
Ripon Cathedral 279 *n. 47.*
Ritson, Joseph 276.
'Robert the Robber' 51, 56.
Robertson, D. W., Jr.
(with Bernard F. Huppé) 'Piers

*Plowman' and Scriptural Tradition* 249, 255, 257-8, 274, 279 *n. 50*; article on 'historical criticism' 277 *n. 17.*
Rolle, Richard 301.
*Roman de la Rose* 228, 278 *n. 30.*
Ross, W. O.
ed. *Middle English Sermons* 279 *n. 42.*
Rushforth, G. McN.
*Medieval Christian Imagery* 185 *n. 3.*
Russell, G. H.
C Text readings 7-8, 44 *n. 19,* 137 *nn. 3, 11,* 224.

Salvation
of Jews and Saracens 104-5; of Wise Ancients 105; universal 109, 148-50, 170, 316; of *lewed* and *lettred* 116; kinds of baptism 117; quality of saving faith 128.
Samaritan
in Passus XVII, 158-9; resemblance to Saviour 163; lesson for the Dreamer 171; story parodied 24.
Samson 168.
Santayana, George 240.
Saul, King 29-30.
Schism, Great 186 *n. 20.*
'Scripture'
wife of 'Clergy' 98; colloquy with Dreamer 103-7; her authority challenged by Trajan 109-10, 209; as personification 252.
Shakespeare, William
*A Midsummer Night's Dream* 198; *King John* (quoted) 256; *2 Henry IV* 35; *As You Like It* (quoted) 313; *Hamlet* (quoted) 55; *Othello* 162; *King Lear* 29, 232; *Macbeth* 48, 224, 280 *n. 55*; Sonnet (17) quoted 223; wordplay 271, 280 *n. 55*; historical scholarship and interpretation 277 *n. 17*; use of anachronism 179; later blank verse 223; mentioned with Spenser and Milton 33.
Shipton-under-Wychwood 12.
Sidney, Sir Philip 193.
Sins, Seven Deadly
in Passus V, 47-51; power over Haukyn 125; an anti-masque 133-4; their repentance followed by con-

fusion 176; headed by Antichrist 182; no power over poverty 202; as individual figures 212; animation of repentance-scene 262.

*see* also *Covetousness*, etc.

*Sir Gawain and the Green Knight* 201, 222, 235.

Sisam, Kenneth
ed. *Fourteenth Century Verse and Prose* 330.

Skeat, W. W.
ed. *The Vision of William concerning Piers the Plowman, etc.* (parallel texts). Punctuation 8; observations cited 35, 56, 97, 181, 186 n. *19*, 224, 273, 279, n. *45*, 325; observations disputed 135, 137 n. *13*, 179; attitude to wordplay 84-5 n. *12*, 274-5, 279-80 n. *55*, 325-7; text departed from (B Text) 43 n. *2*, 44 nn. *15*, *17*, *21*, 137 nn. *6*, *7*, *8*, *10*, 138 nn. *14*, *29*, 154, 186 nn. *21*, *25*, 279 n. *53*, 326; (C Text) 44 n. *19*, 137 nn. *3*, *11*, 224.

*Sloth*
at his devotions 50; his swooning 51; resolved on pilgrimage 54; quality of repentance 119; weds 'Despair' 181; in assault on Unity 182.

Smalley, Beryl
*The Study of the Bible in the Middle Ages* 254.

Socrates 116, 118.

Solomon, King 94, 105, 116, 137 n. *11*.

Spearing, A. C.
article on thematic organization 238 n. *59*.

Spenser, Edmund 33, 242-7, 251, 258, 318-9.

Spitzer, Leo
article on 'I'-narration 320 n. *7*.

Stubbs, C. W.
*The Christ of English Poetry* 219.

'Study'
wife of 'Wit' 94; colloquy with Dreamer 94-99; on dearth of hospitality 100-1, 142; taxing Dreamer with mere curiosity 103, 106, 141, 292; equating learning with self-interest 104, 112, 212, 231, 324;

warning against theological subtleties 105, 220, 268; as personification 252; in situation of cross-purpose 293.

Suddaby, Elizabeth
article on poem 202.

Suso, Henry 301.

Swift, Jonathan 310-12.

Tauler, John 301.

Taylor, Jeremy 15.

Tennyson, Alfred
quoted 223.

Tewkesbury 12.

'Theology'
contests Lady Meed's marriage-contract 23-4; included in her counter-attack 27.

Thompson, Francis, 155.

Thomson, James 233.

'Thought'
colloquy with Dreamer 90-2, 97; his irony 264, 269; effect of his explanation 292.

Tillyard, E. M. W.
*The English Epic and its Background* 240, 307-9; article on English epic tradition 309.

Tolkien, J. R. R.
article on fairy-stories 307.

Tottel, Richard 194.

Tree of Charity
*see under* Charity.

Trajan, Emperor 109-110, 209.

Traversi, Derek
article in *The Age of Chaucer* 199.

Trinity, doctrine of
expounded by Abraham 156; not in old covenant 158; similitude of hand 160, 261, 274, 275; C Text variation 186 n. *9*.

'True-Tongue' 32.

'Truth'
as suitable partner for Lady Meed 23; as *prestest payer* 55-6; approving work done in half-acre 71-2, 232; source of Pardon 72-6; in Harrowing of Hell 85 n. *16*, 166, 213.

Tyrwhitt, Thomas
ed. *The Canterbury Tales of Chaucer* 192.

Vergilian hexameter 193.

Viereck, Peter
article on poet in machine-age 237 *n.*
*20.*

Virtues, Seven 57.

Vision of Mirzah, The 245.

Volpone 47.

Waller, Edmund 236 *n. 1.*

'Wastoure'
warned by Knight 66; abroad in
time of plenty 70.

Wells, Henry W.
*The Vision of Piers Plowman* 203, 248;
article on construction 298.

Whitaker, T. D.
ed. *Visio Will[ielm]i de Petro Plouhman* 119.

Whiteley, M.
article on English prosody 236 *n. 2.*

'Will'
how treated 10; as Dreamer's 'name'
46, 121, 140, 143, 145, 313-4; jocu-
larly used 91; as opponent of *Dowel*
94, 108; relation to 'Kind' and Hope
264-5; as ignorance of self 276;
faculty of will 279 *n. 50;* relation
to 'three lives' 295 ff.; his general
role 303-4, 313-4.
*see also* The Dreamer.

Williams, Gwyn
*The Burning Tree* 307-8.

'Wisdom'
allied with 'Witty' at Meed's examination 36-7, 58.

'Wit'
how treated 10; colloquy with
Dreamer 90-4, 97, 98, 292; contrasted with 'Study' 96, 292; on dangers
of lust 206; as personification 252;
related to 'Will' 264, 328; in situation of cross-purpose 293.
'Witty' ('Wit') and 'Wisdom' at
Meed's examination 36-7, 58,
**266.**

Wordplay
underrated 84 *n. 12,* 280 *n. 55;* func-
tions of 149-50, 177, 265-7, 269-74;
incidence in B (as against A) 327-8;
inherent in role of Dreamer 276, 328.
*abbesse, a.b.c.* 80, 271; *armes* 52,
328; *auance* 266; *belyue* 326; *beloure,*
*[be]louʒ* 326; *bettere, ybette* 266;
*bilow, low* 326; *broke* 267-8; *conformen, confourmen* 212, 238 *n. 34;*
*cosyn* 267; *crosse* 50, 149; *croune,
Crystendome* 269; *faire, fer* 90, 269;
*foule* 270; *good* 84 *n. 12;* grace, grass
267; *incipiens, insipiens* 80, 328;
*Iugged* 181; *loues* 267; *maistrye,
mestus* 279 *n. 55;* *mark* 270; *meteles,
metelees* 274; *metyng* 274; *mone* 270;
*pays, pees* 280 *n. 55;* *prest* 267;
*plante* 327-9; queen, quean 267;
*secte, sute* 52, 57, 110, 134, 164;
*sorwes, sowre* 279 *n. 55;* *spere, vnspered*
279 *n. 55;* *spise* 328; *sterlynge* 270;
*treuthe, trewe(s)* 72, 85 *n. 16,* 328;
*tresore, triest* etc. 274; *vix* 266;
*walkene* 270; *wenten* 270; *wordes,
wortes* 49-50.

Wordsworth, William 200, 219, 233,
247, 317; quoted 246, 312.

Wormynton, John 237 *n. 25.*

*Wrath*
his confession 46-7; description 48;
as convent-servant 49, 50; *pukketh*
echoed 58.

'Wrong'
witness to Lady Meed's marriage-
contract 22; employs 'Wisdom' to
subvert justice 36-7; 'Reason's' attitude 38; not punished 45.

Wyatt, Sir Thomas 9, 194-5, 325.

Yeats, W. B. 189, 234; quoted 215.

'Ymagynatyf'
foretold 97, 231; defined 113-4;
colloquy with Dreamer 114-8, 224,
279 *n. 45,* 292-3.